S0-BYE-749

Fodor's EXPLORING

LONDON

FODOR'S TRAVEL PUBLICATIONS

NEW YORK • TORONTO • LONDON • SYDNEY • AUCKLAND

WWW.FODORS.COM

Important Note

Time inevitably brings change, so always confirm prices, travel facts, and other perishable information when it matters. Although Fodor's cannot accept responsibility for errors, you can use this guide in the confidence that we have taken every care to ensure its accuracy.

Copyright © Automobile Association Developments Limited 2005, 2008 (registered office: Fanum House, Basing View, Basingstoke, Hampshire, RG21 4EA. Registered number: 1878835).

All rights reserved. Distributed by Random House, Inc., New York. No maps, illustrations, or other portions of this book may be reproduced in any form without written permission from the publishers.

Published in the United States by Fodor's Travel, a subsidiary of Random House, Inc., and simultaneously in Canada by Random House of Canada Limited, Toronto. Published in the United Kingdom by AA Publishing.

Fodor's and Fodor's Exploring are registered trademarks of Random House, Inc.

Published in the United Kingdom by AA Publishing.

ISBN: 978-1-4000-1835-2

Seventh edition

Fodor's Exploring London

Author: **Christopher Catling**
Additional Text: **Louise Nicholson**
Revision Verifier: **Hilary Weston & Jackie Staddon**
Revision Editor: **Apostrophe S Limited**
Cartography: **The Automobile Association**
Cover Design: **Tigist Getachew, Fabrizio La Rocca**
Front Cover Silhouette: **Dallas & John Heaton/Corbis**
Front Cover Top Photograph: **AA Photo Library**

Special Sales

This book is available for special discounts for bulk purchases for sales promotions or premiums. Special editions, including personalized covers, excerpts of existing books, and corporate imprints, can be created in large quantities for special needs. For more information, write to Special Markets/Premium Sales, 1745 Broadway, MD 6-2, New York, NY 10019 or e-mail specialmarkets@randomhouse.com.

 This product includes mapping data licensed from Ordnance Survey® with the permission of the Controller of Her Majesty's Stationery Office. ©Crown copyright 2007. All rights reserved. Licence number 100021153.

A03259

Printed and bound in Italy by Printer Trento srl.
10 9 8 7 6 5 4 3 2 1

How to use this book

ORGANIZATION

London Is, London Was
Discusses aspects of life and culture in contemporary London and explores significant periods in its history.

A–Z
Breaks down the city into regional chapters, and covers places to visit, including walks and drives. Within this section fall the Focus On articles, which consider a variety of subjects in greater detail.

Travel Facts
Contains the strictly practical information vital for a successful trip.

Hotels and Restaurants
Lists recommended establishments throughout London, giving a brief summary of their attractions.

KEY TO ADMISSION CHARGES
Standard admission charges are categorized in this book as follows:

Inexpensive	less than £3
Moderate	£3–£5.99
Expensive	£6–£9
Very expensive	
	over £9

ABOUT THE RATINGS
Most places described in this book have been given a separate rating. These are as follows:

▶▶▶ **Do not miss**

▶▶ **Highly recommended**

▶ **Worth seeing**

MAPS
To make each particular location easier to find, every main entry in this book has a map reference to the right of its name. This comprises a number, followed by a letter, followed by another number, such as 176B3. The first number (176) refers to the page on which the map can be found, the letter (B) and the second number (3) pinpoint the square in which the main entry is located. The maps on the inside front cover and inside back cover are referred to as IFC and IBC respectively.

Contents

*De Hems, a Dutch-style pub in
Macclesfield Street*

7

My London

As a child growing up in the city's suburbs, my London was at first a mesmerising dream. My father worked in St. James's and would bring home snippets of London in his briefcase—exotic delicacies from Soho's Italian delicatessens, the Evening Standard newspaper with all the London gossip, blue boxes of perfumed talcum powder from Jermyn Street.

My mother made that dream come true. For one long and glorious day each school holiday, my London was a reality. She had once lived here and wished she still did. So I first saw this great city through her eyes that took on a new sparkle as the train drew into Waterloo station. She introduced me to some of London's secrets. As we hopped on and off buses, dipped into the Underground and went to the great department stores, she pointed out places she loved and recounted tales of her city days. Then, jobs done, we would visit a gallery or museum before catching our train home, laden with parcels.

It was on those days that my ambition to live in London took hold. Later, in the summer of 1976, I packed all my belongings into my Mini and drove to London to make it my home.

My London today is a rich mixture. It is now my turn to show my own children the sights. We sit upstairs on the front seats of a double-decker bus—even seasoned Londoners get a thrill. We clamber to the top of St. Paul's cathedral and spot landmarks in the city laid out before us. We drop into the Museum of London where new finds from Roman London seem to arrive weekly thanks to the developers. On rainy Saturdays we nip off to a matinee theatre performance; on fine ones we picnic in Regent's Park and go rowing on the Serpentine. If it is Chinese New Year, we dance in south Soho; if it is the Lord Mayor's Show we watch the floats and then the fireworks. And we always check out a new sight, be it the BA London Eye, the Somerset House complex or a new Thames ferry service.

Life in London, either living here or just visiting, is what you make of it. My London changes day by day, but it is always exciting, always beckoning. The only frustration is that I cannot possibly squeeze in all that I would like to do.

Louise Nicholson

Louise Nicholson lives in Islington, north London, where she has restored a Georgian house. Her many books on London have been praised for their 'infectious enthusiasm'. She has won the London Tourist Board's Guide Book of the Year Award and their London Book of the Decade Award.

Top: Piccadilly Circus at night

London Is

London is truly cosmopolitan, embracing people of every race and religion. Throughout history, it has served as a magnet for foreign traders, offered a place of refuge to those fleeing persecution, and, as the capital of an empire that once spanned the globe, absorbed great numbers of immigrants. The result is a multi-ethnic, integrated community where a variety of cultures thrive side by side.

As early as the 7th century, the Venerable Bede called London 'a mart of many peoples', and social historians say that the rapid growth in London's population during the Middle Ages can only be explained by large-scale immigration. Among the later migrants were Jews expelled from Portugal and Spain, who arrived via the Netherlands after 1656, when Oliver Cromwell extended an official welcome. Other newcomers were the Huguenots from France, who arrived and settled in the Soho and Spitalfields areas when Louis XIV denied their right to religious freedom by revoking the Edict of Nantes in 1685.

In London's Chinatown

It was during this period that London became the most populous city in Western Europe, overtaking Paris, Venice, Naples and Milan as its total number of inhabitants, increased from around 200,000 in 1600 to 600,000 by 1700.

From the late 18th century onwards mass migration, reflecting the miseries of war and political upheaval, swelled the population of London even further: Refugees came from the French Revolution after 1794, followed by Scottish and Irish settlers during the famine years of the 1840s.

Anti-Semitic pogroms in Russia and Eastern Europe brought Jewish refugees in the 1880s, and another wave arrived in the 1930s fleeing Fascist persecution. Londoners might have reacted antagonistically to all these newcomers but most did not. When Sir Oswald Mosley, leader of the Fascist Blackshirts, tried to march through the streets of the East End in 1936, 500,000 Londoners turned out to stop him.

POSTWAR MIGRATION In the postwar years, many Londoners made homeless by the Blitz were rehoused in new towns (such as Bracknell, Harlow and Hemel Hempstead); others sought a new life in Australia, Canada or New Zealand. To compensate for the labour shortage, Commonwealth citizens were encouraged to settle in London to work in the transport system, the National Health Service or on construction projects. Greek and Turkish Cypriots, Vietnamese, Chinese, Bangladeshi and Ugandan Asian refugees, fleeing from warfare or dictatorship, came to

live in London, although not all of them managed to find work; unemployment in London is highest among ethnic minorities.

INTEGRATION A wide range of ethnic traditions has been absorbed into London life. It has the biggest Caribbean carnival in Europe—the Notting Hill Carnival that takes place during the last weekend in August; the splendid Central Mosque has added to the city's rich architectural heritage; and there is a huge range of good, cheap restaurants serving worldwide cuisines, most notably Chinese and Indian. Thanks to hardworking Asian entrepreneurs, every district has corner shops that are

open all hours; and the Brick Lane area has been transformed into a hub for Bangladeshi Asians, full of street stalls, fabric stores and restaurants.

NEXT GENERATION A new wave of immigration has come to Britain with countries from Eastern Europe joining the EU. It is not uncommon to find Poles , Romanians or Bulgarians working in hotels and restuarants throughout the city.

A city of ethnic diversity

❏ London's population reached a peak of around 8.5 million in 1939. Since then it has fallen to about 7.3 milllion in 2006, but it is still the highest of any city in Europe and about 12 per cent of the total UK population. After a period when people were more inclined to move out to greener suburbs and commute into the city to work, there is now a return to London living, and the latest census is expected to show a significant population rise. Nevertheless, around 1.25 million commute daily from places as far afield as Oxford or Brighton. London also receives 29 million visitors a year. The capital's bus and Underground network carries an amazing 5 million passengers a day. ❏

London is full of symbolic monuments and buildings, none more potent than the Houses of Parliament, known as 'the mother of Parliaments'. To many Londoners, however, politics is not just something that goes on within the House of Commons: It is part of daily life, affecting everything from litter to the state of the city's roads and transport.

In 1986, when the Labour-controlled GLC (Greater London Council) was abolished by Margaret Thatcher's Conservative régime, London became the only major city in the world not to have a single elected administrative body.

In 1997, however, the Conservative party was soundly defeated by Labour, in both national and London polls. Labour immediately announced plans to reintroduce a unified body that would be responsible for those issues that cross borough boundaries, and which therefore have an effect on all of London (e.g. transport and pollution, see page 13). In May 2000, Londoners elected Ken Livingstone Mayor of London. As head of the Greater London Authority he has been responsible for improving four main areas of London life: transport; development and economy; policing; and the emergency services. Never one to duck an issue Livingstone is never far from controversy. Nonetheless as far as most Londoners are concerned his policies seem to have worked and in 2004 he was re-elected for a second four-year term as mayor.

Sleeping on the streets

❏ Visitors sometimes expect to see the city as Dickens described it, its dark medieval alleys made darker still by fog as thick as pea soup. Smog (a mixture of smoke and fog) killed plants and trees, turned honey-coloured buildings black, left encrustations on the varnish covering historic paintings, bleached clothes and ancient fabrics and caused great damage to human health. In the worst winter smogs of the 19th century, theatregoers could hardly see the actors on stage for smoke, and pedestrians could only just see their feet. One of the last smogs to hit the city, the 'killer smog' of December 1952, caused an estimated 4,000 deaths among bronchial sufferers, and the resulting outcry led to London being declared a smokeless zone under the Clean Air Act of 1956. ❏

LITTER AND HOMELESSNESS

Political conflict did not end with the GLC's abolition; it simply moved onto a broader stage. The national government has a powerful grip on the budgets of local authorities and often intervenes, through a process known as 'capping', if any borough threatens to overspend. Some boroughs have responded by cutting expenditure on street cleaning and other services, arguing that limited funds must be spent on essentials, such as housing and education. Litter has thus been turned into another pawn in the political game and is an all too familiar sight in certain parts of the city.

More distressing is the high number of homeless people on London's streets, huddling for shelter in doorways because they have nowhere else to go. The sight provokes puzzlement and anger in Londoners, most of whom are unsure of the causes or the solution. The situation is slowly improving, however. At one time in the early 1990s about 2,000 people slept outdoors; now many of them go to charitable hostels, while others have managed to find more permanent lodgings.

TRANSPORT AND POLLUTION

Another pressing problem is the sheer quantity of traffic and the resulting pollution. London made great strides to solve its pollution problems following the Clean Air acts of 1956 and 1968. Smog, a noxious mixture of smoke, chemical fumes and fog that had characterized London for several hundred years, became a thing of the past when coal burning was banned, and industry

and homeowners were encouraged to switch to oil, gas and electricity for heating and power. Many buildings were cleaned of the soot blackening their stonework—the Houses of Parliament, Westminster Abbey and most other landmarks were restored to pristine condition.

Measures to discourage car use had been discussed for years but finally in 2003 Congestion Charging was introduced to London. A levy of £8 is imposed on every car entering Central London (large red C signs mark the boundaries) between 7am and 6pm Monday to Friday. Estimates of traffic reduction vary from 18 per cent to 30 per cent and it has been hailed by most people as a great success—though some London businesses beg to differ.

Combating vehicle pollution

13

Many of the 29 million visitors to London come for the same reason as the cat in the nursery rhyme: to look at the Queen, or at least to look at the palaces, jewels and ceremonies associated with royalty. Fascination with things royal tends to be strongest among visitors from republican countries, while British people tend to be sceptical about the role of the monarchy.

14

The last decade of the 20th century was a traumatic one for the British royal family. Even the fire at Windsor Castle in 1992 did not provoke much sympathy for the Queen. In fact, there was a public outcry that taxpayers should fund the palace's restoration while the Queen, at the time the richest woman in the world, contributed nothing. In response, the Queen funded it herself by opening Buckingham Palace to paying visitors.

The controversy came at the end of a year that had seen the breakup of two royal marriages and calls for the Queen to pay tax on her vast annual income. This last demand was one to which the Queen did concede, marking an important stage in a long-running saga: the definition of an appropriate role for monarchy in the modern age. The death of Diana (in 1997), and the way the royal family

Trooping the Colour

were perceived to have reacted to it, reopened this debate.

One poll suggested that half Britain's population would like to see an end to the monarchy, and some say that Britain would long ago have become a republic but for the thought of who might be elected President instead.

THE SUCCESSION Charles, Prince of Wales, the heir to the throne, is popular for his involvement with a host of issues, including his much admired youth programme and most things green. Despite the shadow of his marriage to Diana still haunting him, Charles finally married his long-term companion, Camilla Parker Bowles, on 9th April 2005. There have been suggestions that the succession should bypass Charles straight to his elder son, the popular William, who has become something of an icon.

THE ROYAL YEAR The Queen's official life follows an established pattern. The New Year is usually spent at Sandringham, in Norfolk, which was bought in 1861 for the Prince of Wales (later Edward VII). February and March often involve overseas tours but she returns to London, dividing her time between Buckingham Palace and Windsor Castle, for the spring and early summer. On the second Saturday in June she travels down the Mall in a horse-drawn carriage for the Trooping the Colour ceremony in Horse Guards, in celebration of her official birthday (her real one is on 21 April). June is also the month when the Queen goes to the races, often to see her own horses compete, for the Derby and for Ascot Week (when women wear flamboyant hats). In July the Queen hosts garden parties at Buckingham Palace before heading north to Scotland, to visit Holyrood House (Edinburgh), and then Balmoral Castle for the grouse-shooting season. Foreign tours may take place in September, but the Queen is back for the State Opening of Parliament (late October or early November), which takes place in the House of Lords; no monarch has been admitted to the Commons since 1642, when Charles I burst in demanding the arrest of five Members of Parliament. On Remembrance Sunday, the Sunday nearest 11 November, the Queen lays a wreath to commemorate the war dead at the Cenotaph in Whitehall.

❏ The stormy marriage of Prince Charles and Diana, Princess of Wales, was charted daily by the world's press, as was that of Charles's brother Prince Andrew to Sarah Ferguson. Both ended in divorce, and both women continued to live in the public eye, apparently by choice. But after Diana's death in 1997, the press began to exercise some self-control towards Prince Charles's sons, princes William and Harry; and softened their attitude towards Prince Charles's long term affection for Camilla Parker Bowles. The marriage, in 1999, of the Queen's youngest son, Prince Edward enjoyed more privacy. Meanwhile, the Queen herself is more actively in touch with her people, giving the monarchy a new humanity. ❏

The Queen in bejewelled splendour

London is a style capital, giving birth to new ideas that become international fashions. London's position was established during the 1960s style revolution, epitomized by the Beatles and Mary Quant, and confirmed during the emergence of punk in the 1970s, when designers from Tokyo to New York embraced black clothes with studs, zips and safety-pin decoration. Today, London continues to lead in fashion, music and art of all kinds.

London stars in the 1950s were singers such as Tommy Steele and Joe Brown, with their Cockney accents—quite acceptable to most parents. Youngsters dressed like their parents, except for the Teddy Boys, who were generally thought of as a rough crowd.

16

SWINGING SIXTIES By the mid-1960s, youth had begun to create its own fashions. The King's Road and Carnaby Street became the hub of all that was hip and new in the London of the Swinging Sixties. Boutiques like Mary Quant's Bazaar became the trendsetters for those 'dedicated followers of fashion' so pilloried by the

Patriotic punk

well-known Kinks song. London also dominated the music scene, especially after the Beatles made this city their home. They, the Who and the Rolling Stones dominated the pop charts on both sides of the Atlantic at this time.

Thirty years later, the innocent, fun London pictured with its 'Bobbies on their bicycles, two by two' in songs such as 'England Swings Like a Pendulum Do' is just a memory, but anyone nostalgic for the past can join a Beatles Tour (tel: 020-7624 3978), which takes in places such as Abbey Road, where the eponymous album cover was shot, the clubs where they performed, and the rooftop building in Savile Row where they made their last public appearance together in February 1969.

PUNK By contrast, punk's lasting influence is the dynamic and daring experimental street fashion confidently worn by many young people, as if they are moving, living art works. Museum-piece punks hang around the King's Road on summer weekends, but these are semiprofessionals: usually art students who supplement their grants by dyeing their hair lurid colours and posing for photographs (they expect a tip, of course). They have little in common with the raw, anti-establishment music, clothing and attitudes that were born in London during the long, hot summers of 1976 and 1977. However, punk ideas have been absorbed into the amorphous style that characterizes many of today's young Londoners.

YUPPIES AND THE 'ME' GENERATION In the 1980s London took its tune from America, in a new materialism and ostentatious spending. Teenage Porsche owners did global deals over their cellular phones and put down options on penthouse apartments (yet to be built) in the Docklands. Something of this still hangs around among young businessmen who flaunt their designer clothes in fashionable restaurants—but they make less of an impression today.

DYNAMIC VARIETY Changes in the 1990s have prepared the city for the 21st century. London is alive with creative talent working in all styles, leaving Londoners free to enjoy their individuality and particular tastes. London Fashion Week is an important event, when young British designers set the tone for world fashion. Art and crafts are so lively that east London now supports the largest community of artists in Europe, an estimated 10,000 people. Music is vibrant in all its forms—jazz, pop, rock, reggae, trance, salsa, hip hop, garage, house, jungle and many others, reflecting the cosmopolitan culture of the capital, and the consequent club scene is

Yasmin le Bon on the catwalk at London Fashion Week

Mary Quant, 1960s fashion queen

large, fast and ever-changing. Theatre follows a similar pattern, with landmark, innovative productions staged from the top Royal National Theatre down to the small fringe theatres such as the Almeida and Young Vic, with productions regularly moving on to New York. Restaurants, which burgeoned in the 1990s while undergoing a welcome revolution to find more authentic ingredients and recipes, now offer quality dishes from almost all the world's food traditions. Meanwhile, health and the environment have a central position: Diet, exercise, pollution and waste are daily considerations in the lives of many Londoners.

From double-decker buses to soldiers dressed in red tunics and bearskin helmets guarding Buckingham Palace, London is a city steeped in tradition and pageantry. No matter what time of year you visit, there is bound to be some colourful event going on.

The most famous of London's regular events is the Changing of the Guard. It is worth remembering that this takes place in several different locations. In summer the crowds at Buckingham Palace often block the view, and you may prefer the alternative ceremonies at Whitehall or St. James's Palace, while the hour-long event at Windsor Castle, with its marching bands and music, is perhaps the best of all.

January's big event is the Lord Mayor of Westminster's New Year's Day Parade. This only started in 1986 but has become a popular attraction, with floats, bands and American-style cheerleaders, who march from Piccadilly to Hyde Park starting at 12.30pm. On the anniversary of Charles I's execution (30 January) members of the Royal Stuart Society, in appropriate costume, retrace the monarch's route to the scaffold from St. James's Palace and lay a wreath on his statue at the head of Whitehall.

Shrove Tuesday, which usually falls in February, is celebrated with pancake races in Carnaby Street;

Bearskins and bayonets

❏ The Trooping the Colour ceremony takes place in June, but there is a public lottery for the tickets (50,000 people apply for 4,000 seats). To try, write requesting tickets (a maximum of two) with a stamped, addressed envelope to The Brigade Major, Trooping the Colour, Household Division, Horse Guards, Whitehall, SW1A 2AX between 1 January and 1 March. You can also apply for tickets to the dress rehearsals on the two preceding Saturdays, with a better chance of success. ❏

seven weeks later, on Easter Sunday, there is a carnival in Battersea Park, while on Easter Monday there is a parade of working horses (still used to draw brewers' carts) in Regent's Park at noon.

In June more pageantry takes place in Horse Guards Parade, called Beating the Retreat, when military bands mark the setting of the sun and perform by floodlight (advance reservations essential: for details, tel: 020-7839 5323).

Chelsea Pensioners parade in honour of their founder, Charles II, on Oak Apple Day, 29 May (see pages 92–93), and most Wednesday evenings in May and June you can watch Morris dancers performing their routines outside Westminster Abbey.

There are festivals galore in July (one of the best is the City of London Festival, tel: 020-7796 4949 for details) but for something more unusual you can watch the start of the Swan Upping ceremony at Temple Stairs

on the Embankment. From here, the Queen's Swan Keeper travels upriver to Henley-on-Thames to mark the beaks of the newly born cygnets, which are all owned by (and therefore enjoy the protection of) the Queen and the Dyers and Vintners livery companies.

The annual Costermonger's Harvest Festival, held in early October at St. Martin-in-the-Fields, Trafalgar Square, brings together the hardy characters who sell fruit and vegetables from stalls all over London. It is here that you are most likely to see London's famous Pearly Kings and Queens, so called because of their coats covered with buttons made of mother of pearl. They were originally elected by costermongers to act as unofficial community leaders, sorting out disputes between street traders, who were reluctant to involve the police in their affairs.

The Lord Mayor's Show

Today most Pearly Kings and Queens devote their spare time to raising money for charity.

On the first Sunday in November you can watch the start of the London to Brighton Veteran Car Run; only cars made before 1905 can take part, and their owners dress in period costumes. The rally commemorates the abolition in 1896 of the law requiring all cars to be preceded by someone walking with a red warning flag. The second Saturday in November sees the colourful Lord Mayor's Show (see page 163). The State Opening of Parliament, usually held in late October or early November, marks the new parliamentary year with the Queen's grand procession from Buckingham Palace to the Houses of Parliament—this and the indoor ceremonies are televised. Numerous events lead up to Christmas, including carol-singing around the tree in Trafalgar Square (every day at 4pm from mid-December onwards).

19

London is in an almost constant state of flux, as old buildings are knocked down and new ones built in their place, or historic buildings are restored to their former pristine splendour. Here are some of the bigger changes that took place in the latter part of the 20th century. The visitor to 21st-century London will encounter yet more.

FLEET STREET Although Fleet Street still looks the same, the newspaper printworks and the journalists have gone, scattered to various parts of the city, including Marsh Wall (the *Daily Telegraph*) and Wapping (*The Times, Sunday Times, Sun* and *News of the World*). Strikes and violence accompanied the breakup of Fleet Street (and the breakup of the once powerful print unions), as newspaper proprietors, led by Rupert Murdoch, embraced new technology and moved into new premises.

THE THAMES EMBANKMENTS The 1990s revitalization of London is especially striking along the Thames. At Vauxhall Bridge a conspicuous green and white building, completed in 1992, houses the headquarters of the secretive MI6, the government

Lloyd's (by Richard Rogers)

organization responsible for foreign intelligence (or, in plain terms, spying). Further east, Terry Farrell, designed the eight-storey office building above Charing Cross Station, which seems to hover like a giant glowering beetle above the water. On the opposite bank is Nicholas Grimshaw's great glazed and curving arch, the former International Terminal at Waterloo, opened in 1994 to serve the Channel Tunnel. Indeed, the whole south bank of the Thames from County Hall to London Bridge is now revitalized. Stops along the riverside walkway include the London Aquarium, the BA London Eye, the OXO Tower, the Tate Modern and Shakespeare's Globe Theatre.

DOCKLANDS The Port of London was once the world's busiest port. At its peak in 1964, it employed 100,000 people and handled 61.6 million tonnes of cargo in giant enclosed docks. Then, with the arrival of container ships, the port moved downriver to modern, mechanized Tilbury. Between 1968 and 1981 all the docks closed, leaving an area of waterscape 18km (11 miles) long containing 182ha (450 acres) and 88km (55 miles) of water's edge silent and empty. In 1981, the London Docklands Development Corporation was formed, intended as a catalyst to reshape and revive the area, backed by government incentives and tax relief. Two decades and much controversy later, its success can begin to be assessed. More than 80 national and international awards have been won for buildings, landscaping and conservation, including Canary Wharf,

The redeveloped Docklands area

St. Anne's Church and the Royal Docks landscaping, but it is Canary Wharf tower and squares that impress the first-time visitor the most.

THE FUTURE NOW Docklands regeneration launched the revival of east London and, in the following years, the whole of London's riverside. With it came a new way of living: Derelict warehouses were converted into spacious loft apartments with river views. The focus of the capital's new developments is increasingly returning to the Thames. In central London they include Tate Modern, housed in Giles Gilbert Scott's brick power station on Bankside, the revitalization of Sir William Chamber's palatial 1770s Somerset House, and the BA London Eye big wheel. Most eye-catching of all however is the Swiss Re Tower—a stunning 180-m (590-ft) high rounded skyscraper, better known as The Gherkin for obvious reasons. It stands on the site of the old Baltic Exchange in the City, and was completed in 2004. The South Bank has seen the striking City Hall building, and the Royal Festival was completely refurbished in 2007. In the east, the Museum in Docklands fills a waterside Georgian warehouse, while the vast Millennium Dome, reopened by the O2 group in 2007, is a notable landmark. Away from the river, overhauls have been seen at the Royal Opera House, the British Museum, The Wallace Collection and Science Museum. Latest projects include the new International Terminal for Eurostar at St. Pancras and the huge regeneration and building around Stratford in the East End in preparation for the 2012 Olympics to be held in the city.

Charing Cross Station

THE CRADLE OF THE NATION London is a city so steeped in history that it sometimes seems as if every building has its own story to tell, from the humblest pub with its low, beamed ceilings to the grandest palaces and cathedrals.

London has played an extraordinarily dominant role in the history of both Britain and the world. Within living memory it was both the biggest city on the earth and the capital city of an all-powerful empire, spanning

London was

Scala passuum 5 pedum

80 160 240 320 400 480

Spittle fyldes

Aldgate

Merchantaylo.

Haberdashers

Salters.

Ironmongers.

Vintners.

Clothworkers

East Smithfeild

Billyn gate

gally kaye

The tourre

S. Katherynes

Custom house

fluuius

S. Towleys

8. Fanchurche.	14. Fetter lane.	20. Winchester house
9. Marke lane.	15. S. Dunsthous.	21. Battle bridge
10. Mincheyn lane.	16. Themes streete.	22. Bermodsey streete
11. Paules.	17. Lidon stone.	
12. Eastcheape.	18. Olde Baylye.	Ioannes Norden Angl.
13. Fleeshtreete	19. Clerkenwell.	descripsit anno 1593.

the continents, upon which it was said that the sun never set. Since the end of World War II, with the rapid break-up of the empire, Britain and London have diminished greatly in importance and influence. That process seems set to continue, as closer integration with Europe will inevitably mean that less power is wielded by London-based politicians and a great deal more by institutions based in Brussels or Strasbourg. Even so, London retains many reminders of its past history, in its buildings, its museums, its stately palaces, its churches, its statues and works of art. Visiting them reminds us of all the many great events that the city has witnessed in its long history, such as the first performances of Shakespeare's plays.

Little did the Romans suspect that the city they founded on the north bank of the Thames in AD43 would eclipse Rome itself and grow to be the biggest city in the world. Surprisingly enough, substantial remains of that first Roman city can still be seen today, despite 2,000 years of rebuilding and development.

London owes its existence to chance and the building of a bridge. The Emperor Claudius had intended that Colchester, in Essex, should be the capital of Roman Britain, and that is where the Roman invasion force headed in AD43 after landing near the site of today's Richborough, in Kent. To reach Colchester, the seat of King Cunobelin (Shakespeare's Cymbeline), who ruled all of south-east England, the Romans had to cross the Thames at some point. A few years after their triumph, the Romans constructed a wooden bridge near the site of today's London Bridge—in fact, though rebuilt many times since, it has remained close to the spot the Romans originally chose. London's bridge became the focus of the road network that the Romans built to enable troops to be moved quickly

Mithras, the Roman army's cult god

around the newly conquered province of Britannia. Market forces began to operate, for where there is a major road junction, with troops stationed and ships calling, merchants will inevitably set up stores. Before very long, Londinium was a thriving settlement and port.

THE BOUDICCAN REVOLT Londinium was strategically important to the Romans and, as a new settlement, was a symbol of Rome's colonial ambitions. As such it was a target for those disaffected Iron Age peoples who had not welcomed the invasion. They formed an alliance under the leadership of Boudicca (Boadicea), leader of the Iceni tribe, whose territory covered much of modern Norfolk. Boudicca chose her time well, waiting until Suetonius Paulinus, the Roman governor, was putting down a revolt in Anglesey, before destroying Colchester and then marching on Londinium in AD60. The city was burned to the ground and its inhabitants massacred. What happened after that is not entirely known. Flushed with victory, Boudicca's troops pursued the Roman cavalry to a battle site somewhere in the Midlands, where, according to Tacitus, the Romans achieved an easy victory through superior discipline, killing 80,000 British, while only 400 Romans died. Boudicca is said by Tacitus to have poisoned herself, but other contemporary writers suggest that she died of an illness. It is said that the Britons gave her a rich burial, and legend has it that she is buried, complete with chariot and retainers, beneath the round barrow, or burial mound, that sits on Parliament Hill, on Hampstead Heath. Boudicca has

Boudicca, the Celtic warrior queen

become a popular folk figure, a symbol of resistance against tyranny. Ironically, the magnificent bronze statue of her that stands on the Thames at Victoria Embankment was made in the 1850s, at exactly the time when Britain was itself pursuing a policy of imperial expansion.

ROMAN LONDON London was rapidly rebuilt and, because its location was clearly more convenient than Colchester, it became the official administrative capital of Britannia sometime around AD100. As such, London had its full complement of civic buildings, palaces and temples;

the Museum of London (see page 166) has excellent reconstructions showing the appearance and development of the Roman city from this time. Of visible remains, there is the Temple of Mithras (see page 167) and substantial parts of the city wall built around AD200; one well-preserved stretch can be seen just north of Tower Hill, by the Underground station, and there is another good stretch still serving as the churchyard boundary wall next to the church of All Hallows on the Wall, near the corner of London Wall and Broad Street. You can follow the route of the wall (2.8km/1.75 miles) with the aid of the *London Wall Walk* leaflet published by the Museum of London.

25

Major developments took place in the medieval period that have had lasting effects on the shape of London—most notably, the founding of Westminster Abbey and its adjacent royal palace, which was to become the focus of law-making and administration, while the City developed as an important commercial and industrial area.

SAXONS AND VIKINGS The period that followed the withdrawal of Roman troops from Britain in AD410 is one of the most intriguing in history, precisely because so little is known about it. We do know that the first churches were built in London in the 7th century, if not before, and archeological finds suggest that the port of London continued to thrive, exporting wool and cloth.

London appears in the historical record again in the 9th century, when chroniclers noted 'great slaughter' resulting from Viking raids. In 994 the city was again attacked by Sweyn Forkbeard, son of the Danish King, who was eventually bought off—London was a major contributor to the *danegeld* tax that the Danes demanded in return for peace. In the end, Sweyn's son, Canute, was accepted as 'King of all England' in 1017 and crowned in London.

Glass in the medieval Guildhall

❏ **Monarchs and their reigns**

Normans
William I 1066–1087
William II 1087–1100
Henry I 1100–1135
Stephen 1135–1154

Plantagenets
Henry II 1154–1189
Richard I 1189–1199
John 1199–1216
Henry III 1216–1272
Edward I 1272–1307
Edward II 1307–1327
Edward III 1327–1377
Richard II 1377–1399

Lancastrians
Henry IV 1399–1413
Henry V 1413–1422
Henry VI 1422–1461 (deposed); 1470–1471 (restored)

Yorkists
Edward IV 1461–1470; 1471–1483
Edward V 1483
Richard III 1483–1485 ❏

EDWARD THE CONFESSOR London as we know it today began to develop during the reign of Edward the Confessor, who came to the throne in 1042. He devoted his income to a magnificent new abbey church at Westminster, building a royal palace alongside it. This marked a decisive shift away from the old Roman city, and from that time onwards London consisted of two distinct parts: the royal area around Westminster and the commercial area in the City.

THE NORMANS The importance of Westminster was confirmed when William I, the Norman Conqueror, was crowned King of England in the abbey. A huge number of immigrant merchants began to settle in London in the wake of the Conquest, including Jewish bankers, who occupied the area still known as Old Jewry. This street runs down to Cheapside, which was one huge open-air marketplace. Other streets leading off Cheapside were devoted to particular crafts or products, as names such as Bread Street, Poultry Lane, Goldsmiths Row, and Friday Street (the site of the Friday fish market) still recall.

LAW AND LITERACY As a system of law and concepts such as trial by jury were established, London developed new institutions, such as the Inns of Court, built midway between the City and Westminster during the 13th century for the training and housing of law students. While the universities of the period trained students to become clergymen, the Inns of

Geoffrey Chaucer, poet and clerk

Court were more like business schools, turning out advisers to the king, ambassadors and administrators. One such was Geoffrey Chaucer, whose career included spells as Controller of Customs, ambassador to France, and Clerk of the King's Works. In between he found time to write (but never complete) *The Canterbury Tales* (begun around 1387), a book that helped to establish English as a respectable, poetic language, well able to compete with Latin and French. The widespread availability of Chaucer's work resulted from the activities of William Caxton, who studied printing in Cologne. Edward IV encouraged him to set up a press at Westminster in 1476, and between then and his death in 1491 he published a total of 80 books. Caxton's apprentice, Wynkyn de Worde, took over the business and moved the press to Fleet Street in 1500, thus beginning that street's long association with the printed word.

❏ One of London's most impressive medieval buildings is the Guildhall, which dates from around 1411 but is on the site of an earlier, 12th-century building. The size and splendour of this hall reflects the strength of London merchants, who were organized into guilds to protect their interests: They regulated prices and, through apprenticeship schemes, effectively controlled who could enter their lucrative professions. Under the medieval system of government each ward or district of the City appointed an alderman, usually from the elite of the guilds, and together the aldermen ran all the City's affairs, guided by their leader, the mayor. The aldermen and mayor still exist, but their powers are now more limited. ❏

The Tudor period brought far-reaching changes to London, sparked off by Henry VIII's decisive break with the Church of Rome and the dismantling of monastic power. The effect was to usher in the more confident and secular age of Elizabeth I.

HENRY VII The Tudor era began with a great act of piety: the building of a beautiful fan-roofed chapel in Westminster Abbey by Henry VII, a shrewd financier and politician who was determined to strengthen the role of the monarchy. The chapel was still unfinished in 1509, when Henry VII died, and it was completed by his son, Henry VIII.

HENRY VIII AND THE DISSOLUTION
Soon Henry VIII was busy with demolition, rather than building. He produced the final answer to a debate that had been raging since

> ❏ **Monarchs and their reigns**
> **Tudors**
> Henry VII 1485–1509
> Henry VIII 1509–1547
> Edward VI 1547–1553
> Mary I 1553–1558
> Elizabeth I 1558–1603 ❏

early medieval times (and that had resulted in countless wars and the martyrdom of St. Thomas à Becket); he declared himself, rather than the Pope, to be the absolute head of the church in England. Conveniently this meant that he could appropriate the vast wealth of the church; the church tithe (a tax of one-tenth of all crops and revenues) was diverted to the Crown in 1534, and in 1536 Henry dissolved the monasteries, gaining a vast stockpile of property with which to reward his supporters. Religious houses in and around London were converted to mansions by favoured courtiers; Blackfriars, for example, became the estate of the Master of Revels, Thomas Cawarden. A huge amount of property in the City that had previously been owned by the church was sold or given away, so that rents plummeted and houses stood empty.

POPULATION GROWTH AND PLANNING LAWS This situation did not last long, however, for the reign of Elizabeth I was marked by a four-fold growth in London's population, resulting in serious overcrowding and the passing of the first ever planning law. This was issued as a royal proclamation in 1580 (and made law in 1592). It prohibited any new build-

The Tower of London in 1509

Genius at large: Henry VIII

❏ London Bridge was one of the wonders of Tudor London. Since its completion in 1209 it had acquired some unusual features: one was the sheer number of shops and houses packed onto the bridge, resulting in great congestion. Another was the ornate Nonsuch House, built towards the Southwark end of the bridge in 1577; this folly was so called because there was 'none such' like it. The heads of traitors executed in the nearby Tower of London were displayed on poles above the gatehouse of the bridge, having been boiled and dipped in tar to preserve them. This practice ended in 1661, and the bridge itself, having stood for 600 years, was replaced in 1831 by a new bridge designed by Sir John Rennie. In 1972 Rennie's bridge was replaced, only to be sold and re-erected in Lake Havasu City, Arizona. ❏

ing within a 4.8-km (3-mile) radius of the city, and any subdivision of existing buildings. This and similar laws issued in the early 17th century were totally ignored, with the effect that the many monastic gardens and fields that had previously existed within the boundaries of the city rapidly became clogged with shoddy timber buildings. Much of the Elizabethan city was destroyed a century later by the Great Fire, but the spirit of the period lives on in Shakespeare's great plays, and in the comedies of his contemporary, Ben Jonson, whose *Bartholomew Fair* gives a pretty clear idea of the rough nature of life of the early 17th century.

EXPANDING TRADE No area was rougher than Southwark, where Shakespeare's Globe Theatre was built in 1598–1599, alongside the brothels, taverns, bear pits and cock-pits to which apprentices would come for entertainment. This area developed rapidly as London burst beyond its Roman and medieval limits, and the south bank became the place where poorer, semiskilled or manual labourers lived. They were joined by a growing population of sailors and shipbuilders as London's overseas trade contacts expanded. The Royal Exchange was opened in 1570 by Elizabeth I, designed to compete with powerful markets in Antwerp and Amsterdam (though, ironically, the original building was built from Dutch and Flemish materials), and British merchants such as Sir Thomas Gresham made vast fortunes from trade with Russia, the Levant and the East Indies.

The 17th century began with the coronation of James I in 1603; since he was already James VI of Scotland, the two kingdoms were united for the first time and conciliation was the theme of the Jacobean age. But soon Britain would be gripped by civil war and a king would lose his head, while London would be decimated by plague and then destroyed by fire.

THE GUNPOWDER PLOT In the early years of James I's reign an event took place that is still commemorated with bonfires and fireworks all over Britain. Catholic conspirators, who looked to Rome and the Pope as head of the church, sought to further their cause by placing explosives in the cellars beneath the House of Lords, with the aim of killing the King and all the assembled peers. The plan, known as the Gunpowder Plot, failed, and Guy Fawkes was caught before lighting the gunpowder fuse on 5 November 1605.

THE CIVIL WAR Parliament was again the scene of an explosive event on 4 January 1642, when Charles I burst into the House of Commons demanding the arrest of five Members. This was the culmination of a bitter power

A mural depicting the Great Fire of London

> ❏ **Monarchs and their reigns**
> **Stuarts**
> James I 1603–1625
> Charles I 1625–1649
> The Commonwealth 1649–1653
> The Protectorate 1653–1659
> Charles II 1660–1685 ❏

struggle between the King and Parliament, which then erupted into war. London took the side of Parliament in the battles that ensued, and City merchants made a substantial contribution to the cost of the Parliamentary army that finally defeated the Royalists at Naseby. In 1649 the King was beheaded and, after a period of instability, Oliver Cromwell became Lord Protector, imposing a puritanical rule that lasted until his death in 1658. In 1660 the monarchy was restored.

30

THE MAYOR OF LONDON SIR THOMAS BLUDWORTH IS CALLED OUT IN THE EARLY HOURS TO SEE THE FIRE

FIRES LIKE THIS WERE COMMON IN LONDON AND THE MAYOR UNIMPRESSED, RETURNS TO BED. HIS COMMENT BEING 'PISH A WOMAN COULD PISS IT OUT!'

BY THE END OF MONDAY 3RD SEPTEMBER THE FIRE IS RAGING OUT OF CONTROL

WAREHOUSES AT THE RIVER'S EDGE FULL OF STOCKS SUCH AS TAR·OIL·ROPE SPIRITS·PAINT & CANVAS ADD TERRIBLE FUEL TO THE FIRE

PEOPLE ARE ONLY CONCERNED TO ESCAPE TAKING WITH THEM AS MUCH AS THEY CAN CARRY

London's burning

THE GREAT PLAGUE Two great disasters were to hit the city in the 1660s. The first signs of the Great Plague were detected at Christmas 1664 and soon all those who could afford it, including most of the city's doctors, had fled. Many theories were propounded about the cause of the plague—dogs and cats were blamed and killed by official exterminators, which only exacerbated the problem, for the rats, the true carriers of plague, simply multiplied. At the height of the plague, 14,000 people were dying every week, their corpses dumped into vast plague pits.

The cold winter of 1665 brought a decline in casualties, and by February 1666 the King and court had returned to London. At least 100,000 people had died, but the city soon returned to its normal bustle.

THE GREAT FIRE A mere six months later, on the night of 2 September 1666, a baker's shop caught fire in Pudding Lane. The Lord Mayor was alerted but is reported to have said

that the fire was so trivial that 'a woman might piss it out'. Samuel Pepys, on rising from his bed the next day, was horrified to learn that 300 houses were already burned by 'an infinite great fire', and that nobody was attempting to quench the flames. Remarkably, only nine people lost their lives in the Great Fire, which raged for three days, but the damage to property was immense. Nearly every building within the 160ha (395 acres) of the City had been destroyed: 13,200 houses, 44 guildhalls and 87 churches. St. Paul's Cathedral was so badly damaged that repair was impossible. Those Londoners who had survived the Great Plague were now camped in the fields around the smoldering ruins of their city, wondering what further disaster might occur.

❑ The Great Plague of 1665 was only one of a series to hit the city. The Black Death of 1348–1349 carried off at least half of the city's population, and the plague recurred, on and off, for the next 300 years. By-laws were passed banning the slaughter of animals in the city—the waste was thought to be the source of disease. Burning fires in the streets to purify the air and breathing the scent of nosegays made of herbs were tried as preventative measures, and arsenic was prescribed as a cure. Finally the Great Fire put an end to the epidemics by destroying the rat-infested buildings in which the plague had thrived. ❑

Out of the ashes of the Great Fire a new and prosperous city soon arose. During the next 150 years, a huge amount of building took place that totally transformed London's appearance, resulting in the city that we see today.

SIR CHRISTOPHER WREN The task of rebuilding London after the Great Fire fell to Sir Christopher Wren, Surveyor General to the Crown, but all his initial proposals met with resistance. Wren planned a radical redevelopment of the medieval city, replacing the narrow alleys and jumbled wharfs with a new waterfront and graceful public buildings. His visionary scheme foundered on practicality; comprehensive redevelopment was prevented by the complex pattern of land and property holding in the city, and by the fact that Londoners themselves wanted to rebuild their houses and shops as quickly as possible. The city was reconstructed along the existing street pattern, but using brick, stone and tile, instead of timber and thatch, as a precaution against fire.

Wren's scheme for St. Paul's was also frustrated. Faced with the challenge of building the world's first

Wren, the idealistic architect

> ❏ **Monarchs and their reigns**
> James II 1685–1688
> William and Mary 1689–1702
> Anne 1702–1714
>
> **Hanoverians**
> George I 1714–1727
> George II 1727–1760
> George III 1760–1820
> George IV 1820–1830
> William IV 1830–1837 ❏

Protestant cathedral, he produced a building that broke with the past, as his 'Great Model' in the cathedral crypt shows. His clients, however, wanted to cling to their medieval liturgy, which required a processional nave and a chancel, so the design was eventually altered—some would say compromised—in order to meet their wishes.

THE GREAT BOOM Over the next decades, the city developed its own character and became a place where people worked, rather than lived. Looking down from the dome of St. Paul's, a mason employed on its construction in the last years of the 17th century would have seen large private gardens, fields, orchards and grazing animals only a short distance away. Soon that view was to change, for a huge building boom began that continued at breakneck pace for the next century. The private gardens lining the Strand were developed first, followed by Covent Garden, Holborn, Spitalfields and Soho, St. James's and Mayfair. Many of the residential areas built at this time bear the names of landowners who grew rich on bricks and mortar: the Curzons, Portmans, Cadogans, Camdens, Sloanes and Grosvenors.

These residential areas, such as St. James's and Mayfair, were built for wealthy aristocrats and courtiers, with elegant houses set around garden squares. The subsequent building boom was, however, fuelled by the rise of the professional classes. Doctors, lawyers, underwriters, stockbrokers and merchants, even actors, artists and publishers, had the means to move out of the cramped and overcrowded city into West End property. London must have resembled a vast building site for much of the period, especially towards the end of the 18th century and the beginning of the 19th, when major public buildings, such as the Mansion House, the Bank of England and the British Museum, were erected. Two projects epitomize the buoyancy of this era. The architect John Nash undertook the remodelling of a whole

Wren's masterpiece, St. Paul's

❑ Before the Great Fire London was built largely of timber, as the city lacks any local source of good building stone. Stone for prestigious churches such as St. Paul's had to be brought by sea from Portland in Dorset or along the Thames from the Cotswolds. After the Great Fire, new building laws restricted the use of wood. Bricks became the standard material, made locally by extracting clay from farmland on the fringes of the city. The pits were then filled in with domestic garbage and the land leased to speculative builders. By the 19th century, bricks were being brought in by rail or canal, principally from the clayfields and brick kilns of Bedford, Fletton and Peterborough. ❑

swathe of London, from the Mall northwards to Regent's Park, providing the kind of dramatic vistas that London had so far lacked; it also provided the stimulus for London's expansion northwards that eventually linked it to hilltop Hampstead. Meanwhile, Trafalgar Square was cleared of its royal stables and transformed into a public space leading towards Whitehall, where new buildings such as the Admiralty symbolized England's colonial might. One medieval building remained in the midst of the new monuments: the Palace of Westminster. It had such a long history that nobody dared suggest rebuilding it, although it was archaic and impractical. Few were sorry, then, when the palace finally went up in flames in November 1834, marking the end of an era.

Queen Victoria came to the throne in 1837, aged only 18. During the 63 years of her reign London continued its inexorable growth. It was a city at the heart of a vast empire, the financial capital of the world, a city of magnificent buildings and great institutions; at the same time it had a huge population of extremely poor people living in squalid conditions. The word 'slum' first began to be applied to parts of London at this time.

34

THE GREAT EXHIBITION The most spectacular public event of Queen Victoria's reign was 'The Great Exhibition of the Works of Industry of All Nations', staged in Hyde Park in 1851. Six million people poured through the turnstiles between 1 May and 15 October to see the exhibits housed in Joseph Paxton's Crystal Palace. The profits were sufficient for a new museum complex to be set up, including the Victoria and Albert, the Science and the Natural History museums. They were constructed over the former market gardens of South Kensington.

The Great Exhibition, with its emphasis on technology and industry, set many of the themes of the

Queen Victoria

period—even the Crystal Palace itself, basically a greenhouse or conservatory on a massive scale, inspired scores of similar buildings using iron as the core structural material, rather than wood, brick or stone. Examples range from the Agricultural Hall in Islington to covered markets such as Leadenhall, Smithfield and Covent Garden. The same technology was used for railway stations such as the beautifully restored Liverpool Street, or Paddington, the terminus of the Great Western Railway (where restoration work is in progress).

THE TRANSPORT REVOLUTION
Paddington Station was built in its present form in 1854, but the line itself opened in 1838, offering a service to West Drayton. In 1842, Queen Victoria set the royal seal of approval on this new form of transport by taking her first train journey along the same line from Slough to Paddington, a distance of 27km (17 miles), in 23 minutes—an average of 70kph (44mph); Prince Albert is said to have instructed the conductor: 'Not so fast

next time'. By the end of Victoria's reign, 390,000 commuters were being carried in and out of the city every day, travelling a distance of up to 48km (30 miles), an indication of just how far London had spread by then.

Meanwhile, London's docks were expanding rapidly. Smaller boats, mainly carrying cargoes such as coal and grain from other British ports, still used riverside wharves, but congestion on the Thames was such that purpose-built docks were needed to handle the big oceangoing vessels. Whole new villages and communities grew up to serve the docks, but poverty was endemic because wages were extremely low. London was becoming an increasingly stratified city, with a relatively prosperous West End and a poor East End. Model dwellings to house the poor began to appear—the American philanthropist, George Peabody, left substantial funds for their construction—but never enough to make any serious dent in the growing problem of the slums. The situation gave rise to many philanthropic initiatives, such as the founding in 1878 of William Booth's Salvation Army, which set

❏ London lacked any kind of system for disposing of waste until the mid-19th century. Garbage and sewage were dumped into its rivers, earning it the names 'Venice of drains' and 'capital of cholera'. The first covered sewers were introduced in 1858, known as 'the Year of the Great Stink' because they were completely ineffectual. Nobody went anywhere near the Thames unless they had to and the windows of the newly rebuilt Houses of Parliament were draped with sheets soaked in chloride of lime to keep the smell at bay. The saviour of London, whose name is nearly forgotten but who ought to be regarded as a national hero, was Sir Joseph Bazalgette. His system of brick-lined sewers, linked to treatment plants and pumping stations, came into operation in the 1860s. The 208-km (1,300-mile) system, carrying 320,000 litres (70,200 gal) a day, still forms the basis of London's drainage system. ❏

up soup kitchens and hostels to help the very poor. Ultimately, the extreme poverty in London was to have massive and worldwide repercussions: Karl Marx's observations on its causes and solutions were to become the basis for Communist-inspired revolutions in several parts of the world.

Not long after the century turned, Victoria died and modern history began. Cultural values and attitudes began to change, and in place of the laissez-faire *attitude to development, the London County Council began to impose order. All was to be shattered, however, in the Blitz, when German bombers attacked London repeatedly between September 1940 and May 1941, reducing large parts of the capital to rubble.*

The London County Council was officially created in 1888 as a directly elected body with substantial powers. It needed them to tackle the problems of a city that had grown out of control, but it was not until the early 20th century, under Progressive (Liberal) leadership, that it began to show its muscle. Soon the LCC was involved in everything from slum clearance to building houses. It also created many parks and open spaces, including the Green Belt, designed to halt the city's spread. Some of the LCC's housing plans, such as the Boundary Street development in Bethnal Green, became the models for developments in parts of continental Europe.

THE INTER-WAR YEARS The pace of building continued after World War I; in the words of a slogan of the time, Britain needed 'homes fit for heroes'. Increasingly these were high-rise blocks of flats (apartments) of five stories or more and regarded with suspicion because residents of flats enjoyed none of the benefits of street-based community life.

The middle-class dream was to escape the city, made possible by the creation of a comprehensive and cheap public transit system, the Underground, whose first line had opened in 1863. (Its later, deep-dug tunnels gave the system its nickname, 'the tube'.)

Rapid expansion in the 1920s and 1930s enabled more people to live in new suburban housing developments, where houses had running water and electricity. Soon, however,

> ❏ **Monarchs and their reigns**
> Victoria 1837–1901
> Edward VII 1901–1910
> George V 1910–1936
> Edward VIII 1936
> George VI 1936–1952
> Elizabeth II 1952–present ❏

the Underground would serve another purpose: providing shelter for Londoners during nightly air raids at the height of the Blitz.

THE BLITZ The *Blitzkrieg* ('lightning war') was Hitler's weapon for beating Britain into submission, although its effect was to strengthen resistance. Recognizing that aerial bombing would play a major role in the war, the authorities had already evacuated 690,000 children to temporary rural homes in September 1939. Many poor evacuees from the East End thereby gained their first glimpse of farm animals, and rural people discovered that the children of the East End were not the degenerates, the 'people of the abyss', as they were often portrayed.

Meanwhile, German bombs began to rain down, and a nightly pattern was established: A two-minute siren wail would warn Londoners of approaching aircraft, giving them time to take cover in basements, in Anderson shelters (arches of corrugated metal covered with earth) dug in back gardens, or in the Underground. Even Churchill, the wartime leader, had an underground bunker, which is now an intriguing museum,

in the Cabinet War Rooms in Whitehall.

Throughout the Blitz, everyone tried to live life as normal, although bus and train services were constantly disrupted, along with gas, electricity and water supplies. Even so, nightclubs and theatres remained open. The Café de Paris, which optimistically called itself 'the safest nightclub in town' and had mirrored walls copied from the ballroom of the *Titanic*, received a direct hit in March 1941. It was just one event in the raids that left 29,890 dead and 3.5 million buildings in London severely damaged or destroyed.

The worst of the Blitz was over by May 1941. Towards the end of the war, however, a new bombing

Life goes on, despite the war

campaign began. In reprisal for British air raids on German cities, Hitler unleashed his new 'wonder weapons', the V1 flying bomb and the V2 rocket, from June 1944. These created havoc and caused great loss of life in the last months of the war.

ST. PAUL'S Throughout the Blitz, a special effort was made to protect St. Paul's, which survived intact, even when every building around it was flattened. Prompt action enabled potentially dangerous fires to be put out, but luck played a part as well; the cathedral received a direct hit on 12 September 1940, but the bomb failed to explode and was extracted from the foundations three days later. It was then driven to Hackney Marsh and exploded creating a crater more than 35m (115ft) wide.

37

Nikolaus Pevsner, founder of the Buildings of England *series of books, observed that post-war planners and architects caused greater damage to England's historic cities than the Luftwaffe ever did during the Blitz. This sentiment has been repeated by Prince Charles, an outspoken critic of much modern architecture. The post-war rebuilding certainly transformed the city, yet 21st century London has acquired many impressive buildings and developments.*

Immediately following the war, two key pieces of planning legislation were passed to improve the look of London. Under the Town and Country Planning Act of 1947, protection was given to historic buildings, which could no longer be demolished or altered at will. The Civic Amenities Act of 1967 extended this concept to whole areas of London, thus creating the notion of 'conservation areas' within which development was severely restricted. The other great step forwards was the 1956 Clean Air Act, which successfully eradicated London's smog.

BUILDINGS OF THE AGE Set against these triumphs, London acquired a large body of mediocre and alienating buildings, some of which have since been demolished while others face an uncertain future. One example is the South Bank complex, a legacy of the 1951 Festival of Britain. The Royal Festival Hall was put up in a great hurry when this celebration was first conceived as a way of cheering up the nation after the rationing and austerity that followed the war. As a symbol of the bright new world, the Festival Hall is uninspiring; it is, nevertheless, regarded with some affection by Londoners for the simple reason that it is not as ugly as the bunkerlike structures that surround it, such as the Hayward Gallery and the National Theatre. A new facing has been proposed as a way of improving their appearance, but this has not yet been undertaken despite years of complaints.

LONDON'S FIRST AIRPORT
Heathrow Airport was transferred from military to civil use in 1946. In 1955 its first major passenger terminal was completed; this, like much of the airport, was built by Sikh labourers from the Punjab (a region of India and Pakistan), encouraged to move to London to fill labour shortages.

Heathrow quickly became one of the world's busiest freight and passenger airports, making a huge impact on west London and its economy. To cope with the massive increase in air traffic, four other airports have been built: Stansted, Gatwick, Luton and the London City Airport in the Docklands.

Makeshift anti-smog masks

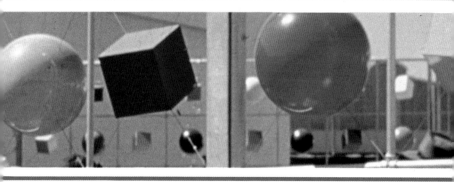

THE DOCKS By contrast, east London went into dramatic decline as manufacturing industries began to relocate out of London, and the docks, much rebuilt after devastating war bomb damage, began to close down with astonishing speed. The increased use of container ships led to the relocation of Port of London to Tilbury, downriver. By 1981 the 17.5-km (11-mile) stretch of docks was entirely closed.

BRAVE NEW WORLD In the four decades following World War II, all but 70 of the City's 270ha (667 acres) have been rebuilt. At first, repairing war damage was a priority. However, after the Big Bang of 1985–1986, a revolution in financial services demanded completely different office space. Meanwhile, the government kick-started the total regeneration of the Docklands area in 1981 and were luring companies eastwards.

The City fathers recognized a threat to their supremacy and responded quickly. In just eight years, from 1986 to 1993, the equivalent of one half of the entire stock of City office buildings had been rebuilt. Just as the centrepiece of Docklands is Canary Wharf, so the City's is Broadgate—37 million sq m (400 million sq ft) of office and recreation space built on disused railway land surrounding Liverpool Street Station.

These massive developments, together with the regeneration of the riverside, especially along the South Bank, have shifted the focus of the capital eastwards, yet kept its financial heart in the City. As the century drew to a close, a host of ambitious Millennium projects, aided by grants from the Lottery Fund, further suggested that London's seemingly infinite expansion westwards has paused and turned around.

Visiting the Festival of Britain

SIGHTSEEING TOURS BY BUS
A tour with the award-winning Big Bus company is as good a way as any to get your bearings. Every bus has a live commentary and also includes a free walking tour and boat tour in the ticket price. There are two different tours; check them out on www.bigbus.co.uk, or look for their various bus stops near central London's major attractions.

Top: there are pigeons galore in Trafalgar Square, even though it is now illegal to feed them

LONDON BY AREA London resembles a giant patchwork quilt, made up of many different districts and communities that have grown up around two ancient, once separate cores: the City of London, known as the City, and the City of Westminster. In and around them, there are parks, monumental palaces, museums and churches. This rich tapestry can seem complex, but today's Central London still retains distinctly discernable districts that reflect the city's amalgamation over the centuries.

WESTMINSTER Its ancient, original purpose remains the political, religious and royal hub of the capital and country. The Houses of Parliament, Westminster Abbey and Trafalgar Square are its historic landmarks, while government offices line Whitehall. Art treasures fill the Tate Britain, the National Gallery, National Portrait Gallery and Banqueting House.

ST. JAMES'S AND THE MALL Privileged Londoners promenade along the Mall, stroll in St. James's Park and frequent gentlemen's clubs, art auctioneers, Floris the perfumer and other long-established stores. With Buckingham Palace as a central point.

MAYFAIR AND PICCADILLY Lying between Oxford Street and Piccadilly, Mayfair was built by the rich for the rich. Today, the grand Georgian streets and squares are temporary homes to the international wealthy. High style is the key-note in the super-deluxe hotels, the Bond Street and Regent Street stores, and the art galleries.

CHELSEA AND KNIGHTSBRIDGE Village Chelsea, inner Knightsbridge, and the core of South Kensington retain their gentle, residential pace. Between them, streetwise shoppers check out the latest fashion statements along the King's Road and around Brompton Cross. Here, too, are Harrods and the great South Kensington museums.

KENSINGTON, NOTTING HILL AND HYDE PARK Built up around the homely Kensington Palace, stuccoed Kensington family homes set the tone. This informal mood pervades Kensington Gardens and adjoining Hyde Park, where Londoners of all ages come to relax, and extends through leafy Holland Park to fashionable Notting Hill and its Portobello Road antiques market.

REGENT'S PARK AND MARYLEBONE The great, elegant swathe of Regent's Park is the back garden for north Londoners, with its roses, zoo, lake and theatre. There is more entertainment nearby at Lord's Cricket Ground, Madame Tussauds and the Planetarium and along Regent's Canal at Camden Lock markets.

BLOOMSBURY AND FITZROVIA In the streets surrounding leafy Georgian squares, university buildings and museums buzz with the hot debates of London's students and intellectuals. The British Museum is its focus; its neighbours include Dickens' House and the British Library.

SOHO AND COVENT GARDEN This amorphous mass of lanes lying between the two cities, London and

London by area

WALKING TOURS
These are a comprehensive, and often very entertaining way to get to know London. The best operators are the Original London Walks (tel: 020-7624 3978), though there are several other companies; see the listings magazine *Time Out* for details.

Westminster, is one big entertainment area. Theatres stage plays and musicals, bars are hives of gossip, and restaurants still serve food to reflect the area's cosmopolitan immigrant past.

HOLBORN AND THE STRAND The riverside strip linking the City to Westminster is punctuated by the quiet medieval Inns of Court and the revamped Somerset House.

THE CITY London began here. It was partly remodelled in the showy 1980s, but today's City traders still walk past Roman temple remains, medieval halls, Wren churches, and Victorian monuments to British imperial power.

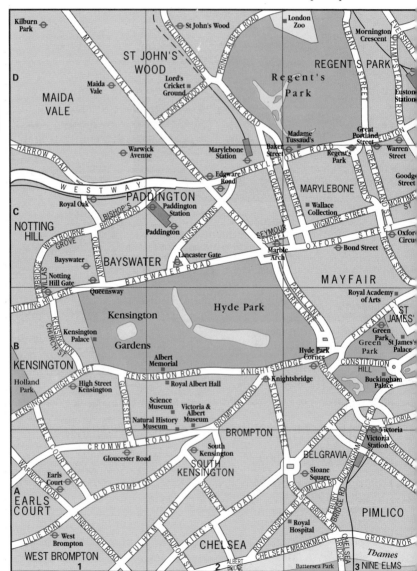

42

CLERKENWELL, ISLINGTON AND THE EAST END
Clerkenwell buzzes with craftspeople, Islington mixes Georgian terraces, avant-garde theatres, and restaurants; the East End retains its grit, wit and immigrant flavour.

DOCKLANDS The river landscape stretching downstream from the City is a blend of old and modern architecture—riverside warehouse apartments criss-crossed by the high-level Docklands Light Railway.

SOUTH BANK A riverside strip of entertainment from Westminster to London Bridge includes concert halls, theatres, the London Aquarium and the BA London Eye.

43

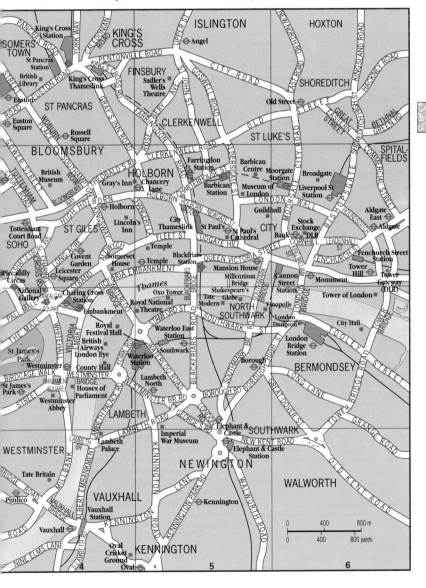

F

Leicester Square

Piccadilly Circus

National Portrait Gallery

National Gallery

St Martin in the Fields

Victoria Embankment Gardens

Cleopatra's Needle

Canada House

TRAFALGAR SQUARE

Charing Cross

Charing Cross

Charing Cross Station

ST JAMES'S

COCKSPUR STREET

Nelson's Column

Embankment Pier

Festival Pier

E

NORTHUMBERLAND AVENUE

Embankment

Royal Festival Hall

Admiralty Arch

Whitehall Theatre

WHITEHALL PLACE

Footbridge

Hungerford Bridge

Old Admiralty

Old War Office

Hispaniola

Banqueting House

HORSE GUARDS PARADE

Ministry of Defence

T h a m e s

Jubilee Gardens

D

St James's

Duck Island

Old Treasury DOWNING ST

British Airways London Eye

Foreign and Commonwealth Office

Cenotaph

Dali Universe

Park

KING CHARLES ST

County Hall

Churchill Museum and Cabinet War Rooms

Treasury

Westminster Pier

London Aquarium

GREAT GEORGE ST

Westminster

WESTMINSTER BRIDGE

BIRDCAGE WALK

PARLIAMENT SQUARE

Big Ben

Florence Nightingale Museum

Guard's Chapel and Museum

Queen Elizabeth II Conference Centre

BROAD SANCTUARY

Westminster Hall

Home Office

St Margaret's

OLD PALACE YARD

Houses of Parliament

C

St James's Park

Caxton Hall

Westminster Abbey

Jewel Tower

St Thomas' Hospital

New Scotland Yard

DEAN'S YARD

ABINGDON STREET

VICTORIA STREET

Westminster School

Victoria Tower

WESTMINSTER

Victoria Tower Gardens

ARTILLERY ROW

GREYCOAT PLACE

MARSHAM STREET

SMITH

Lambeth Palace

B

St John's Smith Square

SQUARE

Royal Horticultural Society New Hall

MILLBANK

Lambeth Pier

Museum of Garden History

HORSEFERRY ROAD

LAMBETH BRIDGE

LAMBETH RD

Royal Horticultural Society Old Hall

Westminster School Playing Field

REGENCY STREET

T h a m e s

ALBERT EMBANKMENT

A

VAUXHALL BRIDGE ROAD

ATTERBURY ST

Tate Britain

0   200 m

0   220 yards

1   2   3

44

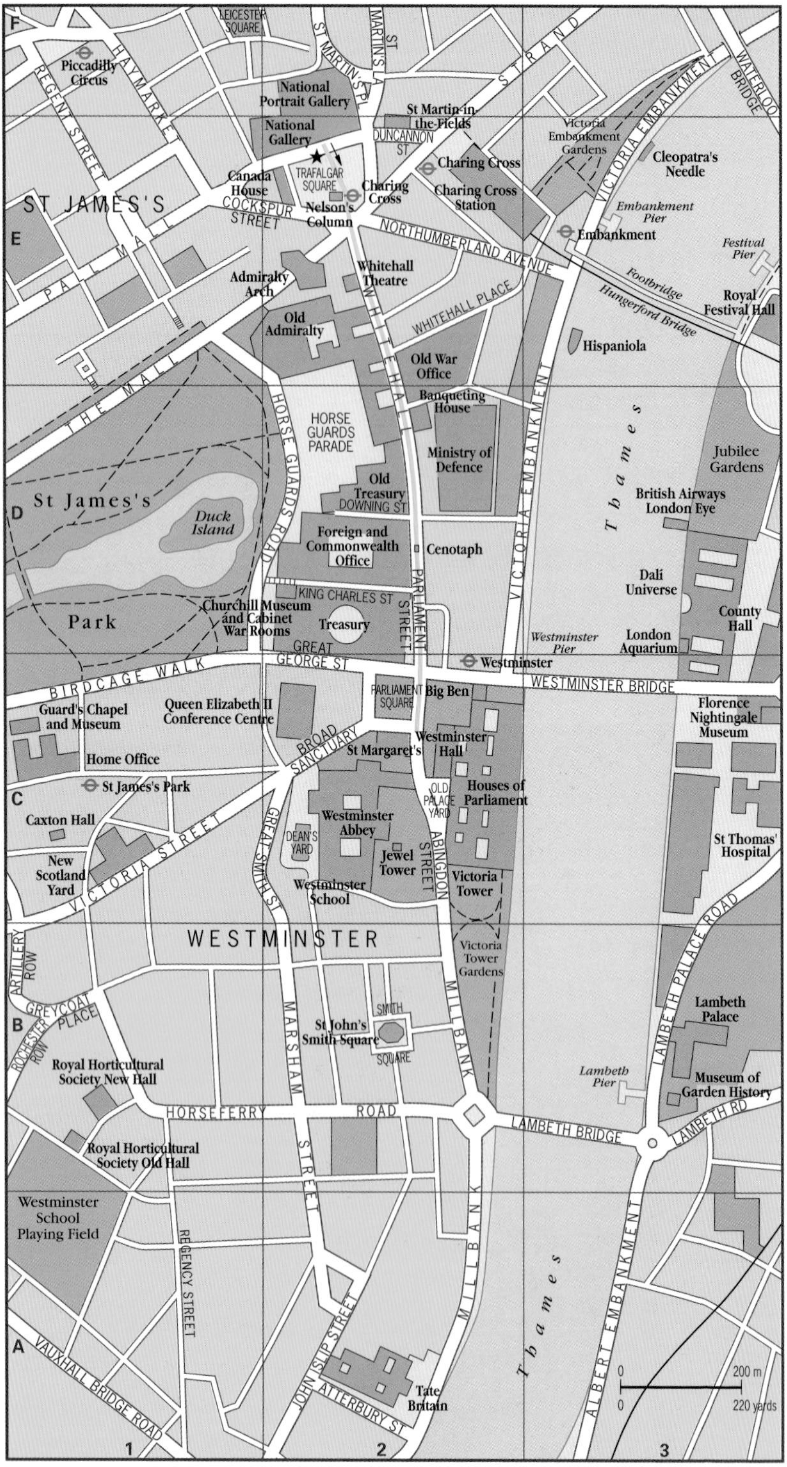

WESTMINSTER Gossip and intrigue—political, royal and religious—have filled the streets and buildings of Westminster since it first developed, 3.2km (2 miles) south-west of the City of London. It was Edward the Confessor who began the original Westminster Abbey after he moved the royal court out of the City in 1042, triggering London's westwards expansion. Since then, Westminster has been synonymous with government. Its major buildings house the Treasury and the Foreign and Commonwealth Office. At its heart stand the Abbey, the Houses of Parliament, Parliament Square, Whitehall and Trafalgar Square

WESTMINSTER WALK Start in Trafalgar Square, on the steps of the National Gallery.

Trafalgar Square is the heart of the city—a bronze plaque in the pavement behind Charles I's statue marks the spot. The square was laid out in 1829 in honour of Lord Nelson's naval victory against Napoleon in 1805. Its centrepiece is a statue of Nelson on a Corinthian column, 53m (175ft) tall. Beyond is a fine view down Whitehall and to the left is the church of **St. Martin-in-the-Fields.**

Walk down into the square, where there is plenty to see: fine reliefs of Nelson's greatest triumphs decorating the base of his column, Sir Edward Landseer's four bronze lions added in 1867, Sir Edwin Lutyens's pools with their playful dolphins added in 1939. Now walk towards **Whitehall.** Stranded on an island at the head of the broad avenue is Hubert le Sueur's animated statue of Charles I on horseback (1633) looking towards Banqueting House, the scene of his execution in 1649. The first building on the right, the **Admiralty**, is fronted by Robert Adam's stone screen (1759) adorned with two sea horses. The country's naval affairs were run from this building when the British fleet was considered the most powerful in the world. Next comes **Horse Guards**, where two members of the Household Cavalry mount guard on horseback daily from 11am (10am on Sunday)—a tradition that survives even though all that remains of the former royal palace is the **Banqueting House** opposite. Beyond Horse Guards is **Downing Street**, the official residence of the Prime Minister (No. 10) and the Chancellor of the Exchequer (No. 11), though the former Prime Minister, Tony Blair, and his family lived at No. 11, which is bigger than No. 10, during his leadership years. Further down Whitehall, in the middle of the road, is the **Cenotaph**, designed by Sir Edwin Lutyens (1920) to commemorate those who died in World War I. Whitehall ends at Parliament Square, with the **Houses of Parliament** to the left and **West-minster Abbey** to the right.

Previous page: Trafalgar Square

THE EXECUTION OF CHARLES I

Charles I is said to have faced death with exemplary courage, wearing two shirts so that he would not shiver in the January cold and give the impression that he was afraid. Andrew Marvell, the poet who witnessed the execution, wrote of the king that 'He nothing common did or mean/ Upon that memorable scene'. Many went to the scaffold, both before and after Charles I, but never an anointed monarch, and many considered his execution an unforgivable act of regicide. To this day, Charles I continues to have his admirers, who place wreaths on his statue, at the head of Whitehall, on 30 January, the anniversary of his death.

Rubens's ceiling paintings in the Banqueting House

▶▶▶ **Banqueting House**   *44D2*

Whitehall, SW1 (tel: 0870 751 5178)
www.hrp.org.uk
Open: Mon–Sat 10–5. Admission moderate, includes acoustiguide. Occasional lunchtime concerts.
Underground: Charing Cross, Westminster, Embankment

The Banqueting House contains one of London's finest rooms. It was built between 1619 and 1622 by Inigo Jones, who had trained in Livorno (Tuscany), and absorbed the influence of the architect Andrea Palladio. He introduced the purity of classical design to London, first with the Queen's House, Greenwich (now part of the National Maritime Museum complex, see page 218), then with this sophisticated and seminal building.

Banqueting House is now hemmed in by other classical buildings. It is difficult to imagine how exotic and different it would once have appeared, crisply faced in white Portland stone, and surrounded by the ramshackle brick and timber buildings of the rambling Whitehall Palace that Henry VIII seized from Cardinal Wolsey. When fire destroyed part of the palace, James I employed Inigo Jones to rebuild it on a massive scale (modelled on the Tuileries Palace in Paris), but only the Banqueting House was completed. The exterior is relatively restrained, except for the frieze of garlands running beneath the parapet. James II added the weathervane on the north side of the roof to warn him when William of Orange might be blown across the English Channel.

The real wonder of the building lies inside and upstairs: the magnificent ceiling paintings commissioned by Charles I and designed by Peter Paul Rubens, who was knighted for this work. Painted in Antwerp and installed in 1635, the nine pictures are intended to emphazise the divine authority of the monarch (a contentious political issue at the time): James I (Charles' father) is shown being received into heaven, while other scenes depict the claimed benefits of his rule: peace, prosperity and the

Union of England and Scotland. This forthright pictorial propaganda is designed to be seen from the doorway, the visitor's viewpoint, as explained on the acoustiguide.

Rubens's ceiling paintings are quite ironic in light of subsequent events, for Charles I went to his execution from this room on 30 January 1649, having fought and lost the seven-year Civil War against Oliver Cromwell and the Parliamentarians. A scaffold was erected outside the north annex (since demolished) of the Banqueting House, and it was from here, through a window, that Charles I stepped out onto the scaffold to meet his death. A bust of Charles I over the staircase entrance marks the spot.

▶▶ Churchill Museum and Cabinet War Rooms *44D2*

Clive Steps, King Charles Street, SW1 (tel: 020-7930 6961)
www.iwm.org.uk
Open: Daily 9.30–6. Admission expensive, includes acoustiguide (children free)
Underground: Westminster

This labyrinth of underground rooms provides an intriguing glimpse of the spartan conditions under which Sir Winston Churchill, the War Cabinet and the Chiefs of Staff operated during World War II. From the cramped confines of this dark basement, they directed the strategies and forces of a global war. The rooms are equipped exactly as they were during this traumatic period. Highlights include the Cabinet Room, arranged as if for a meeting; the Prime Minister's room, which served as a combined office and bedroom; the Map Room containing a map of the world, on which the Allied campaign was charted; and the Telephone Room containing the hot-line telephone on which Churchill discussed his plans with US President Franklin D. Roosevelt.

Here, too, you will find the first national museum devoted entirely to Winston Churchill, giving a unique insight into the great man's life.

Churchill's office and bedroom in the Cabinet War Rooms

▶▶▶ REGION HIGHLIGHTS

Banqueting House *page 46*

Houses of Parliament *pages 48–49*

National Gallery *pages 50–51*

National Portrait Gallery *page 52*

Tate Britain *pages 56–57*

Upriver cruises *page 55*

Westminster Abbey *pages 59–61*

HENRY VIII'S WINE CELLAR
Behind the Banqueting House stands the former Ministry of Defence (MOD) head office. In its basement is a surviving part of the original royal palace of Whitehall; a simple vaulted brick chamber known as Henry VIII's Wine Cellar. This was considered such an important monument that it was moved over 12m (38ft) from its original site when the MOD building was constructed in the 1940s. Sadly, visits are not possible.

Parliament

THE GUNPOWDER PLOT
One of the most celebrated dates in British history is 5 November 1605, when Guy Fawkes and a number of other Roman Catholic conspirators attempted to blow up Parliament, along with James I and his ministers. Effigies of Guy Fawkes (and other unpopular figures) are burned on bonfires at firework parties all over the country on this date, and the cellars of the House are still checked to this day by the Yeomen of the Guard before the ceremonial State Opening of Parliament. The Queen presides over the State Opening from the House of Lords; No monarch has been admitted to the Commons since 1642, when Charles I forced his way in and tried to arrest five Members of Parliament, an event that sparked off the seven-year Civil War between Royalists and Parliamentarians.

▶▶▶ Houses of Parliament 44C2
St. Margaret Street, SW1 (tel: (020-7219 3000/3107)
www.parliament.uk
Open: when Parliament in session, Mon–Fri; see website for precise timings. Admission free. For guided tours, see panel opposite
Underground: Westminster

The public may attend debates when Parliament is in session; visitors should queue at the St. Stephen's porch entrance, which is clearly marked. At other times, the Houses of Parliament are closed for security reasons, but visits can be arranged.

Although access to this monumental building complex is restricted, the exterior alone is a splendid sight. The best views are from the far side of Westminster Bridge, looking across the Thames to the 246m (270yd) frontage, with its symmetrically placed towers and pinnacles. The Parliament Square façade is much more varied, stretching from the Clock Tower (popularly known as Big Ben) to the Victoria Tower. In between lies the low roof of Westminster Hall, constructed by William the Conqueror's son, William Rufus, in 1099, where Parliament met for over two centuries. Its magnificent hammerbeam roof, completed in 1402, is the largest unsupported span in England and the finest medieval timber roof in northern Europe.

Edward the Confessor built the Palace of Westminster on this site in 1049, and successive monarchs used it as their main London residence until 1529, when Henry VIII decided to move to the nearby Palace of Whitehall (see Banqueting House, page 46). Parliament first met in the Chapter House of Westminster Abbey, but transferred its sessions to the vacated Palace of Westminster in 1547, where it has met ever since.

Fire destroyed most of the old Palace of Westminster in 1834, and the design for the new buildings was the subject of a public competition. From 97 entries, Charles Barry's was selected as the winner. A. W. Pugin, the expert on Gothic detailing, assisted him. The result is a palatial construction in the Tudor Perpendicular style, which suits its role as the building from which the nation is governed.

The interior of 'The House', as it is known to those who work in it, is a cramped warren containing 1,100 rooms, 100 staircases and almost 3.2km (2 miles) of corridor. Portcullis House, a precision crafted wing of offices built on top of Westminster Underground Station on Bridge Street, was opened in 2001 and has helped ease congestion; some MPs already have offices just beyond this site, in the Norman Shaw Building. The public areas of the Houses of Parliament are magnificently decorated in neo-Gothic and Arts and Crafts style. The actual debating chambers are so small that seating in the House of Commons can only accommodate 346 of the 659 elected Members of Parliament (the rest have to stand). This intimacy lends the House a clublike atmosphere and encourages the noisy barracking that some regard as undignified, others as an essential feature of parliamentary debate. The layout of the Commons, and of the second chamber, the House of Lords, reflects the fact that parliament formerly met in a chapel: The seating is ranged, like choir stalls, in parallel rows with the Speaker's chair where the altar would have stood.

The House of Lords has been televised since 1985, and the House of Commons introduced the cameras, with trepidation, in 1989.

▶ Jewel Tower   44C2

Abingdon Street, SW1 (tel: 020-7222 2219)
Open: Apr–Oct daily 10–5; Nov–Mar 10–4.
Admission inexpensive
Underground: Westminster, St. James's Park

The Jewel Tower, which was built in 1366, stands opposite the Houses of Parliament, and once formed part of the original Palace of Westminster. The name refers to the fact that it was built as a strongroom to store the royal jewels and other personal valuables during Edward III's reign. It was carefully restored in 1956, after suffering some bomb damage, and is now used to display an exhibition tracing the history of the English parliaments, including a video tour of the Houses of Parliament.

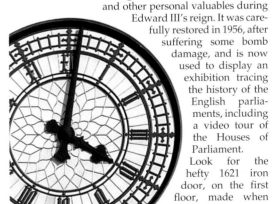

Look for the hefty 1621 iron door, on the first floor, made when the Jewel Tower was still being used to store all parliamentary records.

49

BIG BEN

Big Ben is the bell that tolls out the hours from the clock tower alongside the Houses of Parliament —a sound that is broadcast live at the beginning of some news programmes. The first bell cracked in 1857, after it was cast, and had to be replaced with a new one, made in 1858. Nobody knows how the bell got its name. Some say it was named after 'Big Ben' Caunt, a heavyweight boxer of the day, while others suggest it was named after Sir Benjamin Hall, the rotund man who was in charge of building works at Westminster. The tower has four massive clock faces; the minute hands are nearly 5m (16ft) long and made of hollow copper. Each minute space is 30cm (12in) across. Old British penny coins are used whenever any slight adjustments are needed to the weight of the clock's pendulum—but only rarely has the time been out by more than a fraction of a second. Clocktower tours are given free Mon–Fri but are open to UK residents only and booked throught their own MP, see www.parliament.uk for details.

TOURS OF PARLIAMENT

While parliament is in summer recess (not sitting), usually late July, August and September, you can take an excellent tour of this spectacular building. Guides lead you from the Queen's Tower through the sumptuous House of Lords, the Lobby and the House of Commons, recounting historical events and explaining how Britain's parliament mixes the traditional and contemporary today (tel 0870-906 3773 or see website for information; tours last about 75 minutes. *Admission* expensive)

Left: the king of clocks, high above the Houses of Parliament

The entrance terrace of the National Gallery

NATIONAL GALLERY TOP TEN
Ten pictures in the National Gallery to look out for:
1 *The Wilton Diptych*
2 *The Battle of San Romano* by Paolo Uccello
3 *The Baptism of Christ* by Piero della Francesca
4 *The Virgin and Child with Saint Anne and Saint John the Baptist* by Leonardo da Vinci
5 *Bacchus and Ariadne* by Titian
6 *The Arnolfini Portrait* by Jan van Eyck
7 *Self Portrait* (1669) by Rembrandt
8 *The Haywain* by John Constable
9 *Rain, Steam and Speed* by J. M. W. Turner
10 *Une Baignade, Asnières* (also called *Bathers at Asnières*) by Georges Seurat

▶▶▶ National Gallery   44E2

Trafalgar Square, WC2 (tel: 020-7747 2885)
www.nationalgallery.org.uk
Open: Mon, Tue, Thu–Sat 10–6, Wed 10–9, Sun 10–6.
Admission free (charge for some special exhibitions)
Underground: Charing Cross, Leicester Square

The National Gallery fills the whole of the north side of Trafalgar Square. Few people notice that the building itself is a rather uninspired piece of classical design because there are so many competing attractions in the square. Beyond Sir Edwin Lutyens's elegant fountains, Nelson's Column, the pigeons and the crowds there is a view down Whitehall to the Houses of Parliament; to the right is Canada House (1824), the headquarters of the Canadian High Commission; to the left, the church of St. Martin-in-the-Fields is partnered by Sir Hubert Baker's beautifully crafted South Africa House (1935), the Embassy of the Republic of South Africa. Its façade has lively carvings of South African flora and fauna.

Two bronze statues stand outside the Gallery: Grinling Gibbons's James II (1686), and George Washington, presented by the people of the United States in 1921.

The National Gallery itself was begun in 1824 when the government decided that London needed a national art collection to compete with other European galleries, such as the Uffizi in Florence and the Louvre in Paris. It just happened that John Julius Angerstein's Pall Mall house was for sale at the time, along with his collection of 38 paintings, including works by Raphael and Rembrandt. These were purchased for £57,000 and Angerstein's house was used as the first gallery, until the present building was completed in 1838. In the meantime, a number of important pictures were added to the collection through gifts and bequests, but many of the best known works were acquired by shrewd gallery directors scouring Europe for masterpieces that could be bought cheaply because the artists were temporarily out of fashion.

NATIONAL GALLERY MOSAICS
Do not miss the floor mosaics of the National Gallery's main staircase and halls, designed by the Russian-born artist Boris Anrep between 1928 and 1952. Those in the west hall illustrate the *Labours of Life*. Those in the north hall include portraits of Winston Churchill and T. S. Eliot, exemplifying Defiance and Leisure respectively, in a series entitled *The Modern Virtues*. Best of all, the *Awakening of the Muses* on the half-landing includes portraits of the most beautiful women of the 1930s: Greta Garbo as Melpemone (Muse of Tragedy), Virginia Woolf as Clio (Muse of History) and Diana Mitford as Poly-hymnia (Muse of Song).

Because space in the gallery was limited (originally it was only one room deep), the directors pursued a policy of quality rather than quantity. The result is one of the world's richest art collections, covering most schools and periods of painting up to the 20th century (most British works are housed either in the Tate Britain or the Tate Modern; see pages 56–57 and 204–205). The gallery shops provide a leaflet explaining where to see the 20 most popular masterpieces and you can check on the day's free lectures and guided tours at the information desk, where you can also obtain a room-by-room guide.

If you intend to spend all day at the gallery, enter at the new Sainsbury Wing annex, to the left of the main entrance. The Sainsbury family donated the funds for the building, designed by the American architect Robert Venturi. Since the annex houses Renaissance works (in fact its collection begins *c*1260), the architect incorporated motifs inspired by 16th-century Italian *palazzi*. Brilliantly coloured paintings are dramatically framed by doorway arches carved in gray *pietra serena*, the stone that lends such grace to many of the best Italian Renaissance buildings. Thus the annex makes a fitting and complementary setting for the varied works of Jan van Eyck, Botticelli, Uccello, and for Leonardo da Vinci's entrancing cartoon of the *Virgin and Child*. The Sainsbury Wing also stages an extensive exhibition programme in the basement, has a large ground floor shop, and has a bar and restaurant on the first floor with views over Trafalgar Square.

A bridge leads to the main gallery, where the full riches of European art are displayed. The many works by Rubens include his *Samson and Delilah* and *Le Chapeau de Paile*. Here, too, is Van Dyck's stunning equestrian portrait of Charles I, Constable's *The Haywain* and Seurat's *Bathers at Asnières*. More recent acquisitions include Durer's *St. Jerome*, Stubbs's *Whistle Jacket* and the exquisite *Virgin and Child* by Clarisse Master.

The Arnolfini Portrait
by Jan van Eyck

Gallery of the great and good

52

▶▶▶ National Portrait Gallery   44F2

2 St. Martin's Place, WC2 (tel: 020-7306 0055)
www.npg.org.uk
Open: daily 10–6, Thu, Fri until 9pm. Admission free
Underground: Charing Cross, Leicester Square

Tucked away at the back of the National Gallery, the National Portrait Gallery is a virtual 'Who's Who' of all the famous names in British history, science and the arts. The collection consists of some 10,000 paintings, drawings, sculptures and photographs collected because of the eminence of the subject, regardless of the merits of the artist. Even so, many important artists are represented, from Hans Holbein to David Hockney, and the collection provides an intriguing overview of the development of portraiture from the stylized iconograph representation of early monarchs to the psychological expressiveness of later works. Indeed, the gallery is probably the best place to get an idea of the range of exceptional people who have made up the story of London—and Britain—and continue to do so.

The ingenious new wing tucked into space at the back and designed by Jeremy Dixon and Edward Jones provides visitors with, literally, a tower of treats. At the bottom in the IT room you can explore the collection on screen and set up your own theme tours. The Balcony Gallery and the atmospheric Tudor Galleries occupy the next two storeys, and are topped by the upmarket restaurant (booking essential) with views across Westminster.

The collection is displayed chronologically, with the earliest pictures on the top floor. Here, among the medieval portraits, you will find the poet Geoffrey Chaucer and his patron, Richard II, portrayed as a sensitive young man.

Two towering monarchs dominate the Tudor Galleries: Henry VIII, portrayed by Holbein and surrounded by several wives and advisers who fell from grace; and Elizabeth I, partnered on either side by her favourites, the Earls of Leicester and Essex. The portraits of Elizabeth I are a *tour de force* of political propaganda: Marcus Gheeraerts shows her triumphantly standing on a map of Britain with storm clouds behind (which were intended to represent the defeated Spanish Armada) and bright skies ahead.

Later rooms reveal the faces of writers, artists, scientists, politicians and explorers. There are portraits of Shakespeare, John Donne, Samuel Pepys, Sir Christopher Wren, Sir Isaac Newton and the young Lord Byron. The only known picture of Jane Austen (by her sister Cassandra) and a tender portrait of the Brontë sisters by their brother Branwell are here too.

The late Victorian and 20th-century displays are among the most perceptive and striking. Some pictures are self-portraits (Sir Stanley Spencer, Graham Sutherland, David Hockney, Dame Laura Knight) or depictions of one artist by another (Vanessa Bell by Duncan Grant, Henry Moore by Marino Marini). The ground- and first-floor galleries display the museum's contemporary portraits plus major annual competitive shows. Acquisitions continue today. Recent ones include a photographic portrait of Mr and Mrs David Beckham, and a self-portrait painted by Patrick Heron. It's worth renting the informative audio CD guide.

NATIONAL PORTRAIT GALLERY TOP TEN
1 *Richard II (artist unknown)*
2 *Henry VIII* by Hans Holbein
3 *Elizabeth I* by Marcus Gheeraerts
4 *Sir Francis Drake* by Nicholas Hilliard
5 *Oliver Cromwell* by Samuel Cooper
6 *Emma, Lady Hamilton,* (Nelson's mistress), by George Romney
7 *Lord Byron* by Thomas Phillips
8 *Jane Austen* by her sister Cassandra
9 *The Brontë Sisters* by their brother Branwell
10 *Diana, Princess of Wales* by Bryan Organ

▶ St. John Smith Square 44B2

Smith Square, SW1 (tel: 020-7222 1061)
www.sjss.org.uk
Open: to concert-goers only
Underground: Westminster
This church is hidden away in the residential streets south of the Houses of Parliament, where several Members of Parliament have flats; the area is known as the 'Division Bell' district because many of its pubs and restaurants are wired up to the division bell that rings to summon MPs to vote on issues under debate in the House of Commons. MPs then have exactly eight minutes in which to rush back to the chamber. The church itself is sometimes called 'Queen Anne's footstool' after the story that Queen Anne, when asked how she would like the church to look, tripped over her footstool! Built in 1728, this is in fact a bold example of English baroque architecture. It was bombed during World War II, but has been carefully restored. It is now a busy concert hall, with almost nightly recitals and a licensed restaurant.

▶ St. Margaret Westminster 44C2

Parliament Square, SW1 (tel: 020-7222 5152)
www.westminster-abbey.org
Open: Mon–Fri 9.30–3.45, Sat 9.30–1.45, Sun 2–5.
Admission free. Underground: Westminster
This fine 16th-century church is often overlooked because it stands in the shadow of Westminster Abbey but the stained-glass windows alone make it worth a visit. The

THE MONUMENTS OF ST. MARGARET CHURCH
St. Margaret Westminster contains memorials to many eminent people. A tablet near the altar marks the spot where Sir Walter Raleigh, the explorer and writer, who was beheaded for treason outside the Palace of Westminster in 1618, is said to be buried. Another tablet commemorates William Caxton, the printing pioneer, who was buried here in 1491. James Rumsey, laid to rest in 1792, has a memorial recalling his role as a pioneer of American steam navigation. There are many Elizabethan and Jacobean monuments, of which the best is the alabaster effigy of Mary, Lady Dudley (died 1660) in the south aisle.

53

The handsome church of St. Martin-in-the-Fields

FAMOUS PARISHIONERS

Many famous people are associated with the church of St. Martin-in-the-Fields. George I was the first churchwarden here, and his coat of arms appears on the pediment and above the chancel arch. Charles II was christened in an earlier church on this site in 1630 and his mistress, Nell Gwyn, was buried in the churchyard, as was Chippendale. The original burial ground (and tombs) is gone, however, cleared away in 1829 to make room for Duncannon Street, which runs to the south.

CHURCH ACTIVITIES

54

St. Martin-in-the-Fields is one of London's busiest churches with long opening hours. Its excellent crypt cafe-restaurant is open Mon–Wed 8–8, Thu–Sat 8am–10.30pm (for evening concert goers), Sun 12–8. Evening concerts are in the range of £6–£20 whereas lunchtime concerts (Mon, Tue and Fri at 1.05) are free. A £36 million renewal project will enlarge the crypt café but it will remain open during works.

Choristers from the famous Westminster School, founded c1200

east Crucifixion window was commissioned by Ferdinand and Isabella of Spain and made in the Netherlands around ad1500 for the marriage of their daughter, Catherine of Aragon, to Prince Arthur. Arthur died in 1502 and Catherine became the wife of his brother, Henry VIII. After nearly 20 years of marriage had failed to produce a male heir, Henry sued for divorce (and broke away from the Catholic church in the process), on the grounds that it was not legal to marry your brother's widow. The south aisle windows contain abstract glass by John Piper (1966), while the north aisle window commemorates John Milton, who was married in this church in 1656, as were Samuel Pepys in 1655 and Winston Churchill in 1908.

▶▶ St. Martin-in-the-Fields   *44E2*

Trafalgar Square, WC2 (tel: 020-7766 1100)
www.stmartin-in-the-fields.org
Open: church Mon–Sat 8–6.30, Sun 8–7.30. Admission free
Underground: Charing Cross, Leicester Square

For many people this lovely church is by far the best building in Trafalgar Square. It was designed by James Gibbs and built between 1721 and 1726. Its large portico and soaring spire that rises to 56m (185ft), a fraction taller than Nelson's Column, give it a memorable silhouette. If the arrangement of portico and steeple seems familiar, it is because this architectural masterpiece has inspired the plan of many churches worldwide, especially in early colonial America. Inside, on either side of the chancel, are boxes for members of the royal family (on the left) and the staff of the Admiralty, whose office is nearby in Whitehall. This was the original home of the Academy of St. Martin-in-the-Fields, and their tradition of free lunchtime concerts continues: The quality musicians make this one of the best places to find lunchtime peace in the busy city. The crypt houses a bookstore, brass rubbing activity, art gallery and café, while a daily craft market is located at the rear. St. Martin-in-the-Fields is often referred to as the 'church of the homeless' because Dick Sheppard, vicar from 1914 to 1927, opened a shelter in the crypt just after World War I to help destitute ex-soldiers. Today the work continues with soup kitchens and general assistance for the homeless available in the parish rooms' basement.

Westminster Pier, which extends alongside Westminster Bridge on Victoria Embankment, is the central departure point for trips up and down the River Thames. The number of riverboats is increasing as the river regains popularity, and there are several pier stops between Westminster and the Greenwich Peninsula. Most boats have a bar or café and the best tours are accompanied by a live commentary (though do check first). You can usually buy a ticket on board.

Upriver cruises These run from April to the end of October and go to Kew (for the botanical gardens) and then continue all the way to Hampton Court Palace—you need to set aside a whole day for this trip, and perhaps return by train. They pass through some of the most beautiful rural scenery that London has to offer. Numerous parks (such as Kew, Syon and Richmond) extend to the water's edge. In between are graceful Victorian suspension bridges (notably Chelsea, Albert and Battersea bridges) and fine views of the riverside houses and pubs of Chelsea, Chiswick and Richmond (tel: 020-7930 2062, www.tfl.gov.uk/river or www.wpsa.co.uk).

Downriver cruises By contrast, these run all year and offer fine views of the City skyline, the Tower of London, the rejuvenated Docklands district and Greenwich, home of the National Maritime Museum. Longer cruises continue past the O2 Millennium Dome to the Thames Barrier at Woolwich, a remarkable piece of engineering designed to prevent London from being flooded. The barrier consists of ten movable gates, straddling the river, which can be raised to hold the water back or lowered to let ships through. (For further details about downriver cruises, call Thames River Services, tel: 020-7930 4097 or City Cruises, tel: 020-7740 0400 or check out www.tfl.gov.uk/river).

THE THAMES BARRIER
Each of the Thames Barrier's gates weighs 3,000 tonnes and is 15m (50ft) high. Together they constitute the world's biggest moveable flood barrier. A visitor centre on Unity Way explains the barrier's workings, and you can take a tour around the structure by boat. Visitor centre tel: 020-8305 4188. *Open* daily Apr–Sep 10.30–4; Oct–Mar 11.30–3. *Admission* inexpensive.

55

Thames Barrier

Tate Britain, on Millbank

►►► **Tate Britain**   44A2

Millbank, SW1 (tel: 020-7887 8000)
www.tate.org.uk
Open: daily 10–5.50. Admission free; there may be a charge for some loan exhibitions
Underground: Pimlico

Until 1999, the national collections of British and modern international art were crammed together here. Then, under the dynamic directorship of Nicholas Serota, the collection split in two so that both can have sufficient space. By 2002, the Tate Britain's redevelopment as the new home for the national collection of British art will be complete. Meanwhile, the national collection of modern international art has already left Pimlico and gone to Bankside (see pages 204–205).

The story of the Tate begins with Henry Tate, the sugar millionaire who was determined that London should have a showcase for British art. He offered his own collection of Victorian paintings to get it going, together with funds for a gallery. Finally, the government took up his idea and Sidney Smith's building was constructed on Millbank in 1812–1821. Piecemeal additions and donations followed, including the central cupola and sculpture galleries gifted by the notorious art dealer Joseph Duveen and his son in 1937, and the Rex Whistler Restaurant with its landscape murals by Rex Whistler in 1983.

The Clore Gallery, designed by Stirling and Wilford, opened in 1985 to house the extensive Turner Bequest. It resembles a garden pavilion, and the top-lit galleries bring natural light to J. M. W. Turner's fragile watercolours without damaging them. Turner charted new territory in his depiction of pure light, away from realism and towards abstraction, and is seen as the father of modern British—if not European—painting. He left his personal collection to the nation at his death in 1851, stipulating that the finished

LONDON ARTISTS TODAY
London is at the cutting edge of contemporary art in Europe. Thousands of artists live here, and the commercial galleries reflect the diversity of their work—most stock current copies of the free, thick *Galleries* magazine, which lists them by area, together with useful maps. The annual Turner Prize is the most prestigious (and controversial) art award. Previous winners include Damien Hirst, whose name has become synonymous with pickled or clipped sheep, sharks and cows.

TATE TO TATE
An express boat service connects Tate Britain and Take Modern (see pages 204–205) every 40 minutes. Tickets are moderate price and can be bought from the Tate or on board. The boat also stops at the British Airways London Eye.

works should be displayed together. It took 136 years for that wish to be fulfilled. Now, with the international collection gone, the British collection can spread out. It is not small, however: 3,500 paintings plus prints and sculptures—and always growing. The redevelopment has increased gallery space by a third, but not everything has changed: The popular annual Tate Gallery rehangs begun by Serota in 1990 will continue, when specific aspects of this vast collection are emphasized by rehanging old favourites and exhibiting others unseen for some time.

In all, Henry Tate's vision of an impressive showcase for the range of British art, from the 16th century to the present day, has been realized. The restaurants and shops, already known for their quality, encourage visitors to spend a whole day at the Tate appreciating art in a leisurely environment.

The atmosphere of the Tate has always been relaxed. It is a place that stimulates discussion and delight, disapproval and sometimes disgust. There is the naïve formality of Tudor and Stuart portraits, most strongly visible in *The Cholmondeley Ladies* (1600–1610). There is the passion and realism of the 18th-century paintings of the Enlightenment—William Hogarth's portraits, Stubbs's studies of horses, the aristocratic portraits of Reynolds and liquid brushstrokes of Gainsborough.

These paintings, seemingly calm now, challenged convention in their day; but William Blake's visionary illustrations for Dante's *The Divine Comedy* seem as daring today as when they were created in the 19th century—at the same time as Constable and Turner were painting. The Tate's collection of Pre-Raphaelite paintings is particularly rich, and includes Millais' *Ophelia* (1851–1852). The different paths taken by British art in the 20th century can be seen in the Tate Modern on the other side of the river.

TATE BRITAIN TOP TEN
Ten British artists to look out for in the Tate Britain:
1 William Hogarth (1697–1764)
2 Sir Joshua Reynolds (1723–1792)
3 George Stubbs (1724–1806)
4 Thomas Gainsborough (1727–1788)
5 William Blake (1757–1827)
6 J. M. W. Turner (1775–1851)
7 John Constable (1776–1837)
8 Dante Gabriel Rossetti (1828–1882)
9 Sir John Everett Millais (1829–1896)
10 Rex Whistler (1905–1944)

57

Norham Castle, Sunrise *by J. M. W. Turner*

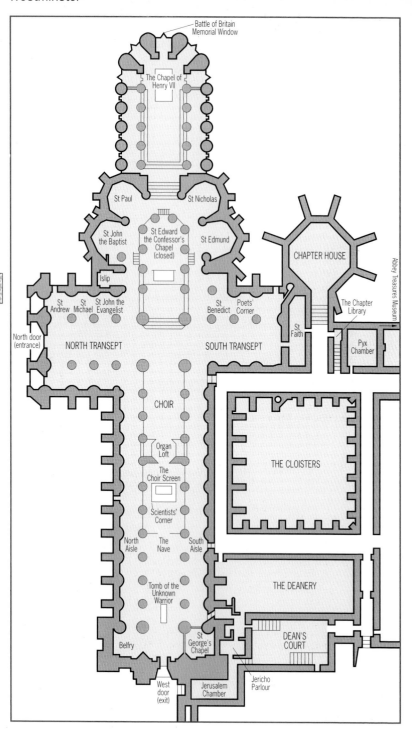

Floor plan of Westminster Abbey

▶▶▶ Westminster Abbey 44C2

Broad Sanctuary, SW1 (tel: 020-7654 4900)
www.westminster-abbey.org
Open: Nave and cloisters daily 8–6. Abbey Mon–Fri
9.30–3.45, Sat 9.30–1.45, Wed 9.30–7, Sun services only
(no sightseeing).
Chapter House, Pyx Chamber, Abbey Museum daily 10–4.
Admission expensive; tours moderate
College Garden Apr– Sep Tue–Thu 10–6; Oct–Mar Tue–Thu
10–4. Admission free
Underground: Westminster

Westminster Abbey is a huge monument, crowded at all times. To experience the full serenity of the building, attend a service and hear the choirboys of Westminster School, accompanied by the abbey organ on which Henry Purcell once played.

History The church that gave its name to Westminster stood here by the 8th century, but the present building was begun by Edward the Confessor around 1050. He died a week after its consecration, on 6 January 1066 and was the first monarch to be buried here. Almost a year later, on 25 December 1066, William the Conqueror was crowned here, confirming the royal status of the church, which has seen the coronation of every subsequent English monarch.

Edward the Confessor was later canonized, and Henry III embarked on large-scale rebuilding in 1245 to make a

The fan-vaulted
Henry VII Chapel

THE TOMB OF THE UNKNOWN WARRIOR
Of the many monuments in Westminster Abbey, the Tomb of the Unknown Warrior, located just in front of the west door, is perhaps the most moving. The simple grave, covered with a black marble slab, contains one anonymous soldier, symbolizing the 765,399 British servicemen who gave their lives in World War I. He was buried here on 11 November 1920, in soil brought from the battlefields of France and Belgium. In front is another simple memorial, to Sir Winston Churchill, who died in 1965 and lies buried at Bladon in Oxfordshire, near his birthplace.

MORE MONUMENTS
The north transept contains monuments to many eminent statesmen, including Peel, Gladstone, Palmerston and Pitt the Elder, while the north choir aisle near the organ is dedicated to musicians, including Purcell, Elgar, Vaughan Williams and Britten. One of the best monuments here is to the relatively unknown Lady Elizabeth Nightingale. She died in 1731 (the monument erroneously says 1734) of a miscarriage, having been frightened by lightning. A dramatic monument by the French sculptor Roubiliac (in the St. Michael Chapel) depicts her lying in her husband's arms as Death aims a spear at her heart.

shrine fit for the veneration of the sainted king. Today's church, greatly influenced by the French Gothic cathedrals of Amiens and Reims, was the result. In 1503, the Lady Chapel at the east end was replaced by the Henry VII Chapel, the architectural high point of the church. The west front was not completed until 1745, when the two towers were built to Nicholas Hawksmoor's design. Visitors enter by the north door and follow a route that ends at the west door.

The Choir and Sanctuary This is the ceremonial heart of the church where services—and royal coronations—take place; you have to pay an admission fee. There are good views of the huge and intricate rose windows of the transepts. The sanctuary itself is railed off. The floor has a very rare cosmati-work pavement, a form of mosaic made of glass and precious stones, dated 1268, but this is usually covered by a carpet.

Henry VII Chapel Continuing round the north side of the sanctuary, you are led first into the north aisle of the Henry VII Chapel to view the white-marble effigy of Elizabeth I (died 1603), who shares a tomb with her half sister, Mary I (died 1558). From the aisle you enter the main part of the Henry VII Chapel. This is the most exciting part of the abbey, with its exquisite fan-vaulted ceiling, and makes an impressive setting for the royal tombs that are arranged

Hawksmoor's towers

around the altar and aisles. Among the finest of these is the tomb of Henry VII, in front of the altar, and of his mother, Lady Margaret Beaufort, near the south aisle altar. Mother and son both died in the same year (1509), and both tombs are the work of the Florentine sculptor, Pietro Torrigiani (who, as a boy, was often involved in fights with Michelangelo). The tombs were the first examples of Renaissance carving to be seen in Britain.

The chapel is used for installing Knights of the Bath, an order founded by Henry IV in 1399, and their banners hang above the flamboyant canopies of the wooden stalls. More down to earth are the stall misericords, which are carved with depictions of mermaids, monsters and a wife beating her husband.

The Confessor's Chapel Access here is restricted, but this is where the king who founded the abbey is buried, along with Henry III, who rebuilt it. Their tombs are plain by comparison with the bronze effigy of Queen Eleanor (died 1290). Here, too, is the wooden Coronation Chair made in 1300, on which all British monarchs are crowned. Until recently it incorporated the ancient Scottish coronation stone, the Stone of Scone, which dates back to at least the 9th century and was captured by Edward I in 1297. Finally in 1996, after years of pressure from Scottish nationalists, the stone was returned north of the border.

Poets' Corner The south side of the sanctuary leads to the south transept, which, since the 16th century, has been where great poets, authors, artists and actors are honoured with memorials (not all are buried here).

The Cloister, Chapter House, Pyx Chamber and Abbey Museum A door in the south choir aisle leads to the cloister, with its fine, flowing tracery and superb views of the flying buttresses that support the nave. The Chapter House is an octagonal building of 1253, whose floor is covered in its original tiles. It was here that parliament met between 1257 and 1547, before moving to the Palace of Westminster. The Norman undercroft, a survivor from Edward the Confessor's original church, houses macabre wax effigies of Queen Elizabeth I, Charles II and Lord Nelson, made using death masks and the real clothes of the people. Some effigies were used to substitute the body for lyings-in-state; others were made in the 18th century to attract visitors to the Abbey. The Pyx Chamber, also part of the original abbey, contains the building's oldest altar, dated *c*1240. It is now home to original pyxes (money chests) and the Abbey's church plate. St. Faith's chapel is for silent private prayer.

The Nave Here you can enjoy the soaring (32-m/105-ft) majestic nave roof. The complex patterning of the vault carries the eye eastwards; only by looking up can you appreciate the enormous length of the building, since at ground level the view is blocked by the 19th-century choir screen. Sir Isaac Newton and other scientists are remembered around this choir screen. The Tomb of the Unknown Warrior and St. George's Chapel are near the west door. Outside the chapel, is a portrait of Richard II (1377–1399), the oldest known true portrait of an English monarch.

The Battle of Britain memorial window (detail)

61

CONCERTS
During July and August free band concerts are held in College garden every Thursday 12.30–2.

POETS' CORNER
Among the best monuments in Poets' Corner are the busts of Dryden, Jonson, Milton and Blake—the last sculpted in bronze by Sir Jacob Epstein in 1957. There is also a fine statue of Shakespeare, paid for by public subscription and made in 1740. Two non-poets, however, have the finest monuments of all, both carved by Roubiliac: the composer Handel, on the west wall, holding pages from his oratorio *Messiah*, and the soldier-statesman John, Duke of Argyll and Greenwich, to the left of Handel, surrounded by figures symbolizing Liberty, Eloquence and Wisdom.

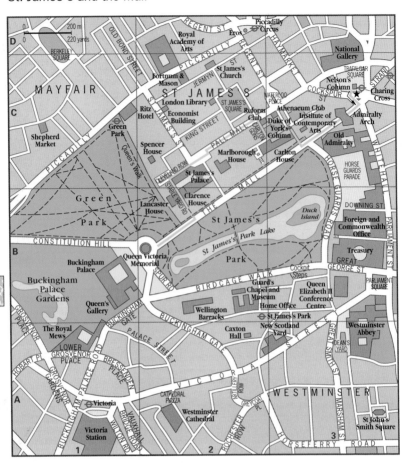

THE GAME OF PELL MELL
The Mall and Pall Mall, which runs parallel to the north, are both named after the game of *paille maille* (French for 'ball mallet'), or 'pell mell' in English. This was a sort of cross between golf and croquet, very popular in the time of Charles II, when London had several such alleys laid out for the game. The aim was to hit the wooden ball through an iron hoop suspended above the alley. No doubt its popularity was partly due to the money that changed hands in the bets that tended to accompany the game.

ST. JAMES'S AND THE MALL If Westminster is the seat of government, then its neighbour, St. James's, is the elegant, formal seat of royalty. Buckingham Palace, the Queen's official London residence, sits at one end of the Mall, a wide avenue laid out in 1660 that forms the ceremonial route taken by the royal family on great state occasions, such as Trooping the Colour and the State Opening of Parliament.

Not far away is the much older St. James's Palace, surrounded by buildings of aristocratic elegance that house such institutions as the Royal Society, the Royal Fine Art Commission and the Institute of Directors. Gentlemen's clubs, such as the Athenaeum and the Reform, dominate Pall Mall and St. James's Street, and the exclusive tone of the whole district is confirmed by Jermyn Street's long-established specialist stores.

ST. JAMES'S AND THE MALL WALK If you begin this walk around 10am you should reach Buckingham Palace in time for the Changing of the Guard ceremony (Apr–Jul daily 11.30am; alternate days for the rest of the year and no ceremony in very wet weather; click on www.royal.gov.uk for information).

Starting from Trafalgar Square, walk through Admiralty Arch, built in 1910 as a memorial to Queen Victoria. Ahead lies Buckingham Palace. On the right is the front of **Carlton House Terrace**, built in 1832 to the designs of John Nash; the **Institute of Contemporary Arts** is at the No. 12, an unlikely-looking site presenting innovative art, drama, film and video. The Duke of York Steps are beside it, at the top of which is the **Duke of York's column**, erected in 1833 to commemorate the son of George III, who commanded the British army during the Napoleonic Wars. Beyond lies **Waterloo Place**, with more memorials, notably an equestrian statue of Edward VII; another, to the right, of Captain Scott, the Antarctic explorer; and, ahead, the Guards' Crimean Memorial, with a statue of Florence Nightingale, the 'lady of the lamp'.

Turn left onto Carlton House Terrace, and take the first right onto Carlton Gardens to reach Pall Mall. On the right corner, the Reform Club's home is Charles Barry's masterpiece, an Italian palazzo adapted for London weather, built 1837–1841. Turn left onto Pall Mall, and keep straight on to Cleveland Row to get to **St. James's Palace**, a surprisingly homey brick mansion built during the reign of Henry VIII. It was the chief royal residence until Queen Victoria moved to Buckingham Palace in 1837, and it is now the London residence of Prince Charles, his sons and his wife, the Duchess of Cornwall. **Clarence House**, to the west of the palace, was the home of Queen Elizabeth the Queen Mother until her death in 2002 (see page 71).

Walk past the gatehouse and turn left onto Stable Yard Road, passing **Lancaster House**, on the right. This was the venue for the Lancaster House Conference of 1978, when Lord David Owen, then Foreign Secretary, presided over talks that led to the end of white rule in Rhodesia (now Zimbabwe). The building is currently used by the government to entertain important foreign visitors.

Once you are back in the Mall, turn right and walk up towards Buckingham Palace.

Above: Lock & Co. Below: outside Buckingham Palace

Above: Buckingham Palace and the Queen Victoria Memorial

THE COURT AND THE SEASON

When the Queen is in residence at Buckingham Palace, the Royal Standard (the flag bearing the arms of the British sovereign) is raised. The Queen holds court in London, during 'the Season', April to mid-August. Formerly, young ladies making their first official appearances in public ('debutantes' or 'debs') were 'presented' at court. Other events of the Season, such as Royal Ascot and the Queen's Garden Parties, are still eagerly awaited. Come mid-August, the Queen moves between her other residences at Windsor, Sandringham and Balmoral.

▶▶▶ Buckingham Palace   62B1

Buckingham Gate, SW1 (tel: 020-7766 7300 recorded information); www.royal.gov.uk
Open: Buckingham Palace State Rooms most of Aug and Sep, daily 9.30–3.45 (last tour). Ticket office opens 9 and closes when last ticket sold; tickets operate on an allocated time basis and can be reserved in advance by credit card, tel: 020-7766 7300. Admission expensive.
Queens Gallery daily during exhibitions 10–5.30 (last admission 4.30). Admission expensive.
The Royal Mews Aug–Sep daily 10–5; Oct–Jul daily 11–4 (last admission 45 minutes before closing). Admission moderate.
Underground: Victoria, St. James's Park, Green Park

The royal court has moved several times in the last 900 years: first from the City to the Palace of Westminster under Edward the Confessor, then to Whitehall Palace under Henry VIII, then to St. James's Palace under Charles II. St. James's remained the official residence of the sovereign throughout the 17th and 18th centuries, and it was here that the big state functions took place. Nevertheless, sovereigns often left the cramped Tudor buildings to sleep at Kensington Palace.

It was at Kensington that Queen Victoria lived from her birth in 1819 until her accession to the throne in 1837. She chose Buckingham Palace as the official London residence of the sovereign, as it remains today.

The palace is named after Buckingham House, built for the Duke of Buckingham in 1705. It was purchased by George III in 1761, lavishly remodelled by George IV (1820–1830), and given Sir Aston Webb's £110 million façade in 1913. Against this classical backdrop one of London's most popular events takes place Apr–Jul daily at 11.30am (alternate days for the rest of the year), when sentries of the Guards Division in full dress uniform perform the Changing of the Guard. Spectators watch from the palace railings with their five wrought-iron and bronze gates, decorated with cherubs and erected in 1906. An alternative vantage point is the Queen Victoria Memorial, which stands in the traffic island in front of the palace (although climbing it is forbidden). This marble column, erected in 1911, is topped by the gilded figure of Victory, while Queen Victoria sits facing down the Mall.

The Queen's Gallery Although Buckingham Palace is only open in August and September, you can visit the Queen's Gallery at the rear of the building all year. Opened in 1962, it was originally built as a garden conservatory, then converted to the palace chapel in 1893 and finally turned into an art gallery in 1962. Here you can see exhibitions of paintings, drawings and furniture drawn from the vast Royal Collection, including works by Rubens, Rembrant and Canaletto, as well as watercolours painted by Queen Victoria. The works on display are changed every six months or so. A £10 million refurbishment took place in 2002, so the public can see more of the Royal Collection.

The Royal Mews Located further along Buckingham Palace Road from the Queen's Gallery, these were built in 1824–1825 to house the royal household's horses and coaches. The splendid state carriages used on major state occasions are displayed here. They include the richly carved and gilded Gold Carriage, made for George III in 1762 and used for coronations; the Irish State Coach, bought by Queen Victoria in 1852 and used for the State Opening of Parliament; the so-called Glass State Coach, bought in 1910 and used to carry visiting dignitaries and overseas ambassadors; and the open-top landau used for the weddings of the Prince and Princess of Wales in 1981 and the Duke and Duchess of York in 1986.

VISITING THE PALACE
Buckingham Palace has been open to the public since 1993, for six weeks a year, from approximately mid-August through September (when the Royal Family are away — see panel page 64). The State Rooms on view are furnished with some of the most important pictures and works of art from the Royal Collection (one of the world's finest art collections). There is no need to queue, as timed tickets may be bought in advance (see page 64). Funds raised contribute to the expansion of the Queen's Gallery and other projects to increase public access to the royal palaces.

Mounted officers leaving Buckingham Palace

These two streets are packed with shops that are worth seeing whether you intend to buy anything or not. Some stores have been trading here since the 1760s and several retain their 18th-century frontages and fittings. In keeping with the tone of the whole area, these stores cater largely to traditional, up-market tastes of wealthy men, although there are shops here that have among their merchandise women's clothes, food, antiques and jewellery as well.

BY ROYAL APPOINTMENT
Several stores in the Jermyn Street area display a royal coat of arms, indicating that they have been granted a coveted Royal Warrant of Appointment. Royal Warrants can be granted by the Queen, the Queen Mother, the Prince of Wales and the Duke of Edinburgh. To qualify, the store must have had the royal patron's custom for at least three years. A handful including the Piccadilly booksellers Hatchards and the General Trading Company of Sloane Street hold all four warrants.

Clothes for the fastidious at Turnbull & Asser

From Regent Street westwards, **Jermyn Street** makes a perfect window-shopping stroll, just as it did for courtiers from St. James's Palace when it was laid out in the 1660s. The buildings, although not original, are charming and house some of London's most attractive shops, with gentlemen's goods predominant. On the right, **Herbie Frogg** (No. 18) sells men's clothes of modern cut. Next door is **Geo F. Trumper**, hairdresser to some of the most eminent heads in London, followed by **Bates the Hatter**, selling deerstalkers and Panama hats. Look out for Binks the shop cat, stuffed in 1926, wearing a smart black topper. Next comes **Russell & Bromley's** shoe store (No. 95) and **Charles Tyrwhitt** (No. 92), offering top quality shirts at below £50. At No. 93 is London's oldest cheesemonger, **Paxton & Whitfield** (No. 93). The shop front is mid-Victorian and the company, founded in 1740, stocks a huge array of cheeses, game pies, hams, pâtés and wines. The Queen Mother buys her provisions here, while both the Queen and the Prince of Wales patronize **Floris**, the perfumier (No. 89), founded in 1730 by a Spaniard from Minorca, Juan Fameias Floris, and still a family firm today. These stores all stand opposite the back entrance to St. James's Church (see page 79).

Further down on the right is the short Princes Arcade, built in the 1880s, while further up is the Piccadilly Arcade with its gleaming bow windows, built in Georgian style in 1910.

Passing several more clothing and antiques stores you will come to **Wiltons** restaurant (No. 55), known for its oysters and traditional English cooking (game is a specialty). **Turnbull & Asser** (No. 71), nearly opposite, is a custom tailor specializing in silk and cotton shirts, famous for attention to clients' often idiosyncratic tastes. Established in 1885, they are shirtmakers to Charles, Prince of Wales. For made-to-measure shirts you must allow time for fittings and order a minimum of six; ready-made shirts are also available for the less fastidious. At the end of Jermyn Street, turn left into St. James's Street.

St. James's Street This wide street lined with gentlemen's clubs, long-established shops and new gourmet restaurants, sweeps down to St. James's Palace. Walking down the hill, you will pass the **Economist Building** (No. 25), an example of modern architecture (see side panel) that fits in well with the surrounding 18th-century premises of leading gentlemen's clubs (see pages 68–69). The second left, King Street, leads to **Christie's**, the auctioneers established in 1766 (No. 8).

Back on St. James's Street, you will find **John Lobb** (No. 9) the shoemaker, where the staff make models of patrons' feet in wood for shoes that are a uniquely perfect fit. Inside the shop, a small museum case displays a miniature prototype of the first Wellington boot and the cobbler's last that was used for making shoes for Queen Victoria. **Lock & Co** (No. 6) does the same thing for heads (established in 1700, it made Lord Nelson's famous cocked hats). Two doors down is an alley leading to Pickering Place, a tiny paved courtyard typical of many that once existed in 18th-century London; a plaque records that between 1842 and 1845 the Legation (Diplomatic Ministry) from the Republic of Texas was based here. **Berry Bros & Rudd** (No. 3) is early Georgian and hardly changed; customers scrutinize the wine list, and staff fetch bottles of rare wines and liquors from the cellars below. There is a huge 17th-century scale to the left of the entrance, which was once used to weigh customers, since public scales were not introduced into England until 1799.

The pick of pipes

67

THE ECONOMIST BUILDING

The Economist Building in St. James's Street was one of the first of modern buildings to be listed Grade II. This means that it is considered such an important example of architecture that it may not be altered or demolished without government approval. The complex, designed by Alison and Peter Smithson and built between 1962 and 1964, is grouped around a quiet plaza containing Henry Moore's *Reclining Figure* (1969) and other modern sculptures. The buildings house the offices of *The Economist* magazine, a bank and apartments. They are faced in Portland stone and seem to have a sculptured quality all of their own. The careful siting of the different offices within the complex allows framed glimpses of the Georgian and Victorian buildings that surround it. The building also contains a stunning minimalist bar, called Che.

St. James's contains many of London's most exclusive gentlemen's clubs. Most were founded in the 18th century, when many aristocrats lived nearby, and flourished in an age when men and women led separate social lives, the woman's domain being confined to the home. Some clubs also served as gambling dens, where many an aristocratic fortune was thrown away over an evening's game of cards.

68

EATING AND DRINKING

Though you are not allowed inside London's exclusive clubs, you can at least try one of the nearby restaurants that have a clublike atmosphere. One of the best is Greens (35–36 Duke Street, tel: 020-7930 4566), where they serve the sort of traditional food that club members enjoy: guinea fowl, sticky toffee pudding, for example, as well as excellent fish and seafood. Wiltons (55 Jermyn Street, tel: 020-7629 9955) is renowned for game, seafood, oysters, and fine port wines. Less expensive is the Red Lion (2 Duke of York Street), a beautifully-preserved Victorian pub full of mahogany panelling and cut glass.

As men began to spend more time at home with their families, the appeal of clubs began to decline, and by the 1930s they were known as the last bastion of crusty, reclusive and conservative bachelordom. In recent years, though, clubs have undergone something of a revival, partly because some provide excellent sports facilities and an overnight place to stay. Even so, the main attraction remains the same as ever: the snob appeal of belonging to an exclusive circle (mostly of men, since few clubs admit women as members even today).

Walk westwards down Pall Mall from Trafalgar Square, and you will encounter the **Institute of Directors**, a club for business leaders, and the **Athenaeum**, standing on opposite sides of Waterloo Place. If the buildings seem to echo each other, it is because both are the work of Decimus Burton. The Athenaeum is named after Athena, Goddess of Wisdom; her statue stands on the porch, and a frieze, based on the sculptures of the Parthenon, runs beneath the cornice. Founded in 1824 as a club for writers and artists, the Athenaeum's members today include bishops, scientists and civil servants.

The Athenaeum's neighbours are the **Travellers' Club** and the **Reform**. When the former was founded in 1819, members had to prove that they had travelled more than 800km (500 miles) from London—not so easy in the pre-railway age. The Reform, as its name suggests, was formed by supporters of the 1832 Reform Act, which paved the way for an electoral system based on one person, one vote. Today, its members include men and women. James Barry was the architect for both buildings; despite their measured Renaissance-style exteriors, the interiors are particularly sumptuous.

The same is true of **The Royal Automobile Club** (No. 89), where members enjoy the use of a marble-lined swimming pool. The RAC stands opposite St. James's Square, first laid out in 1663. The houses around the perimeter were intended for members of the nobility who wanted to live close to St. James's Palace, where Charles II used to live.

No. 5 was the Libyan People's Bureau; the flowers in the gardens opposite mark a memorial to Yvonne Fletcher, the policewoman who was killed by a Libyan gunman during the siege of April 1984. **No. 10** (Chatham House) is the former residence of three Prime Ministers, William

Pitt, the Earl of Derby and William Gladstone. The London Library at **No. 14** is not a club, though you do have to be elected to membership and pay a fee. It was founded in 1841 by the historian and polemicist, Thomas Carlyle, and the book collections include many rare and out-of-print volumes. It is much used today by academics, journalists and writers.

Continuing up Pall Mall, you will pass the **Oxford and Cambridge Club** before turning right onto St. James's Street. This street has several of London's oldest clubs, as well as numerous buildings that were built as clubs but have since been turned to other uses. Many are built in Palladian style with fine Venetian windows, columns and balustrades. The **Carlton Club** at Nos. 69–70 includes many Conservative Party MPs among its members. It is a relative newcomer on the scene, having been founded as recently as 1832.

By contrast, **Brooks's Club** (No. 60), started up in 1764; **Boodles** (No. 28), started in 1762; and **White's** (No. 37), the oldest institution of them all, evolved from White's Chocolate and Gaming House in 1693.

THE ARTS AND SCIENCES

Besides its clubs, St. James's houses the premises of several prestigious bodies. The Royal Society, at No. 6 Carlton House Terrace, was founded by Charles II in 1660 as a scientific society with Samuel Pepys, Christopher Wren and Isaac Newton among its early presidents. Today it lists many Nobel Prize winners among its members. Nearby, at No. 17 Carlton House Terrace, you will find the Mall Galleries (tel: 020-7930 6844, www.mallgalleries.org.uk *Open* daily, 10–5 during exhibitions, entrance on the Mall), which display landscapes, portraits and watercolor paintings by members of the Federation of British Artists; most are for sale. This work tends to be traditional, in contrast with experimental works exhibited at the Institute of Contemporcy Arts (Nash House, The Mall; tel: 020-7930 0493, www.ica.org.uk *Open* daily 12.7.30 (Thu until 9pm) during exhibitions. *Admission* inexpensive).

The Athenaeum, on Pall Mall, was founded in 1824

Scott's Government Offices above the trees of St. James's Park

SPENCER HOUSE
Built in 1756–1766 for the first Earl Spencer (an ancestor of Diana, Princess of Wales), Spencer House (27 St. James's Place, tel: 020-7499 8620, www.spencer house.co.uk. *Open* Feb–late Jul, Sep–mid-Dec Sun 10.30–4.45–access by 1 hour tour only. Min age 10. *Admission* expensive) is London's finest surviving 18th-century town house, now fully restored and lavishly furnished under the patronage of Lord Rothschild. Access to its eight opulent rooms is by a one-hour guided tour, of which the highlights are the Palladian gilded Palm Room by John Vardy, and the elegant mural decorations and gilded furniture of the Painted Room by Vardy's successor, James 'Athenian' Stuart, who designed the first-floor rooms. The house also contains a fine collection of 18th-century paintings and furniture.

▶▶▶ St. James's Park   62B2
Underground: St. James's Park

St. James's Park is the most attractive of all London's green spaces. From the footbridge that crosses the lake at the heart of the park there are uninterrupted views westwards to the classical façade of Buckingham Palace, while to the east you see the rear of Sir George Gilbert Scott's classical Government Offices, and the turrets and onion domes of the National Liberal Club, framed by the weeping willows whose branches cascade down to the fringes of the lake. Several varieties of wildfowl make the lake their home; many of the birds are quite tame. You can either take a stroll all the way around the perimeter of the lake, or concentrate on the views from the bridge and then head south to Birdcage Walk, the road that forms the southern park boundary (there were aviaries here in the time of James II).

On the opposite side of the road, Cockpit Steps (a reminder that the birds were also used for sport) lead up to Queen Anne's Gate, a charming enclave of early 18th-century houses, several of them with very ornate wooden canopies over their front doors. There is a statue of Queen Anne in front of No. 15 and blue plaques abound, recording the famous people who were born here or who lived here. No. 36 is the home of the National Trust, England's foremost historic preservation body, which owns and manages many of the country's finest houses and gardens.

At the southern junction of Queen Anne's Gate with Broadway you will find the London Transport Headquarters. It stands above St. James's Park Underground station and has fine façade sculptures: Jacob Epstein's bold figures of *Day* and *Night* flank the entrance, while reliefs symbolizing the winds were carved by five artists, including Eric Gill and Henry Moore.

▶ Wellington Barracks 62B2

Birdcage Walk, SW1 (tel: 020-7414 3428)
Open: Chapel Mon–Fri 9–4, Sun services. Admission free
Guards Museum daily 10–4. Admission moderate
Underground: St. James's Park

This is the headquarters of the Guards Division: the soldiers, resplendent in scarlet dress uniforms and bearskin hats, who perform the Changing of the Guard ceremony at Buckingham Palace. The Guards' Chapel, which has a moving war memorial cloister, was hit by a bomb in 1944, killing 121 people who were attending a service. It was rebuilt in 1963, incorporating the remains of the 19th-century apse.

The Guards' Museum is for those interested in military history. It explains the background of the regiments that make up the Household Division and the duties they perform as the official bodyguard to the Queen.

▶▶ Westminster Cathedral 62A2

Ashley Place, Victoria Street, SW1 (tel: 020-7798 9055)
www.westminstercathedral.org.uk
Open: Mon–Fri 7–7, Sat–Sun 8–7. Admission free
Tower Apr–Nov daily 9.30–12.30, 1–5; Dec–Mar Thu–Sun 9–5. Admission moderate
Underground: Victoria

This exuberant Byzantine-style building, with its echoes of the great Basilica of St. Mark in Venice, is the principal Roman Catholic church in England, the seat of the Archbishop of Westminster. It was begun in 1895 but remains unfinished. It was intended that the whole interior be lined with marble and mosaics but the funds were sufficient only to complete the facing of the lower area, leaving the upper surfaces impressively bare. The fourteen Stations of the Cross, crisply carved by the young Eric Gill in his distinctive style, are on the name piers. For most visitors, the other main attraction is the superb campanile, built, like the rest of the church, of brick alternating with bands of Portland stone, very similar to Siena Cathedral's bell tower. It is 83m (273ft) in height and there are outstanding views from the summit of all the main buildings of central London and far beyond to the surrounding countryside. What's more, you don't have to be in good shape to enjoy the view; there is a lift to take you to the top.

CLARENCE HOUSE
Clarence House was built 1825–27 by John Nash for the Duke of Clarence and has been a royal residence, more or less, ever since. In 1949 it became the London home of Princess Elizabeth (the present Queen) and the Duke of Edinburgh (Prince Philip). Princess Anne was born at Clarence House in July 1950 and it was the early home of The Prince of Wales. When the royal couple moved to Buckingham Palace, Clarence House became the home of Queen Elizabeth the Queen Mother from 1953 until her death in 2002. Today it is the official London residence of The Prince of Wales and the Duchess of Cornwall, and of the Princes William and Harry. Clarence House is open to the public (tel: 020-7766 7303, www.royalresidences.com. *Open* daily Aug–mid-Oct 9–7. *Admission* moderate) and visitors are given a guided tour of the five rooms and gallery spaces. To prepare the building for The Prince of Wales, Clarence House underwent extensive refurbishment and redecoration. Nonetheless the rooms are much as they were in Queen Elizabeth's time, including her works of art and furniture with some pieces from the Royal Collection, and The Prince of Wales' own pieces have been added.

71

Westminster Cathedral, Britain's premier Catholic church, comprises some 12.5 million handmade bricks, without any steel reinforcement

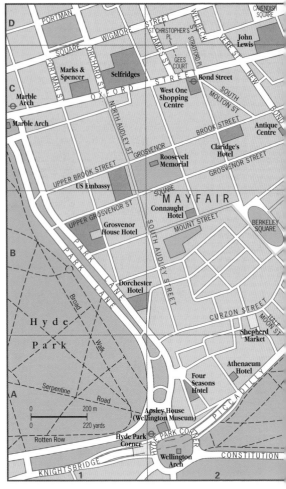

72

MAYFAIR AND PICCADILLY Mayfair contains some of London's most elegant houses, set around leafy squares, but with the exception of several embassies, their original aristocratic tone has mostly been lost as buildings have become offices or upscale apartments. The fine Adam-style architecture of Berkeley Square survives, as do the exclusive stores of Bond Street, Piccadilly and Burlington Arcade. Bordering the north and south sides are Oxford Street and Regent Street, lined with well-known retailers and department stores.

MAYFAIR AND PICCADILLY WALK Starting at Green Park Underground station, walk east along Piccadilly to reach **Burlington Arcade**, the fifth turn on the left. Burlington Arcade is a covered promenade, built in 1819—one of England's first shopping malls. The arcade is Regency in style and atmosphere. Exclusive stores selling antiques and clothing line either side. Rules of propriety are enforced by Beadles, in top hats and great coats, who are retired members of the 10th Hussars regiment.

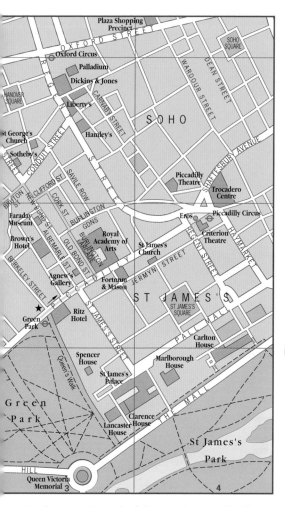

At the opposite end of the arcade, cross Burlington Gardens and walk up Cork Street before turning left onto Clifford Street, past art dealers displaying everything from contemporary art to Old Masters.

Turning right on Bond Street brings you to Bruton Street, on the left; on the corner is the Time-Life Building (1952), with panels carved by Henry Moore set in the terrace parapet. Turn left down Bruton Street to **Berkeley Square**. The west side is lined with Georgian houses; you may glimpse, through the windows, lavishly plastered interiors and grand staircases.

The top left-hand exit out of Berkeley Square leads left onto **Mount Street**. The **Connaught Hotel**—an English country mansion in the city—on the right, is probably London's most discreet super-deluxe hotel.

Turn right at The Audley pub on South Audley Street to reach **Grosvenor Square**, where the forbidding American Embassy on the left is heavily protected.

North Audley Street leads from the top left-hand corner of Grosvenor Square to Oxford Street.

Old and New Bond streets together form a continuous thoroughfare cutting through the heart of Mayfair and lined with fashionable shops. Starting at the Piccadilly end, there is a succession of picture dealers selling quality works. On the left are Thomas Agnew and Marlborough Fine Art. On the right are the Leger Gallery (No. 13), specializing in 18th- and 19th-century British art, and Colnaghi (No. 15), which deals in European paintings and sculpture. Opposite, Gucci's elegant shop, with marble floors and stucco ceilings, sells the best of Italian couture.

SAVILE ROW

Parallel with New Bond Street, three blocks east, is Savile Row, a byword for gentlemen's tailoring. Gieves and Hawkes (No. 1), founded in 1785, was the first establishment; at No. 38 Davies & Son have been court tailors since 1803. At No. 3 the Beatles made their last public appearance, on the roof of the Apple Building in 1969.

Bond Street shops

Bond Street prices are high, but window shoppers can have a field day. Beyond Stafford Street, on the left, is **Gucci**, followed by the cheerful orange-and-white façade of the **Royal Arcade**, where **Charbonnel et Walker** (No. 1) sell their exquisite chocolates, and other shops specialize in silver, paintings and antiques. The Arcade leads to **Albemarle Street** with more art galleries, such as the Albermarle Gallery at No. 49 and Marlborough Fine Art at No. 6, plus **Brown's Hotel** (No. 23), where Eleanor and Franklin Roosevelt spent their honeymoon, and the **Royal Institution** (Nos. 20–21) with its temple-like façade. This was founded in 1799 for the promotion of scientific knowledge. A small museum in the basement is devoted to the pioneering electromagnetic experiments of Michael Faraday (Tel: 020-7409 2992, call for opening times).

2**6** SILVERSMITHS TESSIERS GOLDSMITHS

TESSIER

TESSIER

DEALERS IN ANTIQUE SILVER & JEWELLERY.

VALUATIONS FOR PROBATE.

Back on Old Bond Street, the **Ferragamo** boutique stands on the right, and if you turn down **Burlington Gardens**, then left onto **Cork Street**, you will find several galleries specializing in the works of modern artists.

Asprey & Garrard (Nos. 165–169 New Bond Street) stands at the junction of Old Bond Street (laid out in 1686) and New Bond Street (extended in 1721). Its big windows of plate glass and iron, considered revolutionary when they were installed around 1848, make it ideal for window shopping. A favourite with royalty worldwide, this is where Prince Charles bought the engagement ring for his fiancée, Lady Diana Spencer.

Further up, on the corner of New Bond Street and Bruton Street, is **Hermès**, known for its silk scarves. Beyond Bruton Street, on the left, the thoroughly unstuffy **Fine Art Society** store (No. 148), dating from 1876, sells works by 19th- and 20th-century British artists, and is always worth visiting.

Sotheby's (No. 35), on the right, has a modest entrance for such a well-known auctioneers' house. There are viewings and sales here most days: details inside (or tel: 020-7293 5000, www.sothebys.com). Antiques can also be found at the **Bond Street Antiques Centre** (No. 124) and the **Bond Street Silver Galleries** (Nos. 111–112).

Designer-label clothing and shoe stores predominate in the upper stretch of New Bond Street, where **Fenwicks**, the stylish department store, is to be found on your right at the Brook Street intersection.

Turning right down Brook Street you will enter **Hanover Square**, laid out in 1717 and named for the Elector of Hanover who took the throne as King George I in 1714. Handel, who lived at No. 25 Brook Street, had his *Messiah* performed annually at The Hanover Square Rooms (since demolished). Turn round, back along **Brook Street** and continue towards **Claridge's Hotel**, where frock-coated doormen admit the tidily dressed to its opulent interior. Before you reach Claridge's, take a detour right down the pedestrian area of **South Molton Street**. Here, chic boutiques belie the street's old nickname, Poverty Lane, and in summer there is a festive atmosphere as shoppers enjoy the sunshine from its pavement cafés.

ST. GEORGE'S CHURCH

At the southern end of Hanover Square, in St. George Street, is the church of St. George, built in 1724 by John James and fronted by massive Corinthian columns. The baroque interior retains its 18th-century layout with galleries in the aisles. The Venetian east window is filled with 16th-century stained glass, moved here from a church in Antwerp, showing a Tree of Jesse. St. George's was, and remains, a fashionable place for weddings. Among those married here were Benjamin Disraeli, Mary Anne Evans (better known as the novelist George Eliot), Theodore Roosevelt and the poet Percy Bysshe Shelley.

From Marble Arch in the west to High Holborn in the east, Oxford Street stretches for 2.4km (1.5 miles) to form Europe's longest row of department stores and retail outlets. Leading up to Christmas, when festive lights and decorations are strung across the street, it is the most crowded place in town, with police called in to control not the traffic, which is largely excluded, but the sheer volume of shoppers.

THE ROAD TO TYBURN
Oxford Street used to be known as Tyburn Way because it led to the gallows at Tyburn (at the intersection of Edgware Road and Marble Arch), where public executions took place until 1783. Public hanging was intended to act as a deterrent to the watching crowds, a warning against crime, but it turned into popular entertainment, and high prices were paid for ringside seats.

76

Oxford Street sign on Selfridges' department store, right; the store's clock, below

Oxford Street was so named because it led to Oxford, a name consolidated when the Earl of Oxford bought the open land to the north of it in 1793. Once lined with entertainment halls, it is now Europe's longest retail street, a shopper's delight, even if many stores are chain outlets. One is **Marks & Spencer**, whose flagship store is at Marble Arch (No. 458). The largest and best known store is **Selfridges** (No. 400). The impressive Edwardian building, designed by R. F. Atkinson and Daniel Burnham and built in 1907–1928, introduced American retail ideas to London. Harry Gordon Selfridge, from Chicago, commissioned the steel frame building with its opulent Ionic columns, founding London's only rival to Harrods. The giant art deco clock over the main entrance (by Gilbert Bayes) has the regal figure of *The Queen of Time*, standing on a prow that represents the ship of commerce.
On a completely different scale **Gees Court** and **St.**

Christopher's Place form a narrow pedestrian alley that is easily missed (entered through a tiny archway between James Street and Stratford Place on the north side of Oxford Street). The lane is lined with small shops and sidewalk cafés, a different and more intimate world than the big modern **West One Shopping Centre** above Bond Street underground station opposite.

  Stratford Place, the next left, is another surprising interruption to Oxford Street's almost continuous line of shop fronts. Set back at the end of this 18th-century cul-de-sac is the elegant and untouched Stratford House of 1723, built in Adam style and housing the Oriental Club, founded in 1824 for colonial civil servants.

  Next comes **John Lewis** (Nos. 278–306), another of the street's big stores. Its motto is 'We are never knowingly undersold' and the store will refund the difference if you can buy identical goods more cheaply elsewhere.

Oxford Circus forms the busy intersection of Regent Street and Oxford Street. Note the view northwards to **All Souls Church**, Langham Place (see page 118), with its circular portico and spire, built by John Nash to form the focal point of the view up Regent Street, though today it is rather dwarfed by tall office towers and store signs. Curving façades also give distinction to the buildings of Oxford Circus, but the architecture becomes less impressive as you continue east. In this stretch you will find two well-known music megastores, **HMV** (No. 150) and **Virgin** (Nos. 14–16).

  The eastern end of Oxford Street is dominated by the **Centrepoint** building, a rather gloomy structure too tall for its site (120m/400ft) and set in a windswept plaza. Designed by Richard Seifert, the tower has recently been listed as a building of architectural merit, thus protected from alteration or demolition. The skyscraper marks Oxford Street's junction with Tottenham Court Road, the best place to buy genuine electronic goods at good prices, with reliable after-sales service. From here, New Oxford Street continues east, having sliced through the slums of St. Giles (where the Great Plague of London started in 1665) in 1847 to join up with High Holborn.

  The pretty church of **St. Giles-in-the-Fields** still stands to the south. David Garrick, the Shakespearian actor, was married here, the children of the poets Shelley and Byron were christened here, and the satirist and poet Andrew Marvell lies buried in the churchyard.

MARBLE ARCH
Marble Arch, designed by John Nash in 1828 and inspired by the Arch of Constantine in Rome, was originally intended to form a triumphant gateway to Buckingham Palace. After Nash's death it was moved to make way for a new range of buildings. Now it stands in sad isolation in the middle of a busy traffic circle, and the central gates remain firmly closed most of the time. To this day only members of the royal family are allowed to drive through.

St. Christopher's Place, a stylish enclave from which to escape the madding crowd

Piccadilly's name has its origins in a mansion built here in 1612 for one Robert Baker. He had made his fortune selling 'picadils', a type of stiff collar fashionable with the 17th-century court, and his house (and the area around it) became known as Piccadilly. Today, Piccadilly mixes gaudy neon signs with state-of-the-art entertainment and splendid old stores.

THE TROCADERO

Once home to a lovely old music hall the Trocadero houses a huge indoor entertainment complex on its seven floors (tel: 020-7489 1791. *Open* Sun–Thu 10am–midnight, Fri–Sat 10am–1am. *Admission* free, but charges for attractions). There's a pool hall, white-knuckle, virtual reality rides and experiences, and the huge IMAX (it stands for maximum image) 3-D cinema where audience members wear electronic headsets with surround sound to maximize the feeling of really 'being there'.

78

In Shepherd Market

Piccadilly begins at **Hyde Park Corner**, a spot where cars do battle above while pedestrians get lost in the labyrinthine underpass below. One exit from the underpass leads to the traffic island containing **Constitution** (or Wellington) **Arch**, designed in 1828 by Decimus Burton and intended as a ceremonial gate linking Hyde Park with Buckingham Palace via Constitution Hill. It is topped by animated horses pulling Victory's chariot, a superb bronze sculpture by Adrian Jones (1912). Nearby is a statue of the Duke of Wellington (1888) facing his residence, Apsley House (see page 83). To the north are the luxury hotels of Park Lane; the south side of Piccadilly runs alongside **Green Park**, laid out in the 17th century.

Walking up Piccadilly on the north side, you can detour left up White Horse Street to find the shops, Victorian pubs and many restaurants around **Shepherd Market**. These narrow streets and alleys were built in 1735 by Edward Shepherd on the site of the ancient May Fair that gave its name to the district. Just off the market at 9 Curzon Street is George F. Trumper, London's most elegant gentlemen's perfumier and hairdresser, set in a beautiful 18th-century shop with many original fittings.

Continuing up Piccadilly, **Half Moon Street**, the next on the left, was the home of Bertie Wooster, P. G. Wodehouse's comic creation, as well as of Dr. Johnson's real-life friend and biographer, James Boswell.

Beyond Green Park is the Parisian-style **Ritz Hotel** (1906). Once a haunt of the fashionable set it is still a glamorous place in which to have tea (reservations advised), and its dining room overlooking Green Park is one of London's most beautiful. Further along on the left are Old Bond Street and Burlington Arcade, the latter dates from 1819, London's oldest 'shopping mall', (see page 72). Opposite Piccadilly Arcade was built in 1910; it too has bow-fronted shops, specializing in china, rare books and clothing. Next on the right comes **Fortnum & Mason**, the grocery shop founded in 1707, lit by chandeliers and lined with mahogany panelling. Its shelves are piled high with displays of delicious foods. Look for the clock above the entrance: On the hour, music strikes up and Mr Fortnum and Mr Mason pop out of their niches and bow to each other. A veritable London institution, this is a marvellous place for browsing, with a marble-pillared food hall second only to Harrods. It made its name as a supplier of foodstuffs to the British Empire notably to the Raj (the British Empire in India) and in some respects little has changed since then. Most visitors don't explore

any further, which is a pity as the upper floors have excellent women's fashion, perfumery and fine china. If you make it to the fourth floor there are seasonal exhibitions and antiques. **Hatchards**, next door, with its 18th-century shop front, is one of London's best stocked and most congenial bookshops. Opposite is the Royal Academy (see page 82) and further down on the right, slightly set back, is Sir Christopher Wren's church of **St. James's.**

Piccadilly Circus itself is a somewhat confusing sight, which planners have remodelled repeatedly since Nash laid it out in 1819. It marks the junction of five major streets but lacks the coherence of design to make this clear. These days it is a rather shabby, overcommercialized place, famous for its enormous, illuminated advertising signs and for Alfred Gilbert's tiny figure of a winged archer, popularly known as Eros, the god of Love, but actually designed as the *Angel of Christian Charity*. This was erected in 1893 as a memorial to the philanthropic Earl of Shaftesbury, who did much to improve the lot of factory and mine workers (especially children) in the mid-19th century.

The Angel of Christian Charity, *mistakenly known as Eros, watches over Piccadilly Circus*

79

ST. JAMES'S CHURCH

St. James's Church (tel: 020-7734 4511, www.st-james-piccadilly. org; *open* daily 8–6.30) was the last of some 55 churches that Sir Christopher Wren designed for London and the one that he himself liked best. It was bombed in 1940 but has been superbly restored (you would not guess that the spire of 1968 is made of fibreglass). Its gallery-lined interior contains work by the great carver, Grinling Gibbons, including the angels of the organ case, the Garden of Eden font, and the altarpiece. St. James's today is more than a church: There is a coffee shop and its courtyard is the venue for a crafts market (art, knitwear, gifts) Wed–Sat, and an antique market on Tuesday. Music lovers should check out the free lunchtime recitals (Mon, Wed and Fri 1.10; full concerts on most Thu, Fri and Sat evenings).

Regent Street, named for the Prince Regent, later George IV, was laid out by John Nash between 1813 and 1816 to form a grand boulevard linking Regent's Park with the royal palaces and aristocratic mansions of Carlton House and Pall Mall. Although most of the original buildings have been replaced, Regent Street retains its grandeur, especially at the Piccadilly Circus end. Here, it bends dramatically to the left, obscuring the buildings that lie beyond but promising much. From here up to and beyond Oxford Circus, this grand street is devoted to quality shopping.

Above: mural in Carnaby Street
Right: Regent Street, facing south

The eastern side of Regent Street has many of the best buildings. The **Café Royal** (No. 68) opened in 1865 and soon became the haunt of Aubrey Beardsley and Oscar Wilde; the Brasserie retains something of its sumptuous beau monde atmosphere. **Mappin & Webb** (No. 170) is one of London's longest-established goldsmiths, silver-smiths and jewellers. Nearby on both sides of the street, are well-known clothes shops, including **Aquascutum** (No. 100), **Austin Reed** (No. 103) and **Burberry** (No. 165). Opposite Burberry is **Wedgwood** (No. 158), selling quality fine bone china, crystal and cutlery. Further up, **Hamley's** (Nos. 188–196), established in 1760, is thought to be the largest toy shop in the world; despite its size, expect it to be packed, with queues well down the street before Christmas. More for the young can be found farther down at **Mamas and Papas** (No.256–258). **Liberty's** comes next with its trademark fabrics (the store front is, in fact, on Great Marlborough Street, not Regent Street itself and the Regent's Street façade now has other fashion outlets). The range of tempting stores continues with **Laura Ashley** (No. 256), a prime source for clothes, fabrics and furnishings. The former department store **Dickins & Jones** (No. 224) is being converted into a range of retail shops. Popular high street shops in Regent Street include Mango, Zara, Gap, French Connection and Karen Millen.

CARNABY STREET
Running parallel with Regent Street, to the east, is Carnaby Street, a byword for trendiness in the Swinging Sixties, when Mary Quant was the fashion queen and everyone came here to buy paisley flower-power shirts and bell-bottomed trousers. As fashions changed, so Carnaby Street declined to the point where it became a seedy eyesore. More than thirty years later, it has been revived to cater to today's fashionable young people.

Liberty's (Regent Street) is a department store unlike any other in London: an Aladdin's Cave housed in a building that is a gem of Arts and Crafts design. A wide and varied range of goods can be bought here, but the distinctive Liberty print fabric is still the main attraction—and carries with it an image of up-market style.

The store fills two buildings, both designed by E. T. and E. S. Hall and built in 1924. The classical part overlooks Regent Street; above the entrance, a frieze shows Britannia receiving goods from the nations of the world. Inside, the basement is packed with the Japanese ceramics, textiles and prints that were Arthur Lasenby Liberty's trademark when he opened the store in 1875. The floors above offer a profusion of goods from around the world, from African tribal jewellery to exotic silk fabrics, arranged to re-create the atmosphere of a bazaar. The ground floor stocks Liberty handkerchiefs, scarves and ties.

The top floor, by contrast, resembles an informal museum. On one side you can browse among Arts and Crafts furniture, known for its quality craftsmanship and its straightforward, clean design. On the other, glass cases line the walls, filled with antique silver and pewter pieces specially commissioned from artists such as Archibald Knox; his flowing, Celtic-inspired designs were so popular that 'Liberty style' became synonymous with art nouveau. In between is the central stairwell, where you can peer over the banister and look down on oriental carpets and Liberty's own range of fabrics.

Liberty's Tudor-style wing dates from 1924 and is built of timbers salvaged from HMS *Impregnable* and HMS *Hindustan*. A bridge across Kingly Street, linking the store's two parts, has a clock where St. George and the Dragon do battle every hour. Above the Great Marlborough Street entrance is a gilded caravel, the sailing ship that once carried cargoes of silks, porcelain and spices.

Liberty's weathervane depicts a caravel, the ship that once sailed the oceans in search of spices and silk. Below, Liberty's stock, laid out like an eastern bazaar

82

THE ROYAL ACADEMY SUMMER EXHIBITION

The Royal Academy Summer Exhibition is one of the high points of the London Season: Tickets to the fashionable and exclusive private preview are much sought after. The exhibition (Jun–mid-Aug) displays the paintings, sculpture and architectural drawings of living artists, and much of the work is for sale. Of the 10,000 or so works submitted, the Academicians select just over 1,000 for public display. They have, in the past, been criticized for conservatism and for preferring representational works, while ignoring the abstract. Today, the choice tends to be more adventurous and wide-ranging.

▶▶ Royal Academy of Arts   73B3

Piccadilly, W1 (tel: 020-7300 8000)
www.royalacademy.org.uk
Open: daily 10–6 (Fri 10–10). Admission free
John Madejski Fine Rooms Tue–Fri 1–4.30, Sat–Sun 10–6
Underground: Green Park, Piccadilly Circus

Burlington House, Piccadilly's most imposing building, was built as a Palladian palazzo (mansion) for the Earl of Burlington around 1720. Today it is the home of the Royal Academy of Arts, whose members include many distinguished British artists and architects. Major international exhibitions loaned from collections around the world fill two suites of galleries for most of the year; art in the Summer Exhibition (see side panel) is for sale. Recent major exhibitions have included Monet's late works and Picasso's ceramics.

Burlington House is set back from the street, with a courtyard in front that has a statue of Sir Joshua Reynolds. He was elected first President of the Royal Academy when it was founded in 1768, under the patronage of George III, with the twin aims of raising the prestige of the arts and of teaching promising painters (Constable and Turner were among the first students). The two wings on either side house other learned bodies, including the Society of Antiquaries.

The statues that adorn the Royal Academy's façade represent Raphael, Titian, Wren, Vinci and others. The Academy's entrance hall has ceiling paintings by former Academicians—notably Benjamin West's *The Graces* and *The Four Elements*.

The main exhibition rooms are on the first floor and many of them have splendid door frames, ceiling decorations and fireplaces. The top floor of the building, the Sackler Wing, which is reached by glass lift or steps, has been remodelled by Sir Norman Foster, himself an Academician, and is used for smaller exhibitions, including shows by living artists. Here, and not to be missed, is Michelangelo's *Madonna and Child with the infant St. John*, a circular relief carved in marble in 1504–1505 and generally considered to be one of his most beautiful works. The Royal Academy shop stocks a range of art books, and sells cards, posters, artists' materials and gift items.

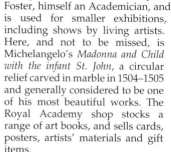

83

The Iron Duke, a national hero after his defeat of Napoleon Bonaparte

THE IRON DUKE

The Duke of Wellington is popularly known as the 'Iron Duke' but not, as is often supposed, because of his military achievements. Instead the name dates to the later period in his life when, having served as Prime Minister from 1828 to 1830, he resigned in opposition to parliamentary reform and the extension of democracy. This refusal to support the Reform Bill made him so unpopular that rioters broke the windows of Apsley House. Iron shutters were then put up to prevent a reoccurrence—hence the sarcastic nickname.

▶▶ Wellington Museum (Apsley House)   *72A2*
Hyde Park Corner, W1 (tel: 020-7499 5676)
www.english-heritage.org.uk
Open: Apr–Oct Tue–Sun 10–5; Nov–Mar Tue–Sun 10–4. Admission moderate
Underground: Hyde Park Corner

When the Duke of Wellington (1769–1852) finally defeated Napoleon at the Battle of Waterloo in 1815, he became the nation's hero. Parliament, in gratitude, voted to give Wellington £200,000 (then a very substantial sum), which he lavished on alterations to his home, Apsley House. The original house was built of brick by Robert Adam in 1778. Wellington's architects (Benjamin Dean Wyatt) wrapped it in Bath stone, added the giant Corinthian portico and pediment, and designed the vast Waterloo Gallery.

Apsley House, known as 'No. 1, London' in Wellington's day, is today a museum that combines two pleasures: the opportunity (surprisingly rare in London) to see inside an aristocratic 18th-century home; and the chance to admire the Duke's art collection (some of it looted as the spoils of war, some of it bought legitimately, some of it given to Wellington by grateful allies freed from Napoleon's yoke). Yet, in the midst of all this splendour and opulence, it is Napoleon who manages to steal the show: Canova's heroic 3.35m (11-ft) marble statue of the French emperor, nude except for a fig leaf, stands at the base of the staircase. Napoleon himself commissioned the work but did not like it because the figure of Victory, in the statue's right hand, appears to be flying away. The statue remained in storage in the Louvre until the British government bought it in 1816 and presented it to Wellington.

Equally intriguing is Goya's *Equestrian Portrait of Wellington*, hung in the Waterloo Gallery. X-rays have shown that this originally depicted Joseph Bonaparte, Napoleon's brother; he was made king of Spain in 1808 but defeated by Wellington at the Battle of Vittoria in 1813, and Goya hastily painted Wellington's head over the original.

WELLINGTON ARCH

Designed by Decimus Burton in 1827–1828 as a northern gate to the grounds of Nash's Buckingham Palace, this monumental arch with its later addition of London's largest bronze sculpture, winged Victory (1912), now stands on the huge traffic island at Hyde Park Corner. Recent renovations have breathed new life into this forlorn monument. Access to its island site is now easy, and the space inside has been transformed to create three exhibition spaces. These show the history of both this and Marble Arch; the richness of London's street monuments and statues; and temporary exhibitions. In addition, specially commissioned Commonwealth Gates remember soldiers of Commonwealth countries who gave their lives in the two world wars. (Hyde Park Corner, tel: 020-7930 2726. *Open* Wed–Sun 10–5; Nov–end Mar 10–4. *Admission* moderate.)

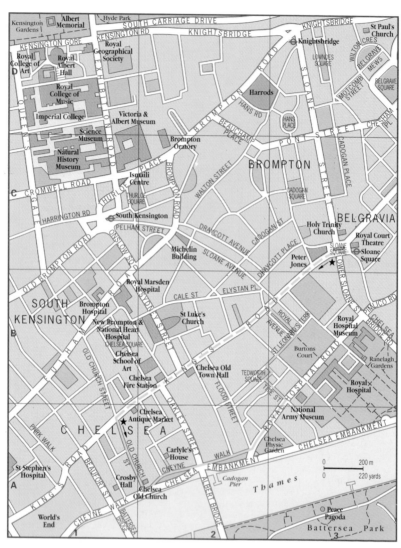

84

CHELSEA AND KNIGHTSBRIDGE These upmarket residential areas are kept immaculate for Londoners and temporary residents from abroad. But Chelsea's King's Road, by a twist of irony, continues to stand for youthful, very British rebellion. Its boutiques were the first to sell mini skirts and hippie gear in the 1960s, and punk was born here in the following decade. By contrast, the South Kensington museums complex on Cromwell Road presents a wealth of objects, events and images that stimulate curiosity, while London's best-known department store, Harrods, is just a short step away, in Knightsbridge.

CHELSEA AND KNIGHTSBRIDGE WALK This walk starts and ends at the King's Road, taking in a range of buildings spanning nearly 500 years of Chelsea's past.

Take Bus No. 22 from Sloane Square Underground station down the King's Road, getting off near the cinema, on the corner of Old Church Street. Walking south down Old Church Street, you will pass two important examples of Modern Movement architecture set among pretty Georgian brick houses: **No. 64** (by Mendelssohn and Chermayeff) and **No. 66** (by Gropius and Fry) were both built in 1936.

Turn left at the end of the street to reach **Chelsea Old Church**, which has a memorial to Sir Thomas More, Henry VIII's Chancellor, who lived near here from 1524 until he was executed in 1535. It is said that Henry VIII secretly married his third wife, Jane Seymour, in this church in 1536. There are many other important monuments at Chelsea Old Church, including an unusual shrouded effigy of Sara Colville (1631).

Turn left from the church onto Cheyne Walk; to the right there is a good view of the Albert Bridge (built 1873).

Cheyne (pronounced 'Chainy') **Walk** is lined by early Georgian houses, many with elegant railings and balconies. The second street on the left (Cheyne Row) has more modest houses but of the same early 18th-century

date, including **Carlyle's House** (see page 90). Cheyne Walk continues on the other side of Oakley Street. The most splendid of the houses (**No. 16**) was once the home of Dante Gabriel Rossetti.

Nearby, on Chelsea Embankment, **Swan House** (No. 17), built in 1875, and its neighbour, **Cheyne House** (1876), are pioneering examples of Norman Shaw's Queen Anne style, with oriel windows.

Continue up Royal Hospital Road and take the third left into **Tite Street**, whose playful houses and studios were popular with a number of artists in the late 19th and early 20th century. Oscar Wilde wrote several of his best-known plays at **No. 34**, Whistler lived at **No. 46**, John Singer Sargent at **No. 31** and Augustus John at **No. 33**.

Turn right onto Tedworth Square (Mark Twain lived at No 23) and right onto St. Leonards Terrace, with its fine 18th-century houses (Nos. 14–32). Turn left onto Royal Avenue to return to the King's Road.

Left: elegant Albert Bridge

Some of the world's best-known designers have their boutiques among Brompton Road's chic shops and restaurants. Once lined with rural market gardens, it is now a window shopper's dream—Harrods' window dressing is exceptionally sumptuous. At the same time, some of the buildings themselves warrant a closer look.

BROMPTON ORATORY

Brompton Oratory (tel: 020-7808 0900. *Open* daily 6.30am–8pm. *Admission* free) is the work of Herbert Gribble, who designed this large and flamboyant baroque building in 1876, when he was a young and almost unknown architect. The huge Carrara marble statues of the Twelve Apostles in the nave, carved in the 1680s by Giuseppe Mazzuoli, originally stood in Siena Cathedral. On a more intimate scale is the Chapel of St. Wilfrid, with its triptych by Rex Whistler of the *Martyrdom of St. Thomas More and St. John Fisher* (1938).

If you start at South Kensington tube station, it is a short walk down Pelham Street to Fulham Road and the **Michelin Building** (No. 81), a striking art deco building of 1911, decorated with ceramic-tile panels of racing cars. It was built for the French tyre company and rescued from the threat of demolition in 1985; now it houses the **Conran Shop**, specializing in imaginative furnishings, and **Bibendum**, an upscale restaurant and Oyster Bar.

To the south, down Fulham Road, there are other interior furnishings shops. To the north, Brompton Road leads towards Harrods, passing stylish boutiques such as **Joseph** (No. 315), **Issey Miyake** (No. 270) and **Emporio Armani** (No. 191).

The huge Italianate baroque church, known as the Brompton Oratory (see panel), stands at the busy intersection of Thurloe Place and Brompton Road. This is a fashionable church for London's Roman Catholic community. Choral mass is held here every Sunday at 11am, and the sermons are often highly theatrical, and very entertaining and interesting.

The fourth right turn beyond the Brompton Oratory leads to another enclave of chic clothes shops and smart restaurants: Beauchamp Place. Try Caravela or O Fado (for Portuguese food) or Patara Thai for excellent Thai cooking. Borshtch 'n' Tears is a long-established, quirky Russian restaurant serving variable food, but usually has a great party buzz. Designer **Caroline Charles** has a shop at No. 56–57, and opposite, **Janet Reger** (No. 2) sells fine lingerie.

At No. 52 is the London branch of Hamilton and Inches, Scotland's leading jewellers and specializing in watches, silver and gifts. **Bruce Oldfield** (No. 27), one of the established stars of modern British fashion, will create something original—at a price.

Bibendum in Michelin House: from French tyre headquarters to shrine of modern cooking

Harrods, at 87–135 Brompton Road, is more than just a shop: It is a miniature kingdom, over which the princes of high finance have fought bitter battles. Its vast, terracotta building (famously illuminated at night) has grown to occupy 6ha (15 acres)—a far cry from its origins as a small grocer's shop founded by Charles Henry Harrod in 1849.

Harrods has 330-plus departments, more than 5,000 staff, and has been known to take in £16 million in a single day (in 1997), although normal turnover is a more modest £1.6 million a day. Harrods' Latin motto (*Omnia, omnibus, ubique*—everything, for everyone, everywhere) sums up the philosophy of a shop that attracts visitors from around the world and sells almost everything the world produces.

Pick up the *Store Guide* (from information desks at the entrance) for exhibitions, author signings and product demonstrations or visit www.harrods.com.

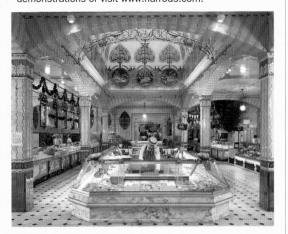

For many, the street-level food halls are the highlight, partly for the range of good foods on display, but also for W. J. Neatley's tiled ceilings above the fish, meat and poultry halls, illustrating *The Hunt* and dating from 1902.

Equally lavish art deco ceramics decorate both the men's hairdressing rooms and the women's lavatories. The shop's Egyptian owners have added the highly elaborate central escalator, inspired by the art of Ancient Egypt. Children in particular will enjoy the pet shop and Toy Kingdom.

There is a price to pay for so much free entertainment—the crowds can be unbearable, and the shop is best visited early in the day. If you want to take tea in Harrods' 400-seater Georgian Restaurant, it is best to book; otherwise, try any of the other restaurants, cafés and bars—28 at the last count. Harrods is not open on Sundays.

HARRODS SALES
At the legendary January sale, reductions are huge, but so are the crowds, and some people are so eager to secure a bargain that they will camp outside the entrance over Christmas. Once inside the shop, even dignified and aristocratic ladies lose all sense of decorum—elbows and fists fly in this test of consumer tenacity that can sometimes resemble a game of rugby.

Harrods' sumptuous food halls are both a tourist attraction and the local shop for Knightsbridge residents

London is among the world's culinary capitals. This has come about through three profound changes: innovative chefs reinterpreting traditional British recipes; customers demanding quality and authenticity; and restaurants competing in service, interiors and food.

SOHO

Soho has a cosmopolitan range of restaurants, but there are some constants that can be relied upon. Alastair Little, 49 Frith Street (tel: 020-7734 5183), modern British, in minimalist setting; Lindsay House, 21 Romilly Street, W1 (tel: 020-7439 0450), modern British, in a sumptuous town-house; Yo! Sushi, 52 Poland Street, W1 (tel: 020-7287 0443), amusing hi-tech Japanese; and Wagamama, 10a Lexington Street, W1 (tel: 020-7292 0990), a no-frills noodle refectory. In Wardour Street, try Mezzonine at No. 100 (tel: 020-7314 4000), the first-floor canteen section of Conran's mega-restaurant, and Spiga at Nos. 84–86 (tel: 020-7734 3444). In Dean Street, find top quality Italian cuisine at Quo Vadis at Nos. 26–29 (tel: 020-7437 9585), part of Marco Pierre White's burgeoning empire.

Here are just a handful of the many good restaurants in town at the moment. The top chefs work in impressive locations; reservations are essential and prices high. The dress code is smart, and men may need to wear jackets and ties; if in doubt, check when reserving your table.

TOP CHEFS AND HAUTE CUISINE In this category the chef is key; if he has moved on, reconsider your choice. Michel and Albert Roux's Le Gavroche restaurant, 43 Upper Brook Street, W1 (tel: 020-7408 0881) was the training ground for many top chefs. Michel Roux Jnr now runs it, serving classic French food in a formal, flawless setting. Marcus Wareing, 'the crown prince of British cooking', has taken Pétrus to the Berkeley Hotel, Wilton Place, SW1 (tel: 020-7235 1200). Gordon Ramsay has moved into the premises formerly occupied by La Tante Claire, now called the Restaurant: Gordon Ramsey, 68 Royal Hospital Road, SW3 (tel: 020-7352 4441) to add to his list of exceptional London restuarants. Renowned

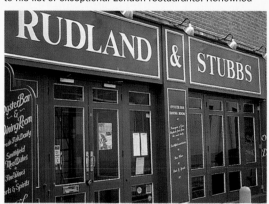

chef Alan Pickett reveals his passion for French cuisine at his restaurant Orrery, 55 Marleybone High Street, W1 (tel: 020-7616 8000. Chef Marco Pierre White now has an empire including: Quo Vadis (see left); Mirabelle (see below); Belvedere, Holland Park, W8 (tel: 020-7602 1238); Criterion Grill, 224 Piccadilly, W1 (tel: 020-7930 0488) and L'Escargot Marco Pierre White, 48 Greek Street, W1 (tel: 020-7437 2679).

Oysters and fresh fish are the speciality of Rudland & Stubbs

BRITISH British food has undergone a revolution. Here is a variety of places to find good dishes. The Ivy, 1 West Street, WC1 (tel: 020-7836 4751), Le Caprice, Arlington

The Quality Chop House: the best of British cooking

House, Arlington Street, SW1 (tel: 020-7629 2239) and J. Sheeky at 28–32 St. Martin's Court, WC2 (tel: 020-7240 2565) are three flawless, professional restaurants. Other restaurants worth investigating include Quality Chop House, 94 Farringdon Road, EC1 (tel: 020-7837 5093); Rules, 35 Maiden Lane, WC2 (tel: 020-7836 5314), for full roasts in Edwardian rooms; St. John, 26 St. John Street, EC1 (tel: 020-7251 0848), for everything traditionally British eaten at communal tables; Tom's Kitchen 27 Cale Street, SW3 (tel: 020-7349 0202) is great for families: plenty of casseroles, sausages and pies, plus some more sophisticated dishes. There's a cocktail bar on the first floor if you come in the evening.

WORLD CUISINES This is a token selection of the choice on offer. For French food, try Marco Pierre White's glamorous Mirabelle, 56 Curzon Street, W1 (tel: 020-7499 4636). For Indian Chor Bizarre, 16 Albemarle Street, W1 (tel: 020-7629 9802), La Porte des Indes, 32 Bryanston Street, W1 (tel: 020-7224 0055), Tamarind, 20 Queen Street, W1 (tel: 020-7629 3561), and Veeraswamy's, 99 Regent Street, W1 (tel: 020-7734 1401) are some of the upscale best. For Japanese, Nobu, The Metropolitan Hotel, 19 Old Park Lane, W1 (tel: 020-7447 4747) is unbeatable; for Italian, try Zafferano, 15 Lowndes Street, SW1 (tel: 020-7235 5800) for Thai, Nahm at the Halkin Hotel, 5 Halkin Street, SW1 (tel: 020-7333 1234).

HOTEL RESTAURANTS Dine in sumptuous surroundings at The Ritz (tel: 020-7493 8181), The Dorchester (tel: 020-7629 8888), Claridges (tel: 020-7629 8860), Savoy (tel: 020-7836 4343), Le Meridien Waldorf (tel: 020-7734 8000) and One Aldwych (tel: 020-7300 1000). Reservations will be necessary for all of these.

BREAKFAST AND AFTERNOON TEA
The British no longer eat huge cooked breakfasts and multi-course afternoon teas with scones and home-baked cakes. However, they are still well prepared in a few restaurants, in particular in the deluxe hotels, which all take breakfast and tea seriously. Away from the hotels, try the full breakfast at Tom's Kitchen, 27 Cale Street, SW3 (tel: 020-7349 0202 Sotheby's Café, 34 New Bond Street, W1 (tel: 020-7293 5077), or the little Italian-run cafés on so many London street corners. For delicious cakes, go to Patisserie Valerie, 44 Old Compton Street, W1 (and other branches throughout London tel: 020-7437 3466) or to the growing number of high quality cafés in museums and galleries, such as those at the V&A, Whitechapel Art Gallery, Tate Modern, the Wallace Collection, Somerset House, the British Museum and Kensington Palace's Orangery.

Chelsea salon; here the Carlyles entertained Charles Dickens

'THE FRENCH REVOLUTION'
Carlyle's most famous work, entitled *The French Revolution* (1837), is a massive tome and a towering achievement, especially since a major part of the book had to be written twice. Carlyle left the manuscript at the house of his friend, the philosopher John Stuart Mill, who lived at No. 17 Kensington Square. To his horror, Mill discovered that his housemaid, thinking that the pile of paper was discarded, was using it to light fires. As a result, Carlyle had no alternative but to sit down and write the whole of the first volume over again.

▶▶ **Carlyle's House**   84A2
24 Cheyne Row, SW3 (tel: 020-7352 7087)
www.nationalturst.org.uk
Open: mid-Mar–Oct Wed–Fri 2–5, Sat–Sun & Bank Holiday Mon 11–5. Admission moderate
Underground: Sloane Square. Bus: 11, 19, 22, 49, 219, 239
Few people today read Thomas Carlyle's thunderously oratorical works, such as his history of the French Revolution, but in his day he was regarded with almost religious reverence. Admirers would come from far away to visit the great man, who was renowned for the high moral tone of his work. His wife, the witty Jane Carlyle, poet and letter writer, attracted an equally eminent bevy of admirers: Dickens, Tennyson, Browning and Thackeray among them. This stream of visitors met for conversation in the upstairs drawing room of Carlyle's house, where he lived from 1834 until his death in 1881.

Visiting the house today, you gain a very real sense of that mid-Victorian era. The house (built in 1703) was described by Carlyle himself as 'old-fashioned, eminent, antique', and some of the rooms, to this day, have no electricity. Heavy furnishings and rose-coloured wallpapers add to the dark but dignified atmosphere. The walls are hung with portraits of the Carlyle family (including a fine early picture by the pioneer of British photography, Julia Margaret Cameron) and of the men about whom Carlyle wrote, most notably Frederick the Great of Prussia.

The top-floor attic was specially built for Carlyle in 1853 and was intended to be a soundproof study, though in fact it actually amplified sound. A touching reminder of domestic life is Carlyle's hat, hung by the back garden door: Thomas was fond of his pipe but had to go into the garden for a smoke, since Jane could not stand the smell.

▶▶ Chelsea Physic Garden

84A3

66 Royal Hospital Road (entrance on Swan Walk), SW3
(tel: 020-7352 5646)
www.chelseaphysicgarden.co.uk
Open: Apr–Oct Wed 12–dusk or 9pm (whichever is earlier,
Thu–Fri 12–5, Sun 12–6; daily during Chelsea Flower Show
(last week in May), noon–5. Admission expensive
Underground: Sloane Square. Bus: 19, 22, 239

Founded in 1673, the Chelsea Physic Garden is a haven of privacy and tranquillity in the heart of busy London. As the name suggests, it began as a place of scientific research, planted with species valued for their medicinal properties, under the auspices of the Worshipful Company of Apothecaries. That work continues to this day. The beneficial effects of feverfew in the relief of migraine is just one of the many research projects that are currently underway.

Within its high sheltering brick walls, the simple rectilinear beds are planted by genus, according to the method of plant classification established by Linnaeus in the 18th century. (Pick up the useful map by the entrance.) Any suggestion of dull formality is banished, however, by the wild and willful way in which these plants, many of them highly fragrant, thrust their colourful blooms outwards and upwards, spilling out over the paths so that progress around this crowded garden is necessarily slow.

Many rare trees grow here, some of considerable age, such as the striking golden rain tree (*Kolreuteria paniculata*), with its twisted branches. The woodland areas come into their own at the end of the winter, when the ground beneath is carpeted in snowdrops, cyclamen and hellebores. The garden also has the first-ever rock garden constructed in England: It dates from 1772 and is made from basaltic lava blocks brought from Iceland and old masonry from the Tower of London.

SIR HANS SLOANE

A statue of Sir Hans Sloane in wig and gown stands in the middle of the Chelsea Physic Garden (there are others in Sloane Square and the British Museum). London owes much to this extraordinary man, who was physician to Queen Anne and George II, President of the Royal College of Physicians, and immensely wealthy. The British Museum was founded from the collection he bequeathed at his death in 1753. In 1712 he purchased the manor of Chelsea, which included the Physic Garden. Sloane ensured the garden's survival by paying for its restoration (at a time when it was in serious decline), and he made financial arrangements to ensure that the site would never be built upon, but would always remain a garden.

91

Informal beds at the Chelsea Physic Garden

OAK APPLE DAY

Oak Apple Day (29 May) at Chelsea Royal Hospital is one of London's more colourful pageants. The resident veterans parade in their three-cornered hats to honour the birthday of Charles II, their founder. The parade takes place around Grinling Gibbons' statue of Charles II in the Figure Court. The statue is ritually decorated with oak leaves, to commemorate the king's escape from the Battle of Worcester (1651) after defeat at the hands of the Parliamentarians. After hiding in a hollow oak tree, the king was able to escape to France, from where he eventually returned, after the death of Cromwell, to be restored to the English throne in 1660.

The splendid Great Hall, with Charles II looking on from a distance

►►► Chelsea Royal Hospital 84B3

Royal Hospital Road, SW3 (tel: 020-7881 5200)
Open: Mon–Sat 10–noon and 2–4 Sun 2–4 in summer only, plus Sun services. Admission free
Underground: Sloane Square

There is a story that Charles II's mistress, the actress Eleanor Gwyn (also known as Nell Gwyn), persuaded the king to found this hospital because she was moved to tears by the sight of a wounded soldier begging for alms. A more realistic version may be that, with the bitter experiences of the Civil War behind him, Charles II realised the importance of maintaining a standing army that would stay loyal to the Crown. His method of winning the army's loyalty was to provide for aged and injured soldiers, rather than simply throwing them onto the streets without so much as a pension.

The Chelsea Royal Hospital was set up in 1682, an institution modelled on Louis XIV's Hôtel des Invalides in Paris (founded in 1670) to provide food, lodging and medical care for infirm veterans. The architect was Sir Christopher Wren, who, up to now, had concentrated almost exclusively on designing churches for the reconstruction of the City of London after the Great Fire. This was his first full-scale secular work, and he produced a building of almost barracklike simplicity but of great dignity, which was subsequently extended (between 1809 and 1817) by Sir John Soane—see especially Soane's Stables to the right of the entrance.

The central courtyard is known as the Figure Court because of the figure of Charles II standing in the middle; this bronze statue, made by Grinling Gibbons in 1676, was brought here in 1692 and depicts the king as a Roman soldier. The central block of the hospital building has an

Chelsea Pensioners' in their striking uniforms

CHELSEA FLOWER SHOW
The Chelsea Flower Show is one of the great events of the summer season. Established in 1913, it is held in late May and provides a showcase for all that is novel in the gardening world, from the newest rose varieties to the latest in lawnmower technology. Every devoted gardener attends, from the Queen downwards. The horticulturalists who display their stock here spend all year preparing and, by playing tricks with nature, succeed in presenting all the riches of the four seasons in a single week: Snowdrops and sweet-smelling narcissi bloom alongside summer-flowering delphiniums and autumnal chrysanthemums. Often, however, the simplest ideas steal the show—window-box displays or meadow gardens of British native wildflowers. Garden snobs claim the Chelsea Flower Show is now too popular, and too dominated by the big commercial growers. They prefer to attend the other shows organized by the Royal Horticultural Society at their exhibition hall in Vincent Square, at Hampton Court Palace and elsewhere in London. For details of these, contact the Royal Horticultural Society (tel: 0845-260 5000; Chelsea Flower Show hotline tel: 0870-906 3871).

imposing octagonal lobby, with the Great Hall and chapel either side. The panelled Great Hall, where the residents take their meals, is decorated with a huge painting of Charles II on horseback by Antonio Verrio, while the opulent chapel is a typical Wren design with a black and white stone floor, fine plasterwork, choir stalls by Grinling Gibbons and a huge altar-painting—the *Resurrection* by Sebastiano Ricci—in the vault.

Governor's House stands at the river end of the eastern range, its Council Chamber decorated with sumptuous carving and hung with portraits of Charles I and his family (by Van Dyck), Charles II (by Lely) and William III (by Kneller). Lawns sweep down to the Thames and the terrace displays a cannon captured at Waterloo. To the east, the tree-filled Ranelagh Gardens used to be a vast pleasure garden where, in the words of the 18th-century writer Oliver Goldsmith, the public would flock for 'fêtes, frolics, fireworks and fashionable frivolity'. To the west, the more formal gardens serve as the site for the famous Chelsea Flower Show and provide good views across the river to Battersea Park.

Today, Chelsea Royal Hospital is home to about 400 pensioners (veterans), who wear a distinctive uniform—a dark blue overcoat in winter and a scarlet frock coat in summer—dating back to the time of the Duke of Marlborough (1650–1722). Pensioners must be ex-soldiers of 'good character' and are usually at least 65 years old. The pensioners' duties include attending church and occasional parades, in return for which they receive food, lodging, clothing, and a daily ration of beer and tobacco. Chelsea Pensioners sometimes volunteer to show visitors around the Hospital or to pose for photographs, in which case it is customary to give them a tip.

Chelsea Flower Show

THE CRYSTAL PALACE
The Crystal Palace, which housed the Great Exhibition of 1851, stood on the south side of Hyde Park, near the Royal Albert Hall. It was a stupendous building, three times longer than St. Paul's Cathedral (566m/1,858ft) and tall enough (at 33m/109ft) to contain three elm trees that were already growing on the site. Designed by the great landscape gardener, Joseph Paxton, it was a prefabricated greenhouse on a gigantic scale. Sceptics predicted it would crash to the ground in the first strong gale. In fact, six million visitors passed through before the exhibition closed. The Crystal Palace was then dismantled and moved to Sydenham where, unfortunately, it burned down in 1936. Little now remains (see page 215), though the great greenhouses at Kew Gardens (see pages 226–227) convey an idea of what this splendid Victorian building once looked like.

▶ National Army Museum 84B3

Royal Hospital Road, SW3 (tel: 020-7730 0717)
www.national-army-museum.ac.uk
Open: daily 10–5.30. Admission free
Underground: Sloane Square. Bus 11, 19, 239

This museum covers the history of the British Army from 1485 (when the Yeomen of the Guard, the first professional army, was formed) to the present day. Audiovisual presentations and dioramas bring the subject to life, and rather than glorifying war, the museum brings home a sense of the hardships experienced by ordinary and very vulnerable soldiers.

Start in the basement, which deals with the period from Agincourt to the American Revolutionary War, and features the best display of British swords in the country. You can also try on an English Civil War helmet, feel the weight of a cannonball, and listen to some contemporary soldiers' songs. Upstairs is the skeleton of Napoleon's favourite charger, Marengo, alongside personal relics of Wellington and some gory battlefield remnants. The exhibits on the next floor move on to the defence of the British Empire and the role of the British soldier in the 20th century. It includes a reconstructed trench, and explores such diverse theatres of war as the deserts of Africa and the jungles of Borneo.

▶▶▶ Natural History Museum 84C1

Cromwell Road, SW7 (tel: 020-7942 5000)
www.nhm.ac.uk
Open: Daily 10–5.50. Admission free
Underground: South Kensington

The Natural History Museum was created to celebrate the rich variety of life on Earth and is housed in a suitably splendid building of cathedral-like proportions. The idea of creating a museum devoted to natural science was first discussed at a controversial time; plans were drawn up in 1862, only three years after Charles Darwin had published *On the Origin of the Species*, sparking off a fierce debate between scientists who supported evolutionary theory, and those who insisted on the biblical version of the Creation. The debate even influenced the style of the building. Purists maintained that the neo-Gothic style, then in vogue, should be reserved for places of worship and not employed for secular buildings. The architect, Alfred Waterhouse, sidestepped the *Continued on page 98.*

The Road to Waterloo exhibition in the National Army Museum includes a huge model depicting the Battle of Waterloo with 70,000 model soldiers

The Royal Albert Hall and the buildings that surround it commemorate the vision of Prince Albert, Queen Victoria's husband. The Hall is one of the most prominent among the many grandiose buildings added to the cityscape during Victoria's reign, and has become a familiar landmark.

The Royal Albert Hall, home of the Proms and the occasional rock concert

The substantial profits generated by the Great Exhibition of 1851 were used to purchase land to create educational museums, colleges and halls. Presiding over this grand scheme was a Royal Commission, headed by Prince Albert. When Albert died in 1861, the public was asked to donate funds to finance the building of the Albert Memorial (see page 111) and the Royal Albert Hall. The costs of building the Memorial escalated, and plans for the Hall were shelved until 1863, when Henry Cole, in charge of raising funds, hit on the idea of selling 1,300 seats at £100 each, entitling the owners to attend every event staged over the next 999 years! (This arrangement still stands, although the descendants of the original owners often waive their right to attend.)

Finally completed in 1871 (and refurbished in 2003), the immense domed building, 83m (274ft) in diameter and 47m (155ft) high, can seat 8,000. All kinds of events are held here, but to many the Hall is inextricably linked with the Henry Wood Promenade Concerts, better known simply as the Proms, which take place here every evening between mid-July and mid-September, culminating in the emotion and patriotism of the Last Night of the Proms. Essential to the whole concept is the availability of cheap tickets, sold on a first-come, first-served basis; the first few hundred people at the head of the queue can stand in the arena, right behind the conductor. For details www.royalalberthall.com (tours tel:020-7838 3105).

IN THE VICINITY
There are several fine buildings near the Albert Hall. Behind it is the Royal College of Music, where a collection of musical instruments is on public display during the school term (Wed 2–4.30). To the west of the Hall, the former home of the Royal College of Organists has a façade decorated with a frieze of musicians—but no organist! On Kensington Gore, the Royal Geographical Society (1875), and Albert Hall Mansions (1886) together form a good example of Norman Shaw's Queen Anne style of architecture.

The King's Road, as its name indicates, was once a private royal road, linking St. James's Palace and Hampton Court; it was used only by the monarch and courtiers. Humbler folk had to take a boat along the Thames if they wanted to travel west and visit what was then the small riverside village of Chelsea.

SAATCHI GALLERY
This well-renowned gallery moved to its new premises—the former Duke of York's Headquarters on the King's Road—in November 2007 from the South Bank. The state-of-the-art gallery showcases contemporary art from largely unseen young artists and the work of established international artists not normally seen in the UK. Bookshop and café/bar. (tel: 020-7823 2363, www.saachti-gallery.co.uk *Open* call for times. *Admission* expensive).

96

Pottering around in the King's Road

In 1830 the King's Road was opened to the public, and from that time onwards Chelsea began to expand, becoming something of an artist's colony, whose residents ranged from the eminently respectable to the downright eccentric.

This mixture survives to the present day and gives the King's Road much of its character: Shops selling fine antiques or antiquarian books stand cheek by jowl with avant-garde boutiques; punks with weird clothes and outrageous hairstyles parade alongside immaculately tailored grandes dames taking their coiffeured poodles for a stroll. However, multinational chains such as Starbucks and Gap are now prevalent and the cutting edge of fashion and design is no longer here.

The first stretch of the King's Road, leading westwards from Sloane Square, is lined with the display windows of **Peter Jones** department store (see page 102). Opposite are the early 19th-century barrack buildings of the **Duke of York's Headquarters**, designed as a school for soldiers' orphans and founded by Frederick, Duke of York (see page 63), son of George III and now home to the Saatchi Gallery (see panel). The second street on the right, Blacklands Terrace, leads to **John Sandoe Books** (No. 10), which is one of the best of the many small bookshops found all over London.

Further down on the left, there are glimpses towards Chelsea Royal Hospital down Royal Avenue, a leafy

boulevard laid out in 1689, and intended as a route connecting Wren's Royal Hospital with Kensington Palace. This short stretch is all that was built of the route, and it was here that, in Ian Fleming's novels, James Bond had his home. Beyond the entrance to Markham Square lies the **Pheasantry** (No. 152), a distinctive building with Grecian-style caryatids. Only the portico survives from the original 1760s building. Its present name derives from the 1870s when pheasants were kept here for breeding. Between 1916 and 1934 the Pheasantry housed a ballet school run by the Princess Serafine Astafieva, where stars such as Margot Fonteyn and Alicia Markova took their first steps. Today it is a Pizza Express restaurant.

Beyond the Pheasantry are some of the King's Road's most interesting shops: **Antiquarius** (Nos. 131–141) is an antiques market where some 70 stallholders sell everything from postcards to Georgian silver. At **Chelsea Antique Market** (Nos. 245–253) you will find books, maps and prints. Opposite, there is a taste of the country at the **Chelsea Farmers' Market** (May–Oct), with its small food stalls, and the **Chelsea Gardener,** a tiny spot crammed with (very expensive) plants, flowers and pots, on the corner of Sydney Street.

Further up Sydney Street is **St. Luke's Church**, all neo-Gothic frills, where Charles Dickens was married to Catherine Hogarth in 1836. Nowadays fashionable weddings are more likely to take place at the Register Office alongside **Chelsea Old Town Hall**, on the opposite side of the street from the Sidney Street turn off.

Continuing up the King's Road, **Green and Stone** (No. 259), the artists' supplies shop, is handy for students at the nearby Chelsea College of Art, founded in 1891. Beyond are two interior design premises with contrasting styles: chic, state-of-the-art fabrics at the **Designers' Guild** (No. 277) and classic wallpapers and fabrics at **Osborne & Little** (No. 304–308).

The main part of King's Road ends with two innovative shops: **Rococo** (No. 321) sells fantastic confectionery, and **World's End** (No. 430) is Vivienne Westwood's original shop for her humorous and unconventional fashions.

Keeping the Easy Rider *era alive*

97

THE CADOGAN ESTATE

If architecture interests you more than shopping, you should explore the maze of streets that lies to the north of the King's Road, especially the Cadogan Estate, which has some of London's most interesting Queen Anne-style buildings. The style developed in the 1870s in rejection of the flat-brick or stucco-fronted façades of the Georgian and Regency era. Suddenly, Dutch gables, projecting windows, balconies, and all sorts of ornament came into fashion. For typical examples, see the west side of Cadogan Square, particularly the buildings designed by Norman Shaw (Nos. 62, 68 and 72).

WORLD'S END

The main concentration of shops on the King's Road comes to an end at a kink in the road known as World's End, named after the pub of the same name (No. 459). The origin of the name is obscure but, no doubt, the residents of Chelsea feel that the world does end here, on the borders with the less chic Fulham district.

The Natural History Museum

The beast from Wyoming: Diplodocus carnegii: *for some it has become a symbol of the Natural History Museum*

NATURAL HISTORY MUSEUM HIGHLIGHTS
The Natural History Museum has more than 67 million items in its collection, an indication of the sheer diversity of the natural world. Among the most intriguing exhibits, look for the skeleton and reconstruction of the extinct dodo in the Bird Gallery, the weird and spiny coelacanth in the Central Hall, and in the section devoted to dinosaurs the giant flesh-eating monster, *Tyrannosaurus rex*. Biggest of all, however, is the Blue Whale model in the Mammal Hall, which measures almost 28m (93ft) in length. The largest land animal—the African elephant—is dwarfed beside it.

Continued from page 94.
problem by looking to French Romanesque architecture for his inspiration.

Waterhouse chose a style that was less familiar to the British and less loaded with religious connotations. The building is clad in a bravura display of coloured terracotta, with relief panels depicting animals, fossils, plants, and insects running the whole length of the 207-m (680-ft) façade; living species of the time are depicted to the left of the entrance, extinct ones to the right.

Today, the collections include 28 million insects, 27 million animals, 9 million fossils, 500,000 rocks and minerals and 3,200 meteorites.

Stepping through the main entrance, with its twin towers, the sense of entering a cathedral is reinforced by the navelike form of the Central Hall, although the voices of hundreds of excited children exploring the dinosaurs on display is a far cry from the hushed tranquillity of a church. Soaring staircases provide a viewpoint for admiring the profusion of decoration (note especially the monkeys scampering up and down the arches) and for looking down on the plaster-cast skeleton of *Diplodocus carnegii* (who comes from Wyoming), 150 million years old, 26m (86ft) long, and one of the largest land animals ever to have roamed the earth.

Plans displayed in the Central Hall will help you decide what to see, and there is plenty of choice. Many of the most recent displays were designed specifically with children in mind. The favourite is the Dinosaurs exhibition (turn left to Gallery 21) where a high-level walkway brings you eye to eyesocket with some of these ancient monsters. The lighting is low and atmospheric, and for children weaned on *Jurassic Park*, there is an

THE GIANT SEQUOIA TREE
Not all the items in the Natural History Museum are animals. One of the most intriguing exhibits is a section through a Giant Sequoia tree (*Sequoia-dendron giganteum*) displayed on the stairs to the first floor. This was cut down in 1892, by which time it was 84m (277ft) tall and measured 15m (49ft) around the girth. A tree ring count indicates that it was 1,335 years old when felled, having started its life in California in AD557.

99

animatronic re-creation of flesh eaters in action. Moving on to more peaceful matters, the Mammal Hall has the giant life-size blue whale model—another highlight of the museum. Also in this area is the 'Human Biology' exhibition (set in a darkened room that simulates the interior of a womb). The rest of this exhibition explains human reproduction, development and perception using imaginative models, push-button displays and authentic sound effects.

There are more ancient creatures to seek out in the Central Hall, while 'Creepy Crawlies' takes an entertaining look at insects, and the Ecology Gallery, opposite, demonstrates the interdependence of all living things on earth. The Museum has a good restaurant, and the shops stock some excellent souvenirs and gift ideas.

The Earth Galleries section of the museum offers an exciting series of state-of-the-art displays. These include Visions of Earth, a dramatic, if somewhat ethereal space, which depicts the Earth within the solar system. A central escalator leads up straight through a huge globe to the second floor, where displays tell the story of the Earth's formation. Many beautiful mineral and gemstone specimens are also on display. The most popular exhibits, however, are on the top floor; 'The Power Within' focuses on volcanoes and earthquakes, including a simulation of the Kobe earthquake in Japan in 1995, with film footage captured live at the time that shows a supermarket being shaken. The 'Restless Surface' exhibition includes several hands-on stations that demonstrate the forces of wind, water and heat on the landscape. Other galleries focus on the story of Britain from the beginning, including the Earth's natural geological treasury of gemstones, and discuss ways of protecting our world for the future.

SCIENTIFIC ART
Some of the Science
Museum's exhibits
bridge the gulf between
art and technology. One
of them is a painting
Coalbrookdale by Night
by P. J. de Loutherbourg
(1801) hanging in the
Iron and Steel Gallery.
Another is the intricate
Orrery of 1716, a working
model of the solar sys-
tem, demonstrating
the movement of the
planets, made and
named for the Earl of
Orrery. Nature's artistry
is also demonstrated by
the model of the DNA
spiral to be found on the
second floor, while dis-
plays on the same floor
show the futuristic
possibilities of computer-
generated graphics.

►►► Science Museum 84D1

Exhibition Road, SW7 (tel: 0870-870 4868)
www.sciencemuseum.org.uk
Open: daily 10–6. Admission free; IMAX expensive.
Underground: South Kensington

Even the most technophobic visitors to London will find something to interest them in this fascinating museum, since many of the displays are as entertaining as they are educational. This is a wonderful place for families, with plenty of hands-on exhibits, information screens and a variety of free gallery talks. To have a rewarding visit, select one or two areas to explore. Thanks to the clear explanations, you do not have to have any science train- ing to get a huge amount out of a visit: Indeed, the longer you stay, the more your curiosity grows.

If time is short, you could explore two particularly exciting galleries. Firstly, in the Making the Modern World Galleries on the ground floor, find monstrous engines of all kinds, driven by steam, wind or pressure, often pumping or clicking into life during museum hours. Secondly, visit the nearby Wellcome Wing that sits above a favourite basement attraction, Launch Pad, a hands-on children's science and technology gallery.

Devoted entirely to contemporary science and technol- ogy, The Wellcome Wing has three floors of interactive, stimulating exhibitions about science now. You can explore digital technology, human identity, patterns in science or the latest scientific news—ground floor exhibits change regularly to keep right up to date. Visitors can take part in ongoing biomedical research projects in the Live Science section, they are encouraged to play games that question the future of our world and they are invited to consider the possibilities of artificial intelligence and how it already affects our life. There is also an IMAX cin- ema (the museum runs the one on the South Bank, too, see page 202), and virtual voyage trips across the solar system or to establish a colony on Mars.

From the Wright Brothers to Stealth bombers, the Flight Gallery is a museum highlight

Elsewhere in the museum, the basement's Secret Life of the Home explains the intriguing technology of the seem- ingly simple modern home, while the ground floor focuses on the excitement of power and space—the Apollo 10 command module is here, and you can design your own rocket. Upstairs, the first floor focuses on mate- rials, telecommunications, gas, agriculture, surveying, time measurement and weather.

Exploration of the final frontier; from gunpowder rockets to the Apollo missions

SCIENCE AND HISTORY
Among its displays of the cutting edge of technology, the Science Museum also has some ancient exhibits. The oldest of these is the clock mechanism from Wells Cathedral, displayed in the Time Measurement Gallery and still working some 600 years after its construction. An important piece of industrial history is represented by Arkwright's original spinning machine of 1769, one of the pioneering inventions that sparked off the whole Industrial Revolution, with its far-reaching implications for the way we live today.

101

The second floor is more challenging and deserves more time. Here chemistry and physics, nuclear power and computing are explored. Printing, lighting and marine engineering are introduced and explained with exhibits such as an 18th century printer's workshop and an advanced gas-cooled reactor. The collection of intricate model ships is especially fine, and forms a unique historical archive of vessels no longer in existence.

On the third floor, visitors can learn about geophysics, oceanography, flight and optics with intriguing holograms, a delicate model of the first hot-air balloon to carry people and the pioneer pilot Amy Johnson's Gipsy Moth plane, 'Jason'. In the Flight Gallery, you can use working models, computer games and wind tunnels to discover what keeps aeroplanes and helicopters in the air. Here, too, is the On Air radio and sound studio that explains the equipment and mechanisms behind one of the most popular means of communication—radio. Visitors over 12 years old can use the computer simulation to compile their own mix and then hear how it sounds. The fourth floor's galleries tell the story of medical and veterinary history, helped by an Egyptian mummy, an anatomical model of a horse, leech jars and Louis Pasteur's microscope.

Sloane Street offers good shops and interesting architecture. The haunt of caricatured Sloane Rangers in the 1980s—upper-crust girls (and guys) of good breeding—the top half is now lined with haute couture shops that include the classics: Chanel and Valentino.

Pont Street

102

THE MEWS PUBS OF BELGRAVIA

Some of London's most interesting pubs are located in the mews of Belgravia, where they were built to serve the coachmen, grooms and butlers employed by the big houses, and soldiers from the nearby Wellington Barracks. One such is the Grenadier (18 Wilton Row), full of military mementos and said to be haunted by the ghost of an officer flogged to death for cheating at cards. Another is the Star Tavern (6 Belgrave Mews), the very model of a perfect traditional tavern, with open fires in winter and antique furnishings.

At **Peter Jones** department store, on the west side of Sloane Square, you can buy everything necessary for decorating and furnishing your home in a conventional or modern British style. The **Royal Court Theatre** stands on the opposite side of the square, famous for radical drama that often satirises bourgeois values (John Osborne's play *Look Back in Anger* received its first performance here in 1956). In between, at the heart of the square, trees shelter a fountain, which features the figure of Venus (1953, by Gilbert Ledward).

As you head up Sloane Street, one of Chelsea's best-known shops is the **General Trading Company** (2 Symons Street, just off Sloane Square), well stocked with gifts, toys, china, kitchen accessories, furnishings and a very good glass department. The fact that the shop is one of a tiny handful in London to hold all four royal warrants indicates how upmarket it is, but it nevertheless also sells modestly priced crafts from the Far East and Africa.

Holy Trinity Church stands across the street from the General Trading Company, a masterpiece of English Arts and Crafts design, completed in 1890. The huge east window contains 48 panels depicting saints and was designed by Edward Burne-Jones (check the notice board for lunchtime concerts here). Further up on the right are the gardens of **Cadogan Place**: Access is limited to residents of nearby apartments, but you can see over the railings. The view is particularly cheerful when the winter-flowering shrubs and bulbs are in bloom.

From Cadogan Place northwards, both sides of Sloane Street are lined with shops bearing famous names. **Valentino**, **Joseph** and **Versace** are among them, as well as more modestly priced up-to-the-minute fashions at other trendy stores.

It is tempting to dip into the side streets for their characterful buildings. To the west you can walk through Pont Street, Hans Place and Hans Road to Harrods. **Pont Street** has plenty of fine Queen Anne-style houses with Dutch gables and terracotta decorations. St. Columba's Church, built in 1955, with a striking helm roof, stands at the far end of the street.

Hans Place contains houses surviving from the time when Henry Holland first laid out his 'Hans Town' development in 1777, building in an area that then consisted of open fields. **Hans Road** boasts some pioneering examples of Arts and Crafts architecture by Mackmurdo (No. 12) and Voysey (Nos. 14 and 16). Jane Austen lived briefly at No. 23 in the year 1815 when she was entertained by the Prince Regent, to whom she dedicated her novel *Emma*.

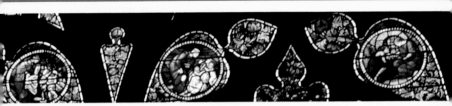

In the opposite direction, the hotel on the corner of Sloane Street and Cadogan Place is where Oscar Wilde was arrested in 1895, following his failed libel case against the Marquess of Queensbury. Beyond lies **Belgrave Square**, at the heart of exclusive Belgravia; many of the huge Regency houses are now embassies or ambassadorial residences. The area was developed between 1825 and 1835 by Thomas Cubitt and is characterized by monumental stucco-fronted mansions, backed by cobblestone mews where horses were stabled and servants lived (today even a simple mews cottage or converted stable is likely to be inhabited by a millionaire). To see the best of this district, visit **Motcomb Street**, with its antiques shops; **Kinnerton Street**, with its pretty courtyards leading off to the left; and curving **Wilton Crescent** and **St. Paul's Church**, Wilton Place, a Victorian neo-Gothic church, popular for high-society weddings, with a fine timber roof and rich decorations.

BELGRAVE SQUARE

Belgrave Square's sunken garden is surrounded by houses designed by George Basevi. For all their monumental proportions, the blank fronts and huge porches have provoked dismissive comments from architectural critics, although the three grand villas at the square's corners (by Kemp, Smirke, and Hardwick) do provide some variety.

103

A stage for satire

The V&A entrance: the lantern was modelled on Victoria's crown

THE GREAT BED OF WARE
Recently restored, the Great Bed of Ware is one of the V&A's most celebrated exhibits, partly because of its prodigious size (3m/10ft wide and nearly 4m/13ft long) but also because of its great age (made around 1590) and its extravagant carved, painted and inlaid decoration. Another celebrated curiosity is the large model tiger in the Nehru Gallery, which is shown in the act of eating a British army officer. Made in 1790, for Tipu Sultan of Mysore, the model incorporates a small organ that imitates the groans of the tiger's victim.

104

Renaissance masterpieces in replica in the V&A's Cast Court

▶▶▶ **Victoria and Albert Museum**　　84C1
Cromwell Road, SW7 (tel: 020-7942 2000)
www.vam.ac.uk
Open: daily 10–5.45, every Wed and last Fri each month
10–10. Admission free; variable charge for exhibitions
Underground: South Kensington

The V&A, as it is affectionately known, is a storehouse of treasures comprising several national collections. Together they form the world's largest collection of decorative and fine arts. Indeed, so remarkable is it that you can easily walk past great masterpieces without even knowing it. Where else under one roof would you find superb examples of textiles from around the world, architectural fragments from French châteaux, Indian chess sets, medieval reliquaries, great photographs and contemporary glass. The immense diversity, eclecticism and idiosyncracy of the collection is astounding.

The origin of the museum goes back to the Great Exhibition of 1851, a celebration of the arts, crafts and

industrial products of the British Empire. Prince Albert, the driving force behind the exhibition, wanted the museum to be a permanent collection displaying the best examples of commercial art and design, which would be a source of inspiration to future generations.

The first museum on the site was a utilitarian structure of iron and glass, nicknamed the Brompton Boilers. As the collection grew, the building expanded to its present size (it covers 5.2ha (13 acres) and has over 9.6km (6 miles) of gallery space). Queen Victoria laid the foundation stone for the Cromwell Road façade in 1899 (her last public engagement in London), and the building was completed in 1909. The lantern on top of the entrance is shaped like the Queen's imperial crown.

Wandering at whim through the galleries will probably leave you tired and confused—it is best to pick up a plan at the entrance, make a rigorous selection and then set off. Alternatively take an introductory tour.

Starting at the main hall, the central corridor houses medieval art, one of the best collections of its kind in the world, ranging from 5th-century ivories to Saxon goldwork and Carolingian gospel bindings. This leads to the Pirelli Garden, a good place to rest weary feet. The garden is overlooked by the Renaissance galleries, while straight ahead you will find the Morris, Gamble and Poynter rooms. These were, originally, the museum tearooms and restaurant, and they retain their Minton tile work, William Morris furnishings and Edward Burne-Jones stained glass. Running to the right of the entrance hall are galleries displaying Art and Design in Europe and America from 1800 to 1890. The 20th-century galleries, on the second floor, bring the story of design right up to date (and also have changing exhibits of recent material).

Do not miss the Toshiba Gallery of Japanese art, the Nehru Gallery of Indian Art, or the T. T. Tsui Gallery of Chinese Art, the Cast Court and the Raphael Cartoons (all on the ground floor), or the British galleries upstairs. The Nehru Gallery displays a tiny fraction of the immensely rich and exotic Indian Art Collection; see especially the carved and inlaid Mughal jade, the fine textiles and the exquisite miniature paintings. The Cast Court is peopled by a magnificent collection of specially commissioned copies intended for study; many are life-size and they include Michelangelo's David and Trajan's Column. The Raphael Cartoons, brought to England by Charles I in 1623, are Raphael's full-scale preparatory drawings for seven huge tapestries intended for the Sistine Chapel in Rome and remain Britain's most important large piece of Renaissance art. As for the British Galleries, their total renovation highlights the V&A's unrivalled collection of 16th-to 19th-century British design. More than 3,000 objects representing the best of all periods have been selected. Furniture, textiles, dress, silver, metalwork and ceramics have been given sumptuous settings. These, together with paintings, sculptures, books, prints and drawings, tell the story of British design while focusing on four themes: style, taste, innovation and fashion.

Opened in 2006, the Jameel Gallery displays a superb Islamic art collection. New for early 2008 is the dazzling Jewellery Gallery, reached by a glass spiral staircase, with a stunning collection of over 3,000 jewels.

THE YALTA MEMORIAL

To the south of the Victoria and Albert Museum, a garden in Thurloe Square contains a moving memorial (1982, by Angela Conner) to the Yalta Victims, the many thousands of people who were forcibly repatriated to the Soviet Union and Eastern Europe between 1944 and 1947, only to face imprisonment and death.

TAKE A BREAK

When hunger sets in, head for the restaurant, one of the best of any London museum. Save some time for the excellent shop, which sells jewellery, ceramics and crafts by some of the most innovative designers working in Britain today.

105

Morris wallpaper

[Map of Kensington, Notting Hill and Hyde Park area, with grid references A–C and 1–3. Labels include: Kensal Green, Market, BAYSWATER, Bayswater, Queensway, Notting Hill Gate, Ladbroke Square Gardens, NOTTING HILL, Holland Park, KENSINGTON, Kensington Gardens, Round Pond, Kensington Palace, The Broad Walk, The Dial Walk, Holland Park, King George VI Youth Hostel, Holland House, Queen Elizabeth College, Kensington & Chelsea Town Hall, Linley Sambourne House, St Mary Abbots, High Street Kensington, Leighton House, Edwardes Square, Victoria Road, Gloucester Road, and various street names. Scale: 200 m / 220 yards.]

KENSINGTON SQUARE

Kensington Square was one of the first developments in the former village after William III moved to Kensington Palace. Nos. 11 and 12, originally one house, are the best preserved and date from 1693. Among the square's early residents was Richard Steele, founder of *The Spectator*. Hubert Parry, composer of *Jerusalem*, lived at No. 17. Edward Burne-Jones, the artist, lived at No. 41 and John Stuart Mill, the political philosopher, lived at No. 18: it was here that Thomas Carlyle's first manuscript of *The French Revolution* was burned by accident (see page 90).

Busking in the park

KENSINGTON, NOTTING HILL AND HYDE PARK The great tract of Hyde Park separates the West End from Kensington, which maintains an air of being apart from the rest of central London. Immaculate stucco houses set in leafy avenues make it easy to imagine how 17th-century Kensington really was just a small rural village. Its transformation began in 1689 when William III came to live at Kensington Palace. Today, many of the fine houses have been converted into apartments. The High Street, once a country lane, is now a wide thoroughfare lined with fashionable shops, and the antiques shops of Kensington Church Street stretch unchecked to Portobello Road.

KENSINGTON WALK This route leads from Kensington Palace Gardens, which provide a glimpse of some of the most aristocratic dwellings surviving in the royal borough, to the present-day focus of Kensington life: the High Street shops.

Start in **Kensington Palace Gardens**, a leafy avenue laid out in 1843 on the site of the kitchen gardens of Kensington Palace. It is closed by entrance lodges at either end to reinforce the sense of privacy and exclusivity. In the 19th century its opulent houses earned it the nickname 'Millionaires' Row'. Several houses have now been converted into embassies.

Head south towards Kensington High Street. At the southern end of Kensington Palace Gardens (Palace Green) look for **No. 1**, which was designed by Philip Webb in 1863 as an experiment in Arts and Crafts style; and **No. 2**, built for the novelist William Makepeace Thackeray in 1860.

Turn right on to Kensington High Street; then take the next major turning on the right into Kensington Church Street. On Kensington High Street, **St. Mary Abbots Church** stands on the site of Kensington's original village church. It was rebuilt by George Gilbert Scott in the 1870s in a style intended to reflect the area's wealth and has a fine spire, which at 76m (250ft) is the tallest in London. Don't miss its famous *Healing* stained-glass window.

Take the second left, Duke's Lane, which still has some cottage-style houses reminiscent of the old Kensington. Turn left again onto picturesque Gordon Place, which has houses originally built for coachmen serving Kensington Palace. Gordon Place quickly leads you to Holland Street, where you turn right. Holland Street retains some unspoiled 18th-century houses (**Nos. 10, 12, 13 and 18–26**) and, at its far end, a left turn down the delightful Kensington Church Walk leads back to the bustle of Kensington High Street. Here, by the tube station, is the former famous department store, **Barker's**, with its splendid art-deco façade (built 1937–1938) and domed atrium. Once as famous as Harrods, it is now a galleria, occupied by a variety of retailers including the House of Fraser department store and well-known high street names.

Above: Kensington Church Street

*A peacock, one of the
many birds roaming free
in Holland Park*

HOLLAND HOUSE
Until it was blitzed in
World War II, Holland
House was one of the
finest Jacobean mansions
in London and the glittering hub of political and
literary society. During the
Commonwealth, when
Cromwell ruled England,
plays were performed here
privately in defiance of the
Puritan ban on all forms of
theatrical activity. In the
early 18th century it was
home to Joseph Addison,
one of the founders of *The
Spectator*, who composed
his articles for the magazine while strolling up and
down the 35-m (116-ft)
Long Gallery, taking a sip
of wine for inspiration
from the glasses he kept
at each end. During the
first decades of the 19th
century it was famous for
the salons hosted by Lady
Holland and attended by
the leading intellectuals of
the day, including Byron,
Talleyrand, Prince
Metternich and Macaulay.
Lady Holland was a
passionate supporter of
Napoleon. During his brief
exile on Elba, she sent
him jars of plum jam,
books and a refrigerator,
as tokens of her belief in
his cause.

▶▶ **Holland Park**   106B1
*Holland Walk, off Kensington High Street (tel: 020-7631 3003)
Underground: High Street Kensington, Holland Park
(entrances to the park are on Holland Park Road, Abbotsbury
Road, Holland Walk and Kensington High Street)*
Flower-filled formal gardens and wilder woodland areas
can both be enjoyed in this varied 22-ha (55-acre) park
hidden behind the grand houses of Kensington and
Holland Park. It used to be the private garden of Holland
House, built in 1606–1607 (see panel). All that remains of
the house today is the ground floor and the orangery,
which has been beautifully converted into the Belvedere
restaurant. The east wing has also been splendidly
restored to house London's best sited youth hostel (see
page 276). The terrace in front of the house, known as the
Holland Park Theatre, is used in the summer months for
outdoor plays (including a Shakespeare festival), ballets,
operas and concerts (see www.rbkc.gov.uk/Holland
Park). Surrounding the house are a rose garden, a Dutch
garden—laid out in 1812 with flower beds bordered by
box hedges—and an iris garden. In one corner there is a
small 18th-century building believed to have been an ice
house. Peacocks and other ornamental birds wander
freely about the park, adding their colour to the scene. The
woodland areas to the north are best in May, when the
rhododendrons and azaleas are in full bloom, complemented by the pink and cream spires of horse-chestnut
blossom. The Japanese Kyoto Garden created in 1991 is
especially tranquil, while for children there is an adventure playground with tree-walks and rope swings.

▶▶ **Leighton House Museum**   106A1
*12 Holland Park Road, W14 (tel: 020-7602 3316)
www.rbkc.gov.uk/leightonhousemuseum
Open: Wed–Mon 11–5.30. Admission moderate
Underground: High Street Kensington*
Leighton House is the most remarkable of a cluster of
artists' houses in the leafy district of Holland Park. George
Aitchison designed it in 1864–1866 for his friend, the artist
Frederick Lord Leighton, as the ultimate up-to-date bache-
lor's indulgence—with only one bedroom as he did not
want to be bothered with house-guests. The result was
London's first full architectural expression of the English

Aesthetic Movement. Leighton was 34 years old when he built the house. Born in Scarborough, Yorkshire, he roamed Europe as a young man, returned to England and, aged 25, achieved success by having his Early Renaissance-inspired painting *Cimabue's Madonna* exhibited at the Royal Academy Summer Exhibition. Better still, Queen Victoria bought it. His future sealed, he became a fashionable painter, was appointed President of the Royal Academy (1878–1896) and was created Baron Leighton of Stretton a month before he died in 1896.

During the 1860s Leighton had travelled widely in the Near East. His fondness for things Oriental is immediately apparent. Behind the plain brick exterior, lies one of London's most idiosyncratic rooms, the wonderful Arab Hall, designed by George Aitchison and based on a Moorish banqueting hall in Palermo, Sicily. The hall is lined with tiles, dating from the 13th to the 17th centuries, which Leighton collected on his travels in Damascus, Cairo and Rhodes; these are supplemented with equally exotic tiles designed by William de Morgan. The domed hall has a fountain at its heart, a Romanesque mosaic frieze by Walter Crane, and marble columns with capitals carved by Edgar Boehm. Other rooms, less exotic, but finished with red walls and ebonised wood, are hung with paintings by Leighton and his leading Pre-Raphaelite contemporaries.

The huge studio upstairs where Leighton worked is used for concerts and exhibitions. Leighton's sculpture, *Athlete struggling with a python* (1877), stands in the walled garden, where visitors may picnic, but you have to seek permission first.

ARTISTIC KENSINGTON

Kensington—Melbury Road, in particular—was once a hotbed of artiness. George Frederick Watts lived at No. 6, where he made the equestrian figure, *Physical Energy*, now in Kensington Gardens (see page 111). No. 9 (now No. 29) was built by William Burges for himself in 1875–1880 and reveals his preoccupation with Gothic detailing. William Holman Hunt, whose painting *The Light of the World* hangs in St. Paul's Cathedral, lived at No. 18. Nearby, No. 8 Addison Road was built in 1906–1907 for Sir Ernest Debenham, founder of the department store, and covered in colorful William de Morgan tiles, earning it the nickname Peacock House.

109

Leighton House—the Arab Hall

Hyde Park and Kensington Gardens together form an expanse of trees, flowers and greenery covering 248ha (615 acres). They are divided by the road that runs from Alexandra Gate in the south, over the Serpentine Bridge, built in 1826, and up to the Victoria Gate in the north. To the west of this road is Kensington Gardens; to the east is Hyde Park.

SPEAKERS' CORNER

Speakers' Corner is at the northeastern edge of Hyde Park, near Marble Arch. Here, on Sundays, soapbox orators harangue the crowds on issues ranging from politics and religion to vegetarianism or the evils of smoking. The tradition of free speech and assembly dates from the mid-19th century. There have been huge gatherings here in the past, including demonstrations against nuclear armaments. According to law, anyone can speak on any topic, as long as they do not blaspheme, use obscene language, incite racial hatred or breach the peace.

110

Kensington Gardens is a relatively quiet area, with surprisingly rich wildlife. Herons and grebes can be seen on the willow-fringed Long Water, to the north of the Serpentine Bridge. Hyde Park is more a place of recreation and entertainment, with boats for rent on the Serpentine in summer; bandstand music at lunchtime in June, July and August; and occasionally fairs, concerts or fireworks parties.

The parks escaped being built upon during the great expansion of London in the 18th century because the land belonged to the Crown. Henry VIII had seized it from the monks of Westminster Abbey at the Dissolution of the Monasteries and had turned it into a huge royal hunting ground. Charles I made it London's first public park, open to 'respectably dressed people' and it became a favourite resort of Samuel Pepys, among others.

A good place to begin a stroll around Hyde Park is Hyde Park Corner. Here, behind Apsley House (see page 83), you can enter through Decimus Burton's 1828 triple-arched screen or the gates created in honour of the Queen Mother. The road inside is Rotten Row—a linguistic corruption of *route du roi* (King's Road)—built to link rural Kensington Palace to Piccadilly and St. James's Palace.

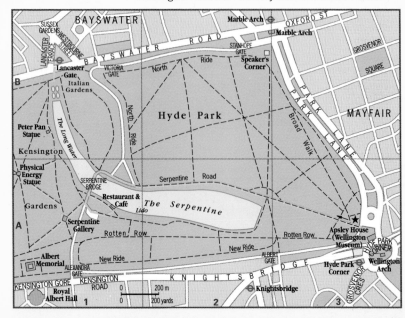

Audience participation at Speakers' Corner, Hyde Park

111

It is now used by the Household Cavalry Brigade for exercising their horses; at around 10.30am (9.30am) on Sunday) and noon, members of the Brigade ride to and from the Changing of the Guard ceremonies, which take place at Buckingham Palace and Horseguards.

Serpentine Road leads straight ahead to the northern shore of the Serpentine. This lake was created by damming the River Westbourne. A beautiful bridge, built in 1826 by George Rennie, spans the water. Swimming in the Serpentine is allowed at the Lido, on the opposite bank, for a couple of months in summer (tel 020-7706 3422 for dates). Hardy members of the Serpentine Swimming Club come here for a daily morning swim, even in the depths of winter, and a few always take a dip on Christmas Day.

Nearby is the Serpentine Gallery, which hosts exhibitions of contemporary art (tel: 020-7298 1501. *Open* daily 10–6 during exhibitions. *Admission* free). Walk north to see two sculptures: *Physical Energy* (1904) by George Frederick Watts is a powerful equestrian figure, and *Peter Pan* (1912) by George Frampton commemorates the hero of J. M. Barrie's play for children, written in 1904—the boy who defied adulthood is depicted playing his pipes among fairies and woodland animals. Lancaster Gate exit is nearby. Head southwest from the Serpentine Gallery to visit the restored Albert Memorial (see panel); or go west to the Round Pond, where children and adults come to sail model boats at weekends, and from there to the more formal gardens of Kensington Palace.

THE ALBERT MEMORIAL
George Gilbert Scott's flamboyant monument to Prince Albert, husband of Queen Victoria, is a reminder of the values of the Victorian age. In the middle is Albert himself, holding the catalogue for the 1851 Great Exhibition, which he organized (see page 95). Completed in 1876, the memorial is crowded with 169 portraits of painters, composers, poets and architects. Its corners illustrate the peoples of Asia, America, Europe and Africa, while allegorical figures represent Albert's interests: Commerce, Manufacturing, Engineering and Agriculture. Weather and pollution caused such serious deterioration that during the 1990s the whole monument was restored by skilled craftsmen.

▶▶▶ Kensington Palace

106B3

Kensington Gardens, W8 (tel: 020-7937 9561/0870 751 5170)
www.hrp.org.uk
Open: Mar–Oct daily 10–6; Nov–Feb daily 10–5. Admission
very expensive, includes acoustiguide
Underground: High Street Kensington, Queensway

The asthmatic William III was the first monarch to set up home in Kensington Palace, in 1689, escaping from the damp and smoke of riverside Whitehall Palace to the cleaner air and rural environment of Hyde Park. He purchased the existing house, built in 1605, and had it enlarged by Sir Christopher Wren. It was further extended, under George I, by William Kent in the 1720s. The result is a roughly rectangular brick building, which is arranged around three courtyards; architecturally it is surprisingly modest, more like a country house than a palace, although the interiors are sumptuous, and the surrounding gardens a great delight. Queen Victoria was born at the palace in 1819 and on her 80th birthday decided that the State Apartments should be opened to view. Today, members of the present royal family still have apartments here, including the Duke and Duchess of Gloucester and the Duke and Duchess of Kent—it is possible you may catch a fleeting glimpse as they depart in their limousines to attend various public engagements in London.

Re-opened in 1998 after major refurbishment, the areas of the Palace open to visitors are the ground-floor Royal Ceremonial Dress Collection and, upstairs, the State Apartments.

The largest of the Queen's Apartments is Queen Mary's Gallery, a spacious panelled room hung with royal portraits and Kneller's forceful picture of Peter the Great of Russia, painted when the Czar visited England to study London's naval dockyards in 1698. A series of smaller private apartments is decorated with 17th-century furnishings and pictures, including the State Bed, in Queen Mary's Bedchamber, with its original hangings.

DIANA MEMORIALS
There was much debate following the death of the Princess of Wales as to what would make a suitable memorial. It was decided, not least because of her work with children, that the Diana, Princess of Wales Memorial Playground would be built in the grounds of her former home at Kensington Palace. A huge pirate ship is the focal point of the playground and much of its equipment has been adapted for children with special needs. It is near Black Lion Gate and open at 10 daily, closing according to the season. Adults are only allowed entry when accompanied by a child, except for 9.30am–10am. On the western edge of Hyde Park, near the Serpentine, a Diana Memorial Fountain was unveiled in summer 2004.

112

Kensington Palace:
modest without but
sumptuous within

The King's State Apartments are very opulent. Italianate in style, the rooms have magnificent ceiling paintings by William Kent. The most magnificent of all is the Cupola Room, with its pillars, figures of Greek and Roman deities, and busts of Roman emperors and ancient philosophers. Queen Victoria was baptised here. Next comes the King's Drawing Room, which enjoys superb views over Kensington Gardens. Through Queen Victoria's bedroom, where a painting illustrates the Queen's marriage to Prince Albert in 1840, an anteroom leads to the King's Gallery. This has ceiling paintings of the adventures of Ulysses, and is decorated and furnished as it was during the 18th century. A curiosity is the wind-direction dial above the fireplace, turned by a weathervane on the roof. After the anteroom is the Duchess of Kent's Dressing Room. Its furnishings and objects date mostly from the 1840s and 1850s and exemplify early Victorian taste.

Courtiers and visitors would have arrived here up the King's Grand Staircase, designed by Wren, with its scrolled wrought-ironwork by Jean Tijou and its walls and ceiling coated in Venetian-style paintings by Kent, inspired by work at Versailles and Blenheim. The trompe l'oeil wall painting of a gallery crowded with figures includes many contemporary portraits of George I's courtiers and servants. One of them, known as Peter the Wild Boy, was discovered living like a wild animal in a forest near Hanover, Germany, and brought to England as a freak curiosity. Finally, the Privy Chamber is painted with the figure of Mars (wearing the order of the Garter) symbolizing the military prowess of George I, and of Minerva, goddess of wisdom, accompanied by figures representing the Sciences and the Arts.

The Dress Collection presents a superb array of court finery, including a permanent collection of dresses belonging to Diana, Princess of Wales. Visitors are taken through the elaborate process of dressing for court; from a replica of a shop where materials were chosen, to a visit to the seamstress for a final fitting.

KENSINGTON PALACE GARDENS
William III was a keen gardener and lavished much affection on the 10-ha (25-acre) garden he had laid out, in Dutch style, immediately around Kensington Palace. This has now gone, and in its place is the pretty sunken garden, made in 1909, surrounded by an alley of pleached lime trees on three sides, with flower beds framing the central lily pond (to which there is No. public access). The north side of the garden is closed by the red-brick Orangery of 1704. Facing south to catch the sun, this is where Queen Anne used to take tea, as visitors still can—part of the Orangery serves as a restaurant. Beyond lies Kensington Gardens (see page 110). An attractive walk from the palace leads up the Broad Walk to Black Lion Gate and Queensway tube station, passing the playground, site of the Elfin Oak, a tree trunk carved by Ivor Innes in 1928 with elves, foxes, frogs, rabbits and secret doorways.

113

A glimpse through the gilded gates of Kensington Palace

▶▶ Linley Sambourne House 106A2

18 Stafford Terrace, W8 (tel: 020-7602 3316, ext: 300)
www.rbkc.gov.uk/linleysambournehouse
Open: Sep–late Jun. Visits by guided tour only Sat, Sun 11.15
(conventional), 1, 2.15, 3.30 (costumed). Prebooking advised as
tours limited to 12 persons. Admission expensive
Underground: High Street Kensington

Anyone interested in the Victorian period should make an effort to see this excellent museum. Alternatively, see the Merchant-Ivory films based on E. M. Forster's novels for many scenes in both were shot in this house. It is named after Edward Linley Sambourne, the chief political cartoonist for *Punch* magazine who also produced the illustrations for Charles Kingsley's *The Water Babies*, published in 1885. Sambourne bought the house in 1874, soon after it was built, and lived here until his death in 1910. His family continued to use it until 1980, when it was opened as a museum, and throughout the intervening years the house and its furnishings remained almost totally unaltered. The museum is a time capsule, preserving its over-furnished, cosy, late Victorian and Edwardian appearance and atmosphere. The rooms still have their original William Morris wallpapers, and the walls are hung with a mass of paintings, cartoons and photographs. These combine to create a sense of cluttered richness, so beloved by the Victorians, which is further enhanced by the Oriental rugs, the stained-glass windows and the heavy, Gothic-inspired furniture.

Although much is undistinguished in the house, there are some gems on the walls, including paintings by Sambourne's friends—such as Watts, Millais and Alma-Tadema—and drawings by other well-known illustrators, such as Kate Greenaway and Sir John Tenniel. Vintage fixtures can be seen in the bathroom and lavatories, and one of the most charming rooms is that of 'Roy' Sambourne, the artist's son, which is complete with pin-up pictures of popular Edwardian actresses and his former girlfriends.

NOTTING HILL CARNIVAL
The Notting Hill Carnival was founded in 1966 as a local neighbourhood festival but has since grown to be the biggest Caribbean-style carnival in Europe with processions of colourful floats, street stalls, steel-band music and non-stop dancing. In deference to the English climate it is held over the August Bank Holiday weekend (usually the last weekend in the month), rather than the traditional carnival date of Mardi Gras (Shrove Tuesday), which falls in chilly, wet February. Marred in the past by racial tension, the carnival is a largely peaceful event, but take the usual precautions against pickpockets.

The drawing room, Linley Sambourne House

▶▶▶ Portobello Road Market   off 106C1

Portobello Road, W11 and W10, and surrounding streets
Open: Antiques Sat 5.30am–4.30pm; general Mon–Wed 8–6,
Fri–Sat 7–7, Thu 8–1; organic market Thu 11–6; clothes and
bric-a-brac Fri–Sun 9–4; Golborne Road market Mon–Sat 9–5
Underground: Notting Hill Gate, Ladbroke Grove

Portobello Market is more than just one market; it is a collection of smaller markets, each with its own character. Furthermore, the antiques shops spill over through Notting Hill and down Kensington Church Street. It is a far cry from its origins at the end of the 19th century, when gypsies traded horses and herbs along the track leading down to Porto Bello farm, named after the Caribbean city of Puerto Bello. Ironically, after World War II, as the British

Empire was disbanded and people from former colonies chose to take up their option of British citizenship, it was the Caribbeans who settled in this area. Meanwhile, the market had thrived, and when Caledonian market in north London closed, its antiques dealers came west to trade here instead.

Today, Portobello Road's Saturday antiques market combines shops and stalls, and is one of Britain's longest markets. This is the best day to come, and it is a full day's outing. At the top (Notting Hill) end, only the cleverest bargain hunters will strike lucky from the all-knowing antiques dealers. Down the hill, they may do better, and there are plenty of pubs and cafés, such as Tom's Delicatessen on Westbourne Grove, where you can pause to consider which of your finds might be worth buying. Here, too, are collectibles such as records, antique clothes and toys, and walking sticks. Along the side streets are contemporary art and ceramics shops, and designer clothes and jewellery outlets (Ledbury Road and Westbourne Grove). The best way to enjoy it is simply to poke about, keeping eyes sharp for attractive and unusual souvenirs.

Further down, find fruit and vegetables in Golborne Road, together with bicycles, household goods and new clothes. Here, too, is a favourite local institution, Lisboa Patisserie, a Portuguese café, perfect for a break from bargain hunting. Alternatively, snack on the excellent tapas at Galicia, also on this stretch of Portobello.

KENSAL GREEN CEMETERY
Kensal Green Cemetery (on Harrow Road, reached from Kensal Green tube station) is, like Highgate Cemetery, full of interesting tombs beside tree-lined avenues. This was the first private cemetery in London (1833) and became fashionable after two of George III's children were buried here. Other notable tombs are those of Thackeray and Trollope, the novelists; Isambard Kingdom Brunel, the engineer; and the tightrope-walker, Blondin. Here too is the grave of James Barry who, after a successful career as an army surgeon, was made Inspector General of the Army Medical Department; only after 'his' death in 1865 was it discovered that James Barry was actually a woman.

115

Art meets junk in the Portobello Road

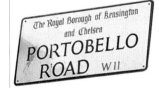

Map labels: C, B, A, 1, 2, 3

Regent's College · Regent's Park · York Bridge · Royal College of Physicians · Euston Centre · Park Square · Park Road · Outer Circle · Euston Rd · Sherlock Holmes Museum · Royal Academy of Music · Ulster Pl · Regent's Park · Great Portland Street · Cleveland St · Marylebone Station · Madame Tussaud's · York Gate · Baker Street · St Mary's Church · Harley Street · Park Crescent · London Telecom Tower · Marylebone · Marylebone Road · Marylebone High Street · Devonshire Street · Portland Place · RIBA · Clipstone Street · University of Westminster · Town Hall · York St · Paddington St · Weymouth Street · Broadcasting House · Crawford Street · New Cavendish Street · Wimpole Street · Harley Street · Chandos Street · Langham St · All Souls · Seymour · Bryanston Square · Montagu Square · George Street · Portman · Wallace Collection (Hertford House) · Marylebone Lane · Thayer Street · Queen's College · Cavendish Pl · St George's Hotel · Manchester Square · Wigmore Hall · Cavendish Square · University of Westminster · The Heinz Gallery · Portman Square · Wigmore · James St · Welbeck St · Royal College of Medicine · Regent St · Oxford Circus · Edgware Road · Selfridges · Oxford Street

200 m / 220 yards

ELIZABETH BARRETT BROWNING
No. 50 Wimpole Street (parallel to Portland Place) was the home of Elizabeth Barrett, whose *Poems* (1844) attracted the attention of the younger poet, Robert Browning. A correspondence and a meeting followed, and the two fell in love. Elizabeth's tyrannical father disapproved, so she married Robert secretly in St. Marylebone Church, and the pair later escaped to Italy in one of literary history's most romantic elopements.

REGENT'S PARK AND MARYLEBONE In 1812 work began on a bold scheme to transform the West End of London and remodel the Crown-owned lands of Marylebone Park. John Nash, the Prince Regent's architect, cut a swathe through the heart of the metropolis, from Carlton House Terrace north via Regent Street and Portland Place, to Park Crescent. Beyond, he laid out the huge Regent's Park and intended to build a whole garden city of Italianate villas and grand terraces. The project, although never completed, gave the city a new focus, and extended smart London northwards. The benefits of Nash's great project are enjoyed by north Londoners today. Regent's Park is their back garden, used for walks, sport and picnics. It is a place to meet friends, to go boating, to delight in the roses, to exercise and play games, and to relax after visits to the Zoo.

MARYLEBONE WALK The contrasts of Marylebone are sampled on this tour, which starts with Georgian elegance and ends with shops and cafés.

Take the tube to Regent's Park station, near **Park Crescent**, a daring 1821 design by John Nash, who intended it to be completely circular, in contrast to the squares that characterize Georgian London. Only half of the circle was built, but the curving terrace, with its impressive colonnade of Ionic columns, hints at what Nash envisaged—to change the axis from the already busy east–west Marylebone Road to a south–north one running uninterrupted into Regent's Park; however, the builder of the circle went bankrupt, which was why it was never completed.

In James Adam's speculative **Portland Place** (1776–1780), the best of the original houses lie between Weymouth and New Cavendish Streets. Beyond are **Broadcasting House** and **All Souls Church** (see page 118), the **Langham Hilton Hotel** then **Saint Georges Hotel**, whose rooftop restaurant offers extensive views over London.

Turn right onto Cavendish Place, which leads to Cavendish Square. Lord Nelson lived for a time at No. 5 Cavendish Square, but the best buildings are on the north side (**Nos. 11–14**), built in 1770 and originally designed as part of a mansion for the Duke of Chandos. The archway between the two has a large bronze *Madonna* by Jacob Epstein. In Chandos Street, running north from the square, **Chandos House** (1771) is one of Robert and James Adam's finest private town houses. **Harley Street**, which also leads off Cavendish Square, has been synonymous with medicine since the mid-19th century. Medical practitioners, dentists, psychiatrists and plastic surgeons have their prestigious consulting rooms here, for the reception of private clients. On the same street (No. 64) the artist Turner lived from 1804 to 1808, and Queen's College (No. 43) was founded in 1848 as the first college of higher education for women in England.

Leave the square via Wigmore Street, which has interesting shops, as well as beautiful **Wigmore Hall** (1901), originally built by the piano maker Friedrich Bechstein next to his showrooms and still a place to hear fine recitals. Further on, to the right, the rigid grid pattern of Marylebone's streets is broken by the serpentine shape of **Marylebone Lane**. This once threaded through the heart of the original medieval village of St. Mary by the Bourne (the River Tyburn). The lane leads to Marylebone High Street, lined with shops and galleries. Try **Pâtisserie Valerie et Sagne** (No. 105), a café that has changed little since it opened in the 1920s.

The elegant semicircular sweep of Park Crescent

▶▶▶ **REGION HIGHLIGHTS**

London Zoo *page 125*
Regent's Park
pages 122–123
Wallace Collection
pages 126–127

TELECOM TOWER

Of all the spires and towers that pierce the London skyline, the Telecom Tower is one of the most dominant. It was completed in 1964, attracting crowds of tourists and Londoners who came to enjoy superb views from the revolving restaurant near its 176-m (580-ft) high summit. After a terrorist bomb exploded in the restaurant in 1975, public access was prohibited; too much is at stake to risk another such incident. The tower is used to transmit and receive satellite phone calls between the City and other financial markets. It also handles London's radio and TV signals.

The Telecom Tower, below; the spire of All Souls, right

▶ All Souls   116A3

Langham Place, W1 (tel: 020-7580 3522)
Open: Mon–Fri 9.30–6, Sun 9–6.30, but check times of services before visiting. Closed to visitors 1 Jan, Easter, 26, 28–31 Dec, but open for services. Admission free
Underground: Oxford Circus

All Souls Church was built in 1822–1824 by John Nash—his only church—to provide a focal point for the view up Regent Street, and a means of turning the road to join it on to Portland Place, which had already been built. This is a job it has done supremely well. The curving portico both arrests the eye and guides it to the left. The church was ridiculed in its time because Nash mixed together a classical portico with a Gothic spire and was therefore accused of breaking all the rules of architectural propriety, despite the fact that the combination works so well. The silhouette of the spire once dominated the skyline, but bigger buildings, notably Broadcasting House (see page 119), have since diminished its impact. There is a bust of Nash on the exterior south wall.

▶▶ Jewish Museum   123C3

129 Albert Street, NW1 (tel: 020-7284 1997)
www.jewishmuseum.org.uk
Open: Mon–Thu 10–4, Sun 10–5. Closed: Bank Holidays and Jewish holidays. Admission moderate
Underground: Camden Town

Exhibits and an audiovisual programme impart the long history of the Jewish community in England. People of the Jewish faith have been here since Norman times, and in the past were sometimes treated with suspicion. Some ostensibly converted to Christianity and many became wealthy as wool merchants.

The museum has an outstanding collection of ceremonial objects, which is considered the best in the world. It dates mostly from the end of the 17th century, when Oliver Cromwell removed the prohibitive laws on Jewish settlement, although there are earlier objects, such as the 13th-century bankers' tallies and 16th-century hardwritten scrolls. There is a second Jewish Museum in Finchley, North London (tel: 020-8349 1143. See panel on page 221).

The British Broadcasting Corporation (BBC) is one of Britain's best-loved institutions and, at the same time, one that is much criticized. It is known affectionately as 'Auntie Beeb' because of its tendency to take a high moral tone, sometimes at the expense of the preferences and tastes of the licence-payers. This attitude is very much in the tradition of its founders.

The BBC was set up in 1922 in a deliberate government plan to prevent radio broadcasting in Britain from developing along commercial lines, as it had in the US. The BBC's first Director General, Lord Reith, was a dour figure with strong views about the BBC's missionary role; Christian morality and serious culture were the keynotes. As the 'voice of the nation', BBC announcers and presenters were trained to speak 'formal' English and regional accents were looked down upon. High seriousness was pushed to ridiculous extremes. In the early days of the BBC, radio announcers and newsreaders were expected to wear full evening dress when in front of the microphone.

Despite this, the BBC won the heart of the nation and continues to set high standards of journalistic integrity. Until the coming of television, almost everybody in Britain listened to the BBC, was entertained and educated by it, and many had their lives, ideas and thoughts shaped by it. The wireless gadget was hugely popular. Nine million licenses were held by 1939, and the following year Bush House at Aldwych became home to the globe-encompassing BBC World Service. Television followed, and BBC TV Centre is in West London.

Today the BBC no longer has a monopoly over broadcasting, and British audiences can choose from dozens of channels thanks to digital, cable and satellite stations. (Following historical tradition, the BBC's digital service is exceptionally good.) The BBC is currently funded by the revenue from selling TV licences to every television owner in the country, rather than from advertising, and is thus free to produce programmes 'in the public interest'. This principle never fails to arouse passionate debate.

HOME OF THE BBC
Broadcasting House in Portland Place was built in 1931, and echoes the shape of All Souls Church (see page 118), although its curving façade is topped by a radio mast rather than a spire. G. Val Myers's elegant building of Portland stone bears a sculpture by Eric Gill over the main door, showing Shakespeare's Prospero sending his ethereal creation Ariel out into the world (see below). Ariel was chosen in the early days of the BBC as an appropriate symbol for the new medium of radio broadcasting.

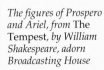

The figures of Prospero and Ariel, from The Tempest, *by William Shakespeare, adorn Broadcasting House*

► **Madame Tussauds**   *116B2*

Marylebone Road, NW1 (tel: 0870-400 3000)
www.madame-tussauds.co.uk
Open: Mon–Fri 9.30–5.30 (last admission), Sat–Sun 9–6.
Admission very expensive.
Underground: Baker Street

Madame Tussauds, a quirky eccentricity, is one of London's favourite attractions, with more than 2 million visitors annually. To beat the queues, which are especially long in summer, you can make a reservation in advance by credit card.

Madame Tussaud (1761–1850) perfected her craft during the French Revolution by taking death masks of guillotine victims, including Louis XVI and Marie Antoinette. She was a friend of Louis XVI's sister, so the Revolutionary authorities must have derived some satisfaction in assigning her this gruesome task. In 1802

The foggy Victorian London of Jack the Ripper comes to life at Madame Tussaud's

ROYAL INSTITUTE OF BRITISH ARCHITECTS
Grey Wornum's Swedish-inspired building of 1932–1934 somehow finds sympathy with Adam's palatial mansions strung along Portland Place. Founded in 1824, the RIBA, as it is fondly known, thrives on controversy, particularly when the coveted annual Gold Medal is awarded— Norman Foster, who won it in 1983, and Richard Rogers, in 1985, are both now dominant influences in London's biggest building projects. Past presidents have included George Gilbert Scott, Charles Barry and Edwin Lutyens. It is well worth visiting the current exhibition, the architecture bookshop and the upstairs RIBA café and restaurant and (tel: 020-7580 5533; *Open* (exhibitions) Mon–Fri 8–6, Sat 8–5. *Admission* free).

she fled Paris and arrived in Britain with her macabre collection, first touring the country, then setting up an exhibition of historic figures, living and dead, in London in 1835. In 1884 the collection moved to its present Marylebone Road site. The collection is continually extended to encompass famous figures from every age, but they are made using techniques that have changed little in 200 years. More recent additions include Tony Blair, Brad Pitt and Kate Moss. In 2007 a new 'green' up dated version of Prince Charles was put on display, his former model being resculpted using clay and natural beeswax in keeping with his desire to combat global warming.

Madame Tussauds also has a special ride called the 'Spirit of London' experience. It uses audio-animatronic figures to help re-create the sights, sounds and smells of the city, and there is a spine-chilling Chamber of Horrors (see panel). The oldest figure on display is Sleeping Beauty, made in 1765, based on Louis XV's mistress, Madame du Barry. Overall, Madame Tussauds is great fun—a chance to meet and be photographed with your own personal favourite, whether that be Arnold Schwarzenegger, the Queen, or even Madame Tussaud herself, whose self-portrait can be seen in the Great Hall. Meet various A-list celebs in the Blush exhibition area and stars of the silver screen in Premier Nights; brush shoulders on the World Stage with JFK, Gandhi, Princess Diana, Mohammed Ali and the like.

THE END OF AN ERA came when the London Planetarium finally closd as a separate attraction. Completed in 1958, it was the first planetarium in Britain and one of the largest in the world. Its remit was to explain the mysteries of astronomy on the inside of its green copper dome. Failing visitor numbers mean it has now been incorporated into Madame Tussauds having launched its new Stardome experience in July 2006. Joining forces with Oscar winning animators, Aaardman, Madame Tussauds has produced a new visitor experience that transforms the dome into a galaxy of stars—human, alien and astrological.

121

▶ Regent's Canal

The Regent's Canal is a branch of the Grand Union Canal, cut between 1812 and 1820 through the north of London from the Paddington Basin to Limehouse, in the Docklands. It soon became the busiest stretch of the innovative network of canals in England, but the arrival of the railways in the 1860s reduced its work to carrying building materials for the expanding city. Today, a number of companies run canal trips, including crusies from Walker's Quay with the tour boat Jenny Wren (*Open year round but weekends only Nov–Mar; tel: 020-7485 4433, www.walkersquay.com; check first for availability*) and Jason's Trip (*Open Apr–Oct; tel: 020-7286 3428, www.jasons.co.uk*).

THE CHAMBER OF HORRORS
Human fascination with death and criminality makes the Chamber of Horrors at Madame Tussaud's one of the most popular attractions, despite the gory nature of its subject matter. Exhibits include Vlad the Impaler (the 'real life' Count Dracula); Joan of Arc, burning at the stake; Guy Fawkes, hanged, drawn and quartered; genuine artefacts from London's brutal Newgate Prison; Jack the Ripper (see opposite); and a scene that Madame T would have been familiar with—execution by guillotine. Sweet dreams! The Chamber also now features live actors who pop out just when you least expect it. Children must be 13 to enter here though you have the option of buying a cheaper ticket that excludes this delight.

On a narrow boat chugging down the Regent's Canal

'More like a work of general destruction than anything else'. This was how one newspaper described the scene in 1817 as Regent's Park was being laid out. Soon, however, it was described as 'among the magnificent ornaments of our metropolis', and so it remains to this day: A beautiful park of 188ha (465 acres), a fine place for a stroll at any time of year, but especially in summer, when the roses and flower beds are at their best.

122

CAMDEN LOCK

Camden Lock lies just to the north of Camden Town tube station, off Chalk Farm Road, and is famous for its lively and atmospheric daily market. Here you can browse among stalls selling crafts, hand-knitted and period clothes, antiques and secondhand books. The lock was built as a branch off the Regent's Park Canal, where barge owners could unload and store their cargoes of lumber, brick and coal. Many of the original Victorian warehouses have been turned into craft studios, cafés and shops, while another has been converted into Lock 17 (formerly Dingwalls nightclub), offering live rock and comedy. The markets have spilled out from the Lock along neighbouring roads, and at weekends this area rivals Petticoat Lane in size, scope and general jollity.

The York Gate entrance, which is served by Baker Street station, lies just beyond **Madame Tussaud's**. As you walk up you will notice, on the right, the **Royal Academy of Music**, founded in 1822, where some of the world's finest musicians, singers and composers perfected have their art.

On York Bridge, look back to see **St. Mary's Church**, on Marylebone High Street. When Nash laid out Regent's Park he deliberately aligned the York Gate axis to take in a view of the church, with its majestic Corinthian portico and circular tower. York Bridge continues past **Regent's College**, on the left, a school, part of which is the UK's largest for European business studies and formerly part of Bedford College, founded 1849 and a pioneer of the women's education movement. Beyond lies **Queen Mary's Garden**. Here, Nash had intended a temple dedicated to the memory of all who had contributed to British history and culture. Instead, the 6.8-ha (17-acre) circle contains London's finest rose garden planted to honour George V's wife, Queen Mary, and the much-loved **Open Air Theatre**, founded in 1932 (*Open* late May–mid-Sep; tel: 0870 601 811 in season for information, see panel 123).

To the west is the Y-shaped boating lake, and if you walk around the upper part of the lake you will come to **Hanover Gate**. Here are the park's newer buildings. The **London Central Mosque**, to the north, with its splendid dome and minaret, was designed by Sir Frederick Gibberd and opened in 1978 as the principal mosque in Britain. To the south, fronting the Outer Circle, you can see Quinlan Terry's villas (completed in 1992), which are disappointingly nostalgic and unimaginative, and compare poorly to Nash's theatrical flair.

The minaret and golden dome of the London Central Mosque

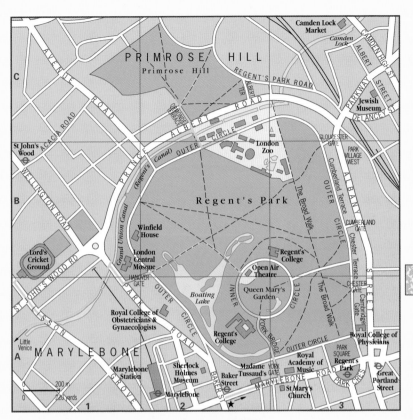

Summer dreams, Regent's Park

The towpath of **Regent's Canal** (a branch of the Grand Union Canal) leads around the northern perimeter of the Park to **London Zoo** (see page 125). From there you can cross over Prince Albert Road to Primrose Hill, whose summit has superb views. Alternatively, follow the canal westwards to St. John's Wood. Star attractions are **Lord's Cricket Ground**, St. John's Wood Road, with a gallery of cricketing memorabilia (guided tours daily noon and 2pm (also 10am Apr–Sep), except match days) and the MCC Museum, and **Little Venice,** around Blomfield Road and Maida Avenue, with its waterside pubs and narrowboats.

OPEN AIR THEATRE
One of the nicest ways to sepend a London summer evening is at the Open Air Theatre in Regent's Park. With entertainment ranging from *A Midsummer Night's Dream* to *Camelot*, to *Wind in the Willows*, or stand-up comedians, all ages and tastes are catered for. For more details visit http://openairtheatre.org

John Nash planned a utopian city for Regent's Park, with houses for the wealthy and for the working classes set in landscaped gardens around a lake. Most of the terraces remain, but only six of the villas. They can be seen on a stroll round the park's eastern fringes.

Regency fanlight

THE BROAD WALK
If you leave the hurly-burly of Oxford Street via Portland Place for a quiet stroll in Regent's Park, you arrive at the southern end of the park's main south-north thoroughfare, The Broad Walk. Here you find a large chunk of the park totally restored to its 1864 layout by William Nesfield, an idea first instigated by Prince Albert. Nesfield followed the highly ornate Victoria bedding schemes that were then at their most complex. The Broad Walk passes between densely planted beds that blossom from spring to autumn and are flanked by outer rows of wych elms. Some of the original ornamental tazzas and vases for plants still exist. The inner row of horse chestnuts stretches all along the Broad Walk, a stunning sight when the trees are in bloom in late spring.

Corinthian capitals and gleaming white stucco

Great Portland Street and Regent's Park underground stations are both close to Park Crescent, a beautiful curving terrace built between 1812 and 1818 (see page 116). Opposite is Park Square, with two long terraces by Nash (1823–1825). Three houses on the eastern side of the terrace were built to house the Diorama, once a popular attraction.

Just beyond, on the right, is the Royal College of Physicians, in St. Andrew's Place, completed in 1964 to the designs of Sir Denys Lasdun. To the north is Cambridge Gate, built in 1876–1880 on the site of the famous Colosseum. This temple-like structure displayed a circular view of the London panorama, painted by a Mr Horner from the top of St. Paul's. The Colosseum was hugely popular at first, but Londoners soon lost interest, and it was demolished in 1875.

Continue north to Chester Gate; look for the bust of John Nash mounted on the left-hand wall. His Chester Terrace (1825) comes next, a handsome row of houses fronted by great Corinthian pillars, all in gleaming stucco. Nash intended the façade to be decorated by 52 statues but then decided that this would look too fussy. Cumberland Terrace (1826–1828) is slightly shorter but much more dramatic, and here Nash did place statues over the pediment of the central block.

Beyond Gloucester Gate you can leave the park, cross Albany Street, and turn right to look at Park Village West. Here, Nash embarked on his scheme for a series of villas set in gardens—notably Tower House, No. 12, once home to Dr. Johnson, physician to William IV.

The London Zoological Gardens opened in 1828, the world's first institution dedicated to the study and display of animals. In its heyday in the 1950s, it received more than 3 million visitors a year. Today, study takes precedence over display, and visitors benefit from informed talks and hands-on demonstrations.

Before you start your tour look at the daily events programme and try to be in the right place at the right time for feeding times and Animals in Action presentations. Across the road from the main entrance are the Cotton Terraces, where giraffes, zebras, okapi, oryx and other African grazers may be seen. Behind is the landmark Snowdon Aviary, which you can walk through in the company of a variety of birds, and adjacent are the charming small nocturnal inhabitants of the Moonlight World house.

Back on the main site, near the entrance, are the noisy primates, the silent and often beautiful world of the aquarium, and the reptile house. The Mappin Terrace (with sloth bears, monkey-like langurs and muntjac deer) was designed by the radical architects Belcher and Joass in 1931; Joass had also designed a new Aquarium for the zoo in 1924.

The big cats are found beyond the children's zoo section. The Asian lions have their own open terrace, which is a nice contrast with most of the zoo where the animals are kept in sad, small barred enclosures. On either side are birds galore, including friendly wandering pelicans who happily (and harmlessly) munch on visitors' arms and feet! The penguin pool, always crowded at feeding time, was designed by Lubetkin and Tecton in 1931. Opposite, there are pony rides on the Riding Lawn, where there are also demonstrations and displays. If it is elephants and rhinos you want to see, however, you will be disappointed. These have been moved to roomier accommodation at London Zoo-owned Whipsnade Park up the M1. However, be sure not to miss the £5.3 million gorilla enclosure, Gorilla Kingdom, opened in March 2007 and the zoo's most significant investment for 40 years.

The giraffes at ZSL London Zoo are a popular attraction

ZSL LONDON ZOO
Back in the 1860s Jumbo the elephant gave children's rides, before he was sold to Phineas Barnum, the American showman. Today, the zoo's focus has changed: Its Web of Life, opened in 1999, is a conservation and preservation centre designed to encourage awareness of the world's fragile biological diversity and interdependence (tel: 020-7722 3333 www.zsl.org. *Open* daily, Mar–Oct 10–5.30; Nov–Feb 10–4. *Admission* very expensive).

125

The famous fictional
detective at home

**IN THE FOOTSTEPS OF
SHERLOCK HOLMES**
Anyone hooked on *The
Adventures of Sherlock
Holmes* can eat and sleep
with the ghost of their
hero. The Sherlock
Holmes pub, 10
Northumberland Avenue,
is a shrine to the
detective. Its walls are
covered with Holmes mem-
orabilia, and its upstairs
room, next to the restau-
rant, has a re-creation of
Holmes' study, with a
model of the man himself
seated in front of the fire
reading a copy of *The
Times*. Sir Arthur Conan
Doyle used to drink here
himself, and the pub fea-
tures in *The Hound of the
Baskervilles* (Chapter 4)
under its old name, the
Northumberland Hotel. The
restaurant serves food
with a Holmesian theme.
After dinner here you could
retire to the Sherlock
Holmes Hotel, 108 Baker
Street, a refurbished
deluxe boutique hotel
(tel: 020-7486 6161).

The collection of 18th-
century Sèvres porcelain
in the Wallace Collection
is one of the finest of its
kind in the world

▶ **Sherlock Holmes Museum**   116B1

221b Baker Street, NW1 (tel: 020-7935 8866)
www.sherlock-holmes.co.uk
Open: daily 9.30–6. Admission expensive
Underground: Baker Street

This small museum, lovingly created by the Sherlock Holmes International Society, is dedicated to Sir Arthur Conan Doyle's famous sleuth. A faithful re-creation of the detective's home is furnished with his personal possessions and memorabilia from his most important cases, including his trademark deesstalker and pipe, violin, chemistry equipment, note-book, Persian slippers and disguises. Visitors can sit in Homes's armchair by the fireside for a photograph (pipe not provided!). A 'policeman' in period costume is posted outside the front door.

▶▶▶ **Wallace Collection**   116A2

Hertford House, Manchester Square, W1 (tel: 020-7563 9500)
www.wallacecollection.org
Open: Daily 10–5. Admission free
Underground: Bond Street

This world-class collection of art—with its especially remarkable armour, ceramics and French paintings and furniture—was amassed by the Hertford family who over four generations and is displayed in their atmospheric mansion. It is one of London's hidden gems and is now even more attractive thanks to its delightful Sculpture Garden and French brasserie restaurant, The Wallace, in the stunning courtyard.

Living as a recluse in Paris at the time of the French Revolution, the 4th Marquess of Hertford, with his illegit-imate son, Richard Wallace, avidly bought French art to add to his inheritance of Sèvres porcelain and paintings by Canaletto and Gainsborough. In the post-Revolution chaos, some of France's best 18th century paintings, porcelain, furniture and even chunks of Paris mansions were being sold off quickly and cheaply. The result is that the Wallace Collection has London's finest collection of French art, including pictures by Fragonard, Boucher, Watteau, Lancret and Poussin.

Richard Wallace inherited the collection in 1870 and brought it to England because of the unstable political sit-uation in France. He added many fine examples of Renaissance ceramics, bronzes, armour and jewellery,

The Laughing Cavalier *(1624) by Frans Hals, much underrated by the public in its day*

HERTFORD HOUSE
The house that holds the Wallace Collection deserves as much study as the paintings. It was built in 1777 for the Duke of Manchester and acquired by the 2nd Marquess of Hertford in 1797. His flamboyant son, the 3rd Marquess, collected many of the 17th-century Dutch paintings in the collection and was able to do so because of his wife's wealth. She was illegitimate—more often than not a barrier to fortune, but in this case two very rich men claimed to be her father (the Duke of Queensberry and George Selwyn) and both left her vast sums of money. The house was refurnished when Richard Wallace moved the collection here. An important feature is the opulent white-marble staircase. This is flanked by a magnificent balustrade, made of wrought iron and bronze in 1723–1741 for Louis XV. It was originally installed in the Palais Mazarin (now the Bibliothèque Nationale) in Paris and was acquired by Wallace when it was sold for scrap in the chaotic world of mid-19th-century Paris.

and his widow left the collection to the nation in 1897, on condition that it remain intact. The rooms are packed with all sorts of objects, from paintings, furnishings and fittings originally made for the palaces of Fontainebleau and Versailles, to 18th-century saucepans and cabinets packed with guns. There are magnificent wardrobes and cabinets designed by André Charles Boulle, which are some of the finest surviving pieces of 18th-century French furniture.

In the Great Gallery is one of London's finest picture galleries. Here hang about 70 paintings from the 17th and 18th centuries. These include *The Laughing Cavalier* by Frans Hals (1624). The subject, whose identity remains unknown, wears an almost arrogant smirk beneath his carefully combed moustache, the sense of swagger emphasized by the hand on the hip and the rich lace collar. In the same room is the beautiful *Lady with a Fan* (1634–1636) by Velázquez, and Rubens's *Rainbow Landscape* (c1636). Here too is the Poussin painting, *Dance to the Music of Time* (1639–1640). It shows an allegory in which dancers represent Pleasure, Poverty, Riches and Work, while the two-headed column on the left represents past and future; in the sky, Aurora (dawn) draws the chariot of Apollo (the sun), followed by the Hours. Don't miss Fragonard's famous frothy extravaganza *The Swing* (1767).

Less obvious is the collection of European arms and armour, the world's finest, much of it embellished with fine inlay decoration and made by specialist metal workers. Elsewhere, Hertford family portraits bring those great collectors alive. In the basement galleries, the reserve collection gives you a new intimacy with the collection while the special exhibitions are always interesting.

The map shows Bloomsbury and Fitzrovia area with the following labels:

Euston Station, Euston, British Library, The Place, ST PANCRAS, Eastman Dental Hospital, KING'S CROSS RD, HAMPSTEAD ROAD, EUSTON ROAD, UPPER WOBURN PLACE, JUDD ST, HUNTER ST, GRAY'S INN ROAD, CALTHORPE ST, Friends' House, British Medical Association, St George's Gardens, Euston Square, TAVISTOCK PLACE, Warren Street, University College, GORDON SQUARE, Church of Christ the King, Percival David Foundation, Brunswick Shopping Centre, Thomas Coram Foundation, Coram's Fields, BRUNSWICK SQ, PENTON, University College Hospital, Petrie Museum, Dillons, WOBURN SQUARE, University of London, BERNARD ST, Russell Square, GUILFORD STREET, Hospital for Sick Children, LAMB'S CONDUIT ST, GT ORMOND ST, The Charles Dickens Museum, Fitzroy Square, Vanbrugh Theatre, TORRINGTON, MALET ST, RUSSELL, BLOOMSBURY, National Hospital, British Telecom Tower, Pollock's Toy Museum, GOWER ST, CHENIES ST, MONTAGUE PL, SOUTHAMPTON ROW, THEOBALD'S ROAD, RED LION SQUARE, Middlesex Hospital, CHARLOTTE ST, GOODGE ST, Goodge Street, COLVILLE PLACE, WINDMILL ST, TRINITY ST, BEDFORD SQUARE, British Museum, MONTAGUE ST, BLOOMSBURY SQUARE, BURY PLACE, PROCTER ST, SIR JOHN SOANE'S Museum, MORTIMER ST, RATHBONE PL, GOODGE STREET, BLOOMSBURY ST, GREAT RUSSELL STREET, MUSEUM STREET, SOUTHAMPTON PLACE, HOLBORN, Holborn, Sir John Soane's Museum, Lincoln's Inn, Lincoln's Inn Fields, OXFORD STREET, Tottenham Court Road, Dominion, GREAT QUEEN ST, KINGSWAY, NEW OXFORD ST, Centre Point, ST GILES HIGH ST, COPTIC ST

0   200m
0   220 yards

Street entertainer

BLOOMSBURY AND FITZROVIA Bloomsbury has the breeze of intellectual curiosity wafting through its leafy squares. The vast British Museum, Britain's most visited museum, is at its heart. The University of London occupies many of the Georgian terrace houses, and students spill out from within, books in hand, to visit the British Library or relax in the public gardens and squares. While Bloomsbury is associated with early 20th-century writers Virginia Woolf, E. M. Forster, Lytton Strachey and John Maynard Keynes, Fitzrovia, across Tottenham Court Road, was the haunt of hard-drinking Bohemian writers, journalists and artists in the 1940s and 1950s, including Dylan Thomas, George Orwell, Cyril Connolly and Anthony Burgess. They coined the name Fitzrovia to suggest the antithesis of genteel Belgravia.

BLOOMSBURY AND FITZROVIA WALK Charlotte Street, where this walk begins, is full of Bohemian atmosphere, with its pubs and inexpensive restaurants serving Greek, Turkish, Indian and Italian food, and its pavement tables lending something of a Mediterranean feel to the area on sunny days.

Turn onto Colville Place, a Georgian alley that leads off Charlotte Street just south of Goodge Street; this threads through to Tottenham Court Road. To the right, leading south, **Tottenham Court Road** is lined with brash stores specializing in everything electronic at rock bottom prices. To the north a number of design-conscious stores include **Paperchase**, **Habitat** and the more upmarket **Heal's** (No 196), with its big, curved windows (built in 1916). True to the philosophy of its founder, Ambrose Heal, the store specializes in top-quality furnishings,

including reproductions of its original Arts and Crafts designs.

Walk up Torrington Place, to the right beyond Heal's. This leads to **Waterstone's** bookshop (82 Gower Street), with a vast and comprehensive stock. Beyond Waterstone's, the tree-filled **Gordon Square** opens up on the left. Its garden is a favourite for students of the nearby Institute of Archaeology. Some of the square's rather dour houses were once centres of Bloomsbury intellectual life: No. 46, the home of Virginia Woolf, Vanessa Bell and Clive Bell, was the meeting place of the Bloomsbury set, an élite circle that embraced Roger Fry, Duncan Grant and E. M. Forster, among others. On the opposite, western side of the square is the Dr. Williams Library, where documents relating to the history of Nonconformity are preserved. On the southwestern corner, the University Church of Christ the King (1853) is a huge building with an ornate interior, whose intended spire was never built. Immediately south of Gordon Square is Woburn Square, lined with restrained Georgian-style terraces. Walking through **Woburn Square**, you will pass the more modern buildings of the **School of Oriental and African Studies** (known as SOAS).

Continue to **Russell Square**, which was laid out in 1800 and is one of the largest in London. Do not miss Westmacott's statue of the 5th Duke of Bedford. The east side has two hotels: the **Hotel Russell**, of 1898, modelled on a French château, and the **Imperial**, the modern building that replaced the old Tudor Gothic-style hotel in 1966. The west side of the square has some of its original houses, designed by James Burton, and an entrance to the **Senate House** (begun in 1932), with its massive stone tower. The Senate is the governing body of the 50 or so colleges and faculties that together make up the University of London, Britain's largest university, with more than 95,000 students.

From the southwest corner of Russell Square, Montague Street leads to Great Russell Street and the front entrance to the British Museum (see pages 131–133).

The streets south of the museum (Coptic Street, Museum Street, Bury Place and Galen Place) are worth exploring for their good bookshops and art galleries, as well as their cafés and pubs.

▶▶▶ REGION HIGHLIGHTS

British Library
page 130
British Museum
pages 131–133

The British Library,
Isaac Newton statue

BRITISH LIBRARY ART
The British Library's public spaces have a number of specially commissioned works of art. In the piazza, Eduardo Paolozzi's bronze statue of Isaac Newton was inspired by William Blake's image. It shows him seated and bending forwards to plot the immensity of the universe with a pair of dividers, a symbol of the British Library's purpose: to preserve a record of man's endless search for truth. The entrance foyer has a more whimsical piece: Bill Woodrow's bronze and brass bench in the shape of an open book, titled *Sitting on History*. Here, too, is a facsimile of Louise Roubiliac's statue of William Shakespeare. Up the steps, find R. B. Kitaj's large tapestry, *If not, not*, incorporating a host of literary references on an idyllic background inspired by Giorgione's landscape paintings. Beyond it, four manuscript donors to the British Museum in its early years are remembered with busts: Sir Robert Cotton, Sir Joseph Banks, Thomas Grenville and Sir Hans Sloane.

▶▶▶ **British Library**   *off 128C2*

96 Euston Road, NW1 (tel: 020-7412 7332)
www.bl.uk
Open: Mon, Wed–Fri 9.30–6, Tue 9.30–8, Sat 9.30–5, Sun 11–5. Admission free
Underground: King's Cross/St. Pancras/Euston

Britain's national library, formerly housed in cramped conditions in the British Museum, gained its own purpose-built complex in 1997. It houses a collection that has been growing since the early 18th century, and is now supplemented by the National Sound Archive. Professor Sir Colin St. John Wilson's design has given Londoners a stunning new package of a welcoming, spacious piazza, three public galleries, new public art works, two restaurants, an excellent shop and plenty of activities and tours. In all, it is a breakthrough in the British idea of the library. There is nothing fusty about the BL; manuscripts and books have been shown to be as interesting as they really are.

Before entering the galleries, go up the steps by the information desk and walk around the floor-to-ceiling central glass shaft to enjoy some of the beautiful bindings of the King's Library, George III's 65,000 volumes donated by George IV in 1823. The outer walls store the British Library's stamp collection, the world's finest, and you can pull out the vertical trays of stamps to examine specimens more closely.

The John Ritblat Gallery displays more of the Library's treasures. Here you can see various editions of the Magna Carta, the only surviving manuscript from Shakespeare's own pen and the Gutenberg Bible, and listen to such sounds as rare bird song, or a Winston Churchill speech.

The Workshop of Words, Sounds and Images explains how books and newspapers are created and printed, and how sound is recorded. Finally, the Pearson Gallery interprets and enlivens the library's great collections and is the location for special exhibitions.

Behind all this are the reading rooms, where those with passes have access to the whole collection, including every book printed since 1911. This was the year when the Copyright Act was passed. It dictated that one copy of every book, periodical or newspaper published in Great Britain must come to the British Library. Currently, the BL has about 150 million items; some 8,000 are added each working day.

▶▶▶ British Museum

Great Russell Street, WC1 (tel: 020-7323 8000)
www.thebritishmuseum.ac.uk
Underground: Holborn, Tottenham Court Road
Open: Galleries Sat–Wed 10–5.30, Thu–Fri 10–8.30. Great
Court Sun–Wed 9–6, Thu–Sat 9am–11pm, Sun 9–6. Reading
Room daily 10–5.30, first Thu of month 10–8.30. Admission free

128A2

Sir Robert Smirke's grand building (1823–1847), as its elaborate Grecian-style façade declares, is a temple to the arts and achievements of the world's civilizations. The British have always been avid collectors and this national museum is the result of over 200 years of erudite collecting, kleptomania, excavation or downright looting. It is unrivalled in the world for the variety and quality of its treasures.

The museum's origins go back to the 'curiosities' that were bequeathed to the nation in 1753 by the wealthy physician, Sir Hans Sloane (see page 91). At the time it consisted largely of natural history specimens but also contained coins and trinkets that formed the nucleus of a historical collection. The museum's holdings grew rapidly thanks to enlightened benefactors, energetic travellers and enthusiastic historians and archaeologists.

The British Museum's recent ambitious redevelopment, the completion of the Great Court, has made it probably the most user friendly national museum of its scope in the world. With the departure of the British Library, the central Great Court has been restored, glassed over to create a huge internal square and plays a double role: It is the central information area and it is the crossroads between all the galleries and between the north and south entrances. Other major new developments include the Wellcome Gallery of Ethnography with its famous Easter Island statue and the restored King's Library, a magnificent neoclassical space housing a permanent gallery devoted to the formation of the British Museum. For the 6 million or so visitors each year, a visit to the British Museum is now a quality experience in every way.

The main focal point of the Great Court is the stunning circular Reading Room, added by Sir Robert Smirke's son

ASSYRIAN ART

The rooms in the British Museum devoted to Near Eastern art (6–10) are less well known than those of the Greek antiquities but no less striking. One has a huge winged bull that once guarded the palace and temple complex at Nimrud, built around 880 BC, and the theme of the lion hunt features in several narrative friezes. Sculptures from the throne room at Nimrud can be seen in Room 7, and in Room 9, displaying magnificent carvings from the palace at Nineveh (7th century BC). These latter scenes seem almost modern in their clean, fluid lines, and their naturalistic portrayal of wounded lions writhing in agony.

131

The Elgin Marbles

A fitting welcome to the world's greatest collection of antiquities: the frieze depicting the Progress of Civilization *on the museum's façade*

CURIOSITIES UPSTAIRS
On the upper floors, the Prehistory Gallery displays the perfectly preserved 2,000-year-old body of Lindow Man, nicknamed 'Pete Marsh' by the archeologists who found him in a waterlogged peat bog in Cheshire. Elsewhere are ancient Egyptian coffins and their contents: not just human mummies but also those of sacred animals—crocodiles, cats, dogs, fish, an ape, an ibex and even a bull. Still upstairs, you can compare the dice, mosaic gaming board and counters from ancient Ur, made around 2,600BC with the mid-12th-century Lewis chessmen, carved in ivory. Many of the clocks, watches and musical timepieces shown in the European Galleries are still working.

Sydney in 1857. Surrounding the Reading Room, beneath the curved roof composed of 3,500 triangular pieces of glass held in a steel frame, cafés and shops provide refreshment, relaxation and simply places to meet—the ground floor galleries stay open late on Thursdays and Fridays. From here, too, stairs go down to the Clore Education centre containing the lecture theatres.

The museum's collections are arranged by geography, culture and theme. Once you have decided what you want to see, if you set off from the Great Court you should be able to find it quickly and easily.

Thus, go north, you find the new Africa galleries, the John Addis Gallery of Islamic Art on the ground floor, the spectacular Joseph Hotung Gallery of Asian Art displaying objects from India eastwards upstairs and displays of Korean art above that. Here, too, are the temporary exhibitions taken from the museum's fine collection of prints and drawings.

In these galleries, highlights to look out for include gilded and enamelled pilgrim flasks in the John Addis Gallery. Here, too, you can see the bold designs of Iznik pottery dishes, a huge jade turtle found in a Mughal palace at Allahabad in India, or the brass astrolabe inlaid with copper and silver made in 13th century Cairo. It is always worth seeing what drawings and prints are on display, since the collection represents most of the great masters including Michaelangelo, Raphael and Durer.

Moving west from the Great Court, you find a host of galleries on the ground floor, basement and upstairs displaying treasures from Ancient Egypt, the Ancient Near East, Greece and Rome. Some of the museum's best-known treasures are here including sculptures from the Parthenon frieze made in the 5th century BC for the Temple of Athena in Athens. Also on the ground floor are the astounding panels from the Assyrian palace at Nineveh, depicting royal life in the 7th century BC (see also panel on page 131). The Museum's Egyptian collection is considered the finest outside Cairo. Among the tombs and

THE MUSEUM'S BACK DOOR
Some of the British Museum's most fascinating galleries cover the less popular Asian art and prints and drawings; when some galleries are crowded, these often remain quiet. If you want to concentrate on these, go north from the Great Court or slip into the museum by the back door on Mongague Place. On the ground floor, right by the door, you find the John Addis Gallery which displays treasures from the Islamic world. There is brass from Syria, jade from India and refined pottery. Look, too, for 13th century astrolabes and globes used by astronomers, and for jewel-encrusted hookahs, once known as 'hubble bubbles'. Upstairs, the vast Joseph Hotung Gallery (Room 33) is devoted to Asian art including Chinese grave horses, 10th century Chola bronzes of the Hindu god Shiva dancing, and intricate Buddhist stone carvings from Amaravati in south India.

statues you can search out the Rosetta Stone, found in 1799, whose 196BC inscription of the same text in Egyptian (hieroglyphic and demotic scripts) and Greek gave scholars the key to deciphering hieroglyphs. Fragments of wall-paintings from Egyptian tombs reveal the daily life of Egyptians—their fashion, their methods of hunting birds and fish and harvesting flax and barley, their prayer and dancing—as do the delightful models of ships, ploughmen and houses made for tombs, intended for the next world.

East of the Great Court, above the King's Library, the upstairs galleries house objects related to Roman Britain and to Europe from medieval times to the present day; there are also galleries devoted to Prehistory and to the intriguing story of money and medals. (The western and northern upstairs galleries house some of the Egyptian, Ancient Near East, Greek and Roman collections.)

It is worth seeking out the 7th century Sutton Hoo treasure, found in Suffolk. Like much of the Egyptian art, this was part of a burial, this time in a huge ship for Redwald, King of the East Angles; highly skilled craftsmen made the swords, helmets, buckles, bowls, drinking horns and bronze cauldron. Other highlights include the Mildenhall Treasure's 4th century silver tableware, the 1st century Battersea shield and, in the European Galleries, the intricate and often still working clocks and watches—some even chime on the hour (see also the panel on page 132). Take a look at the HSBC Money Gallery, which tells the story of 2,000 years of Britain's commercial life.

This beautiful piece of jewellery, made in the 1st century BC, is just one example of the Celtic craftwork to be found in Room 50

Bust of Charles Dickens

LAMB'S CONDUIT STREET
A very short walk west from Dickens house, off Guildford Street, Lamb's Conduit Street is a delightful traffic-free precinct with many shops, pubs and restaurants. The Lamb (No. 94) is an unspoiled Victorian pub with its original woodwork and glass screens and photographs of music-hall stars on the walls, and The Sun (No. 63) stocks a great range of beers made by small independent breweries.

The house where Dickens wrote Oliver Twist

▶▶ The Chrles Dickens Museum   128B3

48 Doughty Street, WC1 (tel: 020-7405 2127)
www.dickensmuseum.com
Open: Mon–Sat 10–5, Sun 11–5. Call for information of special events outside opening times. Admission moderate
Underground: Russell Square, Chancery Lane

Charles Dickens (1812–1870), the great 19th-century novelist, is one of that handful of writers who have shaped and moulded our vision of London. His descriptions of the fog-bound haunts of torpid lawyers, of the criminal underworld of Fagin and his thieves, the cramped and crooked home of Little Nell or the Old Curiosity Shop, are as vivid now as they were 150 years ago. It only takes a little imagination to conjure up visions of Dickensian London as you wander the city's streets, and a visit to the house where Dickens wrote allows you to pursue the illusion further.

The house is the only surviving London home out of several in which Dickens lived and worked. He moved here in 1837, a year after his marriage to Catherine Hogarth. By 1839, such was Dickens's growing wealth that the family was able to move on to 1 Devonshire Terrace (since demolished), a more impressive house overlooking Regent's Park. In the time that Dickens lived here he was characteristically prolific: He completed the *Pickwick Papers*, wrote *Oliver Twist* and *Nicholas Nickleby*, and began *Barnaby Rudge* all in under three years.

His house, which was bought by the Dickens Fellowship in 1924, retains the heavy Victorian colour scheme and the desk and chair where Dickens wrote surrounded by the hustle and bustle of family life (he possessed the remarkable gift of being able to write even with the dis-

tractions of noise, visitors and conversation all around him). Other Dickens memorabilia on display include first editions of his work, the copies he used for his public readings, marked with cues for gestures and intonation, and Lionel Bart's score for his musical version of *Oliver Twist*. A good shop sells Dickens's works.

▶ **London Canal Museum**   *182B1*
King's Cross Basin, New Wharf Road, N1 (tel: 020-7713 0836)
www.canalmuseum.org.uk
Open: Tue–Sun 10–4.30. Admission moderate
Underground: King's Cross
A small but evocative collection housed in a Victorian warehouse pays tribute to one of the city's hidden (and so far wasted) assets: the extensive canal network that runs all the way around north London, and links the capital to the industrial cities of the Midlands, such as Birmingham, Leicester and Nottingham. Some parts of the canal network—around Little Venice, Regent's Park and Camden Lock—are very picturesque and attract many visitors. This museum, by contrast, is located in the rather scruffy area at the rear of King's Cross station, which is slowly being made more attractive by the local community. The warehouse was built in around 1850 by Carlo Gatti, an Italian immigrant who made his fortune importing ice from Norway and storing it here in deep wells. Exhibits tell the story of Gatti and canal life. Developers plan to build a 'model city of the future' in this area.

While the haggling goes on, local community groups, working with the London Wildlife Trust, have established a flourishing nature reserve at Camley Street, just west of the Canal Museum. The reserve (*Open* Thu–Sun 10–5, or dusk if earlier, daily in school holidays) has attracted birds, butterflies, reptiles and self-sown wildflowers. Its backdrop is formed by the brightly painted King's Cross gasholders, some of have been declared listed buildings and are therefore protected from alteration or demolition.

TRAIN STATIONS
Euston, St. Pancras and King's Cross stations stand almost side by side along the northern edge of Euston Road, each built in the 19th century by the independent railway companies that competed with each other until they were brought together to form British Rail. Euston was wholly rebuilt in the 1960s; all that survives of the terminus are two lodge houses, part of the original formal entrance to the station. St. Pancras, by contrast, survives in its original form and is fronted by the Midland Grand Hotel, a magnificent monument of neo-Gothic architecture, bristling with towers and spires and built in 1868–1872 by George Gilbert Scott. The station has undergone a huge development project with the new Eurostar International, opened in Nov 2007, part of a regeneration of the whole area. King's Cross is a much more utilitarian building, designed by Lewis Cubbitt and built in 1851–1852.

Ornate barges on Little Venice canal

135

Sometimes it seems that there is no building or stretch of street in London that has not witnessed some historic event or been the home of an eminent person. Statues abound and hundreds of buildings bear blue commemorative plaques. Tracking these down can reveal a few interesting surprises—people you never knew lived in the city at all, for example—such as the Italian artist Canaletto (at 41 Beak Street) or the US President John F. Kennedy (at 14 Prince's Gate).

BLUE PLAQUES

The idea of placing plaques on the houses or sites where distinguished people once lived was devised in 1866 by William Ewart; the scheme was originally run by the Royal Society of Arts, then by the Greater London Council. The first plaque was placed on the birthplace of Lord Byron in Holles Street. The person commemorated by a blue plaque must have been dead for over 20 years and born more than 100 years ago and conform to other conditions outlined by English Heritage (see www.english-heritage.org.uk).

Charlie Chaplin in Leicester Square, right

In total, London has more than 1,700 statues and 400 blue plaques, originally chocolate-brown but now standardized to a present-day Wedgwood blue with white lettering (see panel).

Alfred the Great In front of Holy Trinity Church (now the Henry Wood Hall) in Trinity Church Square (SE1) is a 14th-century statue of the 9th-century King of England; this is London's oldest commemorative statue.

David Ben-Gurion Israel's first prime minister lived at 75 Warrington Crescent, Maida Vale (W9).

Simon Bolivar The Latin-American revolutionary is commemorated by Hugo Daini's 1974 statue in Belgrave Square (SW1).

Boudicca (Boadicea) The rebellious queen of the Iceni tribe, who burned down Roman London in AD60, is depicted in a stirring bronze statue by Thomas Thornycroft on Westminster Bridge (west end).

Sir Charles Spencer Chaplin Better known as Charlie Chaplin, the comic star, has a statue in Leicester Square by John Doubleday (1987), appropriately surrounded by movie theatres.

Frédéric Chopin The Polish-born composer gave his last ever public concert at London's Guildhall and is commemorated by a statue alongside the Festival Hall on the South Bank.

General Charles de Gaulle A plaque at 4 Carlton Gardens declares that this was the headquarters of the Free French Forces, led by de Gaulle from June 1940 until the end of the war.

Elizabeth Garrett Anderson The first woman ever to qualify as a doctor in Britain had her home at 20 Upper Berkeley Street.

SIR WINSTON CHURCHILL ...ed in a house ...n this site ...921-1924

Captain Robert Scott, Antarctic explorer

Wolfgang Amadeus Mozart The child prodigy composed his first symphony at 180 Ebury Street.

Florence Nightingale A statue of the pioneer of nursing, who was christened 'the lady of the lamp' by her soldier patients, is part of the Crimean Memorial on Waterloo Place; the house in which she lived and died is at 10 South Street (off Park Lane).

Captain Robert Scott Scott of the Antarctic set off for his last fateful expedition from his house at 56 Oakley Street, Chelsea. Scott is portrayed, wearing the clothes he wore for the trip, in a bronze statue made by his widow, Lady Scott, in Waterloo Place.

Princess Pocahontas The Algonquin Indian princess, who saved the life of Captain John Smith in 1602, is remembered with a bronze statue in Red Lion Square (off Holborn). She married John Rolfe, came to England in 1614, and was a great success at the Jacobean Court, but lacked immunity to western diseases and died in 1617, aged 22.

Bertrand Russell Also in Red Lion Square is a bust of the philosopher, who lectured in nearby Conway Hall.

Sun Yat Sen The father of Chinese republicanism, who led the Kuomintang to overthrow the Qing dynasty in 1911, spent time in exile in a house on the site of 4 Gray's Inn Place.

Oscar Wilde Maggie Hambling's statue, opposite Charing Cross station, unveiled in 1998, confirms the Irish writer's long-awaited reacceptance.

Voltaire A plaque recalls the fact that the writer and philosopher whose ideas inspired the Enlightenment once lodged at a house on the site of 10 Maiden Lane, in Covent Garden.

POSTMAN'S PARK
The churchyard of St. Botolph's Church, Aldersgate, is locally known as Postman's Park, since this is where workers from the nearby Postal Sorting Office came to enjoy their lunchtime sandwiches. The park was laid out in 1900 as a national memorial to ordinary men and women whose heroic deeds might otherwise have been forgotten. A long wall contains memorial plaques telling the stories of just a few of those people. One records that Alice Ayres, a labourer's daughter, gave her own life to save three children from a burning house; another commemorates Thomas Simpson, who died of exhaustion in January 1885, having rescued scores of skaters from drowning when the ice broke at Highgate Ponds. Michael Ayrton's sculpture, the *Minotaur*, stands in the park.

137

CORAM'S FIELDS

The Thomas Coram Foundation fronts onto Coram's Fields, a 3-ha (7.5-acre) garden full of trees where the children of the Foundling Hospital used to play until the institution moved to more rural premises in Berkhamsted in the 1920s. The garden is entered by the original gates of 1752, and a sign warns that no adult may visit the gardens unless accompanied by a child.

▶▶ Percival David Foundation of Chinese Art   128B2

53 Gordon Square, WC1 (tel: 020-7387 3909)
www.pdfmuseum.org.ulk
Open: Mon–Fri 10–12, 1.30–5. Admission free
Underground: Russell Square

One of London's most wonderful small museums lurks in an anonymous Bloomsbury terraced house. It is devoted to a permanent exhibition of Chinese ceramics which date from the Sung/Song (10th century) to the Qing (19th century) dynasties and are consumate in their craftmanship. The collection of more than 1,500 pieces was assembled by Sir Percival David (1892–1964) and is the finest outside China. Very early pieces include a Tang dynasty hare. Ru and Guan pieces are especially fine, as are the two David vases made in the 14th century. In all, this is a feast of the finest craftsmanship. There are plans for a new museum in the Institute of Cultural Heritage building due to open in 2010.

▶ Petrie Museum of Egyptian Archaeology   128B1

Department of Egyptology, University College, London, Malet Place, WC1 (tel: 020-7679 2884)
www.petrie.ucl.ac.uk
Open: during university termtime Tue–Fri 1–5, Sat 10–1. Admission free
Underground: Goodge Street, Russell Square, Euston

The Petrie Museum of Egyptian Archaeology, well worth the effort of finding, comprises Egyptian antiquities collected by Amelia Edwards and Sir Flinders Petrie (1853–1942). Its sequence of Predynastic pottery provided the means of dating Egyptian ceramic styles. In the rows of traditional glass cabinets are displays of cat figures, notable relief carvings and a child's linen dress dating, incredibly, from around 2800BC. See the burial pot complete with skeleton, and a mummy with eyebrows and lashes still intact.

Pollock's toy theatres as once sold by Benjamin Pollock; 'a penny plain, twopence coloured'

▶▶ Pollock's Toy Museum   128A1

1 Scala Street, W1 (tel: 020-7636 3452)
www.pollocks.co.uk
Open: Mon–Sat 10–5. Admission moderate
Underground: Goodge Street
Robert Louis Stevenson wrote: 'If you love art, folly, or the bright eyes of children, speed to Pollock's.' He was referring to the shop (since gone) where Benjamin Pollock sold printed sheets that Victorian and Edwardian children stuck to wood or cardboard to create miniature theatres. This child-friendly, small museum, set in two creaky adjoining houses dating from 1760, with a shop below, displays Pollock's theatres and other toys, some from the 18th century. Reproductions of toys from around the world are sold.

Captain Thomas Coram, granted a royal charter in 1739 to care for London's abandoned street children (foundlings)

▶▶ Thomas Coram Foundation   128B3
(Foundling Museum)

40 Brunswick Square, WC1 (tel: 020-7841 3600)
Open: Tue–Sat 10–6, Sun 12–6. Admission moderate
www.coram.org.uk/heritage
Underground: Russell Square
The Thomas Coram Foundation was set up to provide shelter and education for orphaned and abandoned children. Its founder was the remarkable Captain Thomas Coram, shipbuilder and master mariner. Returning to London in 1732, he was appalled by the sight of abandoned children and infants 'left to die on dunghills'. He devoted the remainder of his life to working on their behalf, establishing the Foundling Hospital. George II was a patron, Handel gave a copy of *The Messiah* score, and Hogarth, Gainsborough, Reynolds and others gave pictures. Many of the works are on charitable themes and are now displayed in the present 1930s building, whose governors' courtroom is a replica of the original.

139

GREAT ORMOND STREET HOSPITAL
In 1851, philanthropist Dr. Charles West established London's first Hospital for Sick Children in Great Ormond Street. He was, quite rightly, appalled by the child-mortality rate in 19th-century London (of 50,000 deaths recorded annually in the city, 21,000 were children under 10). The hospital was set up to remedy the situation and still receives an important part of its income from the legacy of writer Sir James Barrie. In 1929 Barrie made a gift of the copyright of *Peter Pan* to the hospital, which benefits from royalties every time the book is sold or the play performed on film, stage, television or radio. Although the royalties expired in 1987, 50 years after Barrie's death, a special Act of Parliament was passed in the following year to ensure that the hospital would continue to benefit from them in perpetuity. Of the original Victorian hospital buildings, only the chapel survives, decorated with mosaics and touching memorials.

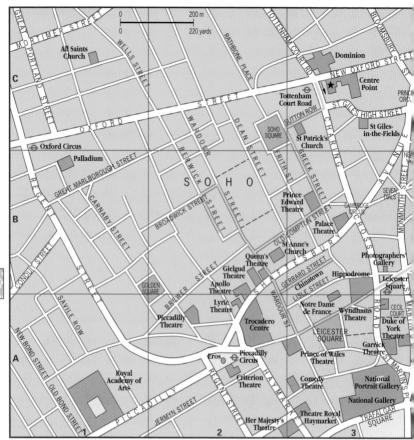

140

A corner of London's Chinatown

SOHO AND COVENT GARDEN Until the 1970s, Soho was a byword for sex clubs and sleaze, and Covent Garden was the run-down haunt of vegetable and flower traders. When the wholesale market moved to Nine Elms in 1974, the local community ensured that the market halls were converted into small shops and stalls. They still watch over the street performers and pavement cafés in the pedestrianized Piazza. Meanwhile Soho was cleaned up and blossomed, too, and the large Chinatown quarter at its heart was turned into a pedestrian district. Today, Soho is once again the heart of London nightlife, where people meet in large bars, eat in the many restaurants, dance the night away in clubs and, in summer, simply promenade.

SOHO AND COVENT GARDEN WALK From Tottenham Court Road tube station, walk south down Charing Cross Road. Off to the right is pretty **Soho Square**, where office workers from the film, advertising, and design companies of nearby Dean Street and Wardour Street come to eat lunchtime sandwiches. Executives are more likely to be consuming expense-account lunches in the restaurants of **Greek Street**, which leads southwards out of the square.

Follow Greek Street to **Old Compton Street**, another gourmets' haven. Turn right at the end of Old Compton

Street onto Wardour Street, then take the third left into Broadwick Street for **Berwick Street market**, the best in central London for fresh fruit and vegetables.

To the left at the end of Old Compton Street, Wardour Street continues south of Shaftesbury Avenue and leads to **Gerrard Street**, the heart of London's Chinatown. Chinese restaurants line Wardour Street, which leads to the movie theatres of **Leicester Square**. The mechanical clock on the façade of the **Swiss Centre** is a popular attraction when it performs on the hour.

From Leicester Square, cross Charing Cross Road into Long Acre, Covent Garden's main thoroughfare. The second right turn is **Bow Street**. It was from here that the Bow Street Runners, London's prototype police force, operated in the early 19th century. Across the street, the **Royal Opera House** is home to the Royal Opera, Royal Ballet and the Chorus and Orchestra of the Royal Opera House. Dixon Jones BDP are the architects who have transformed not just the 1858 theatre—where working conditions had improved little since that time—but added new and neighbouring buildings as well, to create one of the world's greatest modern lyric theatres (see page 147). Pavement views of the old and new buildings from Bow Street and Covent Garden Piazza are stunning.

▶ ▶ ▶ REGION HIGHLIGHTS

Covent Garden Central Market
page 142

Neal Street and Neal's Yard
page 143

Royal Opera House
page 147

Covent Garden is a relatively peaceful oasis in the heart of London. The central Piazza and its side streets are pedestrian zones, so people are free to roam without the noise, pollution and danger of traffic. The many shops and market stalls are small, personal, and sell a wide range of interesting products, from buttons and bows to books and works of art.

SEVEN DIALS

Seven Dials stands at the junction of seven streets in a corner of Covent Garden that was once the haunt of prostitutes and thieves. A Doric pillar erected here in 1694, topped by seven sundials, was knocked down in 1773 because of a rumour that a large sum of money was buried at its base. It was later rebuilt on the green at Weybridge in Surrey. A replica, paid for by local residents and carved by trainee masons, was unveiled in 1989. It actually has only six sundials; the seventh is the column itself, which casts its shadow onto the pavement, where the hours are marked by iron posts.

The focal point of Covent Garden is the Central Market. This elegant building, designed by Charles Fowler, was completed in the 1830s, although the iron-and-glass roof over the central arcade was added in the 1870s. The wholesale fruit and vegetable market that operated here closed in 1974 and moved to Nine Elms, in south London. The market building was then converted to provide space for the small speciality shops and cafés that now line the arcade, itself filled with market stalls selling antiques, crafts, toys, jewellery and clothing. The other Victorian market halls lining the Piazza have also enjoyed new leases of life: the refurbished London Transport Museum is in the old Flower Market; Floral Hall is the spectacular foyer of the rebuilt Royal Opera House. The **Punch and Judy** pub, on the southwestern corner of the market, opened in 1980, but its name is a reminder that the first Punch and Judy puppet show was performed in the square below on 9 May 1662—Samuel Pepys was one of those who came to watch the antics of Pietro Gimonde's marionettes. Mr Punch's birthday is still celebrated on the second Sunday in May, as part of the Covent Garden May Fayre festival.

Entertainment takes place here all week from 10am to dusk. The space in front of St. Paul's Church is used by all kinds of street performers—clowns, fire-eaters, musicians and acrobats. The church railings frame the entrance to the Victorian public toilets built below the square, an attraction in their own right.

St. Paul's Church is the oldest surviving building on the square. It was built by Inigo Jones in the 1630s, inspired by the cathedral in Livorno, Tuscany, which Jones had helped to design as an apprentice to the Renaissance architect Buontalenti. His client, the Earl of Bedford, could not afford to spend much money, and told Jones to make the church as simple as a barn. Jones is said to have replied: 'You shall have the handsomest barn in England.' St. Paul's is known as 'the Actors' Church' because, located near the Theatre Royal, Drury Lane, and the Royal Opera House, it is much frequented by playwrights, performers and impresarios. Stars such as Charlie Chaplin, Vivien Leigh and Noel Coward are buried here or commemorated on the wall plaques even if they are not buried here.

To the north of Long Acre, Covent Garden's main thoroughfare, lies a maze of little streets. Some are lined with warehouses once used to store fruit and vegetables, now converted to dance studios, such as **Pineapple Dance**

Studios (7 Langley Street), art galleries and speciality shops such as the **Kite Store**, **Neal Street East**, **The Tea House** and the **Astrology Shop**, all on Neal Street. Turn left off Neal Street onto Short's Gardens and look above the Holland and Barrett shop to see a fascinating water clock. Close by at No. 17 is **Neal's Yard Dairy**, one of England's best dairy shops, selling cheeses made by small producers all over Britain and Ireland. Just around the corner (look for the narrow passageway) is **Neal's Yard**, a wholefood haven set in a small pretty courtyard, festooned with windowboxes. This is one of London's most charming, bohemian spots and on a sunny day it is a joy to sit outside at one of the Yard's cheap-and-cheerful cafés, and escape the bustle and traffic. Excellent snacks and meals (eat in or take out) are served at Neal's Yard Bakery and Tearoom, and World Food Café, where photographer Chris Caldicott's images of his worldwide travels complement the food.

143

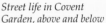

Street life in Covent Garden, above and below

PUBS AND CAFÉS

Covent Garden has scores of pubs and pavement cafés, offering a cosmopolitan range. However, nothing could be more English than the Lamb and Flag (33 Rose Street), a 300-year-old pub serving homemade food, where you are in constant danger of banging your head on the low ceiling beams. That is not why the pub was once known as the Bucket of Blood; bare-knuckle boxing bouts once took place in the upstairs rooms. The Rock Garden, on the Piazza, serves modern British cuisine, and there is live music in the Gardening Club below the restaurant.

Book lovers should have little trouble keeping themselves occupied in the West End of London. For a feast of good bookshops—eccentric, specialist, antiquarian—head straight for Charing Cross Road. But beware of wasting time in a fruitless search for No. 84. Helene Hanff's book 84 Charing Cross Road *was based on her correspondence with the owners and staff of Mark's and Co's secondhand bookshop, but the original shop is no more.*

144

OTHER SPECIALIST BOOKSHOPS

Books for Cooks, at 4 Blenheim Crescent, Notting Hill, is the largest shop in the world devoted exclusively to the culinary arts of every nation. You may also find rare or out-of-print editions among its range of secondhand stock. A short step away is the Travel Bookshop (13–15 Blenheim Crescent), which inspired the setting for the movie *Notting Hill*, selling antiquarian and secondhand titles, as well as all the latest travel literature and practical guides. Another great travel bookshop is Daunt Books for Travellers (83 Marylebone High Street). Shops with an especially good stock on London include Selfridges (in the basement) and Hatchards. For books and magazines in European languages other than English, Grant & Cutler (55–57 Great Marlborough Street), is the place to go; if they don't have what you want, try the European Bookshop (5 Warwick Street; 5 Cecil Court for their Italian bookshop): both shops stock titles from the main French, Italian, Spanish, German and Portuguese publishing houses.

Secondhand book bargains on sale in Cecil Court

One of the most enjoyable ways of spending a wet London afternoon is browsing in a bookshop, and of all the bookshops, **Hatchards** is one of the most pleasant in which to while away a few hours—if the books you buy are too heavy to carry, they can be mailed home. John Hatchard opened his shop in 1797 and made it so inviting that Gladstone, Macaulay and other customers would spend mornings here in front of the fire, reading newspapers and new books. Today, the well-informed staff can, between them, advise usefully on almost any subject.

Nearby, **Waterstone's** Piccadilly shop is the flagship of its chain, the largest book emporium in Europe filling what was the upmarket, long-established Simpson's fashion shop. In-house cafés have transform book-buying into a leisurely experience. Waterstone's even hosts a top quality restaurant and bar, the 5th View Bar and Food. Waterstone's has further shops dotted about central London. This new approach to book-buying is well-established at Borders on Oxford Street, whose café and foreign newspapers make it an international meeting place.

Near here, down Charing Cross Road, home to one of the most famous names in books, **Foyles** (113–119 Charing Cross Road), in business since 1903, at this address since 1906 and still independently owned. On Charing Cross Road you will also find shops with specific themes. **Murder One** (No. 76–78), as its name suggests, has a

Getting arty in Charing Cross Road

A GOOD READ ON LONDON

For information about what's on in London, the weekly *Time Out* magazine provides the most comprehensive listing of all that is going on—although it may take time to find your way round it, and its reviewers may not share your opinions. For another point of view, read the quality newspapers and the *Evening Standard;* first nights of major shows will be reviewed within a day or two of opening. *Time Out* also publishes *Kids Out* (monthly) and *Time Out Eating & Drinking Guide* (annually).

Many visitors to London like to read novels set in the city. To evoke past history, try some Dickens, Thackeray, Galsworthy, Conrad, P. G. Wodehouse, Virginia Woolf or Peter Ackroyd; for more modern fiction, there are Martin Amis, Julian Barnes Michael Moorcock and Iain Sinclair. London diaries abound, the most notable by James Boswell, Samuel Pepys, John Evelyn, Charles Lamb, Norman Collins and Cecil Beaton.

huge stock of crime and detective stories. **Shipley** (Nos. 70) sells books on art, architecture, film, advertising and design. There is scarcely an art book published that they do not stock, although the prices can be as staggering as the sheer weight of some of the beautifully bound and printed volumes. Chek out Caxton Walk where little shops sell secondhand and antiquarian volumes. A word of warning: pickpockets operate here—they know how easy it is to relieve preoccupied browsers of their wallets or purses.

There is one particularly good enclave of antiquarian bookshops on Cecil Court (the narrow alley next to 24 Charing Cross Road, see panel, page 146). From here you can continue up to New Row and into Garrick Street where, across the road in Floral Street, you can go in the back door of **Stanfords**. In this shop, one of the best for travel books, maps and navigational charts, you are quite likely to stumble across well-known explorers and travellers either signing copies of their latest books or buying maps for the next trip. Almost opposite, on Garrick Street, Waterstones Covent Garden has an excellent section on art, architecture and design. But their largest stock is in Bloomsbury at 82 Gower Street (formerly Dillons University Bookshop, nearest Underground station Goodge Street). Well worth a visit.

The London Transport Museum, housed within the old Flower Market in Covent Garden

THE COURTS OF COVENT GARDEN

Although called 'courts', the little lanes that run down from Covent Garden to Charing Cross Road are no more than narrow alleyways, with many a twist and bend where you would have risked a mugging in 18th- and 19th-century London. One example is Goodwin's Court, linking Bedfordbury to St. Martin's Lane, with a row of restored 17th-century houses on one side. Attractive as they look now, this and other courts were known as rookeries because of the sheer number of people who lived in their squalid ghettos. Straight across St. Martin's Lane is Cecil Court, now an enclave of excellent secondhand bookshops where you can buy rare first editions, maps, various prints and illustrated children's books. Cecil Court runs parallel to St. Martin's Court, the home of J. Sheekey's, where diners come to enjoy fish dishes in a setting that has scarcely changed since 1892, when the restaurant opened.

▶▶ **London Transport Museum**   *141B4*

39 Wellington Street, WC2 (tel: 020-7565 7299)
www.ltmuseum.co.uk
Open: Due to open late 2007, call for latest details
Underground: Covent Garden

Housed in the old Flower Market (built in 1870), this is a far more enthralling museum than its title suggests. Children can climb aboard the historical buses, drive the underground train simulator, play on the new Fun Bus and get involved in one of the special events (story telling, model making, face painting, etc). Adults can meanwhile contemplate the sheer immensity and complexity of London's public transport system. Over 6 million passengers a day are carried on buses, trains and underground trains—journeys that encompass more than 800,000km (500,000 miles).

▶▶ **The Photographer's Gallery**   *140B3*

5 & 8 Great Newport Street, WC2 (tel: 020-7831 1772)
www.photonet.org.uk
Open: Mon–Wed, Fri–Sat 11–6, Thu 11–8, Sun 12–6
Admission free
Underground: Leicester Square

This excellent gallery was established in 1971 and has proved to be of London's most popular public galleries and one of the UK's leading venues showcasing photography. It began life in No. 8 Great Newport Street, which houses the gallery's primary exhibition space and the excellent bookshop. Catalogues to accompany exhibitions are also on sale. In the 1980s the gallery acquired further premises at No. 5 Great Newport Street. It contains the Print Sales gallery (closed Sun and Mon), which has a range of prints by over 100 international photographers and a section devoted to British talent. Regularly changing exhibitions and educational programmes has insured photography is now in the mainstream in the major galleries and museums throughout the country. While well-known photographers are represented, this gallery is all about nurturing new talent and future developments include the expansion of the gallery into premises at 16–18 Ramillies Street in Soho.

▶▶▶ Royal Opera House 141B4

Bow Street, WC2 (tel: 020-7240 1200/7304 4000)
www.royaloperahouse.org
Foyer and Amphitheatre Bar open by day. Admission free during the day; admission by theatre ticket in the evening
Backstage tours Mon–Fri 10.30, 12.30 and 2.30, Sat 10.30, 11.30, 12.30, 1.30. Admission expensive
Admission to Floral Hall and temporary exhibtions (Mon–Sat 10–3.30) free.
Underground: Covent Garden

After 30 years of debate and delay, a combination of restoration, rebuilding and building from scratch has produced central London's most exciting new arts forum. The Royal Opera, Royal Ballet and Chorus and Orchestra of the Royal Opera House now present high-quality programmes in modern theatres to a wider audience.

The complex has three parts. First there is the restored original theatre, designed in 1858 by E. M. Barry and decorated with Flaxman's reliefs, which survive from an earlier building that burnt down. Here, what was deemed the 'most inadequate' of the world's great opera houses has been transformed. While the restored auditorium looks much the same (with the addition of air-conditioning), facilities backstage have improved tremendously for performers and the hundreds of people needed to put on a show. More space for sets, rehearsals, dressing rooms and other essentials for both opera and ballet mean up to three performances can be put on at the same time. Second, the 19th-century Floral Hall is now a spectacular foyer. Bars, restaurants, informal music and a spectacular soaring vaulted glass roof make this a great place to meet at any time. From here, visitors can continue into the main auditorium, or pass through a public arcade to Covent Garden Piazza. They can also reach a terrace overlooking the Piazza and the Clore Studio Upstairs (seats 200 for workshops and performances). The adjoining new building, the third element, houses workshops, workrooms, offices, extra opera rehearsal rooms and the Linbury Studio Theatre (seats 420 for concerts and educational events). The backstage tours take about 75 minutes and are fascinating, but reservations are essential.

ELIZA DOOLITTLE AND NELL GWYN

Two of the best-known names associated with Covent Garden both began as street traders. The Cockney heroine of Shaw's play *Pygmalion* (and of the musical based on it, *My Fair Lady*, by Alan Jay Lerner and Frederick Loewe) was Eliza Doolittle, a flower seller. The play opens with Eliza selling violets to pedestrians sheltering from the rain under the portico of St. Paul's Church. Eliza was, of course, a fictional creation, whereas Nell Gwyn really did exist, even if the events of her rags-to-riches life sound like a fairy tale. She started her career selling oranges to the patrons of the Theatre Royal, Drury Lane, then became an actress herself, making her stage debut in the same theatre in Dryden's play *The Indian Queen* in 1665. Although, by some accounts, not a greatly gifted actress, she succeeded in charming King Charles II, becoming his mistress and bearing several of his children, one of whom was made Duke of St. Albans by the King. Her portrait can be seen in the National Portrait Gallery.

147

Royal Opera House, Covent Garden

Some 40 theatres are packed into the area of London known as 'The West End', consisting of the Haymarket, St. Martin's Lane, Shaftesbury Avenue, Charing Cross Road and the Strand. This area pulses with life after dark, as the audiences arrive to enjoy the illuminated façades, glittering interiors and intimate atmospheres of its Victorian and Edwardian theatres.

148

REVIVED AND NEW THEATRES

London may seem to have enough theatres, yet there are often new ones opening. Some are renovations of fine old theatres. Andrew Lloyd Webber picked up The Palace Theatre and returned Collcutt and Holloway's 1888–1889 extravaganza of gilding, marble, alabaster and Doulton terracotta to its original sumptuousness. The Old Vic, originally built in 1816–1818 and once home to the National Theatre under Laurence Olivier, had its interior rebuilt in 1982. The Savoy Theatre, built in the 1880s to stage Gilbert and Sullivan operas, then refurbished in dramatic art deco in the 1920s by Basil Ionides and Frank Tugwell, was painstakingly rebuilt after a fire gutted it in 1990. In the East End, where music halls rocked to full audiences until movies killed them off in the 1930s, Franck Matcham's Hackney Empire and Theatre Royal Stratford East have reopened for music and theatre. Meanwhile, impresario Sally Greene and others have rescued Richmond Theatre and The Criterion Theatre. In Islington the Almeida Theatre was created in a disused literary institute, and Sadler's Wells was entirely rebuilt in the late 1990s.

London theatre has a clear structure. There are the state-subsidized theatres: the Royal National Theatre (three stages, plays and musicals), the Royal Shakespeare Company at the Novello Theatre, Aldwych (plays and musicals) the Coliseum (opera and ballet), and the Royal Opera House (three stages; opera, ballet and related events). Then there are the commercial theatres, located mostly in the West End, stretching from Aldwych to Piccadilly Circus (popular plays and musicals); Shakespeare's Globe is also a commerical theatre. Standing apart from these are the more innovative, avant-garde, 'off–West End' theatres, which are nonetheless commercial, including the Almeida, the Bush, King's Head, Royal Court, Riverside Studios and Donmar Warehouse. This exciting theatre is further explored in the small fringe theatres dotted around London, whose successful shows sometimes transfer to West End theatres (see *Time Out* for details).

To find out what's hot, consult the critical reviews in the daily newspapers; for a comprehensive listing refer to *Time Out*. To buy seats, either telephone the theatre direct, or use a reliable agency such as Ticketmaster (tel: 0870-534 4444, www.ticketmaster.co.uk) or First Call (tel: 0870–840 1111; wwwfirstcalltickets.com); check surcharges. It is best to avoid all ticket touts; if desperate for specific tickets, try Harrods' ticket agency (tel: 020-7730 1234) who almost never fail, even if the surcharge is high. Also, some theatres (such as the RNT and RSC) keep some tickets back for sale on the day of performance. Matinee tickets are often easier to obtain. For half-price tickets, go to the **tkts** Society of London Theatres' Half Price Ticket Booth in Leicester Square where tickets for some West End theatres are sold on the day of performance (*Open* Mon–Sat 10–7 for matinée and evening shows, Sun noon– around 3 matinée only; small service charge). Beware of non-official ticket booths around (and in) Leicester Square.

Historic theatres The Puritans banned theatres from London in 1574, when Bankside, outside the city's precincts, became the entertainment complex and the Globe, Rose and Swan were built. Thus, London's oldest theatre is the **Theatre Royal**, **Drury Lane**, founded in 1663 after Charles II's restoration for Thomas Killigrew and The King's Servants. This and one other in Lincoln's Inn Fields were London's only legal theatres and theatre companies until the great Victorian expansion of the 1840s—all others could be closed at a moment's notice.

Rebuilt several times, David Garrick revived almost forgotten Shakespeare plays here in the 18th century.
Theatre Royal, Haymarket, first built in 1720, was where Henry Fielding's crude satires caused the theatre to be closed and the Lord Chamberlain's powers of censorship to be introduced in 1737, only finally lifted in 1968. Here, in the 1880s, J. G. Phipps built London's first proscenium (picture-frame) stage and converted the pit into stalls. Manager Herbert Beerbohm Tree staged Oscar Wilde's *An Ideal Husband* here in 1895 before leaving to run **Her Majesty's Theatre** opposite, with huge success. This theatre, which was founded in 1705 by architect-playwright John Vanbrugh, staged Handel's oratorios and operas for 40 years. Today, Andrew Lloyd Webber's *Phantom of the Opera* has played here since 1986.

ANDREW LLOYD WEBBER

Andrew Lloyd Webber, the composer of several hit musicals, is one of Britain's most important economic assets. His productions attract so many visitors to Britain, who in turn spend money on hotels and restaurants, that he is single-handedly responsible for a large chunk of Britain's foreign currency earnings. *Cats*, which achieved 8949 performances between 1981 and 2002 held the record for the longest-running musical in theatre history—until superceded by Les Miserables in 2006—and other hits, such as *The Phantom of the Opera* and *Starlight Express* are never off the stage. The secret of Lloyd Webber's success is to write tunes that, instead of sounding new, are instantly familiar. The dividing line between what is and is not genuinely original music is very thin. When Lloyd Webber composed the theme tune for the 1992 Barcelona Olympics he hired lawyers and researchers to ensure that it did not infringe any existing copyright—in other words, to check that he had not subconsciously copied someone else's work.

149

Andrew Lloyd Webber's Cats *received record audience attendance*

Map labels:

Farringdon
Gray's Inn
Gray's Inn Square
St Etheldreda's Church
THEOBALD'S ROAD
SOUTHAMPTON ROW
DRAKE PROCTOR ST
RED LION SQUARE
Field Court
South Square
Chancery Lane
Prudential Assurance Building
HATTON GARDEN
LEATHER LANE
FARRINGDON ROAD
ELY PL
Central London Markets (Smithfield)
HIGH HOLBORN
Holborn
Sir John Soane's Museum
STONE BLDGS
Staple Inn
London Silver Vaults
HOLBORN
HOLBORN CIRCUS
HOLBORN VIADUCT
St Andrew's Church
City Temple
FETTER LANE
SHOE LANE
City Thameslink
BLOOMSBURY WAY
SOUTH HAMPTON
HIGH HOLBORN
Lincoln's Inn
Lincoln's Inn Fields
Lincoln's Inn Chapel
NEW SQUARE
Public Record Office
CHANCERY LANE
STAR YARD
BELL YARD
NEW FETTER LANE
FARRINGDON ST
DRURY
Old Curiosity Shop
KINGSWAY
ST QUEEN ST
Dr Johnson's House
LUDGATE CIRCUS
ENDELL ST
London School of Economics
Royal Courts of Justice
FLEET STREET
St Brides and Crypt Museum
NEW BRIDGE ST
LONG ACRE
BOW ST
Theatre Royal
Aldwych Theatre
St Clement Danes
Temple Church
King's Bench Walk
Covent Garden
Royal Opera House
Bush House
Australia House
Inns of Court and Chancery
Blackfriars
Waldorf Hotel
India House
St Mary-le-Strand
WELLINGTON ST
Covent Garden
London Transport Museum
King's College
Somerset House Galleries
Inner Temple
Middle Temple
Somerset House
Temple
VICTORIA EMBANKMENT
Savoy Theatre
Somerset House
HMS President
Blackfriars Millennium Pier
BLACKFRIARS BRIDGE
Savoy Hotel
EMBANKMENT
HQS Wellington
Thames
Victoria Embankment Gardens
VICTORIA
WATERLOO BRIDGE
Charing Cross Station
Cleopatra's Needle
Riverside Walk
London Television Centre
Oxo Tower

0   200 m
0   220 yards

150

Above: Silver dragons on the City of London's coat of arms
Opposite: St.-Mary-le-Strand

HOLBORN AND THE STRAND Holborn and the Strand form the two main routes linking the City to the West End. The character of this district is heavily influenced by the medieval Inns of Court, with their collegiate buildings and noble open spaces providing a haven of tranquillity a short step away from some of London's busiest thoroughfares. The west end of the Strand is dominated by Charing Cross station, where trains disgorge well over 100,000 commuters into the city every day. The Strand's east end meets Aldwych, where half-a-dozen theatres stand near some of London's most luxurious hotels—the Savoy, the Waldorf Hilton, Number One Aldwych. Here, too, is revived, palatial Somerset House.

HOLBORN AND THE STRAND WALK This route starts at Charing Cross station, which was opened in 1864 and is fronted by the Renaissance-style hotel **Charing Cross Thistle**. Behind it, all is new, however: The station building, with its shopping malls and offices, was rebuilt in postmodernist style in 1990–1991.

Turn right outside the station and walk along **the Strand**. With the coming of the railway, many of the Strand's older riverside mansions were demolished to make way for palatial hotels. One of these is the **Savoy**, near the end of the Strand on the right. The epitome of luxury, it was completed in 1889 by Richard D'Oyly Carte, the impresario who produced the operettas of Gilbert and Sullivan. A striking feature is the hotel's stainless steel art-deco frontage, designed by Basil Ionides. D'Oyly Carte's Savoy Theatre, designed by Ionides and Tugwell in 1929 and meticulously rebuilt after a fire in 1990, stands in the hotel entrance court.

Just beyond, on the right, Lancaster Place leads to **Waterloo Bridge**. The original bridge, built to commemorate Wellington's victory at Waterloo in 1815, was replaced in 1945. Even so, the views to St. Paul's Cathedral and downstream to Canary Wharf, and upstream to the Houses of Parliament are among the city's best. Return down Lancaster Place and continue along the Strand. Opposite the main entrance to Somerset House is an island bounded by the Strand and the great arc of the **Aldwych**. On it are three notable buildings: Herbert Baker's fine **India House** (1928–1930), decorated with India-inspired friezes, **Bush House** (1923–1935)—headquarters of the BBC World Service, and **Australia House** (1912–1918). These huge buildings dwarf the tiny church of **St. Mary-le-Strand**, stuck in the middle of the road, but an exquisite early 18th-century building, designed by James Gibbs. Its counterpart, a little further along, is **St. Clement Danes**, built by Christopher Wren in 1680, with a steeple added by Gibbs in 1720. It was bombed in 1941 but beautifully restored and is dedicated to the Royal Air Force. Its floor is covered in crests carved in Welsh slate, one for each RAF unit. Within the spired and turreted **Royal Courts of Justice** (1874–1882, see page 152), the last major building on the Strand, judges hear some of the most important civil cases in the land; the public is admitted to the viewing galleries and to the Central Hall (*Closed* Aug–Sep).

SIR FRANCIS BACON

The most famous member of Gray's Inn, Sir Francis Bacon was a remarkable polymath—philosopher, scientist, statesman and man of letters. He was part of Shakespeare's literary circle and it is frequently claimed (though never proven) that he was the true author of Shakespeare's plays. His death was no less colourful than his life. While conducting one of the country's first experiments in freezing food (on Highgate Hill in 1606) he caught a chill and died of pneumonia.

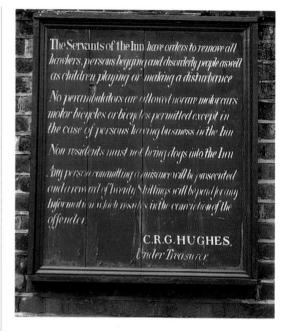

The Servants of the Inn *have orders to remove all hawkers, persons begging and disorderly people as well as children playing or making a disturbance*

No perambulators are allowed nor are motor cars motor bicycles or bicycles permitted except in the case of persons having business in the Inn

Non residents must not bring dogs into the Inn

Any person committing a nuisance will be prosecuted and a reward of twenty Shillings will be paid for any Information which results in the conviction of the offender

C.R.G.HUGHES,
Under Treasurer

THE ROYAL COURTS OF JUSTICE

These cathedral-like buildings, known as the Law Courts, stand at Aldwych, where the Strand and Fleet Street meet. Together they form London's last great Gothic public building, and they solved the old problem of judges and lawyers having to dash around London to various little courts. The campaign for a central court was launched in 1841. Eventually, Parliamentary Bills were passed and the design competition announced in 1866. George Edmund Street won, but the first brick was not laid until 1874. By the time it was completed in 1882, Street had died of a stroke the year before, brought on by the exhausting complexity of the project—it had demanded almost 3,000 drawings.

▶ **Gray's Inn**   *150C2*

High Holborn, WC1 (tel: 020-7405 8164)
Open: Gardens only Mon–Fri 12–2.30. Admission free
Underground: Chancery Lane, Holborn

Gray's Inn is one of the four surviving Inns of Court established in the 14th century to provide accommodation for lawyers and their students. The layout of the Inns resembles that of an Oxford or Cambridge college: Each has a dining hall, chapel and library, and the buildings that house the lawyers' chambers are grouped around courtyards and gardens. Of all the Inns, Gray's Inn suffered most from wartime bombing, but the most important buildings have been well restored. These include the 17th-century entrance gateway, on the north side of High Holborn (at No. 21 and near to the Cittie of York pub, a favourite lawyers' haunt). This leads into South Square, with its statue of Sir Francis Bacon (by F. W. Pomeroy, 1912), who was a member of Gray's Inn from 1576 until his death in 1626 (see panel). The Hall, on the north side of the square, is where Shakespeare's *The Comedy of Errors* was first performed in 1594. Passing through Gray's Inn Square and Field Court, you will reach the extensive gardens. These were laid out by Sir Francis Bacon in 1606, and the catalpa trees are said to have been planted from cuttings brought back from America by Sir Walter Raleigh. The raised terrace was a favourite place to walk during the 17th century and, as Samuel Pepys recorded in his diary, a good place in which to 'espy fine ladies'.

▶ Lincoln's Inn

150B2

Chancery Lane, WC2 (tel: 020-7405 1393)
Open: Chapel Mon–Fri noon–2.30; grounds Mon–Fri 9–6.
Admission free
Underground: Chancery Lane, Holborn

To explore Lincoln's Inn—called an inn because it was originally a 14th–century mansion where barristers and students lived— start at the brick gatehouse, on Chancery Lane. This dates from 1518 and bears the coat of arms of Henry VIII above the original doorways of stout oak.

The narrow pedestrian entrance leads to Old Buildings. To the right is the **chapel** and its stone vaulted undercroft, paved with 18th-century tombstones. Steps lead up from here to the chapel itself, completed in 1623; John Donne, the poet, preached 'a right rare and learned sermon' at its consecration. The east window contains 228 coats of arms of former Treasurers of Lincoln's Inn. To the right is Old Square, leading to **Stone Buildings**, built of crisp, white Portland stone in Palladian style. A low gate to the left leads to **Lincoln's Inn Fields**, a large green area of manicured lawns and statuesque trees. Straight ahead are the **hall** and **library**. They look perfectly medieval but were built by Philip Hardwick in 1845. To the left is New Square, where fig trees and wisteria climb over the late-17th-century buildings. If you walk down the left-hand side of New Square you will reach Lincoln's Inn Archway, sandwiched between the windows of Wildy & Sons, booksellers specializing in legal texts. The windows exhibit fascinating Victorian cartoons and engravings.

The archway leads into Carey Street, once the site of the bankruptcy courts—hence the archaic expression 'heading for Queer Street' ('Queer' being a corruption of Carey) to describe someone in financial trouble. To the right is a pub popular with lawyers, the Seven Stars. To reach Temple (see pages 158–159) turn left on Carey Street, then right into Bell Yard, which leads to Fleet Street. Temple is just opposite.

AROUND HOLBORN CIRCUS

Holborn Circus marks the busy meeting point of several roads leading into the City of London. To the north, Hatton Garden and its side streets are the traditional haunt of jewellers and diamond merchants: Many of the shops here were founded by Jewish refugees fleeing persecution elsewhere in Europe. Leather Lane, running parallel to the west, has an entertaining street market on weekdays where stallholders call out their wares and perform all sorts of antics to attract trade. To the east, in Ely Place, is **St. Etheldreda's Church**, built in around 1290, well worth a visit for its tracery, stained glass and its Café in the Crypt.

153

The 14th-century building of Lincoln's Inn

STAPLE INN

Staple Inn, on Holborn, is one of London's oldest surviving timber-framed buildings (*Open* Courtyard only, Mon–Fri 8–8. *Admission* free). Built in 1545 as a hostel for wool merchants, the gabled building has projecting upper stories with oriel windows, while the shop fronts below date from the 19th century. As you walk through the archway, note the sign on the left saying that the porters have orders to prevent 'Old Clothes Men' and 'Rude Children' from entering. Beyond is a peaceful brick courtyard and a rose garden, a favourite place for office workers to eat their lunchtime sandwiches.

CHANCERY LANE

If you are interested in antiques you should pay a call to the London Silver Vaults, 53–65 Chancery Lane (tel: 020-7242 3844. *Open* Mon–Fri 9–5.30, Sat 9–1)). Originally this was set up in 1885 as a place where valuables could be stored in stout underground vaults, secure from the threat of fire or theft. Today the subterranean labyrinth contains approximately 40 antique dealers specializing in silver-plate and jewellery. Not far away is a curious sight that only male visitors truly appreciate. In Star Yard, up against the high walls of Lincoln's Inn, is an ornate cast-iron urinal, which looks as if it has been transported here from Paris. There are several good secondhand legal bookshops nearby in the alleys linking Star Yard to Chancery Lane.

▶ Lincoln's Inn Fields   150B2

Underground: Holborn

One of the earliest mentions of Lincoln's Inn Fields records that in 1150 this was a jousting ground for the Knights Templar (see Temple, pages 158–159). State-sanctioned violence continued to be a theme of this green and pleasant space for the next five centuries. Many executions were carried out here, most notably in 1586 when Anthony Babington and his 13 co-conspirators were found guilty of plotting against Queen Elizabeth I. A plaque in the bandstand in the middle of the park records the last execution here in 1683, of Lord William Russell, beheaded for treason.

The square of elegant buildings around the park began construction in the 1630s. It is the oldest surviving square in London, and also its largest public square, at just under 3ha (7 acres).

From the 17th century onwards Lincoln's Inn Fields became a very fashionable place to live, though the only original house still standing is No. 59–60. It is a handsome structure, accredited to the great Inigo Jones, and from 1790 to 1807 was the home of Spencer Perceval, the only British Prime Minister ever to be assassinated.

▶ Prudential Assurance Building   150C3

Holborn
Underground: Chancery Lane

Alfred Waterhouse's huge redbrick-and-terracotta building was constructed in 1879, concurrently with his other London masterpiece, the Natural History Museum, which it closely resembles externally. The building occupies the site of Furnival's Inn, one of the Inns of Chancery (preparatory schools for the Inns of Court), which were dissolved in 1817. Just inside the courtyard a plaque and a bust commemorate Charles Dickens, who had lodgings in Furnival's Inn from 1834 to 1837. He wrote most of *The Pickwick Papers* here.

▶▶▶ Sir John Soane's Museum   150C2

13 Lincoln's Inn Fields, WC2 (tel: 020-7405 2107)
www.soane.org
Open: Tue–Sat 10–5 (first Tue each month also 6–9).
Admission free
Underground: Holborn

Sir John Soane (1753–1837) was one of those brilliant architects that Britain produces from time to time, whose buildings are so quirky and original that they defy classification. Examples of his work in London include the Bank of England (see pages 162–163), the Dulwich Picture Gallery (see page 214), and this remarkable house. The house was originally two—he bought No. 13 in 1812 and its neighbour No. 14 in 1824 and remodelled the interiors to serve as his home and as a museum for his paintings, sculpture, architectural models and drawings. Recently the museum has been extended further by the purchase of No. 12, which has been converted to form a gallery for displaying drawings from Soane's massive collection of over 30,000 items. Soane's interior remodelling was brave and experimental: Split-level flooring creates a strange and disorienting experience and anticipates, by 100 years or more, one of the favourite devices of modernist architects.

Bizarre but fun—Sir John Soane's Museum

HOGARTH'S ENGRAVINGS
William Hogarth (1697-1764) was born in London, grew up in Smithfield, and was apprenticed to a goldsmith before becoming an engraver. Through his innovative and hugely popular series of engravings of moral subjects, he painted a ruthless picture of the underbelly of 18th-century London. Using his overflowing imagination and sense of theatre, these satires are sharp, unforgiving and full of wit. As he said: 'my picture is my stage, and men and women my players, who by means of certain actions and gestures, are to exhibit a dumb show'. His first series was *Harlot's Progress* (1732), showing the downfall of a country girl at the hands of wicked Londoners, some of them clearly recognizable to his contemporaries. *Rake's Progress*, *Marriage à la Mode* and *The Election* followed. In addition to the Hogarths on permanent display in Sir John Soane's Museum, you will find Hogarth engravings in several London collections and reproduced in many books.

155

The rooms are crammed with objects and made more bewildering still by the use of mirrors. It's fun just to explore the labyrinthine house and make chance discoveries, but you can also join a lecture tour given every Saturday at 2.30pm (moderate). Not to be missed is the Picture Room, where two of William Hogarth's series of paintings are displayed. *A Rake's Progress* (1732–1733) traces the career of Tom Rakewell in eight canvases, from his life as a happy young man about town to his imprisonment for debt and final home in the Bedlam asylum for the insane (see page 200). *The Election* (*c*1754) presents an equally cynical view of bribery and corruption in British politics illustrated in a series of four pictures.

The fascinating basement has views through the windows to the Monk's Cloister, built in the garden from architectural fragments that Soane rescued when the Houses of Parliament were being rebuilt. Another star exhibit is the Sepulchral Chamber, which contains the Sarcophagus of Seti I (who died around 1300BC).

Manet's Bar at the Folies-Bergère *(1882)*

SOMERSET HOUSE
The rejuvenation of this great riverside landmark has given London a new arts complex. Built in 1776–1786 on the site of the Duke of Somerset's Tudor palace, it housed important offices of state such as the Navy Office and the Exchequer and later became a warren of civil servants' offices, forgotten by most people. Today, however, it is back on the map. The building and its central courtyard have been extensively renovated and provide a variety of activities. The central courtyard has fountains that play all day—the first major public fountains to be commissioned in London since those made for Trafalgar Square in 1845—the outdoor tables for the café and, in the winter, an ice-rink. The rooms overlooking the Thames can be entered either from here or from the grand river façade on the Embankment. An active programme of events includes family trails and guided tours of Somerset House, events and lectures for each collection and workshops for all ages.

▶▶▶ **Somerset House Galleries**   *150A2*
TheStrand (tel: 020-7845 4600)
www.somerset-house.org.uk
Open: Daily 10–6
Underground: Temple, Embankment, Covent Garden
As you enter Somerset House from the Strand it is worth pausing to enjoy the façade and its decoration symbolic of a growing world power. There are sculptures personifying oceans and rivers, the Cardinal Virtues and the Genius of Britain. Once through the grand triple-arched gateway, you will find more triumphant decoration on the courtyard façades

THE COURTAULD GALLERY is housed in rooms that were once home to the Royal Academy (see page 82) and other learned bodies, hence the fine

ceilings in some of its rooms—one has the initials RA and paintbrushes incorporated into the design. The catalyst for this stunning assembly of six private collections was the textile magnate Samuel Courtauld (1876-1947) who in 1931 used his collection to found the Courtauld Art Institute, with the intention that students should be able to study masterpieces such as Renoir's *La Loge* at close quarters. Recently refurbished and reorganized, the collection is filled with top quality pieces.

The first floor's grand rooms house European art from the Early Italian Renaissance to 18th-century British portraiture. Highlights include the richly gilded wooden Italian Virgin and Child, huge painted Italian chests known as cassoni and Botticelli's *Holy Trinity with St. John and Mary Magdalen*. The 16th-century northern European paintings include works by Cranach and Breugel the Elder. A sumptuous roomful of paintings by Rubens follows, including a portrait of his family, and then Gainsborough's thinly-painted, perceptive portraits that perfectly capture England's 18th-century aristocracy. Further up the spiral staircase, a suite of softly top-lit rooms contains a stunning array of Impressionist and Post-Impressionist paintings including eight Cezanne canvases, several Van Goghs and Gaugins, Manet's *Bar at the Folies-Bergère* and a small version of his great *Dejeuner sur l'Herbe*, displayed in Paris's Musee d'Orsay. Other rooms display British 20th century pictures by Roger Fry, Duncan Grant, Vanessa Bell and Ben Nicholson. It is always worth looking at the temporary exhibition on this level.

THE HERMITAGE ROOMS, across the central court, are an innovative idea. The State Hermitage Museum in St. Petersburg is astoundingly rich, yet many people are unable to visit it. Since London is highly accessible and is visited by more than 30 million

THE GILBERT COLLECTION

This collection of decorative arts was given to London, specifically for Somerset House, by Sir Arthur Gilbert and went on display in 2000. Arthur Gilbert was born in 1913 in Golders Green, north London, where his parents had settled in 1893 after fleeing Jewish pogroms in Poland. In 1935 he and his wife, Rosalinde, founded an evening gown business that was so successful they decided in 1949 to retire to California. Ever energetic and entrepreneurial, the Gilberts mixed real estate development with serious art collecting. They concentrated on three areas: Roman and Florentine mosaics from the 16th to the 19th centuries; gold and silver from the 15th to 19th centuries; and gold snuff boxes, mostly made for 18th century aristocrats. Each piece is of the finest quality for, as Sir Arthur says, 'I sought only those objects of great beauty and great value and great history'.

157

THE 'ROMAN BATH' OF STRAND LANE

Strand Lane runs down the east side of King's College; halfway down, at No. 5, you can peer through a window at a curious plunge bath, built of red brick, with a rounded end and measuring about 4m (13ft) by 2m (6.5ft). The bath is fed by a spring that delivers 9,000 litres of icy water every day, then drains into the Thames. Although it was once thought to be of Roman origin, in fact it may only date back to the 17th century.

MIDDLE TEMPLE HALL

This noble building is said to have been opened by Queen Elizabeth I in 1576 and has one of the finest hammerbeam roofs in England. Just as spectacular is the original Elizabethan oak screen at the east end, carved with big bold figures and statues in niches. The serving table, according to legend, is made from the timbers of Sir Francis Drake's ship, the *Golden Hinde*. This is where William Shakespeare took part in a performance of his own *Twelfth Night* on 2 February 1601. *Open* Mon–Fri 10–12, 3–4; closed afternoons if evening function on. *Admission* free).

A dragon's welcome to the City of London at Temple Bar Monument

people a year, as well as having a keen art-going resident population, the museum has made an arrangement to lend objects from its collections to Somerset House, changing them on a regular basis. The first exhibition, for instance, comprised more than 500 works of art—paintings, jewellery, metalwork and antiques—that related to the time of Catherine the Great. Thus, whenever you come to London you can sample a fraction of the Hermitage's collection. Since the exhibitions are temporary and highly popular, timed tickets are often sold in advance.

THE GILBERT COLLECTION (see panel page 157) is reached either by crossing the central court or directly from the Embankment. Comprising more than 800 works of art of the highest quality, this is one of the most important art collections ever given to Britain. To enjoy it fully, take advantage of the free audio-guide.

Given the intricacy of many of the objects, it is helpful that they are divided into small groups, which are displayed separately and are beautifully lit; there are also fold-up stools for use in the galleries. Large pieces of bold mosaic work on the ground floor help you get your eye attuned to what follows. This is the 16th–18th century *pietra dura* (hard stone) inlay using semi-precious stones, an art patronized and developed by the Medici family of Florence.

Upstairs, mosaic is taken to its ultimate refinement, described as micromosaic by Sir Arthur Gilbert. These were created in Rome from the time of the rebuilding of St. Peter's Cathedral, reaching a peak in the 18th century. By this time, as many as 1,500 tesserae might be used in one square inch of a picture. Make time to see some of the 200 tiny and exquisitely decorated snuff boxes and to see the lavish silver and gold tableware, which includes masterpieces by Paul de Lamerie and Paul Storr.

▶ ▶ ▶ Temple　　　　　　　　　　　　　150B3

Inner Temple, EC4 (tel: 020-7797 8250)
Open: Temple Church Wed–Sun 2–4; closed Aug.
Grounds Mon–Fri 12.30–3. Admission free
Underground: Temple (closed Sun), Covent Garden

The Temple takes its name from the Knights Templar, the crusading order whose 12th-century round church survives at the heart of this network of alleys and courtyards. The Temple actually consists of two Inns of Court, the Inner Temple and the Middle Temple, but they are so physically intertwined that they seem like one large collegiate campus, where lawyers in black gowns stroll between their chambers and the Royal Courts of Justice (see page 152), on the opposite side of Fleet Street. Between the Temple and the Royal Courts, in the middle of Fleet Street itself, **Temple Bar Monument** marks the boundary between the City of Westminster and the City of London, guarding the western bound-ary to City of London. Erected in 1880, it is topped by a bronze dragon (the symbol of the City), but is far less imposing than Sir Christopher Wren's original gateway, built in 1672 but taken down when it became an impediment to traffic in 1888.

The Middle Temple, whose past members include Drake, Raleigh, Dickens and Fielding

LAWYERS' HAUNTS
The Wig and Pen (Dining) Club, No. 229 Strand, is a favourite haunt for off-duty lawyers. With its political and legal cartoons in the window, it is set in a tiny timber-framed building of 1625, the only one on the Strand to have survived the Great Fire of London. Nearby, at Nos. 222–225, the Law Courts branch of Lloyd's Bank has a surprisingly ornate interior: Egyptian-style tiles cover the entrance lobby, and the banking hall is decorated with Doulton-tile pictures of flowers, cherubs and historic figures under stucco-work ceilings. All this dates from around 1883 when the building, originally a restaurant, first opened.

159

Near here, on the south side of Fleet Street, a timber-framed gatehouse leads to the calm of Inner Temple Lane. This leads down to the **Temple Church**, past the elaborately carved Romanesque west door, which is no longer used; the entrance is now from the south. The Temple Church's circular nave is known as 'the Round'. It was completed in 1185 and, in common with all the churches built by the Knights Templar, the shape is modelled on the Church of the Holy Sepulchre in Jerusalem. A remarkable series of effigies is set into the floor of the Round. These three-dimensional figures of sleeping knights, dressed in crusading armour, all date from the late 12th and early 13th centuries. The Round was built at the point of transition between Romanesque and Gothic architecture. The chancel, known as 'the Oblong', has the same slender Purbeck marble shafts as the Round, but the style is Early English. Added in 1240, the Oblong has been described as 'one of the most perfectly and classically proportioned buildings of the 13th century in England'.

Leaving the church and turning left past the pretty **Master's House**, you enter **King's Bench Walk**, a fine open space bordered by a handsome terrace designed by Wren in 1677. To the right, in Crown Office Row, is another leafy garden, but this one is strictly for the use of members of the Temple. An archway links Crown Office Row to the cobblestone alley of Middle Temple Lane.

Turn right, then left, into **Fountain Court**, with its tiny, circular fountain itself. Steps lead up on the right to **New Court**, flanked by ornate gas lamps, topped by the lamb and flag symbol of the Middle Temple. Turn right beyond the steps to pass through an arch into Essex Court, then left onto Middle Temple Lane. This brings you to Fleet Street, passing a row of 17th-century timber-framed (but plastered) buildings on the right, whose upper storey juts out to form a covered arcade at street level.

Effigy of a crusading knight in the Temple Church

The City's new face

WEEKEND GHOST TOWN
To enjoy the City's architecture in peace, take a walk through its streets at the weekend. Most churches and public buildings are closed. Exceptions include St. Paul's Cathedral, Broadgate Centre, the Museum of London and the Barbican Centre.

THE CITY The City today still roughly covers the area of the trading city founded by the Romans in AD43, when Emperor Claudius needed a Thames crossing between his ports in Kent and the new Roman province's capital, *Camulodunum* (Colchester). Here, almost 2,000 years later, the City remains the tiny, compact financial heart of Britain. Its soaring modern buildings stand next to medieval lanes and Wren churches; its international businessmen are subject to the rules of the stoically traditional Corporation of London and its Lord Mayor.

THE CITY WALK Starting from Liverpool Street Station, explore the buildings and art of **Broadgate**. Walking down Bishopsgate, turn left into St. Helen's Place to find **St. Helen's Bishopsgate,** London's largest surviving medieval church, with fine memorials. Cutting through to St. Mary Axe, look left up the street to see the Swiss Re Tower (see page 21), then turn right down it and onto Lime Street to see Richard Rogers's **Lloyd's** building (1981–1986), where the marine insurance market founded in the 1680s now insures anything, including a US space rescue operation. Turn right into Leadenhall Place to find busy **Leadenhall Market** and walk through it to Fenchurch Street. Turn left, then right onto **Lombard Street,** with its decorative banking signs.

160

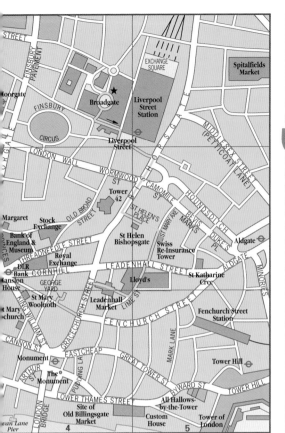

Here, find George Yard on the right and amble through a knot of old lanes, passing the Jamaica Wine House, where the Baltic Exchange began in the 17th century. Turn left onto Cornhill and walk to the junction, **Mansion House Square.** When Britain had an empire, this spot was considered its heart. Here are Nicholas Hawksmoor's beautiful **St. Mary Woolnoth** (1716–1727), Sir William Tite's **Royal Exchange** (1841–1844), and Sir John Soane and Sir Herbert Baker's **Bank of England** (1788–1808 and 1921–1937) with its fascinating little museum round the back, opposite Wren's lovely **St. Margaret Lothbury** (1686–1690). On round Mansion House Square, you can see Stirling and Wilford's controversial rebuilding of **Number One Poultry,** with rooftop restaurant, and George Dance the Elder's **Mansion House** (1739–1752).

Continue by going down Queen Victoria Street, pausing to see the mosaics of the **Roman Temple of Mithras.** Then cut up Bow Lane to Wren's **St. Mary le Bow** (1670–1683), and through King Street to **Guildhall,** whose medieval hall (1411–1440), church of **St. Lawrence Jewry** (Wren, 1670–1687) and clock museum can be visited. Finally, walk along Gresham Street, past lavish **Goldsmiths' Hall** in Foster Lane and some chunks of remaining **London Wall** in Noble Street, to find the **Museum of London** at the roundabout where Aldersgate and London Wall meet.

Bank is to the City what Trafalgar Square is to the West End: a chaotic junction of several roads, surrounded by magnificent public buildings. At the weekend the streets are deserted, but during the week you can stand on any corner at Bank and feel the pulse of this frenetic world of high finance, where international bankers and traders work the investment and money markets worldwide.

DR. JOHNSON'S HOUSE

Tucked behind Fleet Street, tiny Gough Square is a remnant of days when Fleet Street, the artery of information running between the City and Westminster, was alive with printers, publishers, pubs, writers and gossip. Here, between 1749 and 1759, lived the genius Dr. Samuel Johnson (1709–1784). And it was here that he compiled the first comprehensive English *Dictionary*, employing six assistants to help him. Five of them were Scots, and they all worked in the garret on the top floor. When the house fell into disrepair, the press baron Lord Harmsworth bought it in 1911, and it is now a simple tribute to one of London's greatest and most idiosyncratic men, who defined the literary and moral values of his age and is perhaps the greatest English man of letters. Inside, the simply furnished rooms have Johnson's friend Boswell's coffee cup, a teaset from another friend, Mrs Thrale, and portraits of Johnson, Wesley and the actress Mrs Siddons. There is also a portrait of Lord Chesterfield, patron of the *Dictionary*, and a copy of the book itself. (Tel: 020–7353 3745, www.drjohnsonshouse.org *Open* May–Sep Mon–Sat 11–5.30; Oct–Apr Mon–Sat 11–5. *Admission* moderate.)

A good spot for people-watching and admiring the architecture is the triangular space in front of the Royal Exchange, in the angle formed by Threadneedle Street and Cornhill, where there is a statue of the Duke of Wellington (1844). The **Royal Exchange**, built 1843–1844, is a true temple to commerce: The figures carved in the pediment depict Commerce, attended by merchants of all nations, holding the charter granted by Elizabeth I in 1570, the date when the Exchange was first set up to rival that in Antwerp.

Until recently this was where traders in the largest futures market would operate, dressed in coloured waistcoats and using mysterious hand signals and coded shouts. Dealing has now moved to nearby Cannon Bridge Station, Cousin's Lane (no public access) and the Royal Exchange is closed.

With the Royal Exchange behind you, the building on the left is the **Mansion House**, the official residence of the Lord Mayor of London, although today the Lord Mayors use their own homes. Designed and built by George Dance the Elder in 1739–1752, its pediment carvings show London trampling on the figure of Envy (in other words, commercial competitors) and leading in the figure of Plenty. Inside—you can write to Mansion House and reserve a place for the free tours—pictures from the City Corporation's impressive collection hang in the grand rooms. The triangular plot, to the west, on the corner of Poultry and Queen Victoria Street, has been redeveloped. Amid controversy, the Flemish Gothic Mappin & Webb building (1870) was demolished in 1994, to be replaced by James Stirling's landmark office building with its upmarket Terence Conran rooftop restaurant Coq d'Argent.

On the right-hand (north) side of Bank is the vast bulk of the **Bank of England**, after which this whole area is named. The building resembles a fortress: At street level there are no doors or windows in the massive stone walls (except for the main entrance). Sir John Soane' walls (1788–1808) survive surrounding Sir Herbert Baker's rebuilding (1921–1937). Founded in 1694 to fund wars with France, the Bank's role has always been central to the British economy. The Bank is responsible for issuing paper money, raising funds for the government, managing the nation's foreign exchange reserves, setting interest rates and regulating the banking system of the country as a whole. The story of its work is told in an excellent museum in the rebuilt Soane rooms (Bartholomew Lane,

EC2, tel: 020-7601 5545, www.bankofengland.co.uk/ museum. *Open* Mon–Fri 10–5. *Admission* free). Further down Threadneedle Street, Old Broad Street leads left to the **Stock Exchange**. Little did anyone suspect, when this building was opened in 1972, that 20 years later it would have become obsolete. The dealing floor, where jobbers once traded shares in an atmosphere of tense excitement, is empty, since buying and selling is now done by telephone and computer from the offices of brokerage firms.

For a complete contrast, cross Threadneedle Street to explore the alley behind the Royal Exchange leading to **Cornhill**, **Birchin Lane**, and **George Yard**. These little lanes preserve the City's medieval street pattern and are lined with pubs and wine bars. They are a reminder of the days when traders used to do deals in the crowded and congenial coffeehouses, before the markets were institutionalized. Something of the original atmosphere can still be savoured in the oak-panelled upstairs bar of the **Jamaica Wine House**, St. Michael's Alley, Cornhill; this stands on the site of the coffeehouse where traders specializing in West Indian goods, such as rum and sugar, used to meet.

THE LORD MAYOR
The City of London has its own local government, headed by the Lord Mayor since 1192, when Henry Fitzailwyn was installed. Today the mayor is elected to serve for just one year. The election takes place on Michaelmas Day, 29 September, and the mayor is installed in the Guildhall on the Friday preceding the second Saturday in November. The next day the mayor drives through the streets leading the Lord Mayor's Show, a colourful pageant with lavish floats. At the Lord Mayor's Banquet, on the following Monday, the Prime Minister makes an important speech on government policy. The Mayor spends much of the rest of the year attending ceremonial events to raise funds for charity.

163

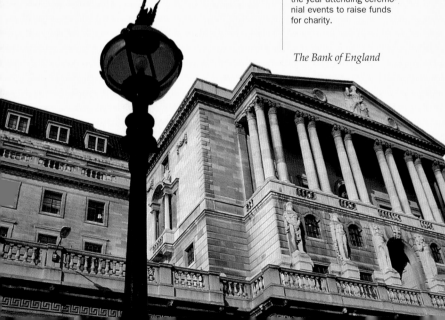

The Bank of England

LONDON'S ROMAN AMPHITHEATRE

In 1988, Museum of London archaeologists unearthed the capital's only Roman amphitheatre in Guildhall Yard. Since the dig finished the remains have been protected in a controlled environment in which they could dry out slowly, thus preventing damage to the ancient masonry. In 2003 the amphitheatre was opened to the public for the first time in nearly 2,000 years via the Guildhall Art Gallery.

Lloyd's of London started life in a humble coffee shop

▶▶▶ Guildhall

160B3

Gresham Street, EC2 (tel: 020-7606 3030)
Open: Guildhall daily 10–5; Clock Museum Mon–Sat 9.30–4.30. Admission free. Guildhall Art Gallery (tel: 020-7332 3700) Mon–Sat 10–5, Sun noon–4. Admission inexpensive; free Fri and daily after 3.30
Underground: Bank

The Guildhall was built in 1411 and, despite severe damage during the Great Fire of London (1666) and the Blitz, its stout medieval walls and impressive undercroft have survived intact. The roof was carefully reconstructed with stone arches by Sir Giles Gilbert Scott in the 1950s. The stained-glass windows incorporate the names of more than 600 past Lord Mayors, and the walls and roof are decorated with the coats of arms and embroidered banners of the City Livery Companies. These are the modern equivalent of the medieval trade guilds, who built the Guildhall for their meetings and ceremonies. The guilds were a powerful force in medieval London, responsible for fixing prices and wages. Today the Livery Companies support the industries they represent (from brewers to weavers) by funding research and education. From their ranks, the Sheriffs and Lord Mayors are chosen to run the City's affairs. The Guildhall is where they are installed. Looking down from the Guildhall's west gallery are two strange figures: Gog and Magog, the mythical giant founders of Albion (Britain). While here, do not miss the Guildhall Art Gallery's pre-Raphelite paintings or the Clock Museum, where 700 finely crafted clocks, watches and clock keys are on show.

Broadgate's hanging gardens, the more acceptable face of 1980s 'Big Bang' architecture

▶ Leadenhall Market   *161A4*

Gracechurch Street, EC3
Open: Mon–Fri
Underground: Bank, Monument

Amid all the markets dealing in stocks, shares, gold, insurance and currencies, Leadenhall Market is a charming oddity that has nothing to do with finance. Traders here sell meat, fish and poultry from shops and stalls on either side of a graceful Victorian arcade designed by Horace Jones in 1881, with highly ornamented façades and a roof of iron and glass. Stallholders mount impressive displays, which could have come straight out of a picture of Victorian or Edwardian London.

▶ Lloyd's of London   *161B5*

Lime Street, EC3
Closed to the public
Underground: Monument

The Lloyd's building, completed in 1986, is one of London's most exciting and controversial modern buildings. Designed by Richard Rogers (also responsible for the Pompidou Centre in Paris), it is a daring building of glass entwined in steel ventilation shafts, cranes, gantries, and staircases. The building is especially thrilling to see at night, when it glows a strange green and purple from concealed coloured spotlights, creating a space-age effect. Ironically, this futuristic building houses one of London's most traditional institutions. Lloyd's evolved in the 1680s as a marine insurance market based at Edward Lloyd's Coffee House on Tower Street.

▶▶ Monument   *161A4*

Monument Street, EC2 (tel: 020-7626 2717)
www.towerbridge.org.uk
Open: daily 9.30–5.30. Admission inexpensive
Underground: Monument

The Monument commemorates the Great Fire of London and was co-designed by Christopher Wren and Robert Hooke. The column was completed in 1677; as the inscription at the base of the column explains, the fire broke out in Pudding Lane, 61m (202ft) away, which is also the height of the column. The gilded bronze urn at the summit symbolizes the flames of the fire. Below the bronze urn is a viewing platform, reached by a dark, spiral staircase of 311 steps. Views stretch to Kent and Sussex.

THE BROADGATE CENTRE

The Broadgate Centre, which wraps around Liverpool Street station at the top of Old Broad Street, is more than just a good example of modern office development. It was a political *cause célèbre*. Begun in July 1985, the first phase of the massive 3.6-ha (9-acre) development was officially opened just two years later. The complex, inspired by Chicago office architecture, is well worth exploring for its elevated walkways, outdoor sculptures, gardens and the amphitheatre used as an ice rink in winter and for open-air entertainment in summer.

SKYSCRAPERS

The 180-m (590-ft) high Swiss Re headquarters 'Gherkin' skyscraper (see page 21) is just the first of a new generation of London skyscrapers that will eventually come to dominate the London skyline. Tallest and most futuristic of all will be London Bridge Tower of 'The Shard of Glass', which at 66 floors and 303m (994ft) will top the current record holder, Canada Tower at Canary Wharf (see page 190) by 16 floors and 66m (216ft). Work has started with completion due by 2009. In the City of London, towering above the existing Tower 42, (184m/604ft) will be the new giants of Minerva Building, which including its spire, will reach a height of 247m (810ft) and the Heron Tower (plus spire) at 222m (728ft).

DIGGING UP LONDON

Laws requiring developers to take archaeology into consideration have meant that as modern London is redeveloped great strides have been made in learning more about earlier periods, especially Roman London. The scale of work going on is huge. The Museum of London's Archaeology Service employs up to 200 archaeologists at any one time; and there are plenty of commercial teams, too. All finds must come to the Museum of London, be it an Iron Age plough tip, a decorated Saxon brooch or an 18th-century Delftware drinking vessel. Roman finds are the most numerous and significant: Since 1985 more than 320,000 sherds of Roman pottery have been found, plus hundreds of other items. Thanks to these digs, we now have a clear picture of the Roman forum and amphitheatre, rebuilt in AD120 to be the empire's largest public building north of Italy (see page 164) in front of Guildhall and now open to the public. We know about the grand Roman baths beneath the remains of Winchester Palace in Southwark, whose wall-painting is similar to those at Pompei. We can plot Britain's Roman roads that all converged on London. Beneath No 1 Poultry, opposite Mansion House, fully equipped shops and houses that lined London's principal thoroughfare in thriving 2nd century London have been unearthed, preserved thanks to the underground Walbrook river. Beneath the Plantation House development, London's largest archaeological dig to date, 43 beautiful gold coins dated AD161–165 were found under a rich merchant's house.

The Roman Gallery

▶▶▶ Museum of London 160C3

150 London Wall, EC2 (tel: 0870-444 3852/0870-444 3851)
www.museumoflondon.org.uk
Open: Mon–Sat 10–5, Sun 11.30–5. Admission free
Underground: St. Paul's, Barbican

This highly entertaining collection is the largest city museum in the world, and traces over 2,000 years of London history through imaginative displays and reconstructions. Check on the extensive programme of special events and lectures on offer before starting your visit. The first gallery, London before London, tells the story of human occupation in the London area from around 500,000BC until the Roman invasion of AD43. Recent archeological excavations (see panel) have provided a wealth of new objects and information, now included in both this and the next gallery on Roman London (don't miss the detailed, large models of London and its port, or the little leather swimming trunks found at the bottom of a 1st-century London well!). A macabre exhibit which appeals to children is the Walbrook Skulls, a collection from the early Roman period found in the Walbrook Stream (now invisible beneath London's streets near the Bank of England). They are thought to mark the site of a pagan ceremony or perhaps to be the heads of pro-Roman Londoners massacred by Queen Boudicca in AD60–61 (see page 24).

Moving on through the centuries, the Early Stuart period (1603–1666) is perhaps the most dramatic time in London's history. The English Civil War, the execution of Charles I, the restoration of the monarchy, the Great Plague and the Great Fire of London are all recalled by relevant pieces: the

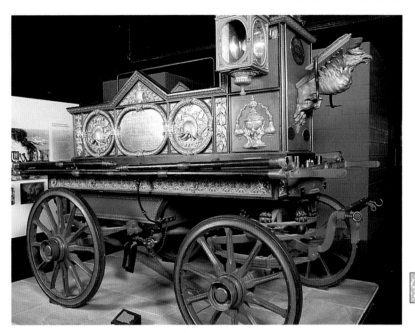

death mask of Oliver Cromwell; a contemporary painting of the procession of Charles II; an actual plague bell, rung to announce the collection of corpses ('bring out your dead'); and the Fire Experience, an audio visual model of London burning to the accompaniment of a reading from the diary of Samuel Pepys, who witnessed the conflagration.

One of the more memorable exhibits from 18th-century London is the reconstruction of dismal Georgian prison cells, complete with graffiti scratched by inmates. By contrast are the costumes of this era and doll's houses that belonged to upper class children. Covering the period from 1789 to 1914 is the World City Gallery, charting the rise of London to become the most important city in the world. Reconstructed streets and shop interiors are the stars.

The growth of the London suburbs is illustrated by 1930s posters and advertisements—many of them art deco exhibits in their own right—extolling the delights of newly built housing subdivisions in the rural-sounding retreats of Golders Green and Hampstead Garden City.

Bringing the story up to date are representations of contemporary London in the permanent galleries and an ongoing series of exhibitions which discuss issues of concern to today's Londoners.

Finally (near the exit, so it can be taken out for ceremonial occasions) there is the Lord Mayor's state coach, made in 1757 and still used for the Lord Mayor's Show every November (see page 163). Before leaving the museum it is worth visiting the well-stocked bookshop, which also sells models and toys.

At time of writing there are major developments in progress and displays may well change. This will cause disruption but some galleries will remain open throughout. The work is due for completion in 2009.

The art of firefighting: an example of an appliance used on the London streets in the 1860s

THE TEMPLE OF MITHRAS
On the raised pavement in front of Bucklersbury House in Queen Victoria Street, you can see one of London's great archaeological finds, dug up nearby in 1954 and reassembled here. It is the ground level of the Temple to Mithras, built in AD240 to serve the growing number of Romano-British followers of this mystical cult that encouraged honesty, purity and courage. (See the sculptures found here on display at the Museum of London.) Several other cults thrived in London at this time together with early Christianity. Many people adopted the Celtic practice of worshipping the mother-goddess or a hunter-god, others kept to traditional Roman gods such as Venus, Mars or Mercury, still others were attracted by the exotic Egyptian goddess Isis and the Asiatic mother-goddess Cybele.

MONUMENTS
Wren did not want his masterpiece cluttered with memorials, but its symbolic importance made this inevitable. One of the most imposing memorials is to Wellington, on the north side of the nave—a huge four poster topped by an equestrian statue. On the opposite side hangs *The Light of the World*, a much-loved painting by Holman Hunt. The tomb of the poet John Donne, on the south side of the choir, shows Donne wrapped in his shroud. It was the only monument to survive the fire that destroyed the medieval cathedral.

▶▶▶ St. Paul's Cathedral 160B2

Ludgate Hill, EC4 (tel: 020-7236 4128)
www.stpauls.co.uk
Open: Cathedral Mon–Sat 8.30–4, Sun services only.
Admission expensive
Underground: St. Paul's

St. Paul's Cathedral is one of the most awe-inspiring sights in London. Its dome, one of the world's largest, dominates the City skyline. The building also manages to communicate a sense of serenity, most notably in the famous (and fabricated) image of 1941 of the dome untouched but wreathed in the smoke and flames of the Blitz. This montage symbolized the undaunted spirit of Londoners during the darkest moments of the war and carried echoes of the cathedral's origins—born out of the flames of the Great Fire of London in 1666.

Wren's English Baroque style mixes High Renaissance ideas of a Greek Cross centralized plan with a traditional long nave demanded by the clergy for their processions—it was a considerable compromise on his original design, a model of which is in the Crypt. It is Wren's dome that gives the cathedral such a wonderfully uplifting atmosphere.

On entering the church it is natural to head for the crossing beneath the dome, with its windows filtering down a

Gibbons' choir stalls

strangely ambiguous golden light. On the pavement below its very heart is a memorial to Wren, composed by his son, which reads *Si monumentum requiris, circumspice* ('If you are seeking his monument, look around you'). The marvellous choir stalls and organ case near John Donne's tomb (see panel) were carved by Grinling Gibbons as part of Wren's original decorative scheme.

Next it is best to visit the crypt, where you can see Wren's actual tomb—a simple black slab—and an audio-visual programme explaining the history and construction of the building, from the laying of the foundation stone in 1675 to the placing of the last stone on the

lantern above the dome in 1708. The crypt is massive, extending beneath nearly the whole of the church. In Painters' Corner the monuments read like a roll call of great artists, from Van Dyck to Constable. George Frampton's memorial is particularly charming and includes a small replica of the Peter Pan statue he made for Kensington Gardens (see page 111). In the middle of the crypt are the ponderous tomb of Wellington and the Renaissance sarcophagus of Nelson. This last was actually made by Benedetto da Rovezzano for Cardinal Wolsey, then confiscated by Henry VIII but never used by him. Instead it remained empty until 1805, when Nelson's body was laid to rest within it, having been brought back from the Battle of Trafalgar pickled in spirits in a barrel. In the Treasury, at the west end of the crypt, you can see Wren's 'Great Model', a scale model in wood of the original design.

After the descent into the crypt the next and most exciting part is the ascent to the dome. In Wren's England the concept of a dome was revolutionary and even today St. Paul's is still the only domed English cathedral. There are 259 steps to the Whispering Gallery. The circular gallery carries sound around so that someone standing on the opposite side will hear your whispers quite clearly after several seconds' delay—though only early visitors will have the peace to test these acoustics properly. There are fine views down to the nave below and up to the frescoes of the dome above.

Continue upwards to the Stone Gallery, which runs around the exterior of the base of the dome. Climbing higher still you pass through the timberwork that rests on the inner dome, supporting the wooden skin of the outer, lead-covered dome. Between these two domes is a third: the brick cone supporting the elegant lantern crowning the whole structure. This can be viewed from the Golden Gallery. There is one last stairway up to the ball, added in 1721, looking over the city from 111.5m (366ft) above the cathedral floor. A hole in the floor of the Golden Gallery lets you look straight down to the cathedral floor.

St. Paul's is undergoing a £40 million restoration programme to coincide with its 300th anniversary in 2008—to prepare the cathedral for its next 300 years.

AROUND ST. PAUL'S
Although St. Paul's itself miraculously escaped major damage in the Blitz, the surrounding area was flattened and then redeveloped in the 1960s with a series of dreary, windswept buildings. These are gradually being replaced with more dynamic architecture. There are also grand schemes proposed for the whole area. They range from the highly modernistic (accused of being out of sympathy with Wren's masterpiece) to the more traditional (accused of being backwards-looking), based on Wren's own plan to surround his church with a series of Italianate piazzas and boulevards. A compromise, the traditional London solution, is likely. If you stand in front of Wren's magnificent façade you, too, may have your own ideas. Here Wren had the word *Resurgam* ('I shall rise again') carved above the door and a phoenix rising from the fire carved in the pediment to symbolize the birth of the new church from the ashes of the old. The baroque twin towers, flanking rows of gigantic columns, a design to which Wren's gifted pupil Nicholas Hawksmoor may well have contributed.

The Great Fire of London broke out at a bakery on Pudding Lane on 2 September 1666. Four days later, when the fire's rage was finally quelled, four-fifths of the City's buildings had been destroyed, including more than 13,000 houses and over 50 churches. The great rebuilding that took place after the fire provided the architects of the day with a wonderful opportunity to create a new city. The churches built by Christopher Wren and his assistants remain one of the great lasting legacies of that age, their spires, towers and domes as much a symbol of the City as the skyscrapers of today's financial institutions.

The mighty bells of Bow, which, according to legend, called Dick Whittington back to the City

THE GREAT BELLS OF BOW
The bells of St. Mary-le-Bow (Cheapside) are of great symbolic importance to Londoners. Only those born within the sound of the 'Great Bells of Bow' qualify as true Cockneys. When the church was hit by a bomb in 1941, sending the bells crashing to the ground, the pieces were saved; in 1962 they were rehung, having been recast, and the church was restored. Of the original Wren church (built 1670–1680), the tower and splendid steeple survive, and below, in the crypt—now home to a very good vegetarian restaurant—restorers found remains of an 11th-century staircase.

St. Martin Ludgate (Ludgate Hill). Built in 1677–1687, this church stands within a short step of Wren's masterpiece, St. Paul's Cathedral. Its spire and portico seem designed to echo the twin towers fronting St. Paul's. Notable features of the interior are the galleries, reached through richly carved doors, and the pulpit.

    St. James Garlickhythe (Garlick Hill). Wren was continually adding spires and towers to his churches in order to improve the London skyline. This church is an example: It was built between 1676 and 1683, but Wren decided to add the graceful spire in the early 18th century. In fact, some architectural historians think the spire may have been the work not of Wren himself but of his assistant, Nicholas Hawksmoor.

    St. Stephen Walbrook (Walbrook). Some consider this to be the most majestic of all Wren's parish churches; it is one in which the architect experimented with ideas later used for St. Paul's, notably the large central dome. Henry Moore's stone central altar was placed below the dome in 1987.

    St. Mary Woolnoth (King William Street). This astonishing building is the work of Nicholas Hawksmoor and was built between 1716 and 1724. Fronted by the powerful west tower, it is a strange and daring building that looks more like a pagan temple than a Christian church. Inside, do not miss the monument to a former rector of the church, John Newton, who died in 1807 having devoted many years of his life to campaigning for the abolition of the slave trade. He also wrote the perennially popular hymn *Amazing Grace*.

St. Mary Abchurch (Abchurch Lane). This is one of the few Wren churches to have remained virtually unaltered, complete with its woodwork. The chief glory is the huge reredos behind the altar, carved by Grinling Gibbons—all the more remarkable when you consider that it was carefully pieced together by restorers in 1948–1953, having been shattered into over 2,000 pieces by a bomb that fell during the Blitz.

St. Helen Bishopsgate (Great St. Helen's). St. Helen is one of the few City churches not to have been destroyed by the Great Fire. Fashionable during the Elizabethan and Jacobean periods, it preserves a remarkable series of 15th-century tomb effigies, including the fine recumbent figures of John and Mary de Oteswich and the wool merchant, Sir John Crosby. A later monument (1636) by Nicholas Stone commemorates the grandly named Sir Julius Caesar Adelmare, a judge in the Court of Admiralty.

St. Katharine Cree (Leadenhall Street). This is another church that escaped the Great Fire, and it is a very rare example of the transition from Gothic to classical, having been built around 1628. The nave arcades are supported on splendid Corinthian columns, but the vaulting is Gothic, as is the splendid rose window, symbolizing the wheel on which St. Katharine was martyred.

SIR CHRISTOPHER WREN
Sir Christopher Wren (1632–1723) was an extraordinary man. In his youth he was regarded as a brilliant mathematician and was appointed Professor of Astronomy at Oxford at the age of 29. With little formal architectural training he launched himself on a glorious career by designing the Sheldonian Theatre in Oxford: He was appointed surveyor general and principal architect for rebuilding the City after the Great Fire, on the strength of a comprehensive plan he drew up. Apart from St. Paul's Cathedral, Wren personally designed 52 churches for the City, of which 23 survived the bombs, Blitz and developers. He also inspired a generation of artists and architects, including Grinling Gibbons, the great woodcarver, and Nicholas Hawksmoor, creator of the English baroque style.

171

CITY LUNCHTIME MUSIC
Many City churches open at lunchtime and stage relaxed, informal concerts played by professionals or students. The City Information Centre, near to St. Paul's Cathedral has a list.

St. Mary-le-Bow, built by Wren, but gutted in 1941. The interior was rebuilt in the 1950s

Vegetarians and the squeamish should be warned that Smithfield is a raw, rough and bloody place—London's main market for meat and poultry. Even those with strong stomachs have been known to blanch at the sight of porters in bloodied aprons running around with great sides of beef or whole pig carcasses slung across their backs. You will also be sworn at in resounding terms if you get in the way— this is a no-nonsense place; visitors are welcome provided they keep in their place.

Above: Rahere's tomb, church of St. Bartholomew-the-Great

172

CLOTH FAIR
Cloth Fair is a quiet little street lined with timber buildings, antiques shops and pubs running down the north side of St. Bartholomew-the-Great. It preserves something of the appearance of pre-Fire London, because the Great Fire died out finally at nearby Cock Lane. No. 43 Cloth Fair was for a long time the home of Sir John Betjeman, Poet Laureate and campaigner for the conservation of Victorian monuments. The house now belongs to the Landmark Trust, an organization that restores historic buildings and rents them as holiday homes (details from The Landmark Trust, Shottesbrooke, Maidenhead, Berkshire SL6 3SW, tel: 01628 825925). The wine bar below and the adjacent pub have walls decorated with Betjeman memorabilia and old photographs of Smithfield. Another excellent pub further down the lane is the tiny Hand and Shears, on the corner of Middle Street, whose wood-panelled rooms, some no bigger than corridors, are usually packed with doctors from St. Bartholomew's Hospital.

Smithfield is the last remaining wholesale market operating in Central London, and it offers a unique example of a sight that was commonplace to Londoners until the 1970s, when cramped working conditions and the difficulties of truck access to London's narrow and congested streets drove long-established markets (such as Billingsgate for fish and Covent Garden for fruit, vegetables and flowers) to new sites on the edge of town. Smithfield (from "Smooth Field") was a livestock market at least as early as 1173, but the sale (and slaughter) of live animals was banned in the 1850s because of the squalor of the streets full of filth and entrails and because the drovers who brought their livestock to the market delighted in terrorizing Londoners by making their charges stampede down the narrow streets. Smithfield has survived on this site because the meat market has declined in recent years, so there is enough space for the traders. Late at night, refrigerated lorries arrive, competing with taxis ferrying Londoners home from the fashionable restaurants and night clubs in Smithfield and neighbouring Clerkenwell. Trade begins in the early hours, when buyers for top restaurants and specialist butchers do their shopping. As dawn breaks they and the market porters enjoy a hearty English breakfast or steak and chips washed down with a pint of beer at one of the local pubs that open at 6.30am.

Trade is finished by 9.30am, when the brightly painted hall falls silent. This glorious building cast-iron and glass building was designed by Horace Jones. Built in 1851–1866, it was revolutionary: Its grand avenue had four huge trading halls, connected to a special Underground railway that linked it to the newly built mainline stations for speedy and healthy distribution through Britain. Later, when refrigeration was introduced, the first consignment of frozen meat arrived from America in 1876.

Alongside the market is **St. Bartholomew's Hospital**, one of the City's four great teaching hospitals. It was founded in 1123 by Rahere, Henry I's court jester, in gratitude for his recovery from malaria, contracted while on a pilgrimage. A small museum is open to visitors (*Open* Tue–Fri 10–4. *Admission* free) where you can see the staircase decorated with paintings by William Hogarth of *The Good Samaritan* and *The Pool of Bethesda*. For a better view however, and also to see the baroque Great Hall, take a guided tour. Outside, over the gateway, you can admire the figure of

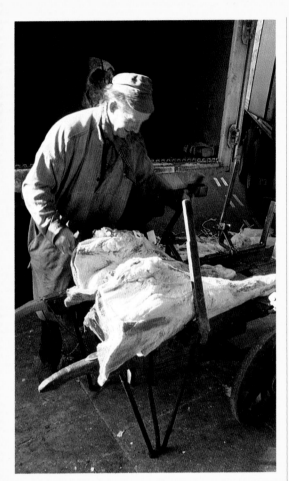

CHARTERHOUSE SQUARE

Charterhouse Square was originally a burial ground for victims of the Black Death, the bubonic plague that decimated London's population in the 1340s. A Carthusian monastery was set up where the monks prayed for the souls of plague victims. The name is an anglicization of Chartreuse, where the Carthusian order was founded. In 1611 the buildings were purchased by Thomas Sutton, who founded the Charterhouse School. (*Guided tours* Apr–Aug Wed 2:15 from main gate; expensive charge. Reservations required in advance tel: 020-7251 5002).

173

The half-timbered 16th-century gate-house leading to the church of St. Bartholomew-the-Great

Henry VIII, the inner courtyard laid out by James Gibbs (1730–1759), and the hospital church of St. Bartholomew-the-Less at any time. (*Guided tours* mid-Apr–Nov, Fri 2pm from main gate; moderate charge; tel: 020-7601 8152).

Just to the east of the hospital entrance is a 13th-century stone archway topped by a timber-framed gatehouse dated 1559. This leads to the quiet churchyard surrounding London's oldest surviving church, **St. Bartholomew-the-Great**, also founded by Rahere, for the Augustinian canons who maintained the hospital. At the Dissolution of the Monasteries, under Henry VIII, the nave was torn down (it stood in the present churchyard and extended to the gatehouse), but the lovely Romanesque choir was allowed to survive, serving as the district's parish church. Rahere himself is buried here beneath the canopied tomb on the north side. On the opposite side, high up on the nave wall, is an oriel window, installed by Prior Bolton at the beginning of the 16th century so that he could observe the monks who were in his charge. The window is carved with a rebus (a pictorial pun) on Bolton's name, consisting of a crossbow bolt and a tun (barrel). The church is closed Saturday afternoons. Tourists are not admitted during services.

London has an extraordinary range of pubs. Some offer live music or theatre, some offer top-quality food at a fraction of the price of a restaurant meal, some have waterside gardens, and many have historical associations and the décor to match.

174

*The pub where
Dr. Johnson drank*

The only surviving galleried inn in London is the **George Inn** in Southwark (77 Borough High Street), now owned by the National Trust. The rambling timber-framed coaching inn dates from 1676 and is unique in preserving its external galleries; Dickens mentions it in *Little Dorrit*. For warm days there is outdoor seating in the courtyard and in summer this is turned into a stage, where excerpts from Shakespeare's plays are performed. The **Black Friar** (174 Queen Victoria Street), on the other side of the river, is worth a visit for its splendid Arts and Crafts decorations (come in the early evening, when it is not too crowded). The interior is a riot of marble, mosaic and woodwork, the walls covered in reliefs of monks at work and play above beautifully lettered mottos exhorting the oblivious drinkers below to reform and improve their dissolute lives. The whole pub is a charming and elaborate joke.

The Counting House (50 Cornhill) in the City is a superb conversion of an imposing bank into a traditional-looking pub, complete with a long horseshoe bar, marble walls, stone mosaics and bare-board floors. It was the first pub to win the prestigious City Heritage Award. Another historic pub to scoop prestigious awards is the **Seven Stars**, built in 1602 and tucked away on Carey Street behind the Royal Courts of Justice. Not surprisingly it fills up with legal types but there are bohemian characters here too and the food as well as the ale is very good.

Even older is the tiny **Olde Mitre** (1 Ely Court, Ely Place), which was founded in 1546. It proudly displays the trunk of a cherry tree around which Queen Elizabeth I is supposed to have danced with one of her favourites, Sir Christopher Hatton, in nearby Hatton Garden. Equally, **The French House** (49 Dean Street) in Soho is easy to visit. A haven for the Free French during World War II, including De Gaulle, it later began to attract writers such as Dylan Thomas and continues its literary associations today.

No historic pub crawl would be complete without a visit to **Ye Olde Cheshire Cheese**, 145 Fleet Street. Built in 1667, it is the least altered 17th-century pub in London, a rambling building of low beams, intimate rooms and sawdust-covered floors. Not all of its original decorations are on display, however. Archeologists researching the fabric of the pub in the 1970s discovered a blocked fireplace in an upper room, which was decorated with a series of 17th-century pornographic tiles. One of the pub's most famous patrons was Dr. Johnson, whose house is just around the corner (see panel on page 162).

MUSIC PUBS

Many pubs have music nights when live bands provide entertainment. Listings magazines provide a comprehensive guide, but the following pubs have well-established reputations for the quality of their acts. The **Half Moon** (93 Lower Richmond Road) in Putney has entertainment every night, usually blues and rock music. The **King's Head** (115 Upper Street) in Islington offers live music as well as adventurous theatrical performances. Jazz lovers in general are very well served, but rarely is good music and good food combined so well as at the **Bull's Head** (373 Lonsdale Road) in Barnes, a huge Victorian pub by the Thames; it is wise to reserve in advance (tel: 020-8876 5241).

Moving closer in to the West End, the **Cittie of York** (22 High Holborn) has several times been voted 'Pub of the Year' by readers of London's *Evening Standard* newspaper. The pub is both huge and intimate, as the drinking area is divided into lots of small, cosy cubicles, designed, it is said, so that lawyers from the nearby Inns of Court can hold confidential discussions with their clients. The large open fireplace intrigues most visitors because it has no chimney (the smoke is carried away by means of a vent in the floor).

A short walk away from the Cittie of York is the **Museum Tavern** (49 Great Russell Street), yet another pub in which you never quite know what famous bottom once occupied the seat you have chosen. As it was so close to the old Reading Room of the British Museum, it was a particularly convenient place for scholars to seek a spot of light relief from their mental labours; even Karl Marx used to slip in here for the odd drink from time to time while writing *Das Kapital*.

Liquid lunch

RIVERSIDE PUBS
There is something truly relaxing about enjoying a pub meal and a pint of beer beside the water. The expanse of The Thames in your view might include rowers, pleasure boats, dredgers or just some seagulls wheeling in the air and some evocative warehouses on the opposite bank. Upriver near Syon House (see pages 232–233), the **London Apprentice** (Church Street, Isleworth) helps you feel a long way from the city. At Richmond, the **White Cross** (Water Lane, Riverside, Richmond) is handy after visits to Richmond Park or Ham House (see page 231). Still in west London, **The Bull's Head** (Strand-on-the-Green, Kew) is perfect after a walk through Kew Gardens (see page 226). In central London, **The Anchor** (Bankside, Southwark) has a large riverside terrace, ideal for a pause between Southwark Cathedral (see page 195) and Tate Modern (see page 204). After a morning at The Tower of London, consider the long established **Prospect of Whitby** (Wapping Wall, Wapping), **The Grapes** (Narrow Street, Limehouse) or the spacious **Captain Kidd** (Wapping High Street, Wapping). At Greenwich, seek out old and charming **Cutty Sark** (Ballast Quay, Lassell Street, Greenwich), while at Canary Wharf in the Docklands, **Via Fossa** is a congenial modern pub (Port East Building, West India Quay).

175

Map labels:

Grand Union Canal (Regent's Canal)
Angel
ISLINGTON HIGH ST
WHARF ROAD
SHEPHERDESS WALK
City Road Basin
St Leonard's Hospital
NEW NORTH ROAD
KINGSLAND ROAD
Geffrye Museum
CITY ROAD
Sadler's Wells Theatre
ROSEBERY AVE
GOSWELL ROAD
JOHN ST
The City University
SHOREDITCH
PITFIELD ST
CALVE AVE
SKINNER ST
PERCIVAL ST
LEVER STREET
BATH STREET
Moorfields Eye Hospital
Old Street
OLD STREET
GREAT EASTERN STREET
CURTAIN ROAD
SHOREDITCH HIGH STREET
Finsbury Leisure Complex
ST JOHN ST
OLD STREET
CLERKENWELL
PEAR TREE CT
CLERKENWELL CLOSE
St James
FARRINGDON RD
CLERKENWELL GREEN
CLERKENWELL ROAD
St John
Wesley's House & Chapel
BUNHILL ROW
WORSHIP STREET
BRITTON ST
ST JOHNS LANE
Museum of the Order of St John
Charterhouse
Bunhill Fields
HATTON GDN
FARRINGDON ROAD
Farringdon
BEECH STREET
ALDERSGATE STREET
Barbican
CHISWELL STREET
Barbican Centre
Guildhall School of Music & Drama
FINSBURY PAVEMENT
Spitalfield Market
HOLBORN VIADUCT
Central Markets (Smithfield)
St Bartholomew's Hospital
The Barbican
St Giles
Moorgate
Broadgate
Liverpool Street Station
MIDDLESEX ST
Petticoat Lane
LONDON WALL
FINSBURY CIRCUS
City Thameslink
NEWGATE ST
Museum of London
MOORGATE
LONDON WALL
BISHOPSGATE
HOUNDSDITCH
Central Criminal Courts
St Paul's Cathedral
St Paul's
Guildhall
CITY
CHEAPSIDE
Bank of England & Museum
Stock Exchange
Tower 42
THREADNEEDLE ST
FLEET STREET

176

1   2   3

CLERKENWELL, ISLINGTON AND THE EAST END

Wrapped around the City to the north and the east are several small communities such as Clerkenwell, Islington, Spitalfields, Whitechapel and Bethnal Green. Each of these communities began as a small village with a parish church, a manor house and cottages around a green. Rapid population growth in the 19th century turned them into one vast metropolitan sprawl. Today, pioneering Londoners have rescued and restored some of the fine buildings, given these distinctive communities a new lease of life, and made them venues for fringe theatre, craftsmen and artists, adventurous restaurants and avant-garde lifestyles.

CLERKENWELL WALK Start at **Farringdon Underground** station, the first Underground station to open in London, on 10 January 1863. Nearby, on Farringdon Road, a Dickensian street market specializes in old books and newspapers. Walking straight up Benjamin Street to Brittan Street, you will see a rare and interesting London addition: a purpose-built townhouse completed in 1987, for the flamboyant TV personality, Janet Street-Porter of the BBC. It has received rave reviews from architects but

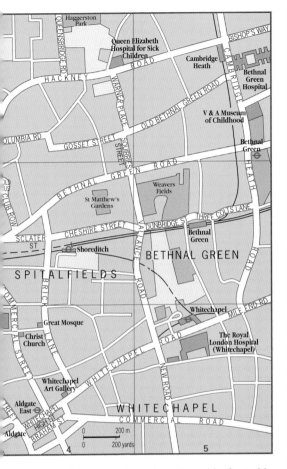

also excited strong reactions from the public for its blue pantiles, brown brick and steel lattice grilles.

Continue up Albion Place, turning left on St. John's Lane to see **St. John's Gate** (1504), the gatehouse of the Priory of St. John of Jerusalem, the English base of the Knights Hospitallers, which evolved into the St. John's Ambulance Brigade. Across Clerkenwell Road is a small **museum** about the Order (tel: 020-7324 4005. *Open* Mon–Fri 10–5; Sat 10–4. *Admission* free. *Guided tours* Tue, Fri and Sat 11 and 2.30. *Moderate donation* requested for tours).

Jerusalem Passage, a narrow alley, links St. John's Lane to Aylesbury Street; turn left to reach **Clerkenwell Green**, where the Palladian-style **Middlesex Sessions House** was built as a court of law in 1779–1782.

Clerkenwell Close winds northwards from the green and leads past another splendid Palladian building: the parish church of **St. James**, built in 1788–1792.

Take the first left, into Pear Tree Court, and left again, to **Farringdon Lane**. Between Nos. 14 and 16, a window reveals the remains of the medieval **Clerk's Well**, after which Clerkenwell is named. The quality of its water accounts for the presence of Booth's gin distillery further down on Turnmill Street, established in the 18th century.

Outdoor terrace at the Barbican

178

THE BARBICAN MAZE
The Barbican's various buildings are linked by a confusing maze of tunnels, elevated walkways and staircases in which it is all too easy to get lost. To improve the situation, yellow markers have been placed on the sidewalks, leading eventually to the **Barbican Centre** arts complex. Alternatively you can use the church of **St. Giles, Cripplegate** for orientation. This Tudor church was left a roofless ruin by the bombing that flattened the surrounding district but was rebuilt in 1952–1960. Surrounded by water, it appears to float on its own island, detached from the massive concrete structures all around. Inside are memorials to people associated with the church: A bust of John Milton, author of *Paradise Lost*, marks the approximate position of his grave. South of the church are remains of the Roman and medieval city walls.

Interior at the Geffrye Museum

▶▶ Barbican Centre   176A2
Silk Street, EC2
(tel: 020-7638 4141). www.barbican.org.uk
Open: Barbican Centre daily 9am–11pm. Admission free
Art Gallery Mon, Wed, Fri–Sun 11–8, Tue, Thu 11–6.
Admission expensive
Underground: Barbican

The Barbican Centre is one of London's most important arts locations. It is the residence of the London Symphony Orchestra who play around 90 concerts here each year, and it mounts important art exhibitions and film seasons. Quite apart from all this there is a full programme of free lobby exhibitions and musical entertainment, weekend activities especially for children, and an excellent bookstore specializing in the arts. The Centre stands on the northern edge of a massive housing complex that is an important example of postwar planning. In 1956, the government proposed that the 14-ha (35-acre) area, left a wasteland as a result of the Blitz, should be developed for housing rather than office buildings. The architects, Chamberlain, Powell and Bon, produced a plan that was very forward-looking in its use of textured concrete. Some 6,500 people now live in the Barbican (which was not finally completed until 1981), many in high-rises over 122m (400ft) high. The buildings are beginning to show their age. It is difficult to imagine how enchanting and futuristic the complex looked when it first opened, with tier upon tier of cascading plants and bright crimson trailing geraniums spilling over every balcony, softening the brutal outlines of the concrete. Most residents have simply given up gardening because of the winds and because so many of them are temporary residents. This gives a certain forlorn, unloved atmosphere to the complex, though the area right around the arts complex is enlivened by sculptures, water gardens, fountains and trees. The best spots to view the Barbican are from the Waterside Café (level 5) or the plant-filled conservatory (levels 8 and 9).

▶▶▶ Geffrye Museum

176C3

Kingsland Road, E2 (tel: 020-7739 9893, recorded information 020-7739 8543)
www.geffrye-museum.org.uk
Open: Tue–Sat 10–5; Sun, Bank Hol Mon 12–5. Admission free
Underground: Liverpool Street then bus: 149, 242, 243, 394

Despite its out-of-the-way location, this treasure of a museum is well worth seeking out. It is like the Victoria and Albert Museum on a very much smaller scale, containing a series of rooms dating from 1600 to the present day, decorated in period style. It was created in 1914 to inspire crafts students in an area that had long been associated with furniture-making. The museum is housed in a row of almshouses grouped around a courtyard, built in 1715 with money bequeathed by Sir Robert Geffrye. At the entrance is a gallery that gives a brief introduction to the displays. Beyond lies the Elizabethan Room, with its rush floor and handsome panelling, beginning a chronological sequence that covers every major period in English history, creating a unique insight into living styles through the centuries.

The later rooms are the most fascinating, especially if you are looking for decorating ideas for your own home. The Mid-Victorian Room, with its bold colour schemes, richly ornamented objects, and busy wallpapers and textiles, may be a little too cluttered for modern living. By contrast the Edwardian Room, named after the Arts and Crafts architect and designer, is furnished with simple pieces whose style has had a major influence on the current generation of furniture designers. Last of all, the extension completed in 1999 includes a fashionable 1990s loft apartment. After the period rooms, explore the Reading Room, restaurant, shop, exhibition gallery and design centre. Don't miss the museum's award-winning walled herb garden (*Open* Apr–Oct) where culinary, aromatic and medicinal plants highlight the traditional past domestic use of herbs. In the summer months there are outdoor concerts.

▶▶▶ REGION HIGHLIGHTS

V & A Museum of Childhood
page 184
Islington
pages 182–183

EAST END PHILANTHROPISTS
Bethnal Green, along with neighbouring Shoreditch and Whitechapel, was notorious in the 19th century for its overcrowded slums and for the poverty of its working-class population. Many attempts were made to improve the quality of life in the East End, not all of them successful or even appropriate. One was the setting up of the Bethnal Green Museum (now the V & A Museum of Childhood, see page 184) in 1875, in an attempt to bring art and culture to the masses. Another was the model housing built at great expense by Miss (later Baroness) Burdett-Coutts, whom Charles Dickens nicknamed Lady Bountiful, after the character in Farquhar's comedy *The Beaux' Stratagem*. These dwellings of the 1860s were themselves condemned as slums a century later and demolished. Model houses of a later period can, however, still be seen in the western part of Bethnal Green. The Boundary Estate, around Arnold Circus (just off Shoreditch High Street), was built in Arts and Crafts style and completed in 1900. The buildings were of such high quality that they inspired urban planners to construct similar complexes to house the poor in Paris, Amsterdam, Berlin and Vienna. A good day to see them is Sunday; the trip can be combined with a visit to the Columbia Road flower market, definitely one of London's most colourful street markets and a place where you can buy top-quality houseplants and flowers at rock-bottom prices (*Open* Sun, 8–2).

179

In addition to hit musicals and popular dramas staged in the West End, London offers a wealth of quality entertainment for lovers of music, theatre, opera and dance. Two of the principal sites for the performing arts are the Barbican Centre and the South Bank Centre. Other venues range from the huge Royal Albert Hall to intimate Wigmore Hall.

The Barbican Centre (see page 178) houses two stages, the large, proscenium Barbican Theatre and the intimate, flexible Pit. The Bite season at the Barbican presents fresh new work that includes a mix of dance and music, as well as theatre.

Sharing the Barbican Centre is the **London Symphony Orchestra**—not only London's oldest orchestra but also the first to be run by its members. The LSO was formed in 1904 by 50 musicians from Henry Wood's Queen's Hall Orchestra, who walked out after a dispute and formed their own self-governing body. Guest conductors are chosen by the orchestra members. The LSO tries to include new or rarely performed works in its Barbican concerts, along with the more popular pieces that are considered essential for attracting large audiences.

On the South Bank, the Royal Festival Hall—the subject of a £91 million revamp, incorporating stunning new acoustics, completed in June 2007— is the place to go for large-scale classical music performances. Top orchestras such as the **Philharmonia** and the **London Philharmonic** perform here regularly, benefitting hugely from the new acoustic. Next door, the **Queen Elizabeth Hall** stages dance, chamber music, opera and the occasional theatrical production, while the intimate **Purcell Room** is the ideal place for piano and song recitals.

The **Royal National Theatre**, also part of the South Bank complex, has three stages and enjoys similar status to the RSC. The building was planned to allow a great variety of production styles, ranging from experimental drama staged in the intimate and flexible Cottesloe Theatre to more traditional productions on the proscenium stage of the Lyttleton, and the large-scale productions in the Olivier Theatre.

The huge **Royal Albert Hall** is used for a wide variety of programmes, ranging from rock and pop spectaculars to mime, ballet,

180

The Coliseum, in St. Martin's Lane, home of the English National Opera

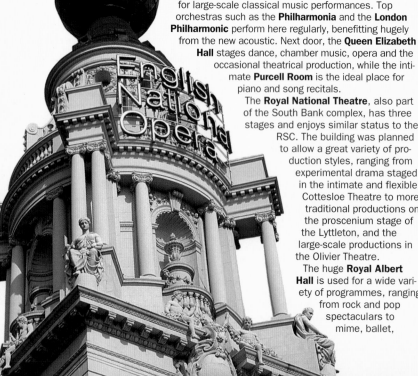

Christmas carol concerts and, most famously, the summer-long season of Henry Wood Promenade Concerts, when tickets at all prices, some sold on the day, fill the auditorium with music lovers every night. In contrast, **Wigmore Hall** was built in 1901 by Friedrich Bechstein, adjoining his piano showrooms and—apart from the churches—is probably London's most sympathetic setting for chamber music and recitals.

For ballet lovers the **Royal Ballet**, based at the Royal Opera House, Covent Garden, may be the best known London company with the most glittering stage (and audience), but it faces healthy competition.

The **English National Ballet** are based at the London Coliseum, St. Martin's Lane, and in particular their performance of the *Nutcracker* (staged every December) is perennially popular. The **Sadler's Wells Theatre** (Rosebery Avenue) reopened in 1998 in a newly built theatre. It presents avant-garde touring international dance companies, as well as a wide selection of home-based talent such as the Rambert Dance Company, the London Children's Ballet and the British Youth Opera.

The Contemporary Dance Trust helped put London in the forefront of modern dance festivals. The major dance festival of the year is staged in October and November by **Dance Umbrella** at various venues (tel: 020-8741 4040, www.danceumbrella. co.uk for details). **Riverside Studios** (Crisp Road, Hammersmith) is a busy and youthful arts venue specializing in new work in all media. Opera has two principal venues: the Royal Opera House (see page 147), re-opened in 2000; and the Coliseum home to the English National Opera (ENO). Visiting companies use these and the splendidly grand Hackney Empire, a Victorian music hall that was revived in 1987.

London also stages a wide variety of festivals. Some districts use them to reinforce local community spirit (see panel). Other events indulge fans of a particular medium: Among the best are the The Times BFI London Film Festival, hosted at venues in London during the last two weeks of October and the Tower Music Festival (popular music) held the Tower of London in June and July (tickets from Ticketmaster tel: 0870-169 187 or personal callers at the Tower of London, daily 10–4, www.towermusicfestival.co.uk). Several London theatres run back-stage tours, including the RNT, Shakespeare's Globe and the Theatre Royal, Drury Lane. For more options see also **Nightlife**, pages 244–245.

ARTS FESTIVALS

One of the most impressive of London's many arts festivals is the City of London Festival (tel: 020-7377 0540), when during the first two weeks of July music, poetry, drama and other arts fill remarkable City buildings often closed to the public at other times. Other festivals include the Spitalfields Festival in June featuring early, new, chamber and world music that reflects the local Bengali/ Bangladeshi community, and the Greenwich and Docklands International Festival held in June, a festival of outdoor performance and artworks. The Kenwood Lakeside Concert season has been under threat with no performances in 2007. It is hoped that they will resume in 2008.

181

Musical treats

Islington has become a chic address for young Londoners. For those who can afford them, its terraces of late 18th- and early 19th-century houses offer elegant living in spacious well-proportioned rooms relatively close to the City and central London. As a result, Islington has a lively atmosphere, with street markets, theatres, restaurants and pubs.

ISLINGTON THEATRES
Half-a-dozen quality fringe theatres include **The King's Head**, 115 Upper Street, one of London's oldest and most vibrant pub theatres, a Victorian gem. The **Almeida Theatre**, Almeida Street, is at the forefront of avant-garde theatre, while puppets of all sizes star at the unique **Little Angel Theatre**, 14 Dagmar Passage, on Saturday and Sunday (closed Aug).

From King's Cross Road, a walk up Vernon Rise soon brings you to the elegant stucco-fronted houses of Percy Circus, developed from 1819, where Karl Marx lived for a time. More genteel houses in the same mould line the streets and squares to the south, such as Prideaux Place and Lloyd Square. Across Amwell Street, Myddelton Square, with its gardens surrounding St. Mark's Church, stands at the heart of the New River Estate. This was developed in the 1820s from the profits generated by the New River Company, which had brought fresh water to London from the River Lea in Hertfordshire, over 64km (40 miles) away since 1613, and still supplies this part of London with drinking water today. It was the brainwave of Sir Hugh Muddleton, a Welsh goldsmith who became a jeweller to James I.

From Myddelton Square, Mylne Street leads north to busy Pentonville Road where the **Crafts Council** has lively exhibitions. A detour here, down to Rosebery Avenue, reaches

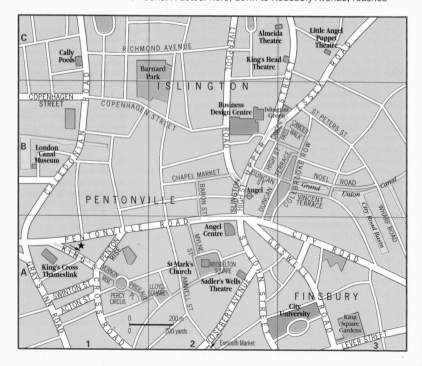

Sadler's Wells Theatre, whose entirely new building opened in 1998, designed by Renton Howard Wood Lewis Partnership. Up Baron Street, you will find Chapel Market, a traditional local street-market where stall-holders sell top-quality fruit, vegetables, flowers and fish. Upper Street leads northwards to Islington Green.

On the left, the cast-iron and glass structure built in 1861–1862 as the Royal Agricultural Hall, a wholesale market for livestock, is now the **Business Design Centre**, a permanent showcase for British design, and usually open to the public.

Across the street, on a more intimate scale, **Camden Passage** is lined with antique shops tucked into Georgian houses. On Saturdays and Wednesdays, street stalls set up here from 7am, selling a mix of antiques and collectables, including jewellery, toys, clothing, books and records. Nearby is the Camden Head (2 Camden Walk), a busy Victorian pub with a patio for outdoor drinking in summer.

Camden Walk leads to Colebrooke Row and the parallel Duncan Terrace, two long rows of town houses, built from 1768 onwards. Halfway down Colebrooke Row, on the left, Vincent Terrace is another pretty spot. It sits alongside the Grand Union Canal at the point where it emerges from the Islington Tunnel. The tree-filled gardens of Noel Road, backing onto the opposite bank of the canal, gives this attractive residential district an almost rural feel, and there are several good pubs serving food nearby, including the Narrow Boat, near Wharf Road Bridge, and the Island Queen, 87 Noel Road.

Those keen on contemporary art should walk northwards along Upper Street to Canonbury, to visit the Estorick Collection of Modern Italian Art (Northampton Lodge, 39a Canonbury Square, N1; tel: 020-7704 9522, *Open* Wed–Sat 11–6, Sun 12–5. *Admission* moderate) and enjoy pictures by Balla, Boccioni and Carra, plus an excellent garden café and gallery shop.

LITTLE ITALY

Rosebery Avenue, leading south from Islington, cuts through the district once known as Little Italy because of the large community of Italians that lived here in the 19th century, many making their living as entertainers and ice-cream manufacturers. Exmouth Market, with its Italianate Church of the Holy Redeemer, its delicatessens, and its market, still has a Little Italy flavour. It was here, at No. 8, that Joseph Grimaldi, one of the most famous pantomime clowns of the 19th century, once lived; he first appeared on stage as a child dancer at the Sadler's Wells Theatre on Rosebery Avenue.

BUNHILL FIELDS

Bunhill Fields, on City Road across from Wesley's House, is the burial place of several Nonconformists, including the author of *Robinson Crusoe*, Daniel Defoe; the poet William Blake; the hymn writer Isaac Watts; and the author of *The Pilgrim's Progress*, John Bunyan. Originally the cemetery was a plague pit, opened up during the Great Plague that hit London in 1665, when people were dying in such numbers that their remains were simply dumped into one huge mass grave. Because it was never consecrated, the burial ground was later favoured by Quakers, Methodists, and other Nonconformists, who could be buried according to their own rites rather than those of the established church. Today the cemetery is a delightful tree-shaded spot full of wildflowers.

184

THE RAGGED SCHOOL MUSEUM

If you are interested in the social history of the East End, pay a visit to the Ragged School Museum (44–50 Copperfield Road, E3; tel: 020-8980 6405, www.raggedschool museum.org.uk. *Open* Wed, Thu 10–5 (also 2–5 first Sun each month). *Admission* free). Ragged Schools were philanthropic Victorian institutions that provided education and two meals per day to children who could not pay their way. This particular school accommodated more than 1,000 pupils and functioned between 1877 and 1908.

▶▶ V & A Museum of Childhood 177C5

Cambridge Heath Road, E2 (tel: 020-8983 5200/5201)
www.vam.ac.uk
Open: Daily 10–5.45. Admission free
Underground: Bethnal Green

This museum of childhood holds one of the largest collection of toys in the world, so there is plenty to justify the trip out to a slightly off-beat area of the East End, perhaps following it with a visit to the nearby Geffrye Museum (see page 179) and Spitalfields (see pages 186–187). A branch of the Victoria and Albert Museum, this collection is housed in an interesting iron-and-glass building that originally stood on the V&A's South Kensington site, but was re-erected here in 1872.

A wonderful collection of 50 doll's houses is displayed in the museum's upper gallery. You can peer into the tiny world of a grand late-19th century country house, stuffed with heavy furniture, or envy the lifestyle of the tiny inhabitants of Whiteladies, a stylish 1930s modernist house.

The lower galleries, collectively The Moving Toy Gallery, are used to display a huge toy collection, grouped by type (dolls, trains, teddy bears, optical and musical toys, for example). The earliest exhibits are 17th-century, and there are toys from every corner of the world.

The upstairs galleries include displays that illustrate the history of childhood and the process of growing up, through exhibits such as baby equipment, nursery furniture, children's clothes and teenage fads and fashions. There is also a collection of children's books from the last three centuries.

Most weekends and during school holidays the museum mounts a programme of activities for children. There is a licensed café and a good shop. Temporary exhibitions take place in the Central Hall. A major restoration scheme has created an excellent and improved facility.

▶ Wesley's Chapel, House and Museum 176B2

49 City Road, EC1 (tel: 020-7253 2262)
www.wesleyschapel.org.uk
Open: Mon–Sat 10–4, Sun 12.30–2. Admission free
Underground: Old Street

John Wesley, the founder of Methodism, lived in this Georgian house from 1779 until his death in 1791, along with several fellow preachers. Methodists from all over the world come here to see the relics of their founder, but the museum is also of interest as a monument to non-conformity. It is interesting to note, for example, that former Prime Minister Margaret Thatcher was married in the chapel attached to the house—as many commentators have noted, the enterprise culture which she espoused during her premiership is a direct product of nonconformist values and the Puritan work ethic. This chapel was designed by Wesley himself and completed in 1778 in a style that he summed up as 'perfectly neat, but not fine'. In the crypt you can watch a video on the history of Methodism, before touring the house. Here you can see portraits of Wesley, his clothes, furniture, pens, annotated books and the prayer room in which he used to kneel at 4am every morning awaiting his daily orders from God. You can also see the electric shock machine that Wesley used in an attempt to cure his bouts of melancholia. Donations are welcome.

▶▶ Whitechapel Art Gallery   177A4

80–82 Whitechapel High Street, E1 (tel: 020-7522 7888)
www.whitechapel.org
Open: Wed–Sun 11–6 (Thu until 9pm). Admission free
Underground: Aldgate East

This gallery in the East End has an international reputation for its provocative exhibitions of modern art. It also stages quality exhibitions of Asian art, reflecting the local Bengali immigrant population. The vibrant bi-annual Whitechapel Open is unique: an exhibition that spreads art from the gallery to include the studios of many of the estimated 10,000 artists living in the area. The building itself is a fine example of the Arts and Crafts style. The gallery was founded in 1901 by the social reformer and ardent missionary, Canon Samuel Augustus Barnett, whose avowed aim was to 'decrease not suffering but sin'. He mounted exhibitions of paintings here that were extremely popular with East Enders. The Whitechapel is undergoing a major development project and the expanded gallery is due to open in 2008.

WHITECHAPEL
Whitechapel was named after its whitewashed parish church and was the place where church bells were cast for parish churches up and down the land. The Whitechapel Bell Foundry, 32 Whitechapel Road, moved here in 1738 and made such notable bells as Big Ben and the original Liberty Bell. The firm now repairs historic bells. In the 19th century Whitechapel was flooded with Jewish refugees from Eastern Europe. Some of their children went on to make a fortune (including Alfred Marks, cofounder of the Marks and Spencer chain). Most moved on to less crowded suburbs, such as Golders Green.

185

The splendid art nouveau building of the Whitechapel Art Gallery, designed in 1899 by Charles Harrison Townsend

A visit to Spitalfields lets you sample the surprising contrasts of London's East End. This neighbourhood has long been a home to refugees. Its character was formed by Huguenot weavers whose houses, many of them still standing today, had skylit attics where weavers worked to produce fine silk cloth. Then came Jewish refugees from Russia and Poland, who specialized in furs and leather. These were followed in the 1970s by Bengali immigrants, who now toil over sewing machines and steam irons, producing garments for sale in London's clothes shops and street markets. Meanwhile, discerning Londoners have restored many of the East End's elegant Georgian houses.

186

JACK THE RIPPER
In modern parlance, Jack the Ripper would be called a serial killer. His six victims were murdered over an eight-week period beginning on 7 August 1888, when the first horribly mutilated body was found by a Spitalfields Market porter in nearby Gunthorpe Street. The Ten Bells pub, near Christ Church on Commercial Street, has a window engraved with the full list of his victims. The police's failure to find the notorious murderer led to the resignation of the London Police Commissioner. The celebrated case stimulated the public's appetite for crime and detective stories, such as *The Adventures of Sherlock Holmes*, which Sir Arthur Conan Doyle began to pen in 1891.

The Spitalfields area lies east of Liverpool Street Station and Broadgate (see page 165), recently restored to its full Victorian splendour. Cross Bishopsgate to Artillery Lane, a narrow alley where No. 56 preserves a rare example of an 18th-century shop front. Turn left and you will reach **Spitalfields Market**, now one of London's trendiest street markets that takes place under a glass roof in Commerical Street and features aromatherapy products, CDs, books, jewellery, crafts, second-hand books, fashion and retro clothing, and antiques (on Thursdays). On Thursday, Friday and Sunday there is a covered Fine Food

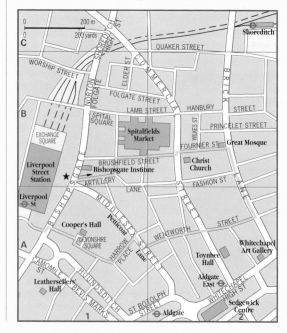

Market (10–5) at **Crispin Place** in the heart of Spitalfields. The market is open weekdays from 10–4 and on Sundays from 9–5. Christ Church, towering above the eastern end of the market, may become the focal point of the development. Built in 1714, this is Nicholas Hawksmoor's masterpiece, and it provokes much debate because of its mixture of classical, Renaissance and baroque elements. Long neglected, and even threatened with demolition, it is now used both as a church and as a concert hall. Some of the gravestones in the churchyard have epitaphs in French, marking the graves of Huguenot refugees who found a haven here after 1685 when the Edict of Nantes, which had guaranteed their right to religious freedom, was revoked. Some grew wealthy as master weavers in the manufacture of silks, damasks and velvets. Their houses can be seen in **Fournier Street**, to the north of Christ Church. Built between 1718 and 1728, several were restored by their owners with a devoted respect for authenticity, rescuing what were regarded as slum properties in the 1970s, faced with the threat of demolition.

Brick Lane is now the heart of a large community of Bangladeshis, who fled their homeland after the demise of East Pakistan. Lined with shops selling exotic groceries, brightly printed fabrics and saris, the simple restaurants serve some of the most authentic Bengali food to be found in London.

On Sundays, this whole area seems like one huge street market. At the northern end of Brick Lane, stalls are set up at dawn. Further south and west, Commercial Street, Wentworth Street and Middlesex Street are crammed with the stalls of Asian, Cockney and Jewish traders on the weekend.

On the way back to Liverpool Street, it is worth seeking out Devonshire Square where, cheek by jowl with the bustling markets, is an office development sited within a group of warehouses dating from the late 18th century and originally built for the East India Company.

PRESERVED HOUSES
In the 1970s, a group of pioneer conservationists, passionate about London's remarkable buildings that were disappearing beneath the developers' bulldozers, bought several of the fine but dilapidated Georgian houses in and around Fournier Street. While restoring their own homes meticulously, they founded the Spitalfields Centre in 1977 (19 Princelet Street, tel: 020-7247 5352), which today continues to identify suitable properties and find new owners who will repair them. One house, 18 Folgate Street, was bought and restored by the late Dennis Severs, and is regularly open to the public (tel 020-7247 4013, reservations essential). Visitors experience the house's own changing atmospheres down the generations as they visit the different period decorations on each floor.

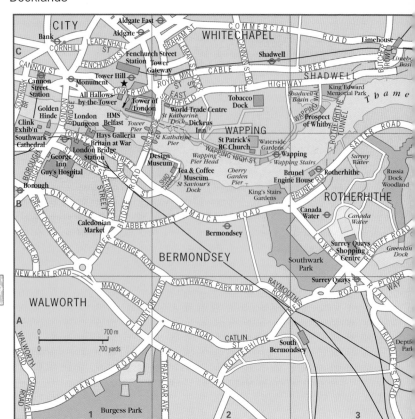

Above: St. Katharine's Dock. Right: Canary Wharf Tower

DOCKLANDS London's former docklands lie to the east of the City, covering an area equal to the rest of central London. When the docks fell silent, a massive project backed by the government started in 1981 to create an infrastructure that would encourage the development of new apartments, offices and leisure facilities. Almost a generation later, despite relentless criticism, this new Docklands is maturing. Set on London's most beautiful natural site, with the Thames snaking through land cut with a patchwork of water-filled docks, it houses 83,000 people—aiming to be 100,000 by 2010—55,000 commute here daily and the occupation rate of the offices is an average of 95 per cent. Canary Wharf, with Cesar Pelli's soaring tower, is the central piece, but many other architects have contributed notable buildings. The high-level Docklands Light Railway skims past these and past urban farms, parks, sports marinas, waterside restaurants and restored dock buildings, including the Museum in Docklands.

DOCKLANDS WALK This walk takes in old Docklands, as well as the remodelled buildings and brand new ones.

From Tower Hill tube station exit to your left and walk towards Tower Bridge. Just before it, steps lead down to the Tower Thistle Hotel. St. Katharine's Dock, beyond, opened in 1828 and closed down in 1968. It then became the first chunk of Docklands to be restored, complete with

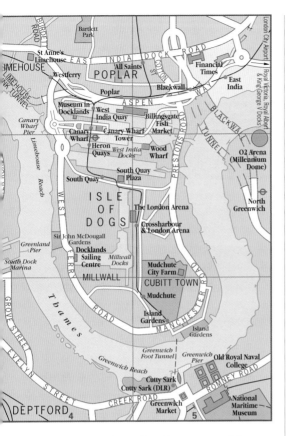

the boat basins and the Dickens Inn, converted from an 18th-century brewery (see page 194).

St. Katharine's Way leads south from the Dock, providing a link to Wapping High Street. This stretch of the route is lined with warehouses built to store tropical spices and valuable hardwoods. Now they have been made into chic loft apartments, although prices have fallen since the 1980s, when a Docklands apartment was the ultimate coveted symbol of success. Further on, **Wapping Pierhead** is lined with Georgian houses, once the homes of wealthy wharf owners. Beyond this, **Waterside Gardens** has views towards Hawksmoor's baroque church, **St. George-in-the-East**. Continue down Wapping High Street, past the Wapping tube station, and turn right on Wapping Wall for the **Prospect of Whitby** pub, once a haunt of Samuel Pepys and artists such as Turner and Whistler, who came to paint the river views.

To enjoy an overview of London's Brave New Docklands World, take a ride on the elevated **Docklands Light Railway▶▶**. It runs from Bank and Tower Gateway Station (by Tower Hill underground station) through the heart of Docklands, under the Thames south to Greenwich, Deptford and Lewisham, east on to Beckton and a branch to London City Airport. To enjoy the riverside Canaletto view of Greenwich, get off at Island Gardens and walk through the Foot Tunnel to Greenwich (see page 216–217).

Tug in retirement in front of the Museum in Docklands

MUSEUM IN DOCKLANDS
This exciting museum celebrates the story of London and its river, port and people from Roman times until today. Indeed, its home is one of its exhibits: a four-floor Georgian warehouse that once stored sugar and rum. Its rich collection is composed of several elements: the Museum of London's huge Port and River Collection, the Port of London Archive including many photographs, and the objects found or saved during the redevelopment of the Docklands, from Medieval vessels and small Roman pieces to giant cranes. One excellent exhibit is a recreated Regency-period panorama of the Port of London, while documentary films include interviews with dock workers. Some children's gallery exhibits even have appropriate smells. (Warehouse No. 1, West India Quay, Canary Wharf, E14; tel: 0870 444 3857, www.museum indocklands. org.uk. *Open* daily 10–6. *Admission* moderate).

▶▶ Canary Wharf and the Docklands   189C4
Canada Square, E14
DLR, Underground: Canary Wharf station
In 1988 the master planners, Skidmore, Owings & Merrill Inc, began to develop this huge site as a new financial complex, a self-contained mini-city covering 28 ha (69 acres). A new railway (the DLR) and airport (London City Airport) were part of the plan. Today, Canary Wharf is central to the revived Docklands. It is well worth a look.

No. 1 Canada Square, Cabot Place and DLR's Canary Wharf station are all designed by Cesar Pelli. Its landmark tower, Britain's tallest, soars 243m (797ft) high, described by the architect as 'a square prism with a pyramidal top in the traditional form of the obelisk—this is the essence of the skyscraper'. The first skyscraper to be clad in stainless steel, it reflects light bounced off the surrounding water. Around it are a number of small squares, with shops restaurants and buildings designed by Troughton McAslan (25 North Colonnade), Terry Farrell (15 Westferry Circus) and Foster and Partners (33 Canada Square and 8–16 Canada Square). There are music and arts events in the public spaces, gardens and parks, and the art commissions include Bruce McLean's Watercourt railings, Richard Chaix's Cabot Square fountain, Guiseppe Lund's Westferry Circus gates and Rod Wales's benches for Wren Landing.

▶▶ Firepower
The Royal Arsenal, Woolwich (tel: 020-8855 7755)
www.firepower.org.uk
Open: Apr–Oct Wed–Sun 10.30–5; Nov–Mar Fri–Sun 10.30–5. Admission moderate
Woolwich Arsenal railway station; ferry from Greenwich
Newly housed in fine historic buildings, the Royal Artillery collections of instruments and accessories of warfare include Roman trebuchets, a Greek ballista and Tudor naval guns, as well as the notorious Iraqi supergun—plus plenty of uniforms, silver, paintings and models.

▶ HMS *Belfast*   188C1

Morgan's Lane, Tooley Street, SE1 (tel: 020-7940 6300)
www.hmsbelfast.imw.org.uk
Open: daily 10–6; Nov–Feb 10–5
Admission expensive, children free
Underground: London Bridge, Tower Hill

HMS *Belfast* is one of the largest warships ever built for the British Navy. Saved from the scrap yard in 1971, the ship is now moored on the Thames and is an outpost of the Imperial War Museum. Today her seven cramped, labyrinthine decks, which once accommodated a crew of up to 800 men, give landlubbers a salty flavour of the rigours of serving at sea. The ship is particularly popular with small children who love scrambling up and down its narrow, steep ladders and exploring its warren of rooms.

▶ Limehouse and Wapping   189C4

DLR: Limehouse station

Once known for ship-building, warehouses, smugglers and Chinese opium-dens, this is now the smartened up link between the City and the Docklands. Elegant Georgian houses and warehouse conversions are the background for old riverside pubs such as The Grapes (76 Narrow Street) and The Prospect of Whitby (57 Wapping Wall). Opposite this pub stands The Wapping Hydraulic Power Station, revived as The Wapping Project, a forum for contemporary arts that includes a theatre, restaurant and exhibitions (tel: 020-7680 2080. *Open* Tue–Sat 12–10.30; Sun 12–6).

Canary Wharf, a monument to market optimism

▶ ▶ ▶ REGION HIGHLIGHTS

Canary Wharf
page 190
Design Museum
page 193
Docklands Light Railway
page 189
Tower Bridge page 196
Tower of London
pages 196–197

ROTHERHITHE
The docklands on the southern side of the Thames, across from Limehouse, have none of the glamour associated with the redeveloped areas of Wapping or the Isle of Dogs, but they have seen their fair share of history. You can get to Rotherhithe by train from Wapping station, passing beneath the river in a tunnel that was first opened in 1843 as a footpath to enable dockers living on the south bank to walk to their places of work in the north. The engineer was Marc Brunel (father of Isambard Kingdom). The Brunel Engine House, a short walk north of Rotherhithe station on Tunnel Road, was built to pump water out of the tunnel during its constru ction. Now it is a lively museum celebrating Brunel's achievement (Railway Avenue, SE16, tel: 020-7231 3840. *Open* daily 10–5. *Admission* inexpensive). Immediately to the west is the Mayflower pub (117 Rotherhithe Street). Near here, the Pilgrim Fathers set sail in the *Mayflower* bound for Plymouth, Massachusetts, in 1620. The pub sells special American postage stamps commemorating the *Mayflower* for the benefit of US visitors. The captain of the *Mayflower*, Captain Jones, is buried in the nearby church of St. Mary the Virgin, among other monuments to merchants, shipbuilders and sailors.

191

London Bridge City is the redeveloped strip of waterfront on the south bank of the Thames, stretching from London Bridge eastwards to Tower Bridge and beyond, into Shad Thames. It is part of Bermondsey, stretching inland, which gained Victorian importance when wharves were built on the south bank to ease shipping congestion. Here, such longstanding institutions as New Caledonian Market survive amid the spunky revival of one of the last areas of inner London to be smartened up.

NEW CALEDONIAN MARKET

Something of the shadowy world of Dickensian London lives on in the New Caledonian Market (confusingly, this is also known as the Bermondsey Antiques Market—it is located at the junction of Long Lane, Bermondsey Street and Tower Bridge Road). The market, which claims to be the biggest of its kind in Europe, opens to the public at 7am every Friday, but long before the ordinary buyers arrive, a huge amount of trading will already have taken place between the stall-holders themselves and the professional dealers who swoop at the crack of dawn to snap up the prize pieces. Everyone involved in the market denies that this is where thieves and burglars dispose of their stolen goods, but the suspicion lingers. This should not stop anyone who is interested in antiques and bric-a-brac from visiting, if only to savour the atmosphere and see the vast array of *objets d'art* on sale. The terms are strictly cash, and persistent haggling is essential if you do not want to pay an exaggerated price. By 9am most of the serious business will be over for the day.

Market-style barrows at Hay's Galleria

Modern, sleek towers of glass in London Bridge City stand hard by survivors from docks days, including several giant warehouses now transformed into fashionable, airy loft apartments.

Starting at London Bridge (see map on pages 188–189) and following the riverside path, called St. Martin's Walk, you will come to **Hay's Galleria**, a stylish if somewhat contrived shopping mall. The original Hay's Wharf has been filled in to create a courtyard for sidewalk cafés and gift stalls, sheltered from the elements by a glass atrium supported on iron columns. The blend of old and new works extremely well. Passing through the Galleria to Tooley Street you will find the art deco façade of St. Olaf's House to the right (west), built in 1931 as the Hay's Wharf Company Offices by the architect H. S. Goodhart-Rendel. The jazzy stripes of this extraordinary building, now fully restored, look exotic among the dark alleys and the utilitarian architecture of the warehouses that surround it.

Going back through Hay's Galleria and turning right (east), it is possible to follow the newly created riverside walk up to Tower Bridge. On the east side of the bridge, is **Shad Thames**, land once owned by the Knights Templar (its name is a corruption of St. John at Thames). Here warehouse walls rise sheer as cliffs, linked, high above, by a network of metal gangway bridges formerly used by warehouse workers to move loads to and from the

interconnecting buildings. Despite the dark and gloomy alleys, the apartments here (which were formerly spice warehouses) are highly prized because of their proximity to the City.

The area between Shad Thames and the river is known as **Butler's Wharf**. It is a huge, exemplary development (1987–1989) by Conran Roche, combining revitalization with conservation to preserve the historical spirit of the spice warehouses. Sir Terence Conran, style guru since the 1960s and founder of Habitat Stores and The Conran Shop, masterminded it, and his first-floor restaurants (marginal river views) and delicatessen open onto the wide riverside promenade.

Right on the bend, where Shad Thames curves round St. Saviour's Dock, is the **Design Museum** (Shad Thames, SE1; tel: 0870-833 9955, www.designmuseum.org. *Open* daily 10–5.45. *Admission* expensive), another brainchild of Sir Terence Conran. The core of the museum, itself a modernist warehouse conversion, examines how design affects our lives. Exhibits include everyday objects, from typewriters and kettles to automobiles, selected as classics of modern design and permanently displayed as a study collection. This is augmented by stimulating temporary exhibitions. The museum has a very good bookshop, and reference library, and the upstairs Blueprint Café (which is actually an upmarket restaurant) boasts wonderful river views. In all, the developers' mixture of dynamic conservation and exciting new buildings on this bank contrasts strikingly with the area east of the Tower, directly opposite.

BERMONDSEY OLD AND NEW

Plans to rejuvenate the Bermondsey embankment of the Thames, from Tower Bridge eastwards, include the creation of an uninterrupted riverside walkway all the way to Cherry Garden Pier. This pier is traditionally the point at which ships passing upstream would sound their horns if they needed the central span of Tower Bridge lifted to let them pass through. Near the pier is one of the area's favourite meeting places, the Angel (101 Bermondsey Wall East), a 15th-century inn with a balcony built out on timber piles enjoying views of the City and the river. Past customers included Samuel Pepys and Captain Cook, while prints on the walls recall the appearance of old Bermondsey. The pub was once a notorious haunt of smugglers and thieves—before the River Police were founded to patrol the river in 1769, it is estimated that nearly half of all the cargo landed on these shores simply disappeared; many port workers and stevedores were allegedly involved in the racket.

Sculptural fantasy on the theme of the sea in Hay's Galleria

▶▶ London Dungeon   188B1

28–34 Tooley Street, SE1 (tel: 020-7403 0606)
www.thedungeons.com
Open: Daily 10–5.30. Admission very expensive
Underground: London Bridge

Horrific sights that would send a chill up the spines of most sensitive adults seem to have the opposite effect on older children, as you will discover if you visit London Dungeon. They will shriek with delight at the realistic portrayals of executions and torture, while adults squirm uncomfortably. The most appalling aspect of this hugely successful attraction is that nearly every display is based on reality—the working models of instruments of torture, the painful scenes of martyrdom (particularly St. George), of hanging, flogging, boiling alive, burning at the stake and disembowelling simply reflect the extraordinarily cruel punishments that human beings have devised and inflicted upon each other. Perhaps children enjoy the spectacle because they know 'it is not real', whereas adults know only too well that it is. The latest addition is the ride, Extremis: Drop Ride to Doom.

One of the less grisly displays in the London Dungeon

WINSTON CHURCHILL'S BRITAIN AT WAR EXPERIENCE
This museum (64 Tooley Street, SE1; tel: 020-7403 3171) re-creates the experience of the Blitz (see page 36) through documentary films, and mock-ups of an underground air-raid shelter and a newly bombed street, complete with choking heat and dust. Exhibits include ration books and gas masks.

▶ St. Katharine's Dock   188C2

St. Katharine's Way, E1.
Open: free access 24 hours
Underground: Tower Hill

St. Katharine's Dock was built in 1824–1828 by Thomas Telford and is the closest dock to the City of London, nestling up against the Tower of London. Here, exotic items such as ostrich feathers, turtle shells and ivory were once stored. This proximity to the financial complex made the dock a prime target for redevelopment when it became obsolete in 1968, and the 19th-century warehouses have been converted to luxury flats for boat lovers, whose yachts are moored in one of the two main basins. Mingled in amongst them are occasional historic vessels, including Thames sailing barges. The dock is a peaceful spot, popular for pub food served at the Dickens Inn, a touristy pub, artfully restored from an 18th-century timber-framed brewery.

▶▶ Southwark Cathedral   *188B1*

Montague Close, Borough High Street, SE1 (tel: 020-7367 6700)
www.dswark.org/cathedral
Open: Cathedral Mon–Fri 7.30–6, Sat–Sun 8.30–6, including all services. Admission free, moderate donation suggested
Underground: London Bridge

Southwark Cathedral, originally the grand Augustinian priory church St. Mary Overie, became thoroughly down-at-heel after the Reformation and might have disappeared entirely when the railways criss-crossed this deprived area in the 19th century. But it was saved, first by devoted 19th-century restoration and then by being given the status of cathedral in 1905. Its fine choir, chancel and east-end chapels mix French, English and revival Gothic styles and can be enjoyed during lunchtime concerts and services. So can the fine monuments, some of which have been gilded and brightly painted as was originally intended. One commemorates John Harvard, who was baptized here. He later emigrated to Massachusetts in 1637 and died within a year. The famous university was renamed after him, following the bequest of his wealth and his library. John Gower, the poet, has a splendidly painted effigy here. The monument in the north transept, to Joyce Austin, was carved by Nicholas Stone in 1633. It uses the harvest as a metaphor for death—flanking the central figure are two girls sleeping in straw hats and flowing robes after a hard day's toil in the fields. As part of the Millennium Project, the cathedral now has a new exhibition, called 'The Long View of London'.

John Gower's tomb

Historic vessels moored in St. Katharine's Dock

VINOPOLIS
This fascinating warren of cellar-shaped rooms is a living museum of wine where people, pictures, equipment and videos recount the story of wine. This continues Southwark's tradition for good entertainment that goes back to medieval times for, in this area, stood the Tabard Inn of Chaucer's Canterbury Tales, the White Hart of Shakespeare's Henry VI and the Queen's Head owned by John Harvard until 1637 when he sold it and emigrated to America (see Southwark Cathedral). Visitors are given a global experience from the Rhone to California, from Australia's vineyards to a lesson in how to taste wine, so allow two to three hours. Tickets include the excellent audio guide plus tasting coupons; an upmarket food shop, wine bar and restaurant adjoin the museum. (Bank End, SE1; tel: 0870-241 4040, www.vinopolis.co.uk; *Open* Mon, Thu–Sat 12–9, Wed, Sun 12–6 (hours subject to change, check ahead). *Admission* very expensive.)

Docklands

196

TOWER TRADITIONS
The Tower has many ancient traditions. One is the nightly Ceremony of the Keys, when the Chief Yeoman Warder locks the main gates of the Tower at 10pm, after which a bugler sounds the Last Post. This ceremony has scarcely changed in more than 700 years, except that it now takes place under flood-lights with an audience (make a reservation well in advance by writing to: The Ceremony of the Keys, Queen's House, HM Tower of London, EC3N 4AB, enclosing a stamped, self-addressed envelope). Sixravens live in the gardens, well cared for by the official Ravenmaster; legend has it that the Tower will collapse if they fly away. On 21 May members of Eton College and King's College, Cambridge put white roses and lilies in Wakefield Tower in memory of Henry VI, who founded both institutions, and who was murdered here in 1471.

►► Tower Bridge   188B1

SE1 (tel: 020-7403 3761)
www.towerbridge.org.uk
Open: daily 10–6.30; Nov–Mar 9.30–6. Admission expensive
Underground: Tower Hill. DLR: Tower Gateway

Tower Bridge has been among London's most famous landmarks since it was completed in 1894 in a Gothic style designed to complement the neighbouring Tower of London. It was then the last road bridge in London, famous for its bascule (seesaw) bridge operation which allowed cargo ships into the Upper Pool of London just to its west.

It was hailed in its day as one of the engineering wonders of the world and the **Tower Bridge Exhibition** shows just how it was constructed. The tour ascends the north tower, moves along the glassed-in high-level walkways (which offer more wonderful river views) and descends the south tower. The tour ends in the impressive original Victorian engine rooms where there are also hands-on exhibits to pull and push.

►►► Tower of London   188C1

Tower Hill, EC3 (tel: 0870 756 6060)
www.hrp.org.uk
Open: Mar–Oct Tue–Sat 9–6; Sun–Mon 10–6; Nov–Feb Tue–Sat 9–5, Mon, Sun 10–5. Admission very expensive
Underground: Tower Hill. DLR: Tower Gateway

In summer the Tower of London can be one of the most crowded spots in London, so get there early to avoid the queues inside; to save queuing outside, buy your tickets in advance from any Underground station. The Tower, Britain's best surviving medieval fort, is important to

The style of Tower Bridge echoes that of the Tower of London

London today for two reasons; it has a long and bloody history and it is home to the English Crown Jewels. In fact only seven people have been privately executed inside the fortress; but more than 300 others suffered publicly on Tower Hill just outside the Tower. Henry VIII's second and fifth wives, Anne Boleyn and Catherine Howard, and Lady Jane Grey, who was pro-claimed Queen of England in 1553 but deposed after nine days, were all executed inside the Tower, while Sir Thomas More and Sir Walter Raleigh were imprisoned here before their final journeys. Prisoners were brought in and out of the Tower by boat through the Traitors' Gate, still visible from the embankment. Several dark deeds were committed in the tower (the 'Princes in the Tower', Edward V and his brother Richard, were murdered in the Bloody Tower, possibly by their uncle, Richard III, in 1483), but the pace of execution really stepped up under Henry VIII. The traditional site of the block was on Tower Green, in front of the Chapel of St. Peter ad Vincula, whose floor was raised in 1876 to reveal a pile of beheaded skeletons, including that of Anne Boleyn. Not surprisingly the Tower is reputedly the most haunted building in London, famous for sightings of the ghosts of Anne Boleyn and Sir Walter Raleigh.

Of course, the Tower was not just a place of execution. It also served as a royal fortress and palace. William the Conqueror began its construction around 1078, building the central keep, known as the White Tower which contains the exquisite 11th-century Chapel of St. John. Henry III kept his menagerie here in the castle, including three leopards given to him by the Holy Roman Emperor.

Most of the Crown Jewels, which are kept in the Jewel House, date from the period after 1660; earlier regalia were melted down after Charles I's execution in 1649. The Imperial State Crown includes the 317-carat Second Star of Africa diamond; the Queen Consort's Crown contains the Koh-i-Noor diamond mined in India. An excellent visual story of the jewels entertains those queuing, and it is possible to repeat the circuit round the actual jewels immediately for a second look at no extra cost. There are many other attractions within the Tower including the Fusiliers Museum, the fascinating Medieval Palace, the amazing Royal Armouries and the Wall-Walk.

The fancily dressed Yeomen Warders ('Beefeaters') have looked after the tower since their appointment by Henry VII in 1485. Today, they conduct tours and are a mine of information about the Tower's history.

ALL-HALLOWS-BY-THE-TOWER
The church that stands a short way west of the Tower, on busy Byward Street, is one of the oldest and most interesting in London (Byward Street, EC3; tel: 020-7481 2928, www.allhallowsbythetower. org.uk. *Open* Mon–Fri 9–6; Sat–Sun 10–5). Its medieval crypt contains a Roman floor and a small museum tracing the church's history from its foundation in the 7th century. Upstairs, the church has fine furnishings including a font cover probably by Grinling Gibbons. Pepys watched the Great Fire of London from the tower of this church in 1666.

197

Beefeaters have been guarding the Tower since 1485

Strand · Savoy Hotel · Victoria Embankment Gardens · Cleopatra's Needle · Waterloo Bridge · Old Barge House Stairs · Oxo Tower · Charing Cross Station · Riverside Walk · London Television Centre · Embankment · Embankment Pier · Northumberland Avenue · National Film Theatre · Queen Elizabeth Hall · Royal National Theatre · Upper Ground · Coin Street · Festival Pier · Footbridge · Purcell Room · South Bank Centre · Hungerford Bridge · Old War Office · Hispaniola · Royal Festival Hall · Hayward Gallery · Stamford · Victoria · Former Ministry of Defence Building · BFI IMAX Cinema · Waterloo East Station · Thames · Jubilee Gardens · Waterloo · Young Vic Theatre · British Airways London Eye · Shell Centre · Norman Shaw Building · Dalí Universe · Waterloo Station · The Cut · Old Vic Theatre · County Hall · Westminster Pier · London Aquarium · Westminster · York Road · Waterloo Road · Big Ben · Westminster Bridge · Westminster Bridge Road · Florence Nightingale Museum · Houses of Parliament · Baylis Road · Lambeth North · St Thomas's Hospital · Victoria Tower Gardens · Kennington Road · St George's Cathedral · Lambeth Palace Road · Archbishop's Park · Mill Bank · Lambeth Palace · Lambeth Road · Imperial War Museum (Tibetan Peace Garden) · Lambeth Pier · Museum of Garden History · Lambeth Bridge · Lambeth Walk

200 m / 220 yards

SOUTH BANK London's south bank has a long association with the theatre. Theatres, bear pits and brothels were banned from the City because authorities felt that apprentices spent too much time playgoing, so the actors moved to the south bank, out of the City's jurisdiction. Today, a long stretch of riverside from Westminster Bridge to London Bridge, and including Bankside, has been regenerated to become a traffic-free boulevard, dotted with museums, galleries, concert halls, theatres, restaurants and shops—and its own new bridge over the Thames.

BANKSIDE WALK From Charing Cross or Embankment Underground stations, on the north side of the river, an

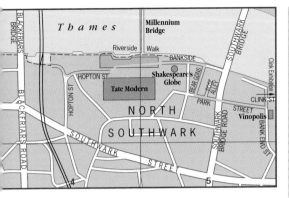

elevated walkway leads across the rebuilt Hungerford Bridge (completed 2000), with good views of Somerset House and the City beyond. Steps descend from the bridge on the south bank to pass in front of the Royal Festival Hall and the South Bank Complex (see page 203). Here you will find street musicians, exhibitions and a crafts market, or you can slip into the Festival Hall for free foyer exhibitions and music recitals.

The walk continues under Waterloo Bridge, past the **National Theatre**, the **National Film Theatre** and the headquarters of **London Television Centre**. It then runs under Blackfriars Bridge to join Hopton Street. Further along, the walk passes the **Tate Modern** and the **Millennium Bridge** (see pages 204–205 for more information on both of these new developments). Next comes Bankside, where a replica of **Shakespeare's Globe** Theatre has been built as faithfully as possible (see page 202).

Bear Gardens leads right (south) from Bankside. In the adjacent Rose Alley, the foundations of the **Rose Theatre** of 1587, which once hosted the plays of Shakespeare and Marlowe, are on public view, preserved in a gallery beneath a new office development.

Walk down Park Street, past the site on the eastern side of Southwark Bridge Road, where Shakespeare's original Globe Theatre stood. Turn left on Bank End. Here you will find a restored pub dating back to the 15th century, the **Anchor Inn**.

Next door, **Vinopolis** is a living museum of the world's wines (see page 195). **Clink Street** was the site of a notorious prison, used from the 16th century onwards to detain heretics, and later thieves, vagabonds and ruffians. The name is said to derive from the 'clinch' irons that were used to pin prisoners to the wall or floor, and 'the clink' has become a slang term for any prison. The **Clink Prison**, nearby, reveals the gruesome nature of prison life. Close by is the St. Mary Overie Dock. Look up and you can marvel at the survival of the tall stone wall and rose window frame of Winchester Palace's Great Hall built in the 14th century; archeologists have found traces of Roman villas beneath it. Further along, the **Golden Hinde** is moored. It is a full-scale replica of the ship in which Sir Francis Drake circumnavigated the world in 1577–1580. In fact the replica has travelled further than the original, twice around the globe before coming to rest in London. There are five decks, and guides in Elizabethan costume.

▶▶▶ REGION HIGHLIGHTS

Imperial War Museum
pages 200–201

London Aquarium
page 205

BA London Eye
pages 201–202

Oxo Tower Viewing Gallery *page 204*

Shakespeare's Globe
page 202

Tate Modern *pages 204–205*

Britain's most famous nurse, Florence Nightingale, tends the Crimea wounded

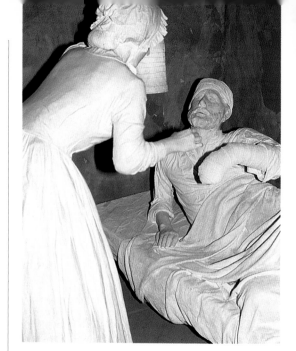

BEDLAM

The building that houses the Imperial War Museum was originally built to house the Bethlehem Royal Hospital, an asylum for the mentally ill, popularly known as Bedlam. The original hospital was founded in 1247 as the Priory of St. Mary Bethlehem, situated outside Bishopsgate. In the 17th century it moved to Moorfields and became a popular tourist attraction. Visitors were allowed in to watch the patients, who were placed in caged cells like animals in a zoo (the last of the paintings in the *Rake's Progress*, by Hogarth, depicts the scene—see page 155). The cruelty of such treatment was not appreciated until the late 18th century; the fact that King George III suffered from mental illness helped to bring about a more humane attitude. The asylum moved to this site in Lambeth in 1816 as part of an overall reform of the treatment of patients with serious psychiatric problems. Criminal patients were then moved from here to Broadmoor in 1864, and in 1930 the remaining patients were moved to new premises in Surrey.

Machines of war, from World War I biplanes to modern missiles

▶ Florence Nightingale Museum 198B2

St. Thomas's Hospital, 2 Lambeth Palace Road, SE1 (tel: 020-7620 0374)
www.florence-nightingale.co.uk
Open: Mon–Fri 10–5, Sat–Sun 10–4.30. Admission moderate
Underground: Westminster

St. Thomas's Hospital, founded in Southwark in 1213, moved to this site in 1868, inspired by hospital reforms recommended by Florence Nightingale. She set up the first school of nursing at St. Thomas's and this museum traces the story of her life using audiovisuals and a series of realistic reconstructions. One recreates the barrack hospital at Scutari, in the Crimea. The famous lamp that earned her nickname 'the Lady of the Lamp' is on display.

▶▶▶ Imperial War Museum 198A3

Lambeth Road, SE1 (tel: 020-7416 5320)
www.iwm.org.uk
Open: daily 10–6. Admission free
Underground: Lambeth North, Waterloo

The bombastic title could mislead you. This is one of London's most interesting museums for the whole family. It tells the story of 20th-century conflict from every social, domestic and military viewpoint, and there are several excellent permanent exhibitions.

Several displays in the basement take a thematic look at the horrors of the two World Wars. You can tramp through the misery and discomforts of a trench from World War I, then relive the Blitz of 1940–1941 among street scenes littered with the rubble of collapsed and burned-out buildings, complete with the acrid smells of charred wood and the sound of air-raid sirens. The displays also cover war as experienced by concentration camp victims living under Nazi tyranny, Royal Air Force pilots and members of the armed services fighting on various fronts, in Europe, Africa, and East Asia. Excellent use is made of audiovisuals and documentary film footage, and the human side of war is also conveyed through the recorded words of war poets and the vivid pictures and sculptures of artists as diverse as Henry Moore and John Piper.

On the first floor the mechanical and technical aspects of war are explored, with huge exhibits of military hardware. The more insidious weapons of germ and chemical warfare are represented, and the display includes John Singer Sargent's large and nightmarish picture of 1918–1919, simply entitled *Gassed*.

Aerial warfare is one theme of the third-floor gallery. There is also an exhibition devoted to clandestine operations and the role of the SAS (Special Air Service) and élite special forces.

Up on the top floor are part of the museum's impressive art collection. Look for works by Stanley Spencer, John Nash, John Piper (both world wars), Peter Howson (Bosnia) and John Keane (The Gulf War).

The museum's newest permanent exhibitions are The Holocaust and Crimes Against Humanity. The latter is an exploration of genocide and ethnic violence (not suitable for under 16s) The former examines the persecution and murder of European Jewry and other groups from 1933 to 1945, a harrowing narrative display unsuitable for anyone under 14 years of age.

►►►BA London Eye   198D1

Jubilee Gardens, South Bank SE1 (tel: 0870-5000 600)
www.ba-londoneye.com
Open: Jun–Sep 10–9; Oct–May 10–8 (see website for exact opening times). Admission very expensive; automated booking and information; reservations for a timed ride essential
Underground: Waterloo, Westminster

COUNTY HALL
County Hall, the former headquarters of the Greater London Council is now home to two hotels and three major tourist attractions.

London Aquarium (Westminster Bridge Road, SE1; tel: 020-7967 8000, www.londonacquarium.co. uk. *Open* daily 10–6. *Admission* very expensive). A subterranean wonderland stocked with the world's aquatic life has as its highlight the three-floor high Atlantic and Pacific displays. Here large sharks and stingrays glide silently between giant sunken Easter Island-style heads. There are myriad colourful fish to enjoy in the Reef and Corals and Indian Ocean exhibits, and children get a real thrill out of stroking a stingray.

Dalí Universe (tel: 0870-744 7485, www.county hallgallery.com *Open* daily 10–6.30. *Admission* very expensive). This is a permanent exhibition of more than 500 works by the Spanish surrealist artists, Salvador Dalí. Lent by various European collectors, they include paintings, drawings, jewellery and sculpture, displayed in dramatic and atmospheric settings.

Museum of Garden History (tel: 020-7401 8865, www.museum gardenhistory.org *Open* daily 10.30–5. *Admission* inexpensive, donations welcomed). In an attractive setting, this museum gives an insight into the history of gardening from Roman times. Plenty of curious implements and garden equipment, and a charming 17th-century knot garden in the churchyard.

The British naval guns that guard the Imperial War Museum were the most powerful weapons of their day

The British Airways London Eye was not only the capital's most successful new landmark for the Millennium, it has already become a symbol of London as iconic as Big Ben or Tower Bridge. A 30-minute ride in the world's highest observation wheel is a great experience. It helps to have seen a little of London beforehand, and to carry a map with you. Those anxious about heights or about claustrophobia should not worry. The wheel moves slowly giving plenty of time to identify sights; and each large capsule is big enough to walk about comfortably. Conceived and designed by Marks Barfield Architects, the precision-balanced 135-m (442-ft) diameter wheel operates on the principles of a bicycle wheel. The first such wheel was built in Chicago in 1893, although the best-known is probably the one in Vienna. But the London Eye charts new technological ground, as each of the thirty-two 20-seater capsules has a solar cell to help provide power for ventilation, lighting and communication.

▶▶▶ Shakespeare's Globe   199D5

New Globe Walk, Bankside, SE1 (tel: 020-7902 1400)
www.shakespeares-globe.org
Exhibition open: mid-Apr to mid-Oct Mon–Sat 9–12, 12.30–5,
Sun 9–11.30, 12–5 ; mid-Oct to mid-Apr 10–5. Admission
expensive (includes tour)
Theatre season: May–early Oct (box office tel: 020-7401 9919)
Underground: Mansion House, London Bridge
Riverboat: Bankside Pier

The dream of Sam Wanamaker, the late American film and theatre director, was finally realized in May 1997: an established likeness of Shakespeare's Globe Theatre (originally erected in 1599) was completed. Late 16th-century construction techniques were used and the circular building (described by Shakespeare as 'the Wooden O') has the first thatched roof in central London since the Great Fire. As in Shakespeare's day, the central part of the theatre is open to the elements, though all seats are covered.

The exhibition brings the Bard's world to life with costume and clothing, special effects, music and printing. It also tells the fascinating story of how the Globe was rebuilt.

SOUTH BANK FILM
Founded in 1952, the National Film Theatre was an early addition to the South Bank concert halls. Today, its three cinemas, shop and riverside restaurant are open to the public. The NFT runs one of the world's most influential film festivals, London Film Festival (November), which aims its programme towards the public rather than the movie business; about 70 per cent of films screened will never have public distribution (Southank, tel: 020-7928 3232).
A short walk away, the IMAX cinema claims to have the world's largest cinema screen—certainly, it is enormous and the film images fill the viewer's vision.

LONDON DUCK TOURS
London has many boat tours and many bus tours but Duck Tours achieves both at once using an original DUKW amphibious craft of a World War II vintage. The 75-minute road tour embarks from behind the London Eye, follows a Westminster itinerary before splashing down into the Thames and a 30-minute cruise. The guides are among London's best and make it great fun for all the family (tel: 020-7928 3132,www.londonduck tours.co.uk. *Admission:* very expensive).

Shakespeare's Globe

▶▶ **Southbank Centre** *198D2*

South Bank, SE1 (tel: 020-7921 0600)
www.sbc.org.uk
Underground: Waterloo, Embankment
Open: daily 10am–approx 10.30pm. Admission free

Grouped along the Thames embankment, either side of Waterloo Bridge, are the buildings of London's most important arts complex. Apart from the concerts, plays and exhibitions held in the main buildings, much use is also made of the lobby spaces and traffic-free riverside terraces.

The first building on this site was the Royal Festival Hall, the centrepiece of the 1951 Festival of Britain. The building itself is sombre, but the acoustics are excellent. Alongside are the Queen Elizabeth Hall and Purcell Room, both used for smaller concerts, and the Hayward Gallery, which stages major art exhibitions. These windowless buildings of weather-stained concrete were built in the Brutalist style of the 1960s, as was the nearby Royal National Theatre, which stages excellent drama and also offers behind-the-scenes tours; for more information, tel: 020-7452 3400.

The architecture of the whole complex has always stirred controversy. Architects admire the spacious, adaptable interiors and the use of modern materials, but the public complain about the unfriendliness of the building. A £91 million revamp to the Festival Hall, completed in 2007, has improved the interior and acoustics significantly.

Bold but brutal—the South Bank arts complex

LAMBETH PALACE
Near Lambeth Bridge is Lambeth Palace, the official residence of the head of the Church of England, the Archbishop of Canterbury. It has been the archbishop's home since 1190, but the main building visible to the public—the brick gatehouse —was built in 1501. The palace has frequently been plagued by controversy. In 1534 Thomas More found himself facing a tribunal in the guard room; despite attempts to persuade him, he refused to sign the Oath of Supremacy recognizing Henry VIII, rather than the Pope, as the head of the English church. For this he was hauled off to the Tower and from there to his execution for treason in 1535. From 1867 until recently the palace regularly hosted the Lambeth Conference, a meeting of all the bishops of the worldwide Anglican church, but the location has now moved as the palace is too small.

Statue of Nelson Mandela on one of the Southbank Centre's walkways

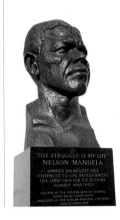

Bankside Power Station has been transformed by architects Herzog & de Meuron

COIN STREET, GABRIEL'S WHARF AND THE OXO TOWER

The section of river frontage just to the east of the South Bank arts complex has been regenerated by the dynamic Coin Street Community Builders. It comprises housing, Bernie Spain gardens, the riverside walkway, Gabriel's Wharf craft market (*Open* Tue–Sun 11–6) and the Oxo Tower. This art deco tower was built in 1930 for the Oxo company, with the letters 'OXO' spelled out in geometrical windows as a permanent advertisement. The Harvey Nichols Restaurant, Bar and Brasserie, a sandwich and deli bar, and a free public viewing gallery (*Open* daily 11am–10pm) are at the top of the tower. Lower down, there is art gallery spaces (tel: 020-7401 2255, www.oxotower.co.uk. *Open:* daily 11–6; closed between exhibitions. *Admission* free).

▶▶▶ Tate Modern
199D4

Bankside, SE1 (tel: 020-7887 8000/7887 8008)
www.tate.org.uk
Open: Sun–Thu 10–6; Fri–Sat 10–10. Admission free (charge for some loan exhibitions)
Underground: Southwark/Blackfriars

This sriking museum is one of the world's leading museums of modern art, comparable to the Metropolitan Museum of Modern Art in New York. Its collection, one of the world's finest, could only be partly appreciated when it was housed with the national British Collection at the Tate Gallery (now Tate Britain, see pages 56–57). Now it is revealed in its full richness, diversity and glory, complemented by further collections at its two provincial sites in Liverpool and St. Ives, Cornwall.

The building is spectacular: George Gilbert Scott's monumental brick Bankside Power Station (1947 and 1963; closed from 1981), whose huge spaces are ideal for exhibiting large-scale works of art in an innovative way. So too is the site: standing on the south bank of the Thames, opposite St. Paul's Cathedral, right in the heart of the capital.

A competition was held to transform the building from power station to international art gallery, and the winners were the Swiss architects Herzog & de Meuron, designers of the Goetz Gallery in Munich and others in Basel and Mulhouse. Their plan respects the old building but provides an appropriately contemporary setting; for instance, a glass structure spans the length of the roof, adding two floors for public facilities and superb London views, and providing extra natural light for upper floor galleries. Entry is by a ramp down to the former turbine hall; the main galleries of various shapes and heights fill three floors above; facilities include a cinema, auditorium, café and shop.

Works exhibited in the galleries continue the story of art where the National Gallery leaves off. They are changed regularly, to allow visitors and Londoners to enjoy a wide range of exhibits, but always include works by the most influential artists of the 20th century, such as Picasso, Matisse, Dalí, Duchamp, Moore, Bacon, Gabo, Giacometti and Warhol. Together, they cover all the significant artistic periods and movements of the 20th century, from Surrealism and Abstract Expressionism to Pop Art and Conceptual Art.

There are pieces by European artists, such as Brancusi's *Maiastra*, Picasso's *The Three Dancers* and Rodin's *The Kiss*. Works by Americans include Richard Hamilton's *The Large Glass* and Andy Warhol's *Marilyn Diptych*. And there are key works of modern British art, showing the different directions it has been developing in. There is Stanley Spencer's mystical painting, Francis Bacon's powerful canvases, Henry Moore and Barbara Hepworth's sculptures, David Hockney's strong draughtsmanship, and Howard Hodgkin's pure colour, alongside seminal works by David Bomberg, Sir Anthony Caro, Ben Nicholson and W. R. Sickert.

As if this were not riches enough, each annual programme includes three special loan exhibitions and a number of mid-scale exhibitions focusing on a single artist, theme or period, with plenty of related events. A day here is a hugely rewarding London experience, and you can take in the City and river views while enjoying a snack or meal on the bankside terrace café or in the upmarket rooftop restaurant.

One more modern work of art sits outside the gallery: this is the pedestrian Millennium Bridge, which crosses the Thames from St. Paul's Cathedral on the north side of the river to its southern anchor point on the riverside walk in front of the gallery. Designed by an unusual team (architect Sir Norman Foster, sculptor Sir Anthony Caro and engineers Ove Arup & Partners), this is London's first new bridge since Tower Bridge, opened in 1894, and the city's first dedicated pedestrian bridge.

The turbine hall of the former power station is now a spacious entrance

The Millennium Bridge links this modern art gallery with historical St. Paul's Cathedral

London may seem to be a vast concrete jungle, but almost every sport takes place in the capital, from tennis to football, from cricket to marathon running. If you wish to play sport during your visit, you can easily find a swimming pool, tennis court, golf course or a park to jog in; just ask your hotel for advice. For spectators, a string of world class sporting events take place in London.

OXFORD VS CAMBRIDGE

Twice a year London plays host to sporting events for Britain's two oldest universities, Oxford (the dark blues) and Cambridge (the light blues). One is the Varsity Rugby Match at Twickenham in December; the other is the Boat Race, held on a Saturday afternoon in Spring, when rowing teams race along the Thames from Putney to Mortlake. Most of the spectators have no connection with the universities; many are not even interested in the sport. The appeal is to attend a traditional event, and visit pretty riverside pubs.

London Marathon

Football (soccer) is the national game, commanding the largest audiences. Tennis challenges cricket for attention throughout the summer. Despite the climate (or perhaps because of it), sport is taken very seriously by most people, whether they participate or merely watch. If England does badly in an international game, the nation goes into a state of gloom, and questions are asked in parliament. Substantial funds raised from the sale of National Lottery tickets are now devoted to providing new sports grounds, sports facilities and better training, with the aid of government money.

Visitors to London who want to watch sport have a wide choice. Football and cricket are plentiful, with top-quality matches in the capital. Cricket fans should look for Middlesex (at Lord's) or Surrey (at the Oval); London's premier league football teams include Arsenal, Chelsea, Tottenham Hotspur (Spurs) and Fulham, although tickets may be difficult to find. Alternatively you can visit a number of sports museums to learn about the record-breaking achievements of past players. One of the best is the award-winning **Lawn Tennis Museum** (*Open* daily 10.30–5 and 1.30–8 during the Championship Fortnight) at Wimbledon, which makes imaginative use of audiovisuals to explain the history of the game. There is a display of

tennis clothing and equipment that vividly shows that the speed and excitement of women's tennis has improved as the players have discarded long skirts and hats (All England Lawn Tennis Club, Church Road, tel: 020-8946 6131, www.wimbledon.org/museum. *Admission* expensive).

Wembley Stadium, the home of English international football as well as the stage for many other events, was finally officially opened on FA Cup Final day on 19th May 2007 after years of delay and controversy. Rugby fans can visit the stadium in Twickenham (see page 234).

For cricket lovers, **Lord's Cricket Ground** (St. John's Wood Road) is almost a place of pilgrimage. The ground is named after the property developer Thomas Lord and not, as is often supposed, because so many early players were aristocrats. Lord set up the first cricket field in what is now Dorset Square in 1787; when the site was developed for housing, he moved the turf of the original ground first to North Bank and finally to the present site in 1811. This and other intriguing episodes in the history of cricket are covered by the **MCC (Marylebone Cricket Club) Museum** at Lord's (*Open* daily; guided tours of the museum and players' facilities are also available, Apr–Sep daily 10, 12 , 2; Oct–Mar 12, 2, except on match days, tel: 020-7616 8656, www.lords.org. *Admission* expensive).

The prize exhibit here is the tiny urn containing the Ashes, the trophy awarded each year to the winner of the England versus Australia test series (the trophy stays at Lord's even when Australia wins). The 'Ashes' are those of a bail symbolically burned by Australian supporters after their defeat at the hands of the Marylebone Cricket Club (MCC) in 1883. Other exhibits include portraits of leading cricketers, such as W. G. Grace, and a stuffed sparrow killed by a fast ball bowled by Jehangir Khan on 3 July, 1936. Lord's itself is particularly interesting from an architectural point of view: The tentlike structure which protects spectators who are seated in the Mound Stand is an innovative example of modern stadium design. Take a look at the startlingly space-age Media Centre, the world's first building to be made of a single aluminium shell. When it was opened in May 1999, the Media Centre, designed by Future Systems, was described as resembling 'a giant radio alarm clock on stilts'.

Wimbledon ball girl

207

THE LONDON MARATHON
Another great annual event that perpetuates the spirit of amateurism is the London Marathon, held in April. The streets that form the route are closed off and thousands of spectators line the route to cheer on the many thousands of runners taking part in the biggest event of its kind. First run in 1981, it has rapidly become a major fixture in the city's calendar. Top international athletes cover the 41.6-km (26-mile) course, from Greenwich/Blackheath to the Mall, in a little over two hours. It is the slower, amateur runners, however, who delight the crowds—celebrities, runners in outlandish costumes, senior citizens and athletes with disabilities. Most raise substantial sums of money for charity, from the friends, families and workmates who agree to sponsor them.

Excursions

Let the train take the strain

TRAVEL INFORMATION
The best bet is the government-run Britain and London Visitor Centre, 1 Lower Regent Street, Piccadilly Circus, SW1 (tel: 0870-156 6366. *Open* Mon–Fri 9.30–6.30, Sat, Sun 10–4, except Jun–Oct, Sat 10–5) which has information on the whole of Britain, visit www.visitbritain.com

EXCURSIONS Inner London holds enough attractions to keep most visitors happy and entertained for weeks on end, but sometimes it is worth escaping for a day to explore delights further afield—the choice is huge whether you like towns or the countryside.

This section highlights the best of the villages, parks, river walks, museums and stately homes within easy reach of central London, from the royal palaces of Hampton Court and Windsor to the botanical riches at Kew Gardens, or the absorbing account of Britain's seafaring history at the Greenwich Maritime Museum. All these sites are well served by public transport and if you buy a one-day Travelcard, from any Underground or British Rail station, you can enjoy unlimited travel by bus, tube, or rail in the London area.

London is also at the heart of the nation's rail and road network, which means that many other historic towns and cities are within easy reach of the capital. Most tour operators offer well-planned day trips to Oxford, Stratford-upon-Avon, Canterbury or Cambridge, and these can often be reserved through your hotel.

Alternatively, you may prefer to travel independently: rail services will take you to faraway towns such as as Bath, York or Edinburgh in a few hours, or to Oxford and Cambridge, which are much closer. Check out the best rail tickets available and early reservations could save money (tel: 08457 48 49 50, www.nationalrail.co.uk. There is also a useful express bus service to Oxford. It is wise to book tickets and reserve seats in advance, if possible.

Renting a car is the least sensible option because of the congested roads, the Congestion Charge (see page 13) and the difficulty of parking within London. On the other hand, a car is essential if you want to see some of England's gardens, stately homes and rural back roads. In this case you should consider taking a train to the region that you want to explore and renting a car locally to avoid driving in London.

In any event, remember that London's roads are busiest during the rush hours (8–10 and 4–7), and long traffic jams are common on the roads that lead out of London on Friday evenings and on routes into the city on Sunday evenings and Monday mornings, as people travel to and from the country. The M25, London's ringroad, is often crowded.

RAIL SERVICES
The following mainline stations in London serve the main cities and regions of Britain:
Paddington for Oxford, Bath and the West Country.
Euston for Stratford-upon-Avon, the Midlands and Glasgow.
King's Cross for Cambridge, York and Edinburgh.
Liverpool Street for Cambridge, Colchester, Ipswich and Norwich.
Waterloo for Winchester, Salisbury, Bournemouth and Portsmouth.
Victoria for Gatwick, Brighton, Canterbury and Dover.
For all rail enquiries tel: 08457-484950.

209

Early morning mists give King's College Cambridge (founded in 1441) a timeless feel

Two of Bath's great attractions, its 16th-century abbey and the adjacent Roman Baths

THE NATIONAL TRUST
Many of England's stately homes, castles, gardens and landscapes are owned by the National Trust—including such London properties as Ham House (see page 231), Osterley Park (see page 228) and Carlyle's House (see page 90). The National Trust was set up in 1895 and has rescued many buildings, areas of countryside and antiquities that might otherwise have suffered from neglect or destruction. Members gain free admission to most of its properties, and receive a comprehensive directory. Details from any National Trust property, from its London Information Centre and store at Blewcoat School, 23 Caxton Street, SW1 (tel: 020-7222 2877) or from The National Trust, Membership Department, PO Box 39, Warrington WA5 7WD (tel: 0870458 4000, www.nationaltrust.org.uk for credit-card membership by phone). You can join from the US via the NT's affiliate, the Royal Oak Foundation, www.royal-oak.org

Days out from London

Here are a few suggestions for day trips out of town that could easily be extended with an overnight stop.

Bath►►► The train ride from Paddington station to Bath takes just under two hours. The magnificent Roman baths and the spa town's elegant Regency buildings, crescents and gardens evoke the age of Beau Nash and the high-society gatherings that took place in the Pump Room, Theatre Royal and Assembly Rooms in the early 19th century. Additional attractions are excellent shops and the American Museum at Claverton Manor.

Brighton►► An hour by train from Victoria station, Brighton was the favoured seaside resort of aristocratic Londoners including the Prince Regent (later King George IV), who built the extraordinary Pavilion, with its Oriental domes and Chinese-style state rooms. Nearby, the shops of the Lanes are a great place to browse. Walk along the Victorian Palace Pier promenade to enjoy the sea air.

Cambridge►►► An hour's train journey from King's Cross or Liverpool Street takes you to Cambridge—a wonderful place to see in spring, when the college gardens backing on to the River Cam are a mass of daffodils, or in summer, when you can rent a boat along the river. Highlights include Kings College Chapel, the Bridge of Sighs and the Mathematical Bridge, designed entirely in wood, although it is now held together with bolts.

Canterbury►► Chaucer's pilgrims, heading for the shrine of St. Thomas à Becket, expected to take several days to journey from London to Canterbury, but now the cathedral city is an hour away by train from Victoria. The cathedral, with its stained glass, sits within the city's surviving Roman walls and not far away from the ruins of St. Augustine's abbey, founded in AD598, when Augustine was sent from Rome to bring Christianity to the British Isles. If you rent a car, Canterbury also makes a good base for exploring Leeds Castle, set on an island surrounded by parkland, and Sissinghurst's magnificent garden, created by Harold Nicolson and Vita Sackville-West.

Oxford►►► Just over an hour's journey from Paddington station, Oxford was described by the poet Matthew Arnold as 'that sweet city with her dreaming spires'. The university town is crowded with ancient collegiate buildings of honey-coloured Cotswold limestone, many of which have lovingly tended gardens. It is also famous for its many good bookshops, its river walks and its lively student atmosphere. If you decide to stay overnight, you could take a bus tour of Stratford-upon-Avon, to see Shakespeare's birthplace, Ann Hathaway's cottage and the poet's grave in Holy Trinity Church, alongside the River Avon.

Salisbury►► Salisbury's glorious 13th-century cathedral has changed remarkably little since John Constable painted its needle-sharp spire rising out of the surrounding water meadows. The cathedral, restored in the 20th century, offers intriguing tours of the roof. Salisbury is just over an hour from London, by train from Waterloo. The 5,000-year-old stone circle at Stonehenge is only 16km (10 miles) outside the city (there is a bus that passes the site and leaves from Salisbury railway station).

Gliding along the tranquil River Cam in Cambridge

ENGLISH HERITAGE
English Heritage is funded by the government and responsible for properties such as Chiswick House (see pages 212–213), Kenwood House (see page 225), and Marble Hill House (see pages 234–235). Membership benefits include free admission to all properties and a comprehensive guide. For details (ask at any property; tel: 0870-333 1181, join on line at www.english-heritage.or.uk or write to Customer Services Department, PO Box 569, Swindon SN2 2YP).

211

THE COTSWOLDS AND BLENHEIM PALACE
You won't be able to see much of the Cotswolds by just taking a day trip out of London, but trips do run from Oxford and Stratford-upon-Avon, which are both on the edge of this area of outstanding natural beauty. Better still, you can rent a car and explore for yourself. Places within easy reach and well worth a visit include Chipping Campden, Broadway, The Slaughters, Snowshill Manor and Burford. Just north of Oxford is one of England's great palaces, Blenheim, where Churchill was born.

Simple domesticity at William Hogarth's House, featuring a picture of the artist and dog

THE HOUSES OF CHISWICK MALL

Chiswick Mall's houses betray the wealth of their original owners, able to afford that rare commodity in London, uninterrupted views of the River Thames and gardens that sweep down to the water's edge. One of the best buildings is Walpole House, a rare example of Restoration-period architecture, built around 1700 for Barbara Villiers, the Duchess of Cleveland, one of Charles II's mistresses. In the 19th century it served as a school, said to be the one on which Thackeray modelled Miss Pinkerton's Academy for Young Ladies in his novel *Vanity Fair*. Another building of note is Kelmscott House, on the Upper Mall, the home of William Morris from 1878 to 1896 and named after his country house in Oxfordshire. It was at the nearby Sussex House that Morris set up the Kelmscott Press to produce beautifully hand-printed, illustrated and bound books.

▶▶ Chiswick   208B2

In the 18th and 19th centuries, Chiswick was a favourite place of residence for artists such as William Hogarth, and it was here that Lord Burlington built Chiswick House, the most perfect example of a Palladian country villa in England. Those interested in Arts and Crafts housing should take a stroll around Bedford Park, designed by E. W. Godwin and Norman Shaw in the 1870s.

The best way to reach Chiswick is by train from Waterloo. From Chiswick station, turn right and follow Burlington Lane for about 1km (0.5 mile) to reach the entrance to Chiswick House, with its fine Italianate gardens.

Chiswick House ▶▶ (Burlington Lane, tel: 020-8995 0508; www.english-heritage.org.uk. *Open* Apr–Oct Wed–Sun 10–5, Sat & hols 10–2; Nov–23 Dec, 1–20 Mar pre-booked tours only. *Admission* moderate. Gardens open daily dawn to dusk. *Admission* free*)*. This delightful villa was built in 1725–1729 by Lord Burlington, a patron of the arts and an accomplished architect in his own right; he had already commissioned Colen Cambell to build his town-house, Burlington House (now home to the Royal Academy of Arts, see page 82). His inspiration was Palladio's Villa Capra, in Vicenza in northern Italy, but the building is far from being a slavish copy. The main east front, for example, has an elaborate double staircase leading to the two-storey portico, unlike any Palladian prototype. Flanking the staircase are fine statues carved by Rysbrack around 1730, representing Palladio and Inigo Jones, the English architect who did so much to introduce the ideals of classical architecture.

There is another homage to Inigo Jones in the obelisks on the roof that surround the central dome. These are, in fact, disguised chimneys and are copied from designs made by Jones for the Queen's House at Greenwich, as are some of the magnificent chimney pieces inside the villa. The upper floor is richly decorated with gilded cherubs, swags and scrolls, statues of classical deities and ceiling paintings by William Kent.

The garden, also designed by Kent, makes a romantic setting for the villa. Although Italian in style, and dotted with temples, statues and obelisks, it marks a departure from the strict geometric Renaissance form to a safer, more idealized version of the Roman Campagna as found in the landscape paintings of artists such as Claude and Salvator Rosa.

Chiswick Mall▶ An underpass leads from beneath the busy Hogarth Roundabout to Church Street and St. Nicholas Church, the burial place of several artists and architects, including Hogarth, William Kent, Colen Campbell and James McNeill Whistler. From the church you can walk along Chiswick Mall, Upper Mall and Lower Mall, admiring some of London's finest 18th-century houses and perhaps stopping at one of several riverside pubs. At the end of the Lower Mall, Hammersmith Bridge Road leads north to Hammersmith tube station for the journey back to central London.

Hogarth's House▶ (Hogarth Lane, tel: 020-8994 6757. *Open* Apr–Oct Tue–Fri 1–5, Sat, Sun 1–6; Nov–Mar Tue–Fri 1–4, Sat, Sun 1–5. Closed Jan. *Admission* donation). Today, Hogarth's House stands to the north of Chiswick House on Hogarth Lane, close to a busy roundabout. The scene was very different when the 'little country box by the Thames' stood in open fields. Hogarth used it as his summer residence between 1749 and 1764, and the simple rooms are hung with copies of his satirical engravings, including *Marriage à la Mode* (1745) and *A Rake's Progress* (1735). In the tiny garden, an ancient mulberry tree, under which Hogarth used to sit, survives and bears fruit.

RIVERSIDE PUBS
As you stroll along the Mall you can choose from one of several historic pubs. The 16th-century **Dove Inn** (19 Upper Mall) is where Charles II and Nell Gwyn are said to have made secret rendezvous. A list of famous customers (including Ernest Hemingway and Graham Greene) is displayed above the great fireplace. This pub earns an entry in the *Guinness Book of Records* for having the smallest public bar in England (a mere 1.5m/5ft by 2.4m/8ft). The **Old Ship** (25 Upper Mall) dates from the mid-17th century and is decorated with nautical relics, and the **Blue Anchor** (13 Lower Mall) is the popular wood-panelled haunt of members of the Amateur Rowing Association, whose headquarters are next door.

213

Chiswick House: Palladian grandeur just a few minutes by Underground from the middle of London

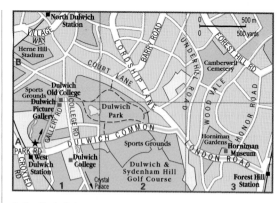

THE HISTORY OF DULWICH PICTURE GALLERY

The remarkable collection of paintings housed in the Dulwich Picture Gallery was put together by the art dealer Noel Desenfans. He was commissioned in 1790 by the king of Poland to buy paintings for a National Gallery that was planned for Warsaw. When the king was deposed, Desenfans offered the collection to the British government, suggesting that it could form the basis of a new National Gallery. The government refused (it finally got around to founding today's National Gallery in 1824), so in 1807 Desenfans left the collection to his friend, Sir Francis Bourgeois, who in turn bequeathed it to Dulwich College in 1811. As a result, an exceptionally fine collection of art, with major works by Rubens, Gainsborough, Van Dyck, Rembrandt and Raphael, fit to grace any national museum, has ended up in a quiet south London suburb.

▶▶ Dulwich

In 1605 Edward Alleyn, an actor-manager who amassed a considerable fortune by running bull- and bear-baiting entertainment as well as theatres, bought the manor of Dulwich. Here he built and endowed Dulwich College, a school for the poor, and ensured the survival of a large expanse of parkland in south London. The attractions in Dulwich today include the Dulwich Picture Gallery, with its collection of Old Masters, and the Horniman Museum, which is renowned for its ethnography collection.

Dulwich Picture Gallery▶▶ (Gallery Road, tel: 020-8693 5254, www.dulwichpicturegallery.org.uk. *Open* Tue–Fri 10–5; Sat–Sun 11–5. *Admission* expensive). Some 300-plus masterpieces, dating largely from the 17th century, hang in the refined neoclassical building designed by Sir John Soane in 1811–1814. This was the first purpose-built art gallery in England, and its highlights include Rembrandt's portrait of *Jacob III de Gheyn* (stolen several times from the gallery but, fortunately, recovered each time), Van Dyck's *Madonna and Child* and Poussin's *Return of the Holy Family from Egypt*. Rick Mather's striking addition, opened in 2000, provides more exhibition space, an education centre and a café overlooking the five-acre garden.

The gallery also serves as a mausoleum: At the rear of the building is the tomb of Noel Desenfans, who was responsible for putting the collection together, and Sir Francis Bourgeois, who bequeathed it to Dulwich College in 1811 (see panel).

Alongside the Picture Gallery, **Dulwich Old College▶** dates from 1619 and now serves as offices. This was the original school founded by Edward Alleyn; the main school today lies 1km (0.5 miles) to the south, housed in Renaissance-style buildings designed in 1866–1870 by Charles Barry, the son of the architect who built the Houses of Parliament.

A path to the Horniman Museum leads through **Dulwich Park▶** from the entrance just east of the Picture Gallery. The park is especially colourful in May, when the azaleas and rhododendrons are in full bloom, but there are fine trees to admire at all times of the year, including statuesque oaks, and a number of more exotic specimens, such as the Japanese pagoda tree.

The path takes you south of the boating lake, café and aviary, and out by the lodge gates on Dulwich Common, which was once a royal hunting ground and is now a golf course. Turn left, then right on Lordship Lane to reach the Horniman Museum on London Road.

Horniman Museum▶ ▶ (100 London Road, tel: 020-8699 1872, www.horniman.ac.uk. *Open* daily 10.30–5.30; Sun 2–5.30. *Admission* free) is very popular with children, not least because of its small animal enclosure.

The entrance to C. Harrison Townsend's 1901 art nouveau building has a large mosaic by Robert Anning Bell: *The Course of Human Life*. Inside, the exhibits reflect the quirky interests of Frederick John Horniman who, as head of his family's tea importing business, travelled widely in the 1870s and collected anything that appealed to his sense of curiosity: these include stuffed animals, fossils, masks, sculptures and assorted tribal artefacts.

Objects representing different cultures have been arranged to illuminate a number of topics, including initiation rites, the use of narcotics, agriculture, crafts, fishing and cooking. Do not miss the excellent newer galleries that include African Worlds, dedicated to African, Afro-Caribbean and Brazilian culture. The latest star is the wonderful new acquarium—well worth a visit.

For the return journey to central London follow London Road left to Forest Hill railway station, where frequent trains depart for London Bridge.

The art-nouveau tower of the Horniman Museum

CRYSTAL PALACE
Once it had served its purpose of housing the Great Exhibition in Hyde Park in 1851, the Crystal Palace Exhibition hall was re-erected on a high hill just to the south of Dulwich. The monumental glass-and-iron building, designed by Joseph Paxton, then became the centrepiece of a huge amusement park, opened by Queen Victoria in 1854. In 1936, the Crystal Palace went up in flames; 90 fire engines failed to quench the ferocious blaze. Today, all that remains of this vast Victorian Disneyland is the boating lake with some life-size models of prehistoric dinosaurs, made in 1854, set on a series of artificial islands. A small museum on Anerley Hill, near Crystal Palace station, covers the history of this fairy-tale building and its sad demise (Anerley Hill, tel: 020-8676 0700, www.crystalpalacemuseum. org.uk. *Open* Sun & hols 11–4.30. *Admission* free). The park now houses a city farm, major sports stadium and concert stadium where pop and orchestral concerts take place daily in summer. Guided tour of the park at 12 first Sun of every month (tel: 020-8676 0700. *Admission* moderate.

215

GREENWICH PUBS

In Greenwich you have plenty of choices when it comes to traditional pubs, many of which serve seafood and have outdoor terraces with river views. Perhaps the best is the **Trafalgar Tavern** (reservations advised for meals, tel: 020-8858 2437) in Park Row, which Dickens describes in *Our Mutual Friend*. The interior is like a ship, with nautical relics on display and large windows overlooking the Thames. Another shiplike tavern, the **Cutty Sark**, is reached by following the riverside path, via Crane Street and Highbridge, to Ballast Quay: it's well worth the walk just for the view northwards up the vast expanse of the Thames to Blackwall. Within Greenwich the choice includes the **Spanish Galleon Tavern** and the **Gipsy Moth**, both on Greenwich Church Street, or the **Coach and Horses**, built in 1730, in Turpin Lane alongside bustling Greenwich Market.

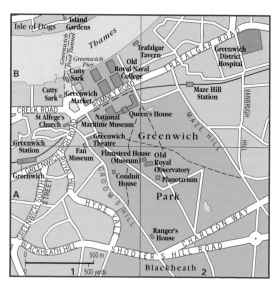

Right: The Cutty Sark.
Below: Early telescope

▶▶▶ Greenwich

Greenwich is as beautiful as its name (a corruption of 'green reach' and pronounced 'Grenitch') suggests. Here, set in parkland that sweeps down to the river's edge, are some of London's most noble buildings: the Queen's House—built by Inigo Jones and now part of the National Maritime Museum; Wren's Old Royal Naval College alongside the Thames, and his Royal Observatory on the hill above. If it's a nice day pack a picnic to take to Greenwich Park. This is the oldest of all London's royal parks, created in 1433. Head to the very top and there are great views over the National Maritime Museum and across the River Thames to Docklands and the City of London. As well as enclosing the Royal Observatory there is a deer enclosure, formal gardens, a boating lake and a children's playground. Greenwich is also home to one of London's best visitors' markets, featuring antiques and collectibles on Thursday, and arts and crafts, food and gifts from Friday to Sunday, all taking place in the covered market built in 1881. All this makes for a pleasant day out from central London.

There are several ways to get to Greenwich: by train from London Bridge; by riverbus from Westminster, Charing Cross or Tower piers; or by Docklands Light Railway, which now goes all the way to Greenwich.

However consider alighting at Island Gardens station so that you can enjoy Christopher Wren's carefully planned view from Island Gardens across the river to the Royal Naval College, with the Queen's House beyond. It is then just a short walk under the Thames through the Greenwich Foot Tunnel to reach all the sights of Greenwich.

Both the foot tunnel and the riverbus bring visitors to Greenwich Pier, where the **Cutty Sark▶▶** (King William Walk, tel: 020-8858 2698, www.cuttysark.org.uk. *Open* daily 11–5, visitor centre and shop only. *Admission* moderate) lies moored in a dry dock. This sleek and handsome ship, with its tall masts and intricate rigging, was built in 1869 as a tea clipper, carrying precious cargoes between Britain and the Orient. In 1871 she broke the world record for sailing between London and China, completing the trip in only 107 days, at her fastest covering 576km (358 miles) in a single day. Tradegy struck in May 2007, when a devasting fire caused immense damage to ship and temporary visitor centre. Miraculously the ship is repairable and the conservation project will include a complete rebuild.

The village of **Greenwich▶** is lined with some early 19th-century buildings that flank the entrance to Greenwich Market. The covered market, built in 1831, is now only open on weekends and specializes in crafts. Another market, selling jewellery, CDs, retro and vintage fashion, operates during weekends on Greenwich Church Street.

A short walk away, splendid wrought-iron gates on King William Walk form the main entrance to the **Old Royal Naval College▶▶** (West Gate, King William Walk, tel: 020-8852 2154, www.oldrnvalcollege.com. *Open* daily 10–5. *Admission* free), originally built as a hospital for infirm and aged seamen. These monumental buildings were begun in 1664, with a riverside wing for Charles II. Christopher Wren, brought in by William and Mary to create a sailors' hospital similar to his one for soldiers in Chelsea (see pages 92–93), evened up the symmetry either side of the court to frame the impressive southward view of the Queen's House. His brilliant design is best appreciated from the Isle of Dogs, at Island Gardens, beside the Greenwich Foot Tunnel.

Two of the buildings are open to the public. The Painted Hall, created by Sir James Thornhill in 1707–1717, has some of the finest baroque paintings anywhere in England. They show William and Mary surrounded by allegorical figures that symbolize the triumph of virtue over vice.

The Chapel (1718–1725), which was originally designed by James Stuart but was rebuilt after a fire in 1779, is in neo-Grecian style and a vast altar painting by Benjamin West, *St. Paul Shaking Off the Viper*, is also displayed here.

MILLENNIUM DOME
Massive optimism took hold of successive governments in the run up to the millennium, perhaps spurred on by London's own self-propelled revitalization. Inspired by the innovative buildings of the 1951 Festival of Britain, they commissioned a design team lead by Richard Rogers to build the world's largest dome. Inside, attraction zones surrounded a central performance area. Opened on New Year's Eve, it failed to attract enough visitors and quickly became a white elephant. In 2001, the attraction was closed, as scheduled, and its contents auctioned off. It was bought by O2 and launched as a leisure complex in July 2007.

217

The domed entrance to the Greenwich Foot Tunnel which leads to the Isle of Dogs

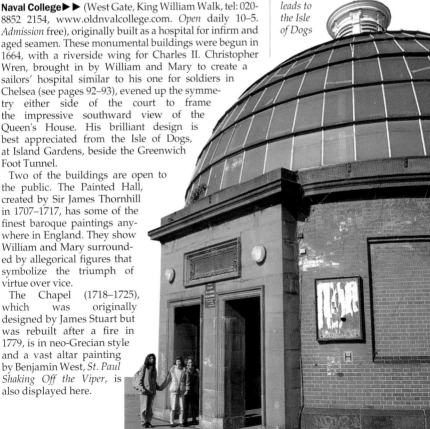

The Greenwich Meridian line, which visitors love to straddle: one foot in the east, one foot in the west

GREENWICH MERIDIAN
The Royal Observatory (see page 219) is the home of the Prime Meridian of the World. A meridian is a north-south line from which astronomer's observe, measure and map the sky. The Prime Meridian marks Longitude zero degrees, from which all other places on earth are measured; it is also the base for calculating Greenwich Mean Time (GMT). Until 1884, when delegates from 25 nations met in Washington to agree on a common time system, most towns in the world kept their own time systems and even varied the length of an hour. It was the railway timetables that demanded a standard time; and it was the fact that 72 per cent of the world's trade depended on sea-charts that used Greenwich as the Prime Meridian that determined the place. On 1 January, 2000, the new millennium began at Greenwich. Visitors can stand on the Meridian and read the latest world news fed by electronic data from *The Times* newspaper's web site.

The principal attraction in Greenwich is the **National Maritime Museum**▶▶▶ (Romney Road, tel: 020-8312 6565, www.nmm.ac.uk. *Open* daily 10–5; Jul–Aug until 6. *Admission* free). Several buildings in Greenwich Park, plus a suite of stunning new galleries, tell the story of Britain's age-old relationship with the sea.

On either side are the State Apartments (the king's to the east and the queen's to the west), furnished in 17th-century style. One of the most intriguing rooms is the Queen's Presence Chamber, where original painted decorations survive, showing the lilies of France impaling the British arms and symbolizing the marriage of Charles I to Henrietta Maria.

Benefiting from a major refurbishment, which was completed in 1999, the 16 galleries and huge glass-roofed Neptune Court of the modern museum tell the 2,000-year history of Britain and the sea. Galleries focus on exploration, trade and empire, luxury liners, naval heroes and more. Among the huge collection of ships (both real ones and models), paintings, navigational instruments and the relics of sailors and explorers, you can seek out the sumptuous state barge made for Frederick, Prince of Wales, in 1732, and the jacket Nelson was wearing when he was shot in the left shoulder and fatally wounded at the Battle of Trafalgar in 1805.

The museum's central building, the **Queen's House**, is an architectural monument in its own right—the first Renaissance building in England to be designed in the classical style, and the prototype for many subsequent public buildings and stately homes. Inigo Jones began the building in 1616 as a rural retreat for Anne of Denmark, James I's queen, but she died in 1619; it was Henrietta Maria, the French wife of Charles I, who presided over its completion in 1635. The finest feature of the interior

is the Tulip Stair, named for the pattern on its balustrade (probably intended to represent fleurs-de-lys, the symbol of France). This leads to the Great Hall, its dimensions forming a perfect cube, with ceiling paintings showing the Muses, the Virtues and the Liberal Arts. The original paintings were moved to Marlborough House, Pall Mall, in the 18th century; these are a computer-enhanced replica.

The **Royal Observatory Greenwich▶▶** situated high on the hill above Greenwich, is an annex to the Maritime Museum (same details as above), consisting of several historic buildings.

The Greenwich Observatory was founded by Charles II in 1675; Flamsteed House was designed by Christopher Wren for John Flamsteed, the first Astronomer Royal. Today the house is furnished to give the impression that Flamsteed and his wife still live there. Early telescopes and time-measuring instruments are on display, there is an astronomy gallery, and the large red ball on top of one tower still drops down its mast at 1am each day, which in the days before accurate timepieces were commonplace enabled navigators on board their ships in the Thames to set their chronometers.

From the start, the Observatory's job was to set standards of measurement for time, distance, latitude and longitude—key components of navigation. The large Gate Clock measures Greenwich Mean Time, the standard by which time is set all round the world. You can stand astride the Greenwich Meridian, marked by a brass strip crossing the Observatory courtyard. This is the dividing line between the earth's eastern and western hemispheres. (If you wish, you can buy a computer printout recording the precise time of your visit.)

Setting the standard— Greenwich Mean Time

THE FAN MUSEUM AND THE RANGER'S HOUSE

The Fan Museum, (Croombs Hill, tel: 020-8305 1441, www.fan-museum.org. *Open* Tue–Sat 11–5; Sun 2–5. *Admission* moderate) is dedicated to the ancient and beautiful art of fan-making. More than 3,000 fans are housed in a superbly restored 18th-century town house. A short stroll away on Chesterfield Walk stands Ranger's House (tel: 020-8853 0035, www.english-heritage.org), a grand 18th-century villa housing Julius Wernher's collection of Renaissance art, funded with profits from diamond mines in South Africa. There are full length Jacobean portraits, jewellery, ceramics and decorative arts. See the website or telephone for opening times.

The National Maritime Museum houses a huge collection of ships

HAMPSTEAD HEATH
In 1829, Hampstead's
Lord of the Manor, Sir
Thomas Wilson, wanting to
capitalize on the popularity
of the village, produced a
plan to build new houses
all over the vast 330-ha
(815-acre) expanse of
sandy heath that he owned
to the north of the village.
This caused uproar, and
opposition to the idea
raged for 40 years until, at
Wilson's death in 1869,
conservationists finally
won the battle to save the
Heath for public
enjoyment. The Heath is a
vast nature reserve, as
well as a public playground
where Londoners come to
walk, jog, ride their horses,
enjoy picnics, fly their kites
and swim in the three
ponds (Kenwood Pond
for women, Highgate Pond
for men, and Hampstead
Pond for mixed swimming).

▶ ▶ ▶ **Hampstead**

Hampstead's pretty lanes and village atmosphere and its
vast expanse of semi-rural heath have attracted many
eminent writers, politicians and intellectuals, past and
present. The tone of the area today is still intellectual,
prosperous and liberal. Hampstead Heath is a fine place
to walk and a popular place for families.

Hampstead Underground station, the deepest in the
system, lies amid the intricate maze of attractive lanes that
cluster around the High Street. Heath Street descends
south to Church Row, with its Georgian houses fronted
by iron railings. Halfway down the Row is the parish
church of St. John, built in 1744–1747. Inside are memorials to many famous former Hampstead residents,
including Keats, Norman Shaw, John Constable and
George du Maurier.

Holly Walk, off Church Row, leads north to Vernon
Hill and Hampstead Grove, and so to 17th-century
Fenton House▶ (Windmill Hill, tel: 020-7435 3471,
www.nationaltrust.org.uk. Open Apr–Oct Sat, Sun, bank
holiday Mon 11–5, Wed, Thu, Fri 2–5; Mar Sat, Sun only
2–5. Admission moderate). A William and Mary house
built in 1695, Fenton House, with its walled garden, is one
of the best of its kind surviving in London. The period furnishings are complemented by some of George Salting's
fine ceramics collection. In addition, the Benton Fletcher
Collection of 17th- and 18th-century keyboard instruments is kept here, and these are used for the regular
concerts given in the house.

The little lanes that run around Hampstead Grove are
worth exploring, and many houses display blue plaques
honouring former residents.

Heading up Heath Street, you will come to New End, a
street on your right. Here is **Burgh House** (New End
Square, tel: 020-7431 0144, www.burghhouse.co.uk. Open
Wed–Sun noon–5. Admission free), a Queen Anne house
built in 1703 by the physician Dr. Gibbons. Its rooms are
now home to Hampstead Museum.

Nearby, Flask Walk and Well Walk are reminders that
Londoners once came here to take the waters at the Pump

House, which has since disappeared. In Flask Walk, the Flask Tavern was the meeting place in the early 18th century of the Kit-Kat Club, a political and literary group. Flask Walk leads to Hampstead High Street, with its good bookshops, boutiques and restaurants.

At the end of Hampstead High Street is Rosslyn Hill where, on the left, Downshire Hill leads to Keats' Grove (formerly known as Wentworth Grove) and the **Keats' House Museum**▶ (Keats Grove, tel: 020-7435 2062, www.keatshouse.org.uk. Closed for final restoration work late Oct 2007–late summer 2008. Check for times). John Keats came to live here in 1818, fell in love with his next-door neighbour, Fanny Brawne, and became engaged to her in 1819. In 1820 he left for Italy for health reasons and died there in 1821. During the short time he lived in this house he wrote some of his best-loved poems, including *Ode to a Nightingale*; the plum tree under which he wrote this poem has gone, but a recent replacement in the garden marks the spot. The rest of the house displays letters, manuscripts and furnishings in period style.

It is worth returning to 2 Willow Road to see London's only Modernist house, complete with its original contents, which is open to the public (tel: 020-7435 6166, www.nationaltrust.org.uk. *Open* Apr–Oct Thu–Sat noon–5; Nov, Mar Sat noon–5. *Admission* moderate). Designed by Erno Goldfinger, he and his family lived here until his death in 1987.

From Keats' Grove it is a short step to Hampstead Heath railway station, or you can walk up Parliament Hill for extensive views over central London—local legend claims that Queen Boudicca (Boadicea) (see page 24) lies buried beneath the hill.

Summertime, and in Hampstead's leafy lanes the living is easy

NEARBY MUSEUMS

Sigmund Freud lived at 20 Maresfield Gardens, in South Hampstead, from 1938, when he escaped from Vienna, until his death the following year. After his daughter, Anna, died in 1983, it opened as a museum (tel: 020-7435 2002, www.freud.org.uk. *Open* Wed–Sun noon–5. *Admission* moderate). Freud's famous couch, along with books, letters and personal relics, are on display. Just north of Hampstead, in Finchley, the Jewish Museum (80 East End Road, tel: 020-8349 1143, www. jewishmuseum.org.uk. *Open* Mon–Thu 10.30–5, Sun 10.30–4.30. *Admission* inexpensive) documents the social history of London's Jewish community. The fine objects and art complement the Jewish ceremonial objects displayed at the Jewish Museum in Camden (see page 118).

Taking a well-earned breather at the Wells Tavern in Hampstead

Hampton Court's vivid mix of styles

THE DOLLS HOUSE

Before you visit the spectacular King's Apartments, it is worth going to Clock Court to see the exhibition recounting their meticulous restoration after the tragic fire of 1986. Do not miss the intriguing dolls house, almost the last exhibit. This is a model of the King's Apartments that, using lever lighting techniques, is peopled with William and Mary's courtiers and visitors and explains how this grand suite of interconnecting rooms was used. The formal and hierarchical structure of the Court in the 1690s meant that a person's progress through the rooms towards an audience with the king was determined primarily by rank but also by wealth, dress, politics and the purpose of the visit. Gentry did not get as close to the king as aristocracy, who in turn were behind ambassadors. After this, you can follow the same route yourself with the costumed guides.

▶▶▶ Hampton Court Palace   208A2

East Molesey (tel: 0870-752 7777)
www.hrp.org.uk
Open: late Mar–Oct daily 10–6; Nov–late Mar daily 10–4.30 (last tickets sold 1 hour before closing). Admission very expensive. Park open daily dawn–dusk. Admission free

Hampton Court is one of the oldest and most interesting of London's royal palaces. Wren's south wing, badly damaged by fire in 1986, has been superbly restored, and the palace, in typical Tudor style, looks like a miniature town that has grown in an organic, unplanned way, unity provided only by the warm reds and browns of the brickwork. The fastest way to reach Hampton Court is by rail from Waterloo station (30 minutes), but a more leisurely journey (of three to four hours) can be made by riverbus in summer, departing from Westminster Pier (tel: 020-7930 2062 for details, see page 55).

The palace Hampton Court is approached through the Trophy Gate, where its vast scale is immediately apparent. The palace was not merely a royal residence. It also housed a huge retinue of courtiers and followers and the warren of courtyards and buildings used to contain 'grace and favour' apartments, where Crown officials, retirees and dependants of the royal family lived. The Landmark Trust also has two holiday homes here that can be rented by the week: Fish Court, which sleeps six, and the Georgian House, which sleeps eight. Details from the Landmark Trust, Shottesbrooke, Maidenhead, Berkshire SL6 3SW (tel: 01628 825925). Ahead is the Great Gatehouse, built by Cardinal Wolsey.

Set in the two side turrets are terracotta roundels depicting Roman emperors. These and Base Court, beyond, date from Wolsey's time. Anne Boleyn's gateway, opposite, is carved with the intertwined initials 'H' and 'A', for Henry and Anne, celebrating a marriage that lasted only four years before Boleyn was beheaded. Clock Court comes next, named after the astronomical clock on the gateway's inner side. On the left is Henry VIII's Great Hall, with its splendid oriel window and an impressive hammerbeam roof. Close to the Great Hall are the Tudor Kitchens, with their vast fireplaces and ancient cooking utensils. Christopher Wren's elegant colonnade is opposite, built for William and Mary. Wren planned to demolish the whole palace and build a new one as grand as Versailles. Luckily, the King could not afford this, and some Tudor buildings were left standing. But the State Apartments (1689–1694), which you enter here are rich indeed, decorated with paintings, furnishings and tapestries. Jean Tijou, a French blacksmith, made the ironwork balustrades of the staircases, Grinling Gibbons made the woodwork and Verrio painted many of the ceilings. The more intimate Queen's Apartments look into Wren's lavish Fountain Court, while the public rooms look over the gardens, with their leafy avenues, canals and fountains. Do not miss the dolls' house model (see panel page 222).

The gardens Like the palace, the gardens are a mixture of styles. To the south, between the Thames and the palace, the Privy Garden was designed for the exclusive use of the royal family and separated from the river by Tijou's handsome wrought-iron screen. The Privy Garden has been accurately restored to its appearance and planting of 1702 when it was completed for William III. Nearby are Henry VIII's Pond Garden and an Elizabethan Knot Garden of aromatic herbs. The Great Vine grows near the Banqueting House; planted in 1768, it still produces Black Hamburgh grapes, on sale in season. To the north of the palace are the Wilderness; the Laburnum Walk; the Maze, planted in 1690; and, to the east, the indoor royal tennis court, built in 1626. The game of royal (or real) tennis, still played here, resembles an amalgam of tennis and squash and was all the rage with the European aristocracy in the 16th century.

Extravagantly decorated Tudor chimneys

CARDINAL WOLSEY AND HAMPTON COURT
Hampton Court started out in 1514 as an ecclesiastical palace, not a royal one, built by Cardinal Wolsey, the son of an Ipswich butcher who rose to fill the highest offices of church and state. As the confidant of Henry VIII he took a leading role in the king's complicated marriage affairs. He amassed great wealth and spent it extravagantly, intending Hampton Court to be the most splendid palace in the land. This spurred the King's envy, however, and Wolsey tactfully decided that it might be wise to present Hampton Court to Henry as a gift, which he did in 1525. This did not satisfy the king who, in 1529, had his former friend arrested on a charge of treason and then seized Wolsey's possessions, including the palace of Whitehall. Disgraced and rejected, the Cardinal soon fell ill, and died at York within a year.

223

The hammerbeam roof of the Great Hall, built in 1532, is richly decorated with pendants, royal arms, badges and a series of carved and painted heads

Memorial to Karl Marx, Highgate Cemetery

DICK WHITTINGTON
On the left-hand side of Highgate Hill, about 250m (275yds) up from Archway tube station, look for the Whittington Stone, set by the roadside. Here, according to legend, Dick Whittington rested with his cat on his way out of London, having failed to make his fortune in the city. Three times, as he rested, he thought he heard the Bow Bells chime 'Turn again, Whittington, thrice Mayor of London', and the third time he decided to return. Thus goes the story; in reality, Richard Whittington was the son of a Gloucestershire squire. He was, indeed, three times Mayor of London (in 1397, 1406, and 1419), but the fable of his rags-to-riches rise seems to have been invented in the 17th century, 200 years after Whittington's death.

►► Highgate   *208B3*

Highgate still retains its village atmosphere, though since the early 19th century it has been swallowed up by London's northward expansion. The core of the village has many opulent 18th-century houses, which set the exclusive tone of the whole area.

To reach Highgate, it is best to take the tube to Archway station and walk up **Highgate Hill**. The ugly hospital buildings soon give way to elegant houses, on the right. On the left, a long wall separates the road from the peaceful oasis of **Waterlow Park**, a hillside garden with fine views towards Regent's Park and central London. At the top of the park, you can visit **Lauderdale House** (Highgate Hill, tel: 020-8348 8716, www.lauderdalehouse.co.uk. *Open*

Kenwood House and its paintings were bequeathed to the nation by the 1st Earl of Iveagh in 1927

Tue–Fri 11–4, Sat 1.30–5, Sun 12–5. *Admission* free), built in 1645 and the home of Nell Gwyn, mistress of Charles II.

Highgate village is grouped around **Pond Square**, which has a delightful mixture of Georgian cottages, grander houses, small shops and restaurants. To one side is the **Flask** pub, so called because travellers used to stop here to fill their flasks for the journey ahead. More Georgian houses can be found in The Grove, a little to the north (the poet Samuel Taylor Coleridge lived at No. 3).

Highgate Cemetery▶▶ (Swain's Lane, tel: 020-8340 1834, www.highgate-cemetery.org. *Open* East cemetery Mon–Fri 10–4.30, Sat–Sun 11–4.30 (3.30 in winter). *Admission* inexpensive. West cemetery admission by tour only (no children under 8) Sat–Sun 11–4 each hour, Mon–Fri at 2 ; Nov–Mar Sat–Sun only 11–3. Tour charge moderate.) You can reach Highgate Cemetery by walking south from Pond Square, down Swains Lane.

A number of famous people are buried here, amid the Victorian landscaping and the fascinating funerary architecture. More than 50,000 tombs, accommodating 166,000 people, lie within its 15ha (37 acres). Opened in 1839, it became an immediate attraction. The best-known grave is that of Karl Marx (who died in Hampstead in 1883), marked by a large head sculpted by Laurence Bradshaw (1956) and the inscription: 'Workers of all lands unite'.

Kenwood House (The Iveagh Bequest)▶▶ (Hampstead Lane; tel: 020-8348 1286, www.english-heritage.org.uk. *Open* Apr–Oct 11–5; Nov–Mar Wed, Fri 10–4. *Admission* free) From the middle of Highgate it is a 10-minute walk along Hampstead Lane to Kenwood House, situated in wooded grounds to the north of Hampstead Heath. This stately home was built in 1616 and remodelled by Robert Adam in 1764 for the Earl of Mansfield (see Adam's fine library ceiling). It was left to the nation in 1927 by the 1st Earl of Iveagh, along with its outstanding collection of paintings. Here you will find Rembrandt's brooding *Portrait of the Artist* (*c*1665), Vermeer's *The Guitar Player* (*c*1676), and Gainsborough's fine portrait of Lady Howe (*c*1764), among many other important works. Open-air summer concerts have been given in the grounds, by the lake, but were not forthcoming in 2007, although it is hoped they will be resumed in 2008.

225

The grave of George Eliot, the nom de plume of Mary Ann Evans (1819–1880), whose novels include Middlemarch, Mill on the Floss *and* Adam Bede

HIGHGATE CEMETERY
Highgate Cemetery opened in 1839 as a commercial enterprise. The Cemetery was immensely popular but in time, with all the burial plots sold and no revenue for maintenance, it fell into neglect. Recently it has been rescued by the Friends of Highgate Cemetery. Tombs in the Western Section (accessible only on tours) include the physicist Michael Faraday (died 1867), the poet Christina Rossetti (died 1894) and Dante Gabriel Rossetti's beautiful wife, Elizabeth Siddal (died 1862).

Excursions

The Palm House, guarded by the heraldic Queen's Beasts, which were carved in 1953

MARIANNE NORTH
Kew has a superb collection of botanical paintings representing the life's work of Marianne North (1830–1890). These colourful pictures (mostly in oil) are crammed into a small gallery on the south-eastern edge of the gardens. Marianne North travelled around the world to paint plants in their natural environment, before her forced retirement to Gloucestershire, caused by a tropical fever.

KEW AND THE RUBBER TREE
Kew has sent seeds all over the world and was actively involved in the introduction of rubber to Southeast Asia. The original rubber-tree seeds were smuggled from Brazil (which did not wish to share this profitable plant), propagated at Kew, and studied by Henry Ridley, who became the director of the botanic gardens in Singapore in the 1870s and persuaded many local landowners to develop new rubber plantations. Rubber is now a staple of Indonesian economies.

KEW PALACE
Within the gardens is delightful 17th-century Kew Palace, the summer home of George III. *Open* late Mar–Oct Tue–Sun 10–4.15. *Admission* moderate (in addition to entrance to the gardens).

▶▶▶ Kew Gardens (Royal Botanic Gardens) *208A2*

Kew, Richmond (tel: 020-8332 5655)
www.kew.org
Open: daily 9.30–shortly before dusk, phone for closing times. Admission expensive

Whatever time of year it is, there is something to see at Kew's Royal Botanic Gardens. Even in the grey depths of winter, the Victorian greenhouses are full of luxuriant tropical growth, while spring and early summer bring massed bulbs, frothing groves of Japanese cherries and magnolias, or swathes of colourful azaleas and rhododendrons. There are plants here from all over the globe and from every habitat, desert, swamp and rainforest.

The gardens were created by combining two royal estates in 1772. Under the patronage of George III they developed into one of the world's foremost centres of horticultural research. The credit for this was largely due to Sir Joseph Banks, who became the King's adviser shortly after returning from a voyage around the world with Captain Cook. During the expedition Banks had recorded a huge number of hitherto unknown plants, which he now brought to Britain, growing them at Kew to assess their value, either as ornamental plants or as sources of food or medicines. The early botanic garden occupied a small part of the total area; the rest was landscaped by Capability Brown (his lake and Rhododendron Dell remain) and dotted with fanciful buildings for the amusement of courtly visitors. The oldest building is the 10-storey pagoda, built in 1761–1762 to the designs of William Chambers. Today, the vistas, royal palace, magnificent glasshouses, mature trees and 120-ha (300-acre) gardens still entrance visitors.

The Palm House Kew began to change after 1841, when the gardens were handed over to the state, and several greenhouses were added. The Palm House, designed by Decimus Burton, opened in 1848.

The Temperate House The next to be built was the Temperate House, also by Decimus Burton, beginning in 1859; by the time it was completed, 40 years later, it was the world's largest greenhouse. It has an elevated gallery from which to enjoy views of brightly coloured plants, including the Chilean wine palm, planted in 1846 and now claimed to be the largest greenhouse plant in existence.

The Princess of Wales Conservatory Opened in 1987, much of this conservatory is below ground level (for insulation) and lit by a series of low, tentlike glass roofs. Computer controls simulate several different environments in the one building, so you pass from arid desert at one end to the orchid-filled tropics at the other. Each climate zone has its own wonderful creations, from the stonelike lithops of the dry regions to the carnivorous pitcher plants of the Asian rain forests. A favourite is the giant water lily, with pads up to 2m (6.5ft) across, grown annually from seed.

Queen Charlotte's Cottage and Gardens (House open on May Day holiday and then Sat–Sun 10–4 until end Sep) British native wildflowers are the theme at this peaceful spot on the southwestern fringes of the site, named after George III's queen, who had a rustic 'cottage' built here in the 1770s. This is now a woodland nature reserve, in accordance with the wishes of Queen Victoria; sheets of bluebells flower here in May.

KEW VILLAGE
The main gate to the Royal Botanical Gardens is on Kew Green, an immaculate triangle where long, lazy games of cricket are played on summer Sundays against a backdrop of late Georgian buildings, provided for members of George III's court. St. Anne's Church, built of yellow brick in 1714, stands on the southern edge of the green and is a quirky, attractive building with an octagonal cupola and Venetian windows. The artist Thomas Gainsborough is buried in the churchyard and two former directors of Kew Gardens, William and Joseph Hooker (father and son), both have unusual memorials of porcelain decorated with ferns and flowers. Two museums stand nearby, on the opposite bank of the Thames. The Kew Bridge Steam Museum (Green Dragon Lane) houses several giant steam engines that once pumped millions of gallons of fresh water a day (tel: 020-8568 4757, www.kbsm.org. *Open* Tue–Sat 11–5. *Admission* moderate, machines in operation on weekends only *admission* expensive). A miniature steam railway runs each Sun, Mar–Nov. Its near neighbour is the Musical Museum with 200 or so mechanical instruments, all in working order. Click on www.musicalmuseum.co.uk for details or tel: 020-8560 8108.

227

The Temperate House is the largest of Kew's glasshouses and contains the huge Chilean wine palm, 18m (60ft) tall

Above: Adam-style finery; below: Tudor turrets, Adam interiors

OSTERLEY STATION
Osterley Park is reached by taking the Piccadilly Underground line to Osterley station; then follow the Great West Road to Thornbury Road. The station itself, a 1930s design by Charles Holden, was modelled on the town hall in the Amsterdam suburb of Hilversum. Other Underground stations by Holden have interesting architecture: He designed the circular concourse of Piccadilly Circus station in 1925–1928, but his best work is on the Piccadilly line from Holloway Road, with its pretty tilework, to Arnos Grove, which is frequently compared to a flying saucer.

228

▶ ▶ ▶ Osterley Park   208B2

Jersey Road, Isleworth (tel: 020-8232 5050)
www.nationaltrust.org.uk
Open: House Apr–Oct Wed–Sun 1–4.30. Admission expensive.
Park daily dawn–dusk. Admission free

Osterley Park, on the western fringes of London, was built in the 1560s for the wealthy City merchant Sir Thomas Gresham. After Gresham's death, the building was untouched. In 1711 Sir Francis Child, founder of Child's Bank, acquired the property to use the Elizabethan vaults to store quantities of money but never actually lived there. His grandsons, Francis and Robert Child, hired Robert Adam to transform the house along neoclassical lines, in 1761. Externally, the final result is a strange marriage of styles: The Tudor brick corner turrets were retained but linked together by a grand open portico with a carved and painted pediment supported by Doric columns and standing above wide, shallow steps.

Inside the house, the sequence of remodelled rooms is exactly as Adam intended, beautifully restored by the National Trust and furnished with superb examples of 18th-century tapestries, chairs and pictures. The classical themes that give unity to the house and its decoration have been meticulously recreated following Adam's original, surprisingly brightly coloured, designs. Even the furniture is arranged around the edge of some rooms, in the Georgian manner. Horace Walpole, the writer, whose own home at Strawberry Hill introduced the neo-Gothic style, found some of the rooms 'too theatric'. On the other hand, Walpole did take a liking to the rich pink, green and gold ceilings of the Drawing Room, with its carpet of similar hues, describing the room as 'worthy of Eve before the Fall'—a rather strange comment to make about such a sophisticated room, which is the exact antithesis of innocent naturalism. The description might perhaps have been more appropriately used for the tranquil garden, with its eye-catching bridge, its lakes, its stately trees, grazing cows, and its long and meandering paths.

London has several small museums and galleries well worth investigating. Some of these are outside the city, and may require a little extra planning to get to—but for those with a particular interest in their collections, or who like to wander away from the tourist track, they provide a refreshing alternative.

The **Fashion and Textile Museum** (83 Bermondsey Street, tel: 020-7407 8664, www.ftmlondon.org. Call for times and prices as closed until early 2008) is dedicated to contemporary fashion and textiles and is the brainchild of London and UK fashion legend Zandra Rhodes who has donated the core collection of around 3,000 garments.

The **Estorick Collection** (39a Canonbury Square, tel: 020-7704 9522, www.estorickcollection.com *Open* Wed–Sat 11–6, Sun 12–5. *Admission moderate*) was founded by Eric Estorick, an American political scientist and writer living in London who, with his wife, Salome, has a passion for 20th-century Italian art. Works on show include figurative pieces by Modigliani, Sironi and Campigli and metaphysical works by de Chirico. Balla, Boccioni, Severini and Russolo, and others represent the Italian Futurists. In addition, temporary exhibitions focus on such subjects as futurism and photography.

The **Royal Air Force Museum** (Grahame Park Way, Hendon; tel: 020-8205 2266, www.rafmuseum.com. *Open* daily 10–6. *Admission* free) is one of the finest collections of historic fighting aircraft in the world. It starts with early experiments with flight (from balloons to man-lifting kites) and comes up to date with high-tech displays on modern fighter aircraft. A whole section is devoted to the Battle of Britain. An art gallery shows works by Elizabeth Frink, Paul Nash, Graham Sutherland and others.

MOTORCYCLE MUSEUM
Bill Crosby's love of motorbikes led him to open his collection to fellow enthusiasts in 1999. From his 1903 Clyde to his 1987 Enfield, some 80 bikes are on display including a Triumph, BSA, Velocette, Ariel and Panther, plus plenty of memorabilia such as vintage oil cans, pictures and magazines. And there's a café, too. (29 Oldfield Lane South, Greenford, Middlesex, tel: 020-8575 6644, www.motorcycle-uk.com/lmm/inventory.html. *Open* Sat–Sun & hols 10–4.30. *Admission* moderate)

229

The RAF Museum in Hendon

RICHMOND BRIDGE
Richmond Bridge dates
from 1777 and holds the
distinction of now being
the oldest in London: All
the other bridges were
rebuilt at some stage in
the 18th and 19th
centuries to cope with an
ever-growing traffic
burden, but Richmond's
elegant five-arch bridge
survives in its original
form. The design itself is
even older—the architect,
James Paine, used as
his model a bridge
designed by the great
16th-century architect
Palladio for the northern
Italian town of Vicenza.

▶▶ Richmond

Richmond is a riverside village west of London, reached by Underground or by boat from Westminster Pier in summer. Its attractions include several good pubs, such as the White Cross on Water Lane or the Rose of York on Petersham Road, with good food and gardens overlooking the Thames. For the more energetic, there are walks along the leafy east bank of the river to Ham House, or up Richmond Hill to the 1,000-ha (2,470-acre) Richmond Park.

If you arrive by train, the river lies to the left as you leave the station, walking down the store-lined Quadrant to the Square. To the right, Duke Street leads to Richmond Green, an open space surrounded by 17th- and 18th-century houses. Northeast of the green is the Little Green, with its late Victorian Richmond Theatre and the Orange Tree Theatre, both part of the vibrant arts scene in Richmond. South of the green, the four houses on Maids of Honour Row were built in 1724 for the ladies-in-waiting of the Princess of Wales. Behind this row, in Old Palace Yard, is the gatehouse of Richmond Palace, most of which was demolished by Parliamentarians after the execution of Charles I.

Little alleys full of antiques shops and boutiques lead south to the river itself, spanned by Richmond Bridge (see side panel). North of the bridge is **Richmond Riverside**, a group of 20 buildings in retro-classical style, arranged

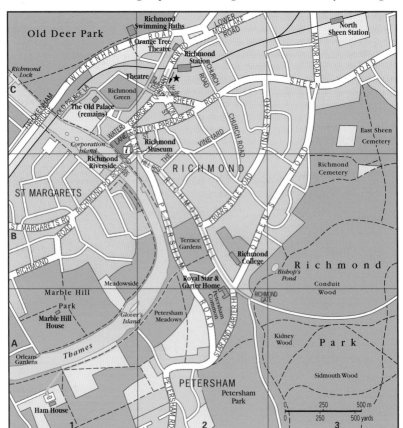

around four courtyards, with shops, a restaurant and a tourist information centre. The development (1988) is the work of Quinlan Terry, an architect who passionately believes in classical values.

A footpath leads south under Richmond Bridge (joining Petersham Road for a short stretch), following the course of the River Thames to **Ham House**▶▶ (Ham Street, tel: 020-8940 1950, www.nationaltrust.org.uk. *Open* House Apr–Oct Mon–Wed; Sat, Sun 1–5. *Admission* expensive. Garden same days 11–6, or dusk. *Admission* moderate) with good views of Marble Hill House (see page 234).

Ham House is a bold Jacobean building, dating from 1610, but remodelled in the 1670s. The sumptuous, grand rooms are remarkable for their ostentatious woodwork, plaster ceilings and furnishings, and the walls are hung with paintings by Lely, Reynolds and Constable. In the restored 17th-century gardens are square lawns, hornbeam hedges, cherry trees and herbs; there is an orangery housing a café.

Richmond Bridge, Hill Rise and Richmond Hill lead upwards for about a kilometre to **Richmond Park**▶ (*Open* 7/7.30 until 30 minutes before dusk. *Admission* free); turn around for views of the river as you climb the hill, which is lined by attractive 18th-century buildings, including Wick House, where the artist Joshua Reynolds lived. The park was enclosed by Charles I in 1637 as a royal hunting ground, and red and fallow deer still wander freely around the grassland, which is dotted with oak trees—some are over 600 years old—and man-made ponds. One enclave, the Isabella Plantation, is spectacular in late spring when the azaleas and rhododendrons are in full bloom, and has many attractive, unusual flowering trees.

Adding to the air of bygone elegance in Richmond

231

RICHMOND RIVERSIDE
Quinlan Terry's classical design for the buildings of Richmond Riverside has proved surprisingly controversial. Many inhabitants of Richmond consider the buildings to be a pleasing addition to their handsome riverfront and a fine complement to the bridge. Architects, however, accuse Terry of being populist and backward-looking. They also claim the development is dishonest: Behind the classical porticos and façades there are ordinary, steel-framed offices. It is an argument that is likely to continue for some time. Competing designs submitted for the redevelopment of the area around St. Paul's Cathedral and Spitalfields, in the City of London, have produced a similar conflict between the classical and the postmodernist approach.

Richmond Theatre, built in 1899 facing the green, has a beautiful interior

Excursions

FROM SYON TO THE SCAFFOLD

Several former inhabitants of Syon House ended up in the Tower of London or with their heads on a block. Before the house was built, it was the site of a convent, which Henry VIII seized at the Dissolution and gave to the Duke of Somerset. In 1541 Catherine Howard, the king's fifth wife, was imprisoned here, falsely accused of adultery, before her trial and execution. Next it was the turn of Somerset himself: he was appointed Protector to the boy king Edward VI at Henry VIII's death but was thought to exercise too much power; accused of conspiracy, he too was beheaded in 1552. Syon then became home to Lady Jane Grey, but only for a short while. Having been proclaimed queen in 1553 she was executed in 1554, one of the victims of the political manoeuvrings of the age.

In the distinguished company of the ancient gods at Syon

►► Syon House and Park   208A2

Brentford (tel: 020-8560 0882)
www.syonpark.co.uk
Open: House Mar–Oct Wed, Thu, Sun & hols 11–5. Admission expensive. Gardens May–Oct 10.30–5 or dusk; Nov–Feb 10.30–4. Admission expensive

A visit here makes an excellent day out: the last privately owned stately home in Greater London, with interiors by Robert Adam, grounds by the famous landscaper Capability Brown, and several other minor attractions. To get there, take the tube to Gunnersbury or train to Kew Bridge, then bus 237 or 267; or go to Syon Lane station and walk down Syon Lane and Spur Road to the London Road entrance.

Syon House From the outside, this historic seat of the Dukes of Northumberland looks slightly forbidding, but the battlemented mid 16th-century building contains some of the most magnificently and elegantly decorated rooms in England. They are the work of Robert Adam, who remodelled the interior between 1761 and 1768, using marble, gilded statues and plasterwork to create a palace fit for one of the country's most powerful aristocratic families.

The Long Gallery was remodelled by Adam, but reflects the original Jacobean House. There is also an excellent collection of portraits of family and royalty, including works by Van Dyck and Lely.

Recently some of the Duke's private rooms, which have not been previously open to the public, have been put on view. These include the Drawing Room with its splendid Adam fireplace, rescued from Northumberland House in the Strand when it was demolished in 1874. Upstairs is the suite of rooms furnished for the young Princess Victoria, to whom the 3rd Duchess of Northumberland was governess, before she became queen.

Syon Park The grounds of Syon House were landscaped between 1767 and 1773 by Capability Brown, who created

Family portraits of the Dukes of Northumberland

LONDON WETLANDS CENTRE (WWT)
This new addition to London's outdoor amenities, opened in 2000, is Europe's largest wetlands centre and comes under the auspices of the Wildfowl and Wetlands Trust (WWT). The hub of the 150 riverside acres is the Peter Scott Centre, with a discovery centre, bird observatory, shop and café. The two principal areas outside focus on the different wetland habitats of the world, including Hawaii and the Tundra, and the ecology and water life of British wetlands. The wild reserve area has 'hides' from which to view London's surprisingly varied bird life. (Queen Elizabeth's Walk, Barnes, tel: 020-8409 4400, www.wwt.org.uk *Open* daily, summer 9.30–6, winter 9.30–5. *Admission* expensive.)

233

an idyllic version of the countryside, with lakes, lawns and fine specimen trees.

The highlight, linking lake and garden, is the Great Conservatory. It has a graceful central dome of glass and iron and two curving side wings and was built between 1820 and 1827. Charles Fowler, the architect of Covent Garden market, designed it, and it perhaps influenced Joseph Paxton's design for the Crystal Palace. The conservatory contains several different gardens, ranging from the damp fernery to the hot, dry cactus beds.

The Rose Garden, between the house and river, was replanted in 1995. More than 8,000 roses, including some rare bushes, are now mature and at their most spectacular in June. Further away, a stroll around the lakes will show you many moisture-loving plants, flowering shrubs and unusual trees.

Other attractions The conservation-driven Tropical Forest is the main draw with fish, reptiles, amphibians and birds in near-natural habitats (tel: 020-8847 4730, www.tropicalforest.co.uk *Open daily 10.30–5.30. Admission* moderate). It's a great day out for the family to see the rescued creatures—often endangered species. There is plenty more to see and do within the grounds, including a giant indoor adventure playground, a garden nursery, a trout fishery and an Edinburgh Woollen Mill outlet.

Syon has a café, or you can picnic in the grounds.

Excursions

TWICKENHAM HOUSES

York House, off York Street, is a late 17th-century mansion built by an Indian tea merchant, Sir Ratan Tata, with delightful gardens stretching towards the river. The building now houses local government officesand is not open to the public.

Pope's Villa, the villa built by the poet Alexander Pope, in which he lived from 1719 to 1744, has now been replaced by St. James's Independent School. But the mineral-lined grotto he created survives from his garden, and can be visited on Sundays by written appointment (tel: 020-8892 2002).

One of Twickenham's most famous houses is **Strawberry Hill** (tel: 0870-626 0402. *Open* by prior appointment early May–Oct, Sun 2, 2.45, 3. *Admission* moderate), now St. Mary's University College. Horace Walpole (novelist and letter writer) bought a simple cottage here in 1747 and, inspired by his studies of medieval buildings, spent the next 30 years turning it into a neo-Gothic castle. The building was enormously influential in reviving the Gothic style and led to the construction of many follies, churches, and even whole houses in the same picturesque Strawberry Hill style.

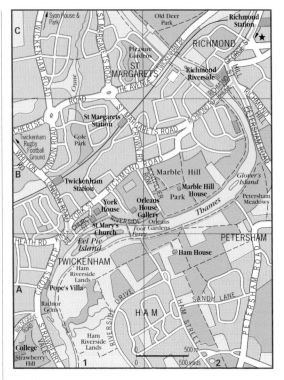

►► Twickenham

Twickenham, to sports fans, means the famous rugby stadium where international matches are held, as well as the Varsity match between Oxford and Cambridge. The stadium lies to the north of the village, with a museum on the history of the game (Rugby Road; tel: 0870-405 2001. *Open* Tue–Sat 10–5, Sun 11–5. *Admission* very expensive. Tours Tue–Sat). The village itself is best reached by taking the Underground to neighbouring Richmond (see pages 230–231) or by riverboat, which sets off from Westminster Pier in summer.

From Richmond station, turn left and walk down the Quadrant, George Street and then Hill Street to cross Richmond Bridge. Take the riverside path south to Marble Hill House, set in its spacious and leafy park.

Marble Hill House► (Richmond Road, tel: 020-8892 5115, www.english-heritage.org.uk. *Open* Apr–Oct Sat 10–2, Sun 10–5; tours Wed 12, 3. *Admission* moderate) is an exemplary Palladian villa, built to make the most of the views over the river towards Richmond Hill. It was designed as a rural retreat for Henrietta Howard, mistress of the Prince of Wales (the future George II) in 1729; later it was given to another royal consort, Mrs Fitzherbert, secretly married to the future George IV in 1785, then rejected by him in favour of Caroline of Brunswick. As with all Palladian villas, the main rooms are on the second floor, the *piano nobile*. The Great Room is a perfect cube, in keeping with the Palladian love of geometry. It is furnished as it would have been in Henrietta Howard's time, when regular visitors included the writers John Gay, Horace Walpole and Alexander

Pope—he advised on the layout of the garden, with its groves of statuesque trees and manicured lawns.

From Marble Hill, visit Montpelier Row, to the northwest, to look at one of the best surviving examples of early terrace housing (row-housing) in London, dating from 1720.

The riverside path continues upstream to the **Orleans House Gallery▶** (Riverside, tel: 020-8892 0221, www. richmond.gov.uk. *Open* Apr–Sep Tue–Sat 1–5.30, Sun 2–5.30; Oct–Mar Tue–Sat 1–4.30, Sun 2–4.30; gardens 9am–dusk. *Admission* free), built by James Gibbs in 1720 and beautifully framed by woodland. The gallery is all that remains of Orleans House, which was demolished in 1927. The Duc d'Orléans (later King Louis-Philippe of France) lived here from 1814 to 1817. Today, the gallery has commercial art exhibitions and art for sale. The Stables have also been converted into a gallery.

From the Orleans House Gallery, continue along Riverside towards **Twickenham Village▶**, passing a good waterside pub that offers food and refreshment, the White Swan. Beyond lie Church Lane, Bell Lane and Water Lane, each lined with Georgian houses. The nearby church of St. Mary is an odd combination of medieval tower and classical nave, rebuilt in 1715. Inside are monuments to the 18th-century poet and satirist Alexander Pope, his parents and his nurse, Mary Beach. Church Street, now pedestrianized, has good stores and is the site of a fair held in May during the Twickenham Week festival. London Road leads north towards the train station; otherwise, you might consider crossing the Thames by ferry from Riverside to visit Ham House (see page 231), and then walking back along the Thames to the tube station at Richmond.

235

The former home of a French king—the Orleans House Gallery in Twickenham

ETON

Thames Street leads from Windsor Castle down to the river, where Windsor Bridge takes you to Windsor's twin town of Eton, on the northern bank. This is the home of Eton College, founded by Henry VI in 1440, the school that has produced 20 prime ministers. During term time you will see the students dressed in their distinctive tailcoats and wing collars. The impressive school buildings include a Museum of Eton Life (tel: 01753-671 177, www.etoncollege.com. *Open* daily Apr–Oct, call for times), with displays on the school's history. The chapel has 15th-century wall paintings and stained-glass windows by John Piper and Evie Hone.

▶▶▶ Windsor   208A1

England's largest castle, painstakingly restored after the devastating fire of 1992, has been a royal home since 1070. The queen lives here for part of the year, usually around Easter and mid-June (when the State Apartments are closed).

A colourful Changing of the Guard ceremony is held outside the castle, May to mid-August daily at 11am, and on alternate days the rest of the year.

Windsor Castle ▶▶▶ (tel: 020-776 7304, www.royal. gov.uk. *Open* Mar–Oct daily 9.45–5.15; Nov–Feb 9.45–4.15. *Admission* very expensive. Some sections may close for royal functions). The castle itself towers above the town on a chalk cliff. Its strategic site was first defended by William the Conqueror in 1070 and for the next 900 years the building was continually enlarged, growing from a medieval castle to a vast and complex royal palace. It took on its present appearance during the 19th century.

There are several buildings to visit. St. George's Chapel is a masterpiece of Perpendicular Gothic architecture, begun in 1478 and completed in 1511. Ten monarchs are buried here. The monument to Princess Charlotte (who died in 1817 in childbirth) in the northwest chapel shows her ascending to heaven with an angel carrying her stillborn child. The Chapel's ceiling is very beautiful; and elaborate 15th-century choir stalls are covered in vignettes (animals, jesters, the Dance of Death and biblical stories) and surmounted by banners of the 26 Knights of

Above: castle guard
Left: Windsor Castle
gatehouse, built by
Henry VIII

LEGOLAND
Based on the original in
Billund, Denmark,
Legoland Windsor
opened in 1996
(tel: 08705-040 404,
www.legoland.co.uk. *Open*
mid-Mar to late-Oct daily
10–5, until 7 in school
summer holidays. Closed
Tue–Wed in Sep–Oct
Admission very
expensive). It's in a beautiful setting of landscaped
and manicured grounds,
with the entrance high on
a hill in Windsor Great
Park, enjoying magnificent
views over Windsor
Castle. Legoland is
designed for children
(ages 2–12) but all the
family will love it. Miniland
is a huge model village of
European landmarks built
with more than 20 million
Lego pieces. Other activity
zones include themed
rides, drive-yourself boats
and cars, dozens of
ingenious working models,
rollercoasters, a Legoland
Driving School, and other
live shows.

On the negative side,
queues can be long (so
bring a picnic of snacks
and drinks to recharge
energy levels during the
wait). On a sunny day this
is undoubtedly the best
day out of London for
young children.

the Garter, whose installation has taken place here since 1348. It was here that the Queen's youngest child, Edward, married Sophie Rhys-Jones in 1999.

The restored State Apartments are hung with works from the Royal Collection, the world's finest private art collection. Do not miss Queen Mary's Dolls' House, designed by Sir Edwin Lutyens and given to the nation in 1923. The furnishings are designed at one-twelfth life-size, the plumbing and lighting really work, and eminent writers and artists contributed handwritten books or miniature paintings to the library.

Windsor town ►► After visiting the castle, it is worth exploring Windsor's shops and public buildings. The Guildhall on the High Street was completed in 1707 by Sir Christopher Wren. Its Tuscan columns, on the ground floor, do not touch the ceiling; apparently, the town council insisted on having them, but Wren left the gap to prove that they were structurally superfluous. Continuing up the High Street you will pass the 19th-century parish church of St. John the Baptist; further on and to the left, St. Albans Street leads to the Royal Mews and an exhibition of the Queen's horses, carriages and state coaches.

Windsor Great Park ►►► You can continue from here up Park Street to the Long Walk, which skirts Windsor Great Park. This 4.8km (3-mile) avenue was laid out by Charles I and planted with elms. The original trees died and had to be replaced in 1945 with chestnuts and plane trees.

Accommodation

The cost of hotel accommodation in central London is horrendously high. You can expect to pay £100 a night for a reasonable room, and the rates begin to soar if you stay at one of London's grand old hotels such as the Connaught, Claridges, the Dorchester or the Savoy. Good value hotels and guest houses do exist, of course (many are listed in the Directory section at the back of this book). Rooms in these hotels are, however, very much in demand, and to get a room you must reserve well in advance—often as much as two or three months prior to your visit.

Many hotels will ask you to confirm your reservation in some way and will charge you a fee if you cancel at short notice or fail to turn up. In some cases you will lose any deposit you have paid and some hotels will charge the cost of the room to your credit card, so advise your hotel as soon as possible of any change of plans.

General tips Here are a few general points to bear in mind when staying in London:
• For relatively cheap but central hotels and guest houses, concentrate on the Bloomsbury area (for example, hotels in Gower Street or Cartwright Gardens, off Russell Square), and the Pimlico–Victoria area.
• Remember that many hotels geared primarily to business travellers offer much cheaper rates at the weekend. It is worth checking to see whether big chains such as the Forte group or Thistle Hotels are offering one of their regular weekend-break discount offers. Some hotels also offer lower rates to guests staying for a week or more.
• London is a popular year-round destination, but rates can be cheaper during February and March, and October and November. London is also generally quieter and less hectic during these months.
• **Visit London** (formerly the London Tourist Board) can reserve accommodation online at www.visitlondon.com. The **British and London Visitor Centre** at 1 Lower Regent Street gives out listings of London and nationwide accommodation that has been inspected by the English Tourism Council, including youth hostels, guest houses, hotels and self-catering accommodation. Visitors may book direct or via the Centre's booking agents (www.lastminute.com), who charge a booking fee. You can also book accommodation at the **London Information Centre** on Leicester Square (tel: 020-7292 2333, www.londontown.com. *Open* 8am–midnight).

238

CHARGES
When making a reservation, check what the room rate quoted includes: Usually the price is inclusive of VAT (Value Added Tax) and a service charge, but it is best to be sure, because these can amount to nearly a third of the bill. Breakfast is often included in the cheaper hotels; the more upmarket you go, the more likely it is that breakfast will be charged as extra.

If you want luxury in London expect to pay top prices

Hotel facilities The biggest problem with London hotels is noise, as many are located on busy streets. Some have double or triple glazing to keep out the sound, but that can make rooms unbearably stuffy, especially since air-conditioning is by no means a standard facility. You should bear this point in mind when choosing a hotel and, if you value peace and quiet, look for hotels on side streets in residential areas; or request a room at the rear of the hotel or higher up in the building.

Most hotel rooms have a private bathroom, television, and direct dial telephone—but beware of very high mark-ups on telephone calls. Laundry service is often slow and expensive. Hotels are increasingly supplying electric kettles and tea or coffee packets so that guests can make their own hot drinks. For other facilities, such as parking, 24-hour room service, gyms and swimming pools, you can expect to pay a very high premium within central London.

The Russell Hotel in Bloomsbury, a grand Victorian landmark convenient for the British Museum

The London Hilton on Park Lane may not be stunning from the outside, but inside guests can enjoy wonderful views

London's cafés and restaurants compare with the world's best

SUNDAY LUNCH
This is a good way to enjoy fine food at a relaxed pace. It can also prove cheaper if you opt for the fixed-price menu. At the top end, try the menu at the Connaught or The Ivy, Tamarind, Chor Bizarre down the price scale; or the slightly cheaper Veeraswamy. Mirabelle does a good set-priced lunch. Most hotels offer a fixed price traditional Sunday roast, too, which include delicious desserts. For a budget alternative, many pubs also offer a whole-some Sunday lunch.

Snacking al fresco in Soho, one of central London's best places for quality casual dining

Food and drink

Eating and drinking in London underwent a revolution that began in the late 1980s and continued throughout the 1990s. Cafés smartened up. Pubs disposed of their smoky, male-orientated image and became places to meet, eat and perhaps drink all day—some even do breakfast. Bars re-invented themselves into upbeat forums. Even in-house museum and gallery eating improved substantially. Meanwhile, restaurants increased in number and became fiercely competitive in setting (well-known architects and designers modelled many), service, and in the authenticity and creativity of their food and drinks. In essence, eating out became an enjoyable and regular experience.

Today, you can sample most of the world's cuisines in central London. Furthermore, their distinctive regional variants are cooked correctly and to a high level, be it north Italian, South Indian, Cajun or Californian. Alternatively, you can enjoy the highly creative cooking of young, imaginative chefs inspired by various countries round the world. Fresh ingredients imported into London from almost every country help ensure quality is main-tained. There is no need to eat badly.

Finding the ideal restaurants for your needs may prove something of a challenge, however. You will almost cer-tainly have a specific setting in mind to suit the mood of the occasion, be it romantic, informal, a family meal or business lunch. Furthermore, this restaurant will need to be in the right place; it is pointless to cross London from an Islington theatre to a Kensington restaurant, only to return to a St. James's hotel. The price must accord with your budget for the occasion.

To add to the difficulties, restaurants open up, reinvent themselves or close down with alarming speed, and chefs move on, which can affect the quality of the fare on offer. Thus, it is wise to start by doing some research (see panel page 241) and to take a few tips from experienced

Food and drink

A combined shopping and dining experience at Covent Garden piazza

SPECIALIST GUIDES
For an idea of the full range on offer, see the *Time Out Eating and Drinking Guide*. For a more personal selection, see the *AA The Restaurant Guide* (of which a selection is listed on page 277–281), *Harden's London Restaurants* or the *Zagat Survey of London Restaurants*, all published annually. The best guide to budget eating is *Time Out Cheap Eats in London*.

241

Londoners—even they have to work to keep abreast of the whole scene.

Finding the good deal Meal deals abound in London. They make a huge difference to the bill, and not even the most comfortable purse will ignore them. Many of London's finest restaurants offer a fixed-price menu at a substantial reduction on the same dishes selected à la carte. They are usually offered for weekday lunches. Some of the best include La Porte des Indes, Veeraswamy, J. Sheekey, Lemonia and Lou Pescadou. There are also good fixed price menus for pre- or post-theatre suppers at venues such as the Savoy Grill, Mon Plaisir and Launceston Place.

Reservations Reserving a table is essential if you want to eat at a specific restaurant at a specific time—which most people do in London. Top chefs, fashionable restaurants and popular locals need to be reserved well in advance. Some will be more likely to have a table at lunch than at dinner. Lunch is eaten from as early as 12.15 or as late as 1.45, and tends to end 2.15–3. If you are meeting for a drink before going to the theatre or out to dinner, try the Waldorf Hilton , the American Bar in the Savoy, Mezzo, One Aldwych and the Dorchester. Some restaurants near the West End theatres—which stretch from Aldwych to Piccadilly, will be quiet and lack atmosphere during performance time; furthermore, they will expect people to leave in time for the restaurant's post-theatre reservations, and this can make dinner more hurried than you might wish. If dinner after the theatre ends very late, you can ask the staff to call a black cab for you.

Fresh fruit and ice-cream at Neal's Yard in Covent Garden

Regent Street decked out for Christmas

Shopping

London offers shoppers a vast range, from mini-city department stores to wheelbarrow bargains and Dickensian speciality shops. Many people come to London just to shop, so Oxford Street and Regent Street can be crammed to bursting point in summer and in the Christmas shopping season, and particularly long queues can be expected at the most popular stores such as **Hamley's**. Remember, there are plenty of other quieter areas to shop.

Opening hours The worst crowds can be avoided by shopping early. Shops tend to open around 10am (though some open at 9am) and you will often find that service is more attentive during the slacker period before lunchtime shoppers begin to arrive. Shops have become increasingly flexible in their opening hours in recent years; it is now common to find them open until 9 or 10pm in the main areas, though the big department stores have late-night opening on only one day of the week (typically Wednesday or Thursday). Increasingly, too, plenty of shops open on Sunday.

242

Bargain time Twice a year, London shops slash their prices in order to sell off the previous season's remaining stock: The January sales start immediately after Christmas and continue well into February. Determined bargain-hunters camp out in the streets for several days in advance to be first in the queue when the sales open at Harrods, Debenhams or Selfridges.

The summer sales begin in June or July and last to the end of August. Strict rules govern the way that sales operate in Britain, and the fact that you bought an item in a sale does not affect your statutory rights as a consumer; you are, for example, entitled to a full refund if the goods

London's markets, such as this one in Berwick Street, are always lively and colourful

prove faulty (unless they were sold as damaged goods) —
but you must retain your receipt as proof of purchase.

Tax-free shopping If the goods you buy are going to be
exported to a non-European Union country you are exempt
from Value Added Tax; this can be a considerable saving
(but you have to spend a minimum amount which varies
from store to store). Most leading stores have details of the
tax-free shopping policy and can help with your claims.

Street vendors With the exception of market traders, you
should beware of street vendors anywhere in London.
The products they sell are often not what they claim to be,
and while you are absorbed in watching their theatrical
sales technique, their accomplices may well be picking
your pockets.

Markets The same advice about pickpockets applies to
crowded street markets, but otherwise London's markets
are enormous fun—the sales banter of stallholders is
refreshingly direct and there are real bargains to be found.
Here is a selection of the best:
• **Berwick Street** (Soho): top-quality flowers, fruits and
vegetables daily except Sunday.
• **Covent Garden**: antiques on Monday, crafts from
Tuesday to Sunday, in and around the central arcade.
• **Camden Lock**: crafts, antiques, books, used clothes
and jewellery; daily.
• **Portobello Road**: fruit and vegetables, but antiques,
used clothes and jewellery; best by far on Saturday.
• **Camden Passage**: antiques, collectables and jewellery
on Wednesday and Saturday.
• **Petticoat Lane** and surrounding streets: a complete
mixture serving City office workers and local East End
residents—everything from silk saris to tacky ties, plus
fruits and vegetables; daily.
• There is more of the same nearby at **Leather Lane**
(weekday lunchtimes) and at **Brick Lane** (Sunday
mornings only).

*The famous Harrods
green livery extends to
the doormen*

243

*Browsing among the
market stalls is a
favourite London
pastime*

London

London's club scene is a melting pot of constant, dynamic change

WORLD AND ROOTS MUSIC

If you're feeling homesick or just want to try another musical culture, the following venues are a good bet:

12 Bar Club, 22 Denmark Place (tel: 020-7240 2120, 020-7240 2622 for tickets), accoustically-driven pop, new folk, new country. Great little venue;

Cecil Sharp House, 2 Regent's Park Road (tel: 020-7485 2206), home to English folk and dance music;

Jazz Café, 5 Parkway London N1 (tel: 0870-060 3777 for tickets), jazz, blues and soul, plus acts from all over the world.

Nightlife

London has a rich and varied nightlife, a fact that is immediately apparent when you flick through the pages of *Time Out* magazine—an indispensable guide if you want to know what is on where, and which clubs, nightspots or discos are active that week. The magazine will also advise you on points of club etiquette, such as dress codes, so that you look the part—most clubs frown on casual jeans, T-shirts and trainers. The preferred dress is smart but casual, although for theme nights you will be expected to dress with flair. Club venues come and go with bewildering speed, and some host different nightclubs or themes on each day of the week. Here are a few venues that have had some staying power:

Koko, 1 Camden High Street (tel: 0870-432 5527); very popular with overseas visitors: vast and fun.
The Gardening Club, 4 The Piazza, Covent Garden (tel: 020-7836 4052). Busy studenty place playing funk, commerical, hip hop, disco and soul.
The Hippodrome, Charing Cross Road (tel: 020-7437 4311); relaunched with a burlesque theme; new and vintage dance.
Ministry of Sound, 103 Gaunt Street (tel: 0870-060 0010); based on a New York prototype, the legendary Paradise Garage, with different styles of music on different nights.

Comedy, cabaret and jazz

The Comedy Store, Haymarket House, 1 Oxendon Street (tel: 08700-602340); founded in 1979, and still going strong, it's the place to see both new talent and more established comedians.

Dover Street, 8–9 Dover Street (tel: 020-7629 9813); food and wine by candlelight with live jazz, blues or soul (and dancing) until 3am every night.

Jongleurs, The Rise Bar, 49 Lavender Gardens, SW11 (tel: all clubs 0870-787 0707). This is the original Battersea venue for one of London's best and longest-running comedy companies. Jongleurs also have clubs at 11 East Yard, Camden Lock and Bow, 221 Grove Road.

100 Club, 100 Oxford Street (tel: 020-7636 0933); trad jazz or indie, depending on which night you go. Drinks at pub prices.

Madame JoJo's, 8–10 Brewer Street (tel: 020-7734 3040); often listed as part of the London gay scene, but it attracts a straight audience as well for scintillating cabaret performed by outrageously camp drag artists.

Ronnie Scott's, 47 Frith Street (tel: 020-7439 0747); famous for top-quality jazz—so it gets very crowded, especially on Saturday, when reservations are essential.

Theatre, music and dance For more information, see Focus on features on pages 148–149, 180–181.

Film Newspapers and listings magazines carry general cinema information; foreign films often experience a delay before being released in the UK. A number of cinemas show a changing schedule of art/classic/cult/kitsch or offbeat films, usually with late-night screenings; try the following:

Barbican, Barbican Centre, Silk Street (tel: 020-7638 7211).
ICA Cinema, Nash House, The Mall (tel: 020-7930 0493).
National Film Theatre, South Bank (tel: 020-7928 3232).
Screen on the Green, 83 Upper Street, Islington (tel: 020-7226 3520).

Bright lights, action, films on Leicester Square: the place to catch the latest Hollywood blockbusters

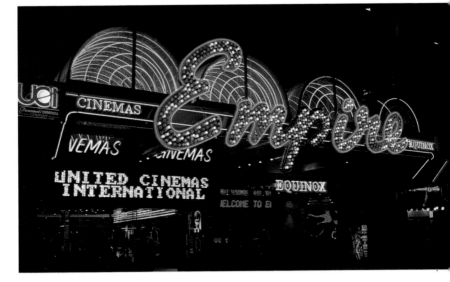

Keep your eyes open for London's colourful old street furnishings, such as this Victorian mailbox

Itineraries

Here are some suggestions for making the most of your time in London.

A weekend in London

Since every minute is going to be precious, do as much advance planning and reserving as possible. Reserve hotels, theatre tickets, and restaurants well ahead, and remember too that you can save time in queues by buying tickets in advance for some of London's most popular attractions, such as the London Eye (see pages 201–202), Tower of London (see pages 196–197), Madame Tussauds (see pages 120–121), and Buckingham Palace (see pages 64–65). Westminster Abbey, St. Paul's and other major churches will be holding services on Sunday, and visits are therefore restricted—if you want to see them, plan to do this on Saturday. Saturday is also an excellent day for sampling markets, such as Camden Lock and Portobello Road. Museums do not open until later on Sunday so use your Sunday morning for a stroll around some intriguing part of London, taking advantage of the relative quiet and lack of traffic to get a good look at the varied architecture.

A week in London

With a whole week at your disposal in London, you'll have a better chance of getting right under the skin of the city. You will probably have your own personal priorities, but consider the following suggestions:

Day 1: Take a guided tour by bus (see page 40) or a river trip (see page 55) to get your bearings.
Day 2: Explore Covent Garden, with its shops, stalls, street performers, museums and restaurants, for a truly varied day. Cross the river to ride on the BA London Eye.
Day 3: Visit one of London's big museums—there are plenty to choose from—in the morning, but plan something different for the afternoon, such as a stroll around St. James's Park and shopping in the Piccadilly/Regent Street area.

The National Gallery, on Trafalgar Square, is London's best free picture show

Day 4: Use the day to hit the popular sights of London, but be prepared to make an early start: buy your ticket in advance but still arrive early at either the Tower of London or Madame Tussaud's; alternatively, skip Madame Tussaud's and pay a visit to the royal wax effigies in the undercroft at Westminster Abbey instead—perhaps combining this with the Changing of the Guard at Horse Guards or St. James's.

Day 5: Get out of town altogether and take a trip to Greenwich or Hampton Court, both very rewarding full-day trips with lots to see.

Day 6: Visit some more museums. If you have not seen the Victoria and Albert or the British Museum, now is the time to do so—you will find so much to see that you will promise yourself a return visit.

Day 7: Your last day may well be spent shopping for presents in Liberty's or the huge department stores, such as Harrods and Selfridges; for something clearly related to your stay in London, find special products in the museum shops of either Tate gallery, the National Gallery, V&A or British Museum, and take a walk along the South Bank for some last memorable views of London.

French-style cafés in Old Compton Street

Best sights for children
1 **Natural History Museum** see pages 94, 98–99
2 **BA London Eye** see page 201–202
3 **London Aquarium** see page 201
4 **ZSL London Zoo** see page 125
5 **London Transport Museum** see page 146
6 **Museum of London** see pages 166–167
7 **V & A Museum of Childhood** see page 184
8 **HMS *Belfast*** see page 191
9 **Science Museum** see pages 100–101
10 **Imperial War Museum** see pages 200–201

Away from the hustle
1 **Chelsea Physic Garden** see page 91
2 **Leighton House Museum** see pages 108–109
3 **Linley Sambourne House** see page 114
4 **The Wallace Collection** see pages 126–127
5 **Sir John Soane's Museum** see pages 154–155
6 **Courtauld Gallery** see pages 156–158
7 **Syon House and Park** see pages 232–233
8 **Dulwich Picture Gallery** see page 214
9 **Fenton House** see page 220
10 **Kew Gardens** see pages 226–227

London

FREE CHILD-FRIENDLY MUSEUMS

Entrance to London's major museums is free, which is great news for families and means you can spend as little time as you like without feeling you have to hang around for hours to get your money's worth. Most children love nature in one form or another so don't miss the Natural History Museum—their dinosaur displays are particularly popular—then change subject by scooting around the corner to the ingenious hands-on stations at the Science Museum. The Museum of London is very child-friendly too and older kids will probably enjoy the British Museum as long as you chose the right subjects—the Eygptian section and its collection of mummies is an evergreen favourite.

Street entertainers

London for free

London can be one of the world's most expensive cities. But those in the know can seek out top quality entertainment without spending a penny.

• Not all museums charge visitors. The National Gallery, National Portrait Gallery, British Museum, the Tate galleries, Wallace Collection, Science Museum, Natural History Museum, Victoria and Albert Museum, Sir John Soane's Museum and many smaller museums are free. If you enjoy yourself, you may like to make a donation.

• It costs nothing to visit the Central Criminal Court (better known as the Old Bailey) or the Royal Courts of Justice (where civil cases are heard) where you can watch the English legal system at work—ask the ushers at the entrance to the public galleries what kind of trial is in progress. Very close by you can also visit the beautiful, ageless Inns of Court where the barristers receive their training.

• Both of the major arts locations—the Barbican and the South Bank—have free lobby exhibitions, children's events, musical performances and other entertainment. Visit the Royal Opera House for their free Monday lunchtime concert.

• If people-watching, clowning, acrobatics, puppetry and pavement musicians are more to your taste, Covent Garden market is the place to go, especially at lunchtime and on weekends in summer. The quality of the street theatre is very high—although you should, in all conscience, contribute a few coins, or more, as gratuities for the actors and performers.

• Go to Harrods or Liberty's or any other of London's great department stores and dream of what you might buy—and perhaps buy it.

• Go to an auction and watch others spend their fortunes —sales at Christie's, Sotheby's, Bonham's or Phillip's are fascinating to watch.

• Attend a free lunchtime concert. There is usually a choice of several, especially in City churches (check with tourist information for details). A popular venue is at St. James's Church Piccadilly, with classical music for free.

Brixton Kennington Whitehall **159**
Trafalgar Square Oxford Street

Marble Arch

VLA 173

ARRIVA

LJ55 BVE

Travel Facts

Arriving and departing

Entry formalities European Union citizens have the right to enter the United Kingdom at will; in theory you need only to carry some evidence of identity, such as an ID card or driver's licence. In practice the United Kingdom authorities are uncomfortable with the idea of open borders, arguing that checks are necessary to combat terrorism, smuggling and illegal immigration. It is therefore advisable to bring your full passport.

Visitors from outside the European Union must have a valid passport to enter the UK. Citizens of most Commonwealth countries, the US, Japan and much of South America do not need a visa, but there are some exceptions (including Nigeria, Ghana, India, Bangladesh, Sri Lanka and Pakistan). If in doubt, check with your travel agent or the British Embassy in your home country.

Airports Most visitors to the UK arrive at Heathrow or Gatwick airports (www.baa.com) where both have good facilities including tourist information, hotel reservations and car hire services. See also information on telephone numbers on page 251.

Gatwick From Gatwick, three train services operate to London. The Gatwick Express leaves every 15 minutes (less often at night) on its 30-minute ride to Victoria. Thameslink trains stop at London Bridge, Blackfriars, City Thameslink, Farringdon and King's Cross. Southern runs between Gatwick and Victoria. National Express Shuttle 025 bus runs hourly by day to Victoria.

Heathrow Train is the fastest way to reach London; you can travel either by Underground on the Piccadilly Line (50 minutes to central London) or by Heathrow Express to Paddington, departing every 15 minutes from 5.10 am–11.25pm (the journey takes 15 minutes). The Airbus bus service (which takes roughly one hour and 15 minutes) calls at all terminals every half hour from around 5.30am until late daily (times depend on which termnal). The route passes by Holland Park, Notting Hill Gate, Queensway, Marble Arch, Baker Street, Euston and Russell Square.

London City This airport (www.londoncityairport.com) mostly used by business travellers, is closest to the central London. Docklands Light Railway (DLR) at London City Airport connects at Bank station for the Underground. There is also a shuttle bus service.

Stansted The Stansted express train departs every 15–30 minutes and takes 45 minutes to reach Liverpool Street station. There is also the A6 bus service to Victoria.

Liverpool Street Station

Black cabs or minicabs run from all airports to central London but are a very expensive option.

London's distinctive black taxicabs are the most pleasant and convenient way to get about town, but can be expensive

> ❏ **Airport information:**
> Gatwick: 0870-000 2468
> Heathrow: 0870-000123
> London City: 020-7646 0000
> Stansted: 0870-000 0303 ❏

Arriving by train Eurostar trains (tel: 08705-186186) arrive regularly at St. Pancras International terminal from Paris and Disneyland Paris, Brussels and Lille.

National trains (tel: 08457-484950) come in to one of the eight main railway stations—Charing Cross, Euston, King's Cross, Liverpool Street, London Bridge, Paddington, Victoria and Waterloo stations—or along the Thameslink line, which connects Luton and Gatwick airports.

Long-distance bus services arrive at Victoria Coach Station (tel: 020-7222 1234). The major bus companies include National Express (tel: 08705-808080) and Eurolines (tel: 08705-143 219).

Other options Visitors from other European countries have a wealth of options for getting to the UK, such as shuttle flights, which operate between smaller regional airports, trans-European train and bus services (including the Channel Tunnel), and ferry services.

It is well worth shopping around for the best deal—you may find that you can save a lot of money. Inclusive packages, covering travel and hotel accommodation, often represent the best value.

Car rental

It is not worth the expense and worry of renting a car in London if you only intend to travel within the city. Using public transport or taxis will cost you far less and save time spent looking for parking spaces and navigating unfamiliar roads. Even for trips out of London, it can be simpler to use train or bus services. If you do decide to rent a car, you will find a huge range of companies and options listed in the *Yellow Pages* telephone directory, and by phoning around you should get a competitive deal.

Some points to bear in mind:
• You must have a driver's licence (an international driver's licence is not required).
• You must be over 18 years old to rent a car (in fact, many companies have an age limit of 21); and you must also have at least 12 months' driving experience.
• Reserving in advance is essential at weekends, especially for the cheaper end of the range (and for cars at the

Many Londoners travel by tube

> ❑ **Leading firms—central reservation numbers**
> Alamo—0870-400 4562
> Avis—0870-010-0287
> Budget—0844-581 2231
> Europcar—08706-075000
> Hertz—0870-844 8844 ❑

top end—Rolls Royces are much in demand at weekends for weddings).
• Car-rental firms prefer you to pay by credit card so that they can check your address and identity—expect to encounter problems if you want to pay by cash or cheque (a very large deposit is usually demanded if this is the case).

Car repairs and servicing

If you hire a car in London, the hire company will usually give you the number of its 24-hour breakdown service. Otherwise, there are two main organizations offering road service in the UK: the Automobile Association (AA) and the Royal Automobile Club (RAC).

If you are a member of a similar organization in your own country, check before you travel to London whether you have the right to use the services of one of these organizations for free—and remember to bring the necessary documentation with you.

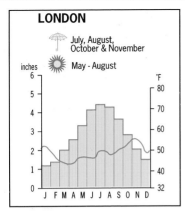

LONDON

July, August, October & November

May - August

Automobile Association:
membership information tel: 08000-852721. For emergency breakdown service tel: 0800-887766 (freefone).
Royal Automobile Club: membership information tel: 08000-722822. For emergency breakdown service tel: 0800-828282 (freefone).

Climate

The British love to talk about the weather simply because it is so variable—changing hour by hour, if not minute by minute. All daily newspapers carry weather forecasts, as do all the TV and radio channels (usually just before or just after the main newscasts of the day) but as every Londoner will tell you, they are not always reliable. London has its own microclimate, because of the great number of heated buildings in the city, so frost and lingering snow are very rare. The temperature seldom falls below freezing, although chilling northerly winds can make it feel cold in the winter. Rain is the biggest problem. Officially the wettest weeks are from late September to the end of November, but it can be just as wet in the middle of summer. As a rule of

A British policeman

thumb, you can usually plan that if you carry full anti-rain gear—waterproof coat and hat, umbrella and boots—the day will probably be dry and sunny, but if you go out unprepared it will pour! Fortunately, you are never very far away from shelter in London—unless, that is, you are caught out in the middle of Hyde Park!

Crime

A substantial amount of petty crime takes place on London's streets by day and night, and visitors are most at risk from pickpocketing and theft of property from parked cars (which is another good reason for not driving in London).

Here are some tips to make your holiday safer:
• Make photocopies of important documents such as your passport, and keep a note of traveller's cheque numbers and credit card details. This record should be kept separately from the original documents and will help you obtain replacements quickly if the originals are lost or stolen.
• Lock all your valuables in a hotel safe. Most good hotels will allocate you a safe with its own key where you can put your money, jewellery, camera, and so on.
• If you must carry valuables, conceal them in a money belt or something similar and keep a tight hold on your camera at all times.
• Be especially wary in crowded situations, such as in street markets, on a bus or subway, or in crowds crossing busy roads, like Oxford Street. Be alert at all times and try not to become so absorbed in window-shopping that you are oblivious to other people around you.
• Trust nobody and be wary of anyone who approaches you, no matter how innocently. Some people operate with accomplices who pick your pocket while you are distracted giving directions. Other thieves hang out wherever there are beggars or street musicians watching to see where you put your hand when asked for money—giving them a clue to where you keep your valuables.

253

If you are robbed you should do the following:
• Report the loss of your credit cards and traveller's cheques to the issuing company as soon as possible.
• Make a report to the nearest police station and obtain a copy of your statement so that you can make an insurance claim. They will issue you with a crime reference number.
• Report the loss of a passport to your embassy or consulate (see page 257).
• It is not sensible to be out in some parts of London late at night on your own. If you must be out, go as part of a group. Do not go to parks or commons after dark and keep to busy, well-lit streets. Buses, trains and the Underground are relatively safe at night, but it is a sensible rule to stay with the crowds, rather than exposing yourself to the risk of attack by sitting in an empty carriage. Most of the public transport system closes down at night; it is better to take a night bus

Enjoying a spot of sunshine

or taxi, despite the expense, than risk being on the streets alone—especially if you are in the city suburbs.

Customs regulations
The import of wildlife souvenirs sourced from rare or endangered species may be either illegal or require a special permit. Before purchase you should check your home country's customs regulations. You will not normally have to pay duty on personal possessions brought into the UK, but some goods, such as tobacco and alcohol, are subject to tax and duty.
Since July 1999 people travelling within the European Union are no longer entitled to import duty-free goods. However, travellers aged over 21 from outside the EU can bring in duty-free goods up to the current EU allowances:
• Alcohol (over 22° vol) 1 litre or

Alcohol (not over 22° vol) 2 litres
• Still table wine 2 litres
• Cigarettes 200 or
Cigars 50 or
Tobacco 250 grams
• Perfume 60 ml
• Toilet water 250 ml
If you think you have goods to declare for duty, either go through the Red Channel at the port of entry (where you can pay any duty levied by credit card), or before you leave for London click on the website of HM Customs and Excise Enquiries www. hmce. gov.uk or tel: 0845-010 9000.

Domestic travel
For travel outside London, see pages 210–211. For travel within London see Public transport, pages 264–265. (For any London travel query click on www.tfl.gov.uk).

Travellers with disabilities
London is a better city than most for people with disabilities. As a general rule, it is a good idea to telephone in

Clamping to deter illegal parking—releasing your car will attract a large fee

advance if you need special help or try www.tfl.gov.uk and follow the links, Passenger Help, Access and Mobility.

Artsline (tel: 020-7388 2227, www. artsline. org.uk) is an organization that offers free information and advice for people with disabilities on all aspects of the London arts and entertainment scene, including museums, galleries, concert halls, theatres and cinemas.

For information on accommodation, contact the **Holiday Care Service** (tel: 0845-124 9971 or write to Tourism for All, The Hawkins Suite, Enham Place, Enham Alamein, Andover SP11 6JS, www.holidaycare.org.uk), which offers a free advisory service.

The most comprehensive specialist guide to London for people with disabilities is *Access in London*, published by Nicholson. It is available in some bookshops or from Access Project, 39 Bradley Gardens, West Ealing, London W13 8HE (www.access project-phsp.org/london). It was written and researched by people with disabilities. For information on tour operators who cater specifically for visitors with disabilities, contact RADAR (the Royal Association for Disability and Rehabilitation, tel: 020-7250 3222, www.radar.org.uk).

Driving tips
The best tip for anyone contemplating driving in London is simple: don't. London already has too many vehicles and it will take you much longer to get around by car than by public transport. Parking spaces are hard to find, meters are expensive, and your car will be clamped (a lock put on the wheel so you cannot drive) or towed away if you park illegally. Theft from cars is the commonest crime in the UK and is still on the increase. If you must drive, then:
• Carry lots of small change to feed parking meters (these are due to be phased out in December 2008 when meters accepting credit cards only will be installed). Do not overstay your allotted time; there are plenty of traffic police around to nab offenders, and the fines are expensive. Meter parking is usually free after 6.30pm, after 1.30pm Saturday and all day Sunday, but restrictions are more

extensive in the West End and busy areas, so check what it says on the meter or on signs at the roadside.

• Don't park on double yellow lines or in areas reserved for permit holders—to do so virtually guarantees that you will have your wheels clamped, or your vehicle towed—a very expensive inconvenience. You should avoid areas with double red lines and anywhere near crossings at all times.

• If you are leaving your car parked in London for any length of time, use a patrolled car park, staffed by attendants, despite the cost involved,

Taking a rest from sightseeing

rather than leaving your car on the streets, where it can be stolen.

• If your car has disappeared when you come back to it, contact the nearest police station. If it was badly parked, you may find it has been towed and you will have to reclaim it from a car pound.

• If your car is clamped, the notice posted on your windscreen will explain how to get it released. If you do not have the time to wait around (and it can take some hours), you can pay someone else a fee to do it for you. Try the **Car Clamp Recovery Club** (tel: 01689 860121).

❏ **24-hour parking garages in central London**
Park Lane (the biggest in central London, below Marble Arch traffic circle—there are usually spaces here even when all other car parks are full.)
Brewer Street
Newport Place
Upper St. Martin's Lane

24-hour petrol stations in central London
106 Old Brompton Road
71 King's Cross Road
104 Bayswater Road   ❏

Electricity

The electrical current in the UK is 240 volts, 50 cycle AC. Plugs are three-prong square. Most hotels also have two-pin 110-volt shaver sockets. To use most American or European appliances you will need to use an adapter.

Embassies, consulates and high commissions

Australia Australia House, Strand (tel: 020-7379 4334)
Canada 38 Grosvenor Street (tel: 020-7258 6600)
France 58 Knightsbridge (tel: 0870-005 6717); visa section: 6A Cromwell Place (tel: 09065 508940)
Germany 23 Belgrave Square (tel: 020-7073 1000)
Ireland 17 Grosvenor Place (tel: 020-7235 2171)
Israel 2 Palace Green (tel: 020-7957 9500)
Japan 101–4 Piccadilly (tel: 020-7465 6500)
Netherlands 38 Hyde Park Gate (tel: 020-7590 3200/visas 09065 540720)
New Zealand New Zealand House, 80 Haymarket (tel: 020-7930 8422)
South Africa, South Africa House, Trafalgar Square (tel: 0870-005 6974)
USA 24 Grosvenor Square (tel: 020-7499 9000)

Emergency telephone numbers

Dial 999 and state whether you need Fire, Police or Ambulance. All calls are free and you can use any telephone—you can dial from a card phone without inserting a card or from a pay phone without inserting any coins.

Health and insurance

In the event of serious illness or injury you can seek medical help at the accident and emergency department ('casualty') of any hospital that has one, and you can call an ambulance by dialing 999. Most of the larger hotels have a doctor on call to deal with more routine problems, but a charge is often made for their services.

Free medical treatment is available to citizens of the European Union and some other countries with whom Britain has reciprocal arrangements. It is advisable to check the precise arrangements before you leave your own country because free treatment is usually only available to those who have completed all the necessary documentation in advance. All other foreign visitors (including those from the US and Canada) are required to pay the full cost of the medical treatment they receive and you are advised to arrange your health insurance before arriving in the UK.

The traditional home of the Prime Minister—No. 10 Downing Street

257

CONVERSION CHARTS

FROM	TO	MULTIPLY BY
Inches	Centimetres	2.54
Centimetres	Inches	0.3937
Feet	Metres	0.3048
Metres	Feet	3.2810
Yards	Metres	0.9144
Metres	Yards	1.0940
Miles	Kilometres	1.6090
Kilometres	Miles	0.6214
Acres	Hectares	0.4047
Hectares	Acres	2.4710
Gallons	Litres	4.5460
Litres	Gallons	0.2200
Ounces	Grams	28.35
Grams	Ounces	0.0353
Pounds	Grams	453.6
Grams	Pounds	0.0022
Pounds	Kilograms	0.4536
Kilograms	Pounds	2.205
Tons	Tonnes	1.0160
Tonnes	Tons	0.9842

MEN'S SUITS

UK	36	38	40	42	44	46	48
Rest of Europe	46	48	50	52	54	56	58
US	36	38	40	42	44	46	48

DRESS SIZES

UK	8	10	12	14	16	18
France	36	38	40	42	44	46
Italy	38	40	42	44	46	48
Rest of Europe	34	36	38	40	42	44
US	6	8	10	12	14	16

MEN'S SHIRTS

UK	14	14.5	15	15.5	16	16.5	17
Rest of Europe	36	37	38	39/40	41	42	43
US	14	14.5	15	15.5	16	16.5	17

MEN'S SHOES

UK	7	7.5	8.5	9.5	10.5	11
Rest of Europe	41	42	43	44	45	46
US	8	8.5	9.5	10.5	11.5	12

WOMEN'S SHOES

UK	4.5	5	5.5	6	6.5	7
Rest of Europe	38	38	39	39	40	41
US	6	6.5	7	7.5	8	8.5

Lost property

Any property left on the bus, in a black cab or Underground system will be taken to the **Lost Property Office** at 200 Baker Street, next door to the Baker Street tube station (Mon–Fri 8.30–4). Either visit in person, tel: 0845-330 9882; fax: 020-7918 1028, or visit www.tfl.gov.uk and click on 'Help'. There is a restoration fee of £3. If you lose property on a train contact the station at which your train terminated (see telephone directory for station telephone numbers).

Insurance companies will expect you to report the loss of money or valuables to the nearest police station as soon as possible.

Media

Overseas newspapers and magazines To keep in touch with events back home through your own favourite newspaper or magazine, the following newsagents pride themselves on having all the leading international papers in stock:

A Maroni & Son, 68 Old Compton Street; Mon–Sat 7am–late and Sun 7am–2pm);

Grays Inn News, 50 Theobald Road; Mon–Fri 4am–5.30pm);

W. H. Smith's, selected branches throughout London, **Borders** bookshops and **Capital Newsagents**, 48 Old Compton Street.

British magazines and newspapers
The publication for all London information is the listings magazine *Time Out*. The British have an unusually large number of national daily newspapers, both broadsheet and tabloid. *The Times*, the *Daily Telegraph*, the *Guardian* and the *Independent* are all serious broadsheets with high standards of reporting on UK and international affairs, and good arts coverage. The *Financial Times*, still printed distinctively on pink paper, covers world business news and all the latest on market prices.

All the above papers have large Saturday editions with plenty of London arts news. In addition, the *Independent on Sunday*, the *Sunday Times*, and the *Observer* all bring out

heavyweight Sunday editions with magazine supplements.

London also has its own newspaper, the *Evening Standard*, which reviews restaurants and pubs as well as performing arts and exhibitions. Many individual areas of London, such as Islington, Hampstead and Highgate, have their own weekly newspapers covering news and events of local interest.

There are magazines available on every subject. Among them, the satirical *Private Eye* and the establishment *The New Statesman* (both weeklies) are an entertaining read. Condé Nast

Signs to look for

The world's news

259

in the UK publish *Vogue, Vanity Fair, GQ* and *Condé Nast Traveller.*

Radio London has several radio stations that are good sources of music and of information about events in the capital. These include the following choices:
Capital Gold 1548AM: golden-oldies 24 hours a day, aimed at a broad range of listeners, but mainly it's for those old enough to remember the Top 40 hits of the 1960s, 1970s and 1980s.
Capital FM 95.8FM: pop music and news 24 hours a day, aimed at

younger listeners—the station you are likely to hear playing in many shops and taxis.

LBC 97.3FM: mainly news, interviews and discussions, plus endless call-ins.

London Live 94.9FM: London's best station for pop music and chat by a long way. Run by the BBC.

In addition there are several national stations. Of these, **Classic FM** (100.99FM) and **Virgin** (105.8FM) are the most important commercial stations. Classic FM broadcasts popular classical music, while Richard Branson's Virgin station delivers 'classic album tracks and hot new music'. Otherwise the BBC still dominates the airwaves with its five channels:

Radio 1 98.8FM: pop music geared mainly for young people.

Radio 2 89.2FM: middle-of-the-road and easy-listening music.

Radio 3 91.3FM: classical music, including live concerts.

Radio 4 93.5FM: news, current affairs, talk shows, radio drama and reviews (*Today* is the flagship news and current affairs programme).

Radio 5 Live 693 and 909MW: the station for sport, with live commentary on major events plus news reports and other features.

Currency dealers abound, but it pays to shop around for the best rates

Television London has its own independent television networks—Carlton and LWT—which broadcast local news, while ITN provides national and international news programmes for this and all other ITV areas. (This arrangement parallels the relationship between local US television stations and the national broadcasting companies.) The other channels are BBC1, aimed at mainstream audiences, BBC2 and Channel 4, both of which show a very broad range of cultural and special interest programmes, and Channel 5, whose output is taking time to get going.

Most hotels supply guests with Cable TV that includes Sky; a few have digital TV.

Money matters

Local currency Britain's currency is divided into pounds and pence (100p = £1). Notes are available in denominations of £50, £20, £10, and £5. Coins come in denominations of £2, £1, 50p, 20p, 10p, 5p, 2p and 1p. A few major department stores will now accept Euros.

Currency exchange Banks give by far the best rates of exchange, whether you are changing currency or traveller's cheques, and only in an emergency should you consider using any other service. Hotels will change money and traveller's

Shop around for the best rates

cheques but give a very poor rate, as do those shops that accept US dollars and other currencies.

There are plenty of *bureaux de change* in London's main tourist haunts, advertising rates that may look more attractive than those of the banks, but once you've paid their hefty commission fees you will usually find that you're actually getting less for your money. If, as a last resort, you decide to use a *bureau de change*, you should seek out a reputable organization like Thomas Cook or Chequepoint. Their 24-hour branches can be found at or near Piccadilly Circus, Leicester Square, Marble Arch and Victoria Underground stations.

Banks There are four main banks in the UK and they have branches all over London: they are the National Westminster, Barclays, Lloyds and the HSBC (formerly the Midland). Most of the major branches have a separate foreign currency window; if not, you can use any window that is open. All branches will allow you to draw cash against your credit card.

Credit cards You can use the four main credit cards (Visa, MasterCard, American Express and Diners Club)

just about anywhere in London, although retailers may not take kindly to, or disallow, your using them for small purchases—say, less than £5, and a few may not accept them at all. One great advantage of using credit cards to pay for goods is the favourable exchange rate. Credit-card companies use the Interbank rate, which can be several percentage points better than the tourist rate, for their exchange calculations. Moreover, by using a credit card, you avoid paying commission on exchange transactions.

These advantages work only if you pay your credit-card bill in full when you receive it and only use your card for purchases, not for cash advances. The high rates of interest charged on cash withdrawals and credit-card balances can more than wipe out any exchange-rate gains.

Money savers For travelling round London, use a Travelcard (see pages 264–265). For trips out of the city, railways offer saver, weekend and supersaver tickets, and hotels have good mid-week deals that may include the rail fare. Consider purchasing The London Pass, which offers entry to over 55 attractions, plus free travel on public transport, and numerous other discounts. Having a prepaid ticket also enables

Credit cards can be used at cash machines

you to jump the queues at some attractions (www.londonpass.com). Consider buying a GoSee Card (on sale at museums and tourist offices; joining English Heritage (see page 211) or the National Trust (see page 210); buying a South Kensington Museums' season ticket (on sale at the museums).

Traveller's cheques These are a safe and convenient method of carrying large amounts of money, since the cheques can be cancelled if they are lost or stolen and you can obtain replacement cheques. Many shops, restaurants and hotels will accept traveller's cheques in payment for goods and services—but do make sure that you are being offered a favourable exchange rate. You can avoid the problem of exchange rates altogether by buying your cheques in pounds sterling in the first place. It is also a good idea to buy some small-denomination cheques so that you don't have to cash a big cheque if you find yourself short of cash towards the end of your trip.

National holidays
Although banks and businesses close on public holidays, the trend in London is for tourist attractions and stores to remain open, except on Christmas, Boxing Day (the day after Christmas), and New Year, when almost everything shuts (and if any of these days falls on a Saturday or Sunday, the next weekday is an additional holiday).
New Year's Day (1 January)
Good Friday
Easter Monday
First Monday in May
Last Monday in May
Last Monday in August
Christmas Day (25 December)
Boxing Day (26 December)

Opening hours
In London the trend is increasingly for stores and sights to open later in the morning—at 10am rather than 9am—but to stay open later in the evenings—until 6pm or later in the major tourist haunts. Late-night shopping, when all stores remain open until 8pm, is on Wednesday in the Knightsbridge and Kensington area and Thursday in the Oxford Street and Regent Street area.

Museums are, as a rule, open Mon–Sat 10–6 and Sun 2–6, but there are many exceptions—check under individual entries first. Some government-run museums are closed all day Monday, and some commercial museums remain open until as late as 10pm.

Pharmacies

Remember that many drugs sold over the counter in other countries are only dispensed in Britain with a prescription from a doctor. If you are not eligible for National Health Service treatment, you will have to go to a doctor with a private practice for a prescription.

Medical Express, 117a Harley Street (tel: 020-7499 1991), offers a private walk-in medical service; or you can ask your hotel to arrange for a doctor to attend to you if you need a prescription (it is also a good idea to know the generic name of any drugs you take regularly, since they may be sold under a different brand name in the UK).

If you have a simple ailment that can be treated with non-prescription drugs, go to a chemist and ask for advice. British chemists are highly trained and knowledgeable people who will do their best to help you. Chemists are to be found all over London. At night, they post a sign on their doors telling you the address of the nearest chemist that will be open late. The following chemists open longer hours than others:
Bliss Chemist, 5 Marble Arch. Daily 9am until midnight (tel: 020-7723 6116);
Boots the Chemist, 44–6 Regent Street. Mon–Sat 8am–midnight (tel: 020-7734 6126).

Places of worship

For a full list of churches, their addresses and where applicable their phone numbers, consult the 'Places of Worship' section of the London *Yellow Pages* telephone directory.

Church of England: St.Martin-in-the-Fields, on Trafalgar Square (tel: 020-766 110), is a friendly and central church popular with overseas visitors. **Westminster Abbey**, Broad Sanctuary (tel: 020-7654 4900), has a fine choir and **St.Paul's Cathedral** is a good place for organ music (tel: 020-723 4128).

Islam: The London Central Mosque, 146 Park Road (tel: 020-7724 3363), is the main religious venue for London's Muslims. Further informa-tion is available from the **Muslim World League** (tel: 020-7636 7568).

Jewish: There are Orthodox, Liberal, and Reformed synagogues all over London (200 in total); for further information contact the Central Enquiry Desk, **Board of Deputies of British Jews**, 6 Bloomsbury Square (tel: 020-7543 5400).

Roman Catholic: Westminster Cathedral, Ashley Place (tel: 020-7798 9055), is the main Catholic church in Britain. **Brompton Oratory**, Brompton Road (tel: 020-7808 0900), has a wide reputation for its particularly good choral music and sung mass in Latin.

Westminster Abbey

263

Police

The days of the friendly London bobby, ever willing to help tourists find their way, have not quite gone, but today's police, overstretched by a rising tide of crime, are often too busy to patrol the streets (although that is what most law-abiding citizens want them to do), and have less time or opportunity to be friendly and helpful. If you report a crime the chances of catching and prosecuting the perpetrators are very slim. If you have your pockets picked or your bag snatched you will receive sympathy but little hope of getting your money back. Still, you should report the crime, if only because insurance companies insist upon it as a policy condition. Look up 'Police' in the telephone directory to find the nearest police station. In an emergency, if you are in danger or under threat of any kind, dial 999 and ask for the police, who will usually respond rapidly.

Post offices

Many ordinary shops and newsagents sell postage stamps and phone cards. Post offices can also provide special services, such as parcel post, registered mail or express deliveries. They are normally open Mon–Fri 9–5.30 and Sat 9–noon; many close on

The unconventional detective

Wednesday afternoons. The branch near Trafalgar Square—24–8 William IV Street (tel: 0845-722 3344)—is open Mon–Fri 8.30–6.30, Sat 9–5.30. Poste restante may also be sent to this office.

Public transport

The Underground, which dates back to the middle of the last century, is the biggest and busiest subway system in the world. The basic choice is between using the Underground system (generally known as the Tube, although strictly this only applies to the deep-dug tunnel sections) or taking a bus. The top deck of a bus is good for sightseeing, and you may actually get to talk to real Londoners. The Tube is usually faster, but it can be extremely crowded during rush hours (8–9.30am and 5–7pm on weekdays).

If you buy a Travelcard, you can switch between the bus and Tube system as you please, since the cards are valid on both, and on the Docklands Light Railway and certain rail services. One Day Travelcards are very economic if you are likely to make more than two or three journeys a day; you cannot use them before 9.30am Mon–Fri and they are not valid on night buses—a slightly more expensive Travelcard permits pre-9.30am travel. They are on sale at all Underground stations and many newsagents.

221b Baker Street

Sherlock Holmes

"We met next day and inspected the rooms at 221b Baker Street.... and at once entered into possession."

A STUDY IN SCARLET
Sir Arthur Conan Doyle

Royal Mail mailbox

Weekly or monthly passes, on the other hand, can be used at any time of day, but to buy one you need a passport-size photograph. There are photo machines at the airport and at some stations in town. Further information on Travelcards can be obtained at any Underground station.

An alternative to a Travelcard is an Oyster Card, which you can buy on arrival and add credit to, so you pay as you go. This is a popular with people living or working in London, but could be useful for those on a long stay. It is valid on all public transport.

Child fares Children under five travel free on the tube and buses. Children up to age 16 qualify for reduced fares but 14- and 15-year olds must carry a Child Rate Photocard as evidence of their age, available free from tube stations (they'll need to have a passport-size photograph and proof of their age).

The Underground The Underground (Tube) runs daily (except Christmas Day). Trains start running at around 5.30am Mon–Sat and 7am on Sun, last trains run just after midnight on weekdays and 11.30pm on Sun (the times of the first and last trains out of

each station are posted in the station entrances). The system is divided into six zones, and you pay more for trips that pass through two or more zones. A table of fares is usually posted close to the self-service ticket

An artistic view

machines. These take coins and will normally give change (if not, a message saying 'exact money only' will be lit). You can also buy tickets from the station ticket office, but expect long queues, especially at during the rush hour. Most stations now have automatic turnstiles, which will not let you through if you have the wrong ticket—for example, if you travelled further than you originally planned and have not paid the correct fare. In these circumstances, seek help from station staff, but be prepared to be treated as a suspected fare dodger.

At the entrance or Public Subway to the Underground, also affectionately known as the Tube

Smoking is prohibited everywhere on the Underground. Technically, playing music and begging for handouts are illegal as well. If you feel you are being harassed, report the incident to station staff or the transport police who patrol the Underground. Most platforms have strategically placed red panic buttons that you can press if you are in danger or feel threatened—you can use them to alert the transport police.

Buses Many people prefer to travel by bus in London, for a variety of reasons. Some people find the Tube too hot and claustrophobic, while others can't deal with the long walks that are often involved between ticket office and platform. Above all, buses offer views, a chance to get to grips with the complex geography of London, and social contact. Visitors to London getting onto a bus will often ask for help and directions from the driver or other passengers; conversations start and soon news, gossip, opinions and family histories are being exchanged.

At main bus stops (signs show a red circle on a white background) you will find information on bus routes and times. The bus will stop here automatically. At request stops (white circle on a red background) you must hold out your arm to stop the bus. Once on the bus, if you want to get off at a request stop, you must ring the bell located on the handrails well before reaching the stop.

Fares are set according to zones. If you do not have a Travelcard (see pages 264– 265), In central London most tickets have to be purchased before boarding any bus. These can be bought at machines at main bus stops (not request stops) and in ticket offices in bus or Underground stations. You cannot buy a 'return' bus ticket. It you are going to use the bus a lot buy a Travelcard or Oyster Card. Keep your ticket safely but accessible as inspectors regularly board buses and check them.

Daytime buses in London run Mon–Sat from around 6am to midnight and Sun from 7.30am to 11.30pm. In theory, buses run at least once every 10 to 15 minutes in each direction along the route, and much more frequently on heavily used routes. But in practice, because of the unpredictable traffic conditions, you can wait for 30 minutes for a bus to arrive, and then three will all arrive at the same time.

Night buses run between 11pm and 6am on main routes through London; all of them pass through Trafalgar Square. A leaflet (called *Buses for Night Owls*) is available from London Transport information centres (see

Performing for the fare

below) detailing the current routes and times.

Docklands Light Railway The computerized and driverless trains of the Docklands Light Railway (DLR) serve the Docklands area to the east of the City. The DLR is part of the Underground system, so Travelcards may be used.

The system operates between Bank or Tower Gateway station (near Tower Hill Underground) and south through the Isle of Dogs and Greenwich to Lewisham, north to Stratford, and east to Beckton and the new extension to London City Airport. Mechanical and engineering faults have dogged the DLR, but it can usually be counted upon to run Mon–Fri 5.40am–around midnight with a more limited service at weekends (tel: 020-7222 1234 for information).

River cruises London's river, the Thames, one of the cleanest in Europe, is being revived as a transport artery. New piers include those at Bankside and the Dome at

Greenwich Peninsula. Riverbuses supply a regular service between Westminster and Greenwich.

One of the most pleasurable ways to travel on the Thames is to use one of the tourist cruise services that operate from Westminster Pier (see page 55). These enable you to enjoy London's skyline from a different perspective. Some cruises go as far afield as the Thames Barrier in the east or Hampton Court in the west. There is a commentary on the sights you pass and boats usually have a bar or café aboard—some have dinner and dancing.

Travel information The main London Transport Information Centre, at Piccadilly Circus Underground Station, is open daily 7.15am–9pm (8pm Sun) and supplies free route maps and schedules as well as information brochures in several languages. You can also phone for information (tel: 020-7222 1234). Travel information centres can also be found at Heathrow Airport, Euston and Liverpool Street Tube stations and at Victoria coach and train stations.

Smoking
On 1 July 2007 it became illegal to

Working out the route

smoke in any enclosed public places, including restaurants, pubs and on public transport. Some hotels will allow smoking in designated bedrooms.

Student and youth travel
If you have an International Student Identity Card you can get special deals on long-distance travel to the UK, such as youth rail passes. Once in London, it is worth looking for the theatres, cinemas and exhibitions that offer reduced rates for students. The listings magazine *Time Out* has good information about student discounts at museums, theatres and clubs, plus advice on getting the best out of the city's sights and entertainment at little cost.

Telephones
There are public telephone booths all over London—in the streets, in pubs and stores, in

museums and on many station platforms. Telephone boxes are provided
by one of the two main telephone
companies. BT (British Telecom)
phones are still the most numerous,
but you will also see other
company's call boxes, which may
have cheaper charges for long-
distance calls.

- **BT coin-operated phones**: These
accept £1, 50p and 20p coins.
- **BT card phones**: These accept BT
phone cards, which can be bought
from post offices and newsagents in
various denominations. More and
more telephone booths will also
accept credit cards.
- **Mercury card phones**: These accept
both credit cards (minimum charge
applies) and Mercury phone cards;
these are sold at the same outlets as
BT cards.
- **Dial tones**: When you lift the
receiver you should hear a continuous

You see more by bus

269

Checking out the bargains in Islington

dial tone. After you have dialled you
will hear ring-ring-pause, ring-ring-
pause to indicate that the number is
ringing at the other end. A series of
rapid bleeps means that the number
is busy; a continuous note means the
number is 'unobtainable'; this will
either be because you have mis-
dialled, in which case you should try
again, or because you have the
wrong number.

- One way to keep the cost of calls
down is to use public telephone
services; hotel phones are horrendously expensive and calls are often
charged at three or four times the
official rate.

The cost of a call from a public
phone depends on what time of day
you make it. The cheapest times for
calls within the UK are Mon–Fri
6pm–8am (evening rate) and at
weekends. The most expensive time
is Mon–Fri 8am–6pm, during the
daytime rate.

The Docklands Light Railway

Time

Between October and March, Britain observes Greenwich Mean Time (GMT); during British Summer Time (BST), which begins in March, clocks are put forward by an hour, reverting back to GMT in October.

❏ **Useful numbers**

International lines dial 00 + country code

Operator (for reverse charge/credit-card calls within UK) 100

International operator (for credit-card calls outside UK) 155

National Directory Enquiries 118 500

International Directory Enquiries 118 505

Emergency calls 999 or 112

Time checks 123 ❏

Tipping

Rates and categories differ only slightly from what is expected in other Western countries. Taxi drivers expect 10 per cent of the fare as a tip, but it is not necessary to tip minicab drivers. The usual tip in restaurants and cafés is 10 per cent, but check to see if service has already been added to the bill.

Other people whom it is customary to tip are cloakroom attendants, hotel doormen, hotel porters and room-service waiters, porters at train stations or airports, hairdressers and barbers and sightseeing guides. Bartenders do not expect tips—although you can, if you wish, offer to buy him or her a drink—nor do theatre or cinema usherettes.

Toilets

Finding a toilet (restroom) in London is not usually too difficult. Museums, department stores, theatres and cinemas all have them, as do restaurants and cafés, although these are usually for customers' use.

Toilets can also to be found at major railway stations, but you may need the correct change for the entrance turnstile. Aluminium 'Loomatic' toilets are also coin-operated.

Tourist information

The London Tourist Board now operate under the name Visit London. As a first port of call log on to to their excellent website www.visitlondon.com.

There are official information centres at the following locations:

Britain and London Visitor Centre

1 Lower Regent Street, Piccadilly Circus, tel: 08701 566366. Mon 9.30–6.30, Tue–Fri 9.30–6.30, Sat, Sun 10–4; Jun–Oct, Sat 9–5. Also personal callers. There is also a useful information centre on Leicester Square (see page 238).

City of London

In the churchyard of St. Paul's Cathedral, no telephone enquiries; personal callers only.

Greenwich

46 Greenwich Church Street, tel: 020-858 6376; Pepys House, 2 Cutty Sark Gardens, tel: 0870-608 2000

Richmond

Old Town Hall, tel: 020-8940 9125. Mon–Sat 10–5, Easter–Sep also Sun 10.30–1.30

Southwark

Vinopolis, 1 Bank End, tel: 020-7357 9168 (see page 195 for opening times). Tate Modern, Level 2, Bankside, tel: 020-7041 5266. Daily 10–6.

Twickenham

Civic Centre, York Street, tel: 020-8891 7272. Mon–Thu 9–5.15, Fri 9–5.

For information on the whole of Britain, go to www.visitbritain.com

Women Travellers

Two organizations provide support in an emergency: **Rape and Sexual Abuse Support Centre** (tel: 020-8683 3300); **Samaritans** (tel: 08457-909090)

One of the city's younger visitors takes a relaxing look at London

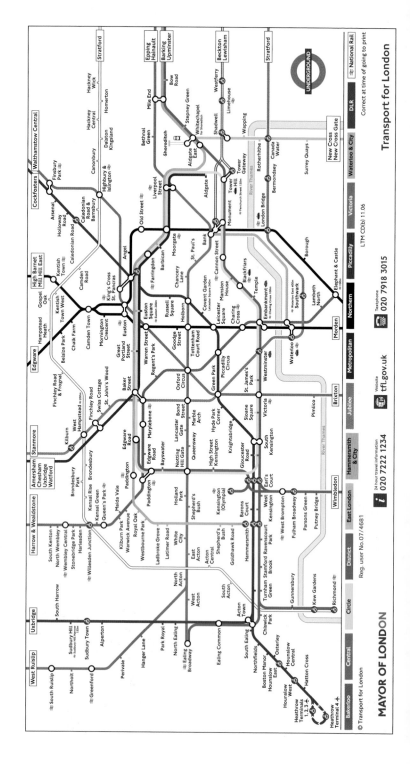

MAYOR OF LONDON

© Transport for London

Reg. user No. 07/4681

Bakerloo   Central   Circle   District   East London   Hammersmith & City   Jubilee   Metropolitan   Northern   Piccadilly   Victoria   Waterloo & City   DLR   National Rail

Transport for London

LTM CD(b) 11.06

Correct at time of going to print

24 hour travel information
020 7222 1234

Website
tfl.gov.uk

Textphone
020 7918 3015

HOTELS

The following recommended hotels have been divided into four price categories based on their stated 'rack' rates. These are the maximum prices and special deals and discount packages are nearly always available. Weekend rates in luxury hotels can be significantly cheaper than weekday rates:
inexpensive (£): a double room for £40–75
moderate (££): a double room for £75–150
expensive (£££): a double room for £150–250
deluxe (££££): a double room for over £250

Full listings of British and Irish hotels and B&Bs available through the service can be reserved at the **AA's internet site**: http://www.theAA.com.

MAYFAIR, PICCADILLY, ST. JAMES'S AND THE MALL

Athenaeum Hotel (££££)
116 Piccadilly, W1 tel: 020-7499 3464, www.athenaeumhotel.com
Elegant hotel overlooking Green Park. Well-equipped bedrooms provide every comfort. Pool, jacuzzi, fitness suite and beauty salon. Good Modern British organic food with a Mediterranean influence in Bullochs Restaurant.

Claridge's (££££)
Brook Street, W1 tel: 020-7629 8860, www.claridges.co.uk
This is the hotel where US presidents, guests of the Queen, monarchs and public figures from around the world all stay; it's one of the country's most prestigious hotels.

Goring (££££)
15 Beeston Place, SW1 tel: 020-7396 9000, www.goring hotel.co.uk
Just beside Buckingham Palace and often used to accommodate royal guests, this is a fine hotel, full of old-world charm.

Le Meridien Piccadilly (£££)
21 Piccadilly, W1 tel: 020-7734 8000, www.lemeridien.com
Popular Edwardian hotel with top-quality restaurants and within easy walking distance of West End theatres and cinemas.

The Ritz (££££)
Piccadilly, W1 tel: 020-7493 8181, www.theritzlondon.com
A byword for stylish opulence and high living, the Ritz is the peak of mirrored and gilded splendour. Live cabaret, tea dances and Palm Court afternoon teas provide ample opportunity for 'putting on the Ritz'.

Stafford (££££)
16–18 St. James's Place, SW1 tel: 020-7493 0111, www.thestaffordhotel.co.uk
Intimate hotel with a club-like atmosphere and a restaurant serving modern British cooking to a loyal clientele of regulars.

22 Jermyn Street (££££)
22 Jermyn Street, SW1 tel: 020-7734 2353, www.22jermyn.com
An elegant town house just minutes from

Piccadilly and Leicester Square. There are some thoughtful extras in the rooms.

The Washington Mayfair (£££)
5–7 Curzon Street, W1 tel: 020-7499 7000, www.washington-mayfair.co.uk
Accommodation in this attractive and air-conditioned modern hotel ranges from state rooms and suites with spa baths to equally comfortable twins and doubles. A wide range of business services

Wigmore Court Hotel (££)
23 Gloucester Place, W1 tel: 020-7935 0928, www.wigmore-hotel.co.uk
Superior class B&B, ideal for families, with large en-suite rooms, and laundry and kitchen facilities available on request. Short walk from Oxford Street.

SOHO AND COVENT GARDEN, BLOOMSBURY AND FITZROVIA, REGENT'S PARK AND MARYLEBONE

Academy (££–£££)
21 Gower Street, WC1 tel: 020-7631 4115, www.summithotels.com
Stylish conversion of Georgian town houses in the heart of Bloomsbury.

Blooms Hotel (£££)
7 Montague Street, WC1 tel: 020-7323 1717, www.grangehotels.com
This elegant 18th-century town house is just around the corner from the British Museum. Comfortable rooms complemented by antique-filled public areas. Lovely garden terrace.

The Bonnington (££)
92 Southampton Row, WC1 tel: 020-7242 2828, www.bonnington.com
This late Edwardian hotel maintains traditional standards in comfortable, modern surroundings. There are rooms suitable for families and for guests with disabilities.

Danubius Hotel Regents Park (££)
18 Lodge Road, NW8 tel: 020-7722 7722, www.danubiuslondon.com
Some of the rooms overlook Lord's Cricket Ground. Rooms are modern and spacious. There is also a fitness area open 24 hours a day and a restaurant—Minksy's New York Deli and Restaurant.

Four Seasons Hotel (£)
173 Gloucester Place, NW1 tel: 020-7724 3461, www.holdiaycity.com/fourseasons
Friendly, family-run hotel in the heart of the West End; comfortable, well-equipped rooms.

Ibis Euston (£)
3 Cardington Street, NW1 tel: 020-7388 7777, www.ibishotel.com
French chain-hotel offering comfort and reasonable prices in the Euston area, with good facilities for people with disabilities.

Melia White House Hotel (££)
Albany Street, NW1 tel: 020-7391 3000, www.solmelia.com
One of London's best-kept secrets, this charming hotel—formerly an apartment building—is well-placed for the West End. The emphasis is on hospitality and comfort.

Mentone Hotel (£)
54–55 Cartwright Gardens, WC1 tel: 020-7387 3927, www.mentonehotel.com
This friendly, family-run guest house features chintzy, fresh bedrooms.

One Aldwych (££££)
1 Aldwych, WC2 tel: 020-300 1000 www.onealdwych.com
Chic and minimalist, this stylish hotel is in a great position in Covent Garden. Choose from 105 luxurious and contemporary bedrooms and suites, all with a host of extras. A truly divine experience.

The Radisson Edwardian Hampshire (£££)
Leicester Square, WC2 tel: 020-7839 9399, www.radissonedwardian.com
This stylish period hotel, built within the existing shell of the Royal Dental Hospital, has a prime location on Leicester Square. Rooms are very comfortable and fully equipped with modern facilities including access to the Internet. The team of staff is particularly friendly.

Radisson Edwardian Mountbatten (£££)
Monmouth Street, WC2 tel: 020-7836 4300, www.radissonedwardian.com
Situated at Seven Dials—well placed for theatregoers. Many rooms are small, but are pleasantly furnished and all have marbled bathrooms. Stylish public areas include a comfortable cocktail bar and restaurant.

HOLBORN, THE STRAND AND THE CITY

Hotel Russell (££–£££)
Russell Square WC1 tel: 020-7837 6470, www.principal-hotels.com
Handy for the British Museum and the West End, this stately Victorian landmark offers public rooms that have great character. Good range of bars, restaurants and lounges.

Savoy (££££)
The Strand, WC2 tel: 020-7836 4343, www.the-savoy-group.com
Founded by Richard D'Oyly Carte, with the profits from staging Gilbert and Sullivan operettas, the Savoy is a majestic hotel, a contender for the title 'best in the world'. Rooms overlooking the river are very much in demand.

Strand Palace (££)
372 Strand, WC2 tel: 020-7379 4737, www.strandpalacehotel.co.uk
Across the street from the Savoy, the Strand Palace is vast (800 rooms) but efficient and offers relatively inexpensive rooms. Convenient for the West End and Covent Garden.

Thistle City Barbican (££)
Central Street, Clerkenwell EC1 tel: 0870-333 9101, www.thistlehotels.com
Well situated for the Barbican arts complex and the City, this is a large and modern hotel with friendly and helpful staff.

WESTMINSTER, SOUTH BANK AND DOCKLANDS

London County Hall Premier Travel Inn (££)
County Hall, Belvedere Road, SE1 tel: 0870 238 3300, www.premiertravelinn.com
This is the perfect place for the family to stay, right next to the London Eye, close to the London Aquarium and near the Houses of Parliament. Excellent value for a great location.

Royal Horse Guards (£££)
2 Whitehall Court, SW1 tel: 0870-333 9122, www.thistlehotels.com
In the heart of central London territory and close to tourist sights, this has refurbished bedrooms and good public areas.

The Tower (££–£££)
St. Katharine's Way, E1 tel: 0870-333 9106, www.guoman.com
Modern hotel enjoying spectacular views of the Tower of London, Tower Bridge, and St. Katharine's Dock. Very convenient for the City.

CHELSEA AND KNIGHTSBRIDGE, KENSINGTON AND NOTTING HILL, HYDE PARK

Abbey Court (££–£££)
20 Pembridge Gardens, W2 tel: 020-7221 7518, www.abbeycourthotel.co.uk
Gracious Victorian mansion in Notting Hill, furnished with antiques in country-house style. Jacuzzi baths add to the comfort.

Beaufort (£££)
33 Beaufort Gardens, SW3 tel: 020-7584 5252, www.thebeaufort.co.uk
Top-class small hotel (28 rooms) with thoughtful personal touches, located on a quiet square in the heart of Knightsbridge.

Berkeley (££££)
Wilton Place, SW1 tel: 020-7235 6000, www.the-savoy-group.com
Splendid hotel on Hyde Park Corner with a rooftop pool emulating a Roman bath and elegant period rooms.

Capital (££££)
22 Basil Street, SW3 tel: 020-7589 5171, www.capitalhotel.co.uk
This very elegant hotel in the heart of Knightsbridge boasts an award-winning restaurant, The Capital, and a tastefully furnished interior.

Jumeirah Carlton Tower (££££)
Cadogan Place, SW1 tel: 020-7235 1234, www.jumeirahcarlton.com
A busy international hotel with health club and swimming pool. Rooms, including a range of suites, are air-conditioned and well equipped.

Halcyon Hotel (£££)
81 Holland Park, W11 tel: 020-7727 7288
The elegant foyer gives a splendid first impression with fresh flowers, fine pictures and antique furniture. Rooms are individually decorated and spacious with sizeable marble bathrooms. Good food in the restaurant.

Hotel 167 (££)
167 Old Brompton Road, SW5 tel: 020–7373 3221, www.hotel167.com
Reserve early for this good-value Victorian terrace home from home. Conveniently placed near to Harrods and the South Kensington museums, the hotel has 19 ensuite rooms. There is an attractive lobby to take your breakfast.

Jumeirah Lowndes Hotel (£££–££££)
21 Lowndes Street, SW1 tel: 020-7823 1234,
www.jumeirahlowndeshotel.com
This chic air-conditioned hotel provides bedrooms and suites with every modern facility.
Good food in the Mimosa Bar and Restaurant.

Mandarin Oriental Hyde Park (££££)
66 Knightsbridge, SW1 tel: 020-7235 2000,
www.mandarin-oriental.com
Palatial public rooms, luxurious décor, and
extensive views across leafy Hyde Park are the
hallmarks of this stately hotel.

Melbourne House (£–££)
79 Belgrave Road, SW1 tel: 020-7828 3516
Another good choice on the Belgrave Road, this
is a small, family-run hotel. Most rooms are
ensuite and the lounge is very pleasant.

Parkwood Hotel (£)
4 Stanhope Place, W2 tel: 020-7402 2241,
www.parkwoodhotel.com
This pretty hotel in a quiet street facing onto
Hyde Park is popular with families, as the
paintings by visiting children, hung in the
'artists' gallery', demonstrate.

Rembrandt Hotel (£££)
11 Thurloe Place, SW7 tel: 020-7589 8100,
www.sarova.co.uk
The ornate architecture of the Rembrandt Hotel
reflects that of Harrods farther along the
road—bedrooms vary in size, but offer real
comfort and style.

Vicarage Private Hotel (££)
10 Vicarage Gate, W8 tel: 020-7229 4030,
www.londonvicaragehotel.com
A family-run hotel in an exclusive area, making
this establishment very good value. Fine period
Victorian house with 18 rooms, some sharing
bathroom facilities. A hearty English breakfast
is included in the price.

OUTSIDE THE CENTRE

La Gaffe (££)
107–111 Heath Street, NW3 tel: 020-7435
4941, www.lagaffe.co.uk
A warm Italian welcome is assured at this
friendly family-run guest house in Hampstead.
Rooms are compact and modestly furnished
but well equipped. There is a popular Italian
restaurant available for guests.

YMCAs and YHAs
YMCA (£)
Trevelyan House, Dimple Road, Matlock,
Derbyshire DE4 3HY tel:01629 592600,
reservations 0870-770 6113,
www.ymca.org.uk
You can write to the above address for details
of all 18 YMCA hotels in London; they are
extremely good value, and it is vital to reserve
at least two months ahead. One of the best is
the Barbican YMCA, 2 Fann Street, a purpose-
built hotel with good sports facilities.

Youth Hostel Association (YHA) (£)
8 St. Stephen's Hill, St. Albans, Herts, AL1
2DY tel: 01727 855215, www.yha.org.uk
Write to the above address for details of the
seven youth hostels in London and reserve at

least three months ahead for summer. The
YHA London St. Pauls hostel is excellent,
located just 100m (100 yards) from St. Paul's,
while the YHA London Holland Park hostel is
converted from the remains of a Jacobean
mansion, set in Holland Park gardens. The
other hostels are at Oxford Street, Earls Court,
St. Pancras and Thameside near Docklands,
some of which are new and purpose-built.

RESTAURANTS

The following recommended restaurants have
been divided into three price categories. Prices
are for a three-course meal per person
excluding drinks:
inexpensive (£): under £15
moderate (££): £15-25
expensive (£££): £25–35
very expensive (££££): over £35
All the restaurants listed here offer vegetarian
meals, unless otherwise stated. See pages
88–89 for additional restaurant selections.

MAYFAIR, PICCADILLY, ST. JAMES'S AND THE MALL

Le Caprice (£££)
Arlington House, Arlington Street, SW1
tel: 020-7629 2239
Reservations are essential at this very chic
restaurant favoured by celebrities, where the
choices range from traditional English dishes
to classic brasserie fare.

Caraffini (£££)
61–63 Lower Sloane Street, SW1
tel: 020-7259 0235
Simple, well-executed Italian food with no pre-
tensions to modernity. Portions of vegetables
are charged separately. All-Italian wine list.

Chor Bizarre (£££)
16 Albemarle Street, W1
tel: 020-7629 9802
Crowded Indian 'thieves market' look and
some unusual regional dishes among the
tandooris and thalis.

The Criterion (£££)
224 Piccadilly, W1 tel: 020-7930 0488
Marco Pierre White's opulent restaurant at the
heart of Piccadilly Circus is stunning and the
place just heaves from 5.30pm till late. Modern
brasserie dishes and fast-paced service.

Foliage (£££–££££)
Mandarin Oriental Hyde Park Hotel, 66
Knightsbridge SW1 tel: 020-7235 2000
Intimate setting within a grand hotel for well-
executed, modern French cooking. The title,
pronounced in the French fashion, emphasizes
the air of exclusivity that prevails in this
elegant dining room overlooking Hyde Park.

Le Gavroche Restaurant (££££)
43 Upper Brook Street, W1
tel: 020-7408 0881/7499 1826
The feel of a discreet, English gentleman's
club with service to match. Michel Roux Jnr has
really made his mark here, his modern French
cooking showing skill and discretion.

Greenhouse (£££–££££)
27a Hay Mews, W1 tel: 020-7499 3331
Several different types of menus to choose
from at this smart, first-rate restaurant, such
as Tasting and Seasonal. One of the best ways
to experience the fine cuisine at Greenhouse is
to have the set menu lunch that is good value.

Green's Restaurant and Oyster Bar (£££)
36 Duke Street, St. James's, SW1
tel: 020-7930 4566
A stylish arrangement of eating and drinking
areas (plus a famous oyster bar) where the fish
and seafood dishes are excellently prepared.

Inn the Park (£–£££)
St. James's Park, SW1 tel: 020-7451 9999
Take breakfast, lunch or dinner overlooking the
lake in the heart of St. James's Park. Good
British cuisine ranges from tasty homemade
cakes to traditional pies and Sunday roasts.
The rooftop bar and terrace gets very busy on
warm summer days.

Langan's Brasserie (££–£££)
Stratton House, Stratton Street, W1
tel: 020-7491 8822
Reservations essential. The boisterous founder
of Langan's Brasserie has passed on, but the
visitors still flock here for live jazz in the bar
and for the food, which ranges from the
famous bangers-and-mash to great seafood.

Maze (££–££££)
10–13 Grovesnor Square, W1
tel: 020-7107 0000
Maze is part of the Gordon Ramsey empire and
here chef Jason Atherthon has brought his talent from his work in both Spain and Dubai. One
speciality is the grilled meats cooked on a
charcoal robata grill. Good wine list.

Mirabelle (££–££££)
56 Curzon Street, W1 tel: 020-7499 4636
One of the most fashionable restaurants in
London, where under Marco Pierre White's
direction, first-class classic French cooking
with a modern twist is delivered. Lunch is good
value. Reservations essential.

Momo (££)
25 Heddon Street, W1 tel: 020-7434 4040
The doyen of North African cuisine, Momo not
only serves authentic Maghreb dishes, they
complement it with faultless service and ambience straight from the Arabian nights.

Nobu (££££)
Metropolitan Hotel, 19 Old Park Lane, W1
tel: 020-7447 4747
New York's Nobuyuki Matsuhisa brings his
pan-American Japanese cooking to the cool
confines of the Metropolitan Hotel. A haunt of
A-list celebrities, so you will need to reserve
well in advance.

La Porte des Indes (£££)
32 Bryanston Street, W1 tel: 020-7224 0055
Dramatic, beautiful establishment with a wide
selection of the sub-continent's finest cuisine.
Intriguing French Indian dishes from the
Pondicherry area are a speciality.

Quaglino's (££–£££)
16 Bury Street, W1 tel: 020-7930 6767
Sceptics scoffed when Terence Conran converted this vast ballroom into a 500-seat
restaurant, yet diners flock here (advance
reservations are vital). Outstanding food and
wine and impeccable service, with less expensive snacks at the bar an alternative to a meal.

Rasa W1 (££)
6 Dering Street, W1 tel: 020-7629 1346
Das Shreedharan's inspired Keralan vegetarian
dishes make a brilliant introduction to this
exciting regional Indian cuisine.

Ristorante L'Incontro (£££–££££)
87 Pimlico Road, SW1 tel: 020-7730 3663
The setting is glamorous and the food has a
price tag to match. The cooking is based on
that of Venice and northeastern Italy, with
dishes such as bean and pasta soup. Pasta is
made on the premises.

Sketch: Gallery (£££–££££)
9 Conduit Street, W1 tel: 0870-777 4488
The most fashionable amd most expensive
restaurant complex in Britain. Sketch is a feast
of all the senses where cutting-edge art, design
and contemporary food—international and eclec-
tic—collide. Starters in the Lecture Room begin
at a staggering £38 but Gallery is affordable to
mere mortals and well worth a try.
Rerservations essential.

Tamarind (££–£££)
20 Queen Street, W1 tel: 020-7629 3561
The most fashionable of London's Indian
restaurants, noted for Atul Kochhar's imaginative regional cooking. The use of specially
imported herbs and spices creates some quite
memorable flavours.

Veeraswamy (££–£££)
99-101 Regent Street W1
tel: 020-7734 1401
London's oldest Indian restaurant makes for
opulent dining. Classical regional Indian food
has a modern twist to suit Western palates.

Wiltons (££££)
55 Jermyn Street, SW1 tel: 020-7629 9955
Very formal and sophisticated, with MPs, aristocrats and royalty among the regular clients.
Renowned for its outstanding fish dishes, and
traditional desserts such as summer pudding.

The Wolsey (££)
160 Piccadilly, W1 tel: 020-7499 6996
This Grand European café-style restaurant, set
in a fabulous 1919 interior next to the Ritz is
the latest inspriation of King and Corbin of Ivy,
Le Caprice and J. Sheekey fame.

Café
Fortnum & Mason (££)
St. James's, 181 Piccadilly W1
tel: 020-7734 8040
Anything from breakfast to afternoon tea is a
treat at this upmarket food-lovers' emporium.
Popular with Londoners and tourists alike, so
be prepared for a queue, especially for lunch
and afternoon tea.

Sotheby's Café (££)
34 Bond Street. W1 tel: 020-7293 5077
Rather more of a restaurant than a café but
nevertheless you can get a stylish club sandwich or a good afternoon tea here. Good
selection of wines to give you nerve before
bidding for that special item.

277

SOHO AND COVENT GARDEN, BLOOMSBURY AND FITZROVIA, REGENT'S PARK AND MARYLEBONE

Acorn House (££–£££)
69 Swinton Street, WC1 tel: 020-7812 1842
Acorn House is regarded as the first truly eco-friendly restaurant in London, dedicated to the use of organic and recycled materials, from the building itself through to the minimisation of waste. Only the best of seasonal ingredients are used and Roux-trained chef Arthur Potts Dawson produces a cuisine he calls 'Modern London'. Lunchtime takeaways include hot soup and wholesome sandwiches. The dining room is stark but the food utterly appetising.

Alastair Little Soho (£££)
49 Frith Street, W1 tel: 020-7734 5183
Excellent Modern Europe cooking. Informal, and reasonably priced set lunches.

Arbutus (££–£££)
63–64 Frith Street, W1 tel: 020-7349 4545
Launched in 2006, this Soho restaurant opened to rave reviews. It's a good venue for a pre-theatre meal, opening for dinner at 5pm and with a special 3-course menu for under £20. The seasonal menus change weekly and the dishes are prepared using the freshest of produce.

Bertorelli's Restaurant/Café Italien (£–£££)
19–23 Charlotte Street, W1 (020-7636 4174
Bertorelli's (upstairs) is an institution; a popular Italian restaurant with affordable prices. The Café Italien downstairs is great for people-watching, with pavement tables in warm weather. Branch at 44A Floral Street, tel: 020-7836 3969.

Café du Jardin (££–£££)
28 Wellington Street, WC2
tel: 020-7836 8760
Buzzing, cosmopolitan brasserie in the heart of the West End with excellent pre- and post-theatre menus. The cooking has an up-to-date European appeal; pianist plays most evenings.

Café Pacifico (££)
5 Langley Street, WC2 tel: 020-7379 7728
Mexican restaurant, located in a cavernous Covent Garden warehouse. Superb range of beers and cocktails.

Christopher's (££–£££)
18 Wellington Street, WC2 tel: 020-7240 4222
This is a popular Covent Garden spot for the classic East Coast Sunday brunch. At other times the All-American menu majors on char-grills. The café does a good line in salads and sandwiches.

L'Escargot (££–£££)
48 Greek Street, W1 tel: 020-7437 2679
This recently revamped Soho institution features in a number of novels, and counts well-known writers and their publishers among its clientele. Classic French food and the choice of a lively brasserie downstairs or a formal restaurant above.

Fung Shing (££)
15 Lisle Street, WC2 tel: 020-7437 1539
Popular restaurant, highly regarded by local Chinatown residents.

Gay Hussar (££–£££)
2 Greek Street, W1 tel: 020-7437 0973
An unchanging pool of calm in the maelstrom of Soho, this popular Hungarian restaurant is noted for its excellent value and good old-fashioned cooking.

The Ivy (££–££££)
1 West Street, WC2 tel: 020-7836 4751
Very much a place to be seen, with stylish 1930s décor and the work of well-known contemporary British artists on the walls. Popular dishes are eggs Benedict and the Ivy mixed grill. Reserve tables several weeks in advance to be sure of getting in.

J Sheekey (££–£££)
28-32 St. Martin's Court, WC2
tel: 020-7240 2565
One of London's best-known seafood restaurants, now owned by the team that is responsible for The Ivy and Le Caprice. Expect traditional English fish dishes and old-fashioned puddings.

Joe Allen (££)
13 Exeter Street, WC2 tel: 020-7836 0651
The Covent Garden haunt of journalists, publishers and theatre-goers, Joe Allen serves chic modern food among some American classics and is particularly renowned for its Bloody Marys.

Kiku (£££)
17 Half Moon Street, W1Y 7RB
tel: 020-7499 4208
This minimalist Mayfair restaurant is noted for imaginative Japanese cooking, good value lunches and the longest sushi bar in London.

Lemonia (££)
89 Regents Park Road, NW1
tel: 020-7586 7454
Popular Greek Cypriot restaurant, more stylish than most. Start with the *meze* hot and cold selection (for two), then try a charcoal grill such as chicken shashlik, lamb or pork souvlaki; or ordikia—quails in olive oil and oregano.

Lindsay House (£££)
21 Romilly Street, W1 tel: 020-7439 0450
Irish chef Richard Corrigan is unique. His Celtic roots are still very evident in a gutsy, almost robust style. This is inspired Modern British cooking from one of London's top chefs.

Locanda Locatelli (£££)
8 Seymour Street, W1 tel: 020-7935 9088
Celebrity chef Giorgio Locatelli, who made his name at Zafferano, is now conjuring the magic at his own establishment where he brilliantly combines rustic and modern Italian.

Masala Zone (£)
9 Marshall Street, W1 tel: 020-7287 9966
Owned by the same people who made Londoners happy by opening Chutney Mary and Veeraswamy, this large dining room is a mouth-watering pan-Indian grazing experience with all sorts of reasonably price mains and downright inexpensive side bowls.

O'Connor Don-Ard-Ri Dining Room (££–£££)
88 Marylebone Lane, W1 tel: 020-7935 9311
In this simple dining room in a popular family-run pub you get traditional Irish dishes (beef

and Guinness casserole) and a great atmosphere.

Orso (££)
27 Wellington Street, WC2
tel: 020-7240 5269
If you do not fancy the trek to Clapham for the Osteria Antica Bologna (see page 281), try Orso instead, conveniently located in Covent Garden and popular (noisily so) for its modern Italian food.

Le Palais du Jardin (££)
136 Long Acre, WC2 tel: 020-7379 5353
Good value *fruits de mer*, plus other French favourites at reasonable prices (it is the wines that send your bill soaring.) Good, very professional service.

Planet Hollywood (££)
Trocadero, 13 Coventry Street, W1
tel: 020-7437 7639
More a movie theme park (with souvenir shop alongside) than a restaurant, but popular with the young.

Rock and Sole Plaice (£)
47 Endell Place, WC2 tel: 020-7836 3785
Maybe a bit rough and ready but this is inexpensive by Covent Garden prices and you do get a good plate of fish and chips. Excellent for a pre-theatre bite to eat or after you've been out for some drinks and need a bit of comfort eating—it's open until 11pm.

Rules (££)
35 Maiden Lane, WC2 tel: 020-7836 5314
London's oldest eating place and a favourite with actors and theatre-goers, drawn by traditional British fare, notably excellent game. Pre-theatre dinners are good value.

Sarastro (££–£££)
126 Drury Lane, WC2 tel: 020-7836 0101
Dine amid a dazzling array of stage props, gilt furniture and silk curtains to the sound of opera (live performers Sun and Mon nights) in this eccentric establishment in the heart of the Covent Garden (you can even reserve a box!). Mediterranean cuisine—strong on fish, vegetarian and Turkish dishes.

Savoy Grill (££££)
Strand, WC2 tel: 020-7592 1600
Many regard the Savoy Grill as their private club, but it is equally accessible to all who wish to experience a real British institution. Since Marcus Wareing brought his Modern British menu here the food has a new edge, while retaining the Savoy's traditional appeal. Smart dress is essential.

2 Sitaaray (££)
167 Drury Lane, WC2 tel: 020-7269 6422
This Bollywood film set is a great venue for some good Indian cooking, a far cry from your average curry house. The set dinner, with nine kebabs and three curries, is excellent value, the food brought to your table in a steady stream.

Spiga (£–££)
84–86 Wardour Street, W1
tel: 020-7734 3444
After a glitzy revamp, pizzas from a wood-fired oven still form the core, but simple pasta and fish dishes are highly recommended. Great atmosphere.

TGI Friday's (££)
6 Bedford Street, WC2 tel: 020-7379 0585
Lively steak, burger and Tex-Mex restaurant, with special children's menu and entertainment on Sunday.

Yming (££)
35–36 Greek Street, W1 tel: 020-7734 2721
Excellent Chinese with the cooking predominantly from the north, around Beijing, plus some regional Szechuan dishes.

Cafés and bars
Bar Italia (£)
22 Frith Street, W1 tel: 020-7437 4520
Anyone with an ounce of italian in them will recognize this famous Soho institution as a piece of their own. Pizzas, paninis, bagels, cappuccinos, Italian beers and wines; open 24 hours Mon–Sat for shoppers, post-pubbers, pre and post-clubbers, you name it, you'll find them here.

Café in the Crypt (£)
St. Martin-in-the-Fields, Duncannon Street (Trafalgar Square), WC2 tel: 020-7766 1158
After a hectic time in the galleries, or tearing around the shops, relax in this oasis of calm in the depths of the church. Perfect for tasty soups, sandwiches and light lunches. You can come later, too, as it is open until 10.30pm Thursday to Saturday.

Mash (££)
19–21 Great Portland Street, W1
tel: 020-7637 5555
Modernistic bar, light, expensive second-floor restaurant and state-of-the-art micro brewery rolled into one. Wide-ranging menu with imaginative pizzas and lots of interesting global influences.

Monmouth Coffee Company (£)
27 Monmouth Street, WC2
tel: 020-7379 3516
One of Soho's best kept secrets: From the front it is nothing more than a shop selling bags of coffee. At the back are eight tables, newspapers to read, and a yummy selection of pastries.

Patisserie Valerie (£)
44 Old Compton Street, W1
tel: 020-7437 3466
Cramped, old-fashioned tea room; a Soho institution. Patisserie is superb, but there are also good salads, croque monsieur and quiches. Branches throughout London.

Union Café and Restaurant (££)
96 Marylebone Lane, W1 tel: 020-7486 4860
Stylish, casual and very popular. Here simple ideas are translated into great food.

HOLBORN, THE STRAND AND THE CITY

Alba (£–££)
107 Whitecross Street, EC1
tel: 020-7588 1798
Smart, modern Italian restaurant a short walk from the Barbican, noted for excellent value at lunch and pre-theatre. Like many City restaurants this one is closed at weekends.

Hotels and Restaurants

Le Café du Marché (£££)
22 Charterhouse Square, EC1
tel: 020-7608 1609
Actually three restaurants under one roof in a converted warehouse on the fringes of the City. Each restaurant has its own separate style and ambience. Reservations are essential though none are taken at the brasserie La Rendezvous at lunchtime.

The Eagle (£–££)
159 Farringdon Road, EC1
tel: 020-7837 1353
Famous food-lovers' pub specializing mainly in chargrilled dishes. Lively and often crowded, so you need to arrive early to secure a table as there are no reservations. This pub gives great value.

Haz (££)
9 Cutler Street, E1 tel: 020-7929 2923
It's nice to find a somewhere to eat in at the weekends in the City and Haz fits the bill. A stylish, slick, busy restaurant serving tasty Turkish cuisine at long communal tables. The set meals—for both meat eaters and vegetarians—are good value.

Imperial City (££)
Royal Exchange, EC3 tel: 020-7626 3437
Within the cavernous vaults of the Royal Exchange, off Cornhill, TV chef Ken Hom's menus include some less familiar dishes.

Miyama Restaurant (£££)
17 Godliman Street, EC4 tel: 020-7489 1937
Just by St. Paul's churchyard, this Japanese restaurant is crowded at lunch and less frequented in the evening. It's typically minimalist in style, with a sushi bar and *teppan-yaki* counter and a main dining area downstairs.

Moro (££–£££)
34–36 Exmouth Market, EC1
tel: 020-7833 8336
An informal, lively setting for food that is largely Spanish and Arabic in origin—the bar serves great tapas. Good raw materials, chargrilled or roasted in a wood-burning oven, produce such great results that it is essential to reserve a table well in advance.

The Peasant (£–££)
240 St. John Street, EC1 tel: 020-7336 7726
Formerly a grand Victorian gin palace, the Peasant has accomplished the difficult trick of becoming one of London's finest gastropubs without losing that real pub atmosphere. Beware the huge portions (no starters needed!).

Quality Chop House (££)
94 Farringdon Road, EC1 tel: 020-7837 5093
Much of the original character remains intact at this former Victorian chophouse. The menu offers a fashionable mix of updated traditional English dishes and French brasserie classics.

St. John (££)
26 St. John Street, EC1
tel: 020-7553 9842/7251 0848 (reservations)
Clerkenwell hotspot close to Smithfield meat market, where Fergus Henderson reworks traditional old English recipes such as pigeon and trotter pie, boiled ham and carrots, and tripe, fennel and bacon.

Cafés

De Santis (£)
11–13 Old Street, EC1 tel: 020-7689 5577
The City's best paninis, washed down with superior Italian coffee, served up by the famous Milanese company of De Santis in sleek stainless steel surroundings.

WESTMINSTER, SOUTH BANK AND DOCKLANDS

Bengal Clipper (££)
Butlers Wharf, SE1 tel: 020-7357 9001
An old cardamom warehouse at Butlers Wharf is a fitting setting for this respected Indian restaurant. The short menu specializes mainly in Bengali and Goan dishes.

Blue Print Café (££–£££)
The Design Museum, Shad Thames Street, SE1
tel: 020-7378 7031
This riverside eatery on the mezzanine floor of the Design Museum is part of Sir Terence Conran's 'Gastrodome'. Eat in the minimalist dining room with its appropriately arty décor, or on the terraces overlooking Tower Bridge. The cooking is modern, the services professional, and the wine list lively.

Butler's Wharf Chop House (£££)
Butler's Wharf Building, 36e Shad Thames, SE1
tel: 020-7403 3403
One of Terence Conran's growing chain of restaurants (see also pages 88 and 193), this one serves traditional English dishes (steak, kidney and oyster pudding), with a stunning view of the river.

Cantina del Ponte (££–£££)
Butler's Wharf Building, 36c Shad Thames, SE1
tel: 020-7403 5403
The mainly Italian-inspired menu brings a simple choice of grilled or roasted meats and fish to this busy, informal Conran eaterie on the quayside by Tower Bridge.

The Cinnamon Club (££–£££)
Old Westminster Library, Great Smith Street, SW1 tel: 020-7222 2555
If you have ever dreamed of sitting in an old Victorian library building (complete with books) feasting on roast turbot in Bengali sauce, or Bombay spiced vegetables, then this splendid Indian restaurant is for you. Interesting twists on traditional dishes.

Cut Bar & Restaurant (£)
Young Vic, 66 The Cut, SE1
tel: 020-7620 2700
Open for breakfast through till dinner, the menu is a mix of classics such as scrambled eggs and smoked salmon to Cal-Ital pasta dishes. Coffee is excellent. Good place to come for a pre-theatre meal.

Le Pont de la Tour (£££)
Butler's Wharf Building, 36d Shad Thames, SE1
tel: 020-7403 8403
In the shadow of Tower Bridge, this large yet surprisingly intimate restaurant is part of Sir Terence Conran's restaurant empire. Expect excellent modern Mediterranean food and spectacular views from the riverside terrace.

RSJ, The Restaurant on the South Bank (££)
13a Coin Street, SE1 tel: 020-7928 4554
An invaluable South Bank destination that is a good choice for after the theatre—a comfortable, contemporary setting with modern Anglo-French cooking that is strong on seasonal ingredients.

Cafés
Caffè Vergnano 1882 (£)
Festival Terrace, SE1 tel: 020-7921 9339
Caffè Vergnano's opened its second branch in the Southbank Centre in 2007. Reputedly the best espresso in town, this Italian coffee blend has been around for almost 125 years. Relax in the sleek interior with whatever coffee takes your fancy.

CHELSEA AND KNIGHTSBRIDGE, KENSINGTON AND NOTTING HILL, HYDE PARK

Adam's Café (£–££)
77 Askew Road, W12 tel: 020-8743 0572
Award-winning Tunisian restaurant in Shepherd's Bush, specializing in couscous served with tender grilled meats and chunky vegetable stew. Good value.

Chutney Mary (£££)
535 King's Road, SW10 tel: 020-7351 3113
Imaginative cooking that draws on regional-Indian cuisine (salmon kedgeree, spicy crab cakes and salads, for example) as well as more conventional Indian dishes.

Clarke's (££££)
124 Kensington Church Street, W8 tel: 020-7221 9225
A new approach here, with set menus offering a choice of three options per course. Clarke's retains its chargrilled meat and fish and still serves dishes with delicious homemade breads (also sold in the store next door).

Fifth Floor at Harvey Nichols (£££)
Harvey Nichols, Knightsbridge, SW1 tel: 020-7235 5250
The top floor of the designer-label department store—a cool, chic space that forms part of a food emporium and popular bar. Simon Shore's cooking reveals imaginative Italian, Middle Eastern and Oriental influences.

Gourmet Burger Kitchen (£)
50 Westbourne Grove, W2 tel: 020-7243 4344
Probably the best tasting and certainly the most varied burgers in the capital. Choose from the Jamaican; the Pesterella (fresh pesto, mozzarella); the Kiwiburger (beetroot, egg, pineapple, cheese, Chicken Camembert & Cranberry ; the Venison; veggie and more.

Racine (££)
239 Brompton Road, SW3 tel: 020-7584 4477
This splendid addition to the capital's Gallic upscale delights, modern but with a nod to its roots, opened in 2003 to rave reviews and best restaurant awards. Service and food is exemplary and the prix-fixe menu is an absolute steal.

Tom's Kitchen (£–£££)
27 Cale Street, SW3 tel: 020-7349 0202
A buzzing, informal restaurant with friendly service. 'Tom' is Tom Atkins, also owner and chef of the smart Chelsea restaurant bearing his name. The lengthy menu at the Kitchen includes breakfasts, meals for children, classic meat and fish dishes, casseroles and organic sausages.

Vama (££)
438 King's Road, SW10 tel: 020-7351 4118
Explore the cuisine of India's North-West Frontier, including interesting vegetarian dishes, at this smart Chelsea haunt.

Veronica's (££)
3 Hereford Road, W2 tel: 020-7229 5079
This Bayswater restaurant is worth seeking out for historically researched English food (the menu will explain what goes into delicious dishes such as salmagundy and watersouchy). Good choice of British cheese and wines.

Zafferano (£££–££££)
15 Lowndes Street, SW1 tel: 020-7235 5800
An air of classy informality permeates this longstanding upscale Italian favourite that specializes in up-to-date interpretations of simple Italian country cooking.

Cafés
The Orangery (£–££)
Kensington Palace, Kensington Gardens, W8 tel: 020-7938 1406
Stunning setting for a classic English afternoon tea—the grandest includes champagne. There's a delicious selection of cakes and light lunches are available between 12 and 2.30.

OUTSIDE THE CENTRE

Kastoori (£–££)
188 Upper Tooting Road, SW17 tel: 020-8767 7027
Family-run vegetarian restaurant specializing in freshly prepared Gujarati dishes and various thalis. Also some African-inspired dishes.

Laicram Thai Restaurant (££)
1 Blackheath Grove, SE3 tel: 020-8852 4710
There is a disarming hospitality and cheerfulness about this neighbourhood Thai restaurant, where diners sit at tightly packed candlelit tables. Children are particularly welcome but reservations are essential.

Osteria Antica Bologna (££)
23 Northcote Road, SW11 tel: 020-7978 4771
This Italian restaurant in Clapham is very popular not least because of the huge range of novel dishes served at honest prices. Lively atmosphere. Can get very busy so often preferable to avoid weekends.

Rani (££)
7 Long Lane, N3 tel: 020-8349 4386
This Finchley restaurant has won awards and high praise because everything is home-made (including the pickles and desserts), and because the East African vegetarian menu contains so many unusual dishes (all well explained). There is a good buffet option too, available from 7pm–9pm.

Index

Index

Index

Acknowledgements

ALLSPORT (UK) LTD 206 London Marathon (S Bruty), 206–7 Lord's Cricket Ground (A Murrell), 207 Ball girl Wimbledon (B Martin). **ARCAID** 204. **BANQUETING HOUSE** 46 Int Banqueting House. **BRIDGEMAN ART LIBRARY** 114 The drawing room/Victorian Society, Linley Sambourne House, London/www.bridgeman.co.uk. **BRITISH MUSEUM** 131 Elgin Marbles, 133 Exhibit. **COURTAULD INST. GALLERIES** 156 Manet's A Bar at the Folies-Bergère. **CROWN COPYRIGHT, HISTORIC ROYAL PALACES** 197 Beefeater, 223b Great Hall Hampton Court. **GETTY IMAGES (HULTON)** 38 Wearing Smog Masks, 38–9, 39 Festival of Britain. **HARRODS LTD** 87b Harrod's Food Hall. **ILLUSTRATED LONDON NEWS** 34 Queen Victoria. **IMPERIAL WAR MUSEUM** 36–7 Aerial view of London, **LONDON DUNGEON** 194 The London Dungeon. **MADAME TUSSAUD'S** 120 Chamber of Horrors. **MAGNUM PHOTOS LTD** 37 London at War (G Rodger). **MARY EVANS PICTURE LIBRARY** 25 Boudicca, 69 Athenaeum Club. **MUSEUM OF LONDON** 24r Carving. **NATIONAL ARMY MUSEUM** 94. **NATIONAL GALLERY** 51 Van Eyck's Giovanni Arnolfini and his Wife. **NATIONAL TRUST** 90 Carlyle's House. **PERFORMING ARTS LIBRARY** 180–1 Ballet. **RADIO TIMES** 119t 1950's Radio Times. **REX REATURES LTD** 15 Queen Elizabeth II,16t Beatles, 16b Punk,17b Mary Quant. **JOHN ROGERS (COURTESY OF THE ROYAL BOROUGH OF KENSINGTON & CHELSEA** 109 Leighton House. **ROYAL GEOGRAPHICAL SOCIETY** 22–3 Old Map, London. **SCIENCE MUSEUM** 100 Flight, 101 Exploring Space. **SPECTRUM COLOUR LIBRARY** 12–13 Traffic, 74 Tessiers, 91 Chelsea Physic Garden, 93b Chelsea Flower Show, 156–7 Somerset House, 224/5 Kenwood House. ©**TATE GALLERY, LONDON 1999** 57 'Norham Castle, Sunrise' by JMW Turner. © **TRANSPORT FOR LONDON** 4, 252 Underground Sign ®. **VICTORIA & ALBERT MUSEUM** 104b Italian Cast Court, 105 "Acanthus" Wallpaper, 184 Engine, Carriage & Tank in V & A Museum of Childhood. **WALLACE COLLECTION** 126b Sèvres Tea Service, 127 The Laughing Cavalier, 224–5 Kenwood House.

All remaining pictures are held in the AA's own photo library (**AA WORLD TRAVEL LIBRARY**) with contributions from: **AA** 27, 28/9, 28, 29, 32, 34/5, 87t, 152, 173t, 218t, 229t, 243t, 257. **P BAKER** 6,168c, 196. **S BATES** 3, 161. **M BIRKITT** 209, 211. **P ENTICKNAP** 18–19, 19. **D FORSS** 222. **D IRELAND** 147b. **R IRELAND** B/C l. **M JOURDAN** F/C t, cl, rcr, 205t, 205b. **P KENWARD** F/C lcl, c, cr, 9r, 21b, 121t, 146. **S & O MATHEWS** 210, 219. **J MCMILLAN** B/C r, 8t, 63b, 241t, 262b. **R MORT** 9l, 12, 26b, 35, 72, 97,116, 135, 136b, 137, 162–3, 164, 165, 171, 175, 176, 183t, b, 213, 216r, 221t, 221b, 240t, b, 241b, 242t, 247, 249r, 254, 265b, 268, 271. **B SMITH** 34a, 61, 64, 66, 78, 84, 96b, 142/3, 144b, 182–3, 200b, 201, 217, 226, 227, 229b, 242b, 255, 263, 267, 270. **N SETCHFIELD** 76t, 121b, 249l. **R STRANGE** 4t, b, 5t, b, 10–11, 10, 11, 13, 21t, 21b, 22, 23, 30, 30–1, 31, 40–1, 48, 49, 52, 53, 55t, 59, 60, 70, 74–5, 76–7, 76, b, 77, 78–9, 79, 80–1, 81c, b, 82, 83, 85, 86t, b, 88t, b, 89, 92, 93t, 95t, b, 98, 98–9, 102–3, 102, 103, 104t, 106, 110–11, 111, 112–13, 113, 115t, b, 117, 118l, r, 119b, 122t, b, 123, 124c, 125t, b, 126t, 128, 132/3, 134t, b, 136t, c, 138, 139, 140, 148–9, 152–3, 155b, 158, 159t, 160, 163, 168b, 169, 172, 173b, 178–179, 181, 185, 186, 187, 191, 224t, 225, 231t, b, 235b, 236, 236–7, 237, 238t, 239t, b, 244, 245b, 246t, b, 250, 251, 252, 253, 256t, b, 259t, b, 260, 261, 262, 265t, 266, 271. **J A TIMS** 80c, 108, 130, 166. **M TRELAWNY** 47, 63t, 68–9, 155t, 159b, 170t, 190, 195t, 212, 228t, b, 232, 233, 269t. **R TURPIN** 129. **V & A MUSEUM OF CHILDHOOD** 184. **R VICTOR** Spine, 18, 180b, 174–5, 195b, 218b, 243b, 248. **W VOYSEY** 20, 45, 54, 66–7, 67, 124b, 142, 143c, 143b, 144–5, 145, 180b, 188, 192, 193, 197t, 203t, 203b, 238b, 269b. **T WILES** 7t, 14–15, 14, 65, 273l. **P WILSON** 50–1, 96t, 150, 151, 174, 200t, 264, 273r. **T WOODCOCK** 20b, 24b, 26t, 33, 55b, 56, 71, 124t, 167, 208, 215, 216l.

Contributors

Original copy editor: Nia Williams   Verifiers: Hilary Weston and Jackie Staddon
Revisions editor: Apostrophe S Limited